Progressive Christians Speak

PROGRESSIVE CHRISTIANS SPEAK

A Different Voice on Faith
and Politics

Progressive Christians Uniting

Edited by
JOHN B. COBB JR.

Westminster John Knox Press
LOUISVILLE • LONDON

Book design by Sharon Adams
Cover design by Eric Walljasper

Published by Westminster John Knox Press
Louisville, Kentucky

This book is printed on acid-free paper that meets the American National Standards Institute Z39.48 standard. ♾

PRINTED IN THE UNITED STATES OF AMERICA

03 04 05 06 07 08 09 10 11 12 — 10 9 8 7 6 5 4 3 2 1

Library of Congress Cataloging-in-Publication Data
Progressive Christians Uniting (Organization)
    Progressive Christians speak : a different voice on faith and politics / Progressive Christians Uniting ; edited by John B. Cobb Jr.
    p. cm.
    Includes bibliographical references.
    ISBN 0-664-22589-6 (alk. paper)
    1. Christianity and politics—United States.   I. Title: Progressive Christians speak. II. Cobb, John B. III. Title.

    BR115.P7 M5442 2002
    261.8—dc21
                                                                    2002028891

Contents

PREFACE   vii

A CONFESSION OF FAITH   xii

1. RELIGION AND THE PUBLIC SCHOOLS   1

2. BASIC RIGHTS FOR OUR CHILDREN   22

3. REFLECTIONS ON ABORTION   36

4. HUMAN RIGHTS AND CIVIL RIGHTS   53

5. HOMOSEXUALITY AND SAME-GENDER UNIONS   76

6. IS SOCIAL SECURITY REALLY BROKEN?   89

7. THE PENAL SYSTEM   107

8. THE WAR ON DRUGS   126

9. THE IMMIGRATION DILEMMA   143

10. DO CORPORATIONS SERVE THE HUMAN FAMILY?   165

11. RESPONDING TO SWEATSHOPS   196

12. THE GLOBALIZATION OF ECONOMIC LIFE   213

13. SHOULD DEBT BE FORGIVEN?   232

14. THE CHURCH AND ENVIRONMENTALISM   249

15. GLOBAL FOOD SECURITY   268

16. THE GLOBAL POPULATION CRISIS   289

APPENDIX: A SHORT POLITICAL HISTORY OF
THE AMERICAN CHRISTIAN RIGHT   306

NOTES   336

Preface

For more than a century, from the antislavery campaign through the civil rights struggle, influential segments of the major Protestant churches in the United States were often leaders in progressive social action. Today Protestantism appears to the public as a bastion of conservatism. What has happened?

One thing did *not* happen. The official positions of the denominations that led in progressive causes in the past have not been reversed. The old-line churches can still be counted on to stand for help to the poor and for justice for ethnic minorities. They support women's rights and have gone through extensive internal change to give women an equal place in their leadership. Even some of the more conservative churches, many of which were slow to support the struggle for civil rights, and are now slow to give equality to women, have repented of their earlier racism, and some of them work very effectively for the poor.

Nevertheless, the image of the churches as weak in their affirmation of progressive concerns and as reacting conservatively to new challenges to inclusiveness and justice is more apt than we would like.

1. Whereas the progressive statements of mainline churches and ecumenical bodies once expressed the views of many of their members and carried weight with the public, now there is suspicion that these statements speak only for a small leadership group. Politicians believe that they can ignore the official positions of what are now the old-line churches, whereas they attend to those of the religious right on the assumption that these express the views of millions.
2. The issues at the forefront of public discussion today are different, and on these issues even the formerly progressive denominations are deeply

divided. These churches are torn apart by opposing views of homosexuality, and the conservatives win most of the votes. When this conflict within the old-line churches is combined with a solid phalanx of the more conservative denominations, the public understandably judges that "the church" is against full inclusion of gay and lesbian persons.

3. Even with respect to the poor, the formerly progressive churches fail to speak clearly. Earlier they supported social welfare legislation to ensure that all would have some minimum of economic support. When the negative effects of this legislation became apparent (and were grossly exaggerated by its critics), these churches were caught off guard and divided in their response.

4. The global situation has changed drastically, both economically and ecologically. There have been efforts to understand and respond at ecumenical levels and also by the leadership of some denominations. Unfortunately, little of this work has filtered down to most local churches. Few lay people have received guidance on these matters. Since these global changes have profound effects locally as well, this failure of the churches to guide their membership renders their opinions largely irrelevant to many important issues of our time.

5. Meanwhile, the formerly mainline churches are losing members and income. Declining in these ways, they turn inward. They do not expend the resources they once did to guide society toward greater justice and righteousness. More conservative segments of the Protestant community, on the other hand, have flourished and have entered the political arena. They have dominated the media.

Concerned about these developments, a group of progressive Protestants in the Los Angeles region organized the Mobilization for the Human Family—now known as Progressive Christians Uniting. Progressive Christians Uniting believes that one reason our old-line churches are declining is their loss of nerve in facing this changing situation. To address it seriously would require honest thinking about the new issues, as well as the old ones, and clear articulation of what we are called to be and do. The failure of most congregations to engage in this reflection is one reason that our own youth do not take our churches seriously as agents of God's salvation.

Progressive Christians Uniting responds to these problems on an ecumenical level. We are progressives who are convinced that our support of progressive movements is an expression of our Christian faith. We think that too many progressive Christians who share this conviction have failed to articulate it effectively. How and why does the gospel call us to respond positively to new challenges? If we cannot show the connection between our faith and our politics in a well-reasoned and persuasive way, we do not deserve to be taken seriously. "Knee-jerk liberals" are as uninteresting as "knee-jerk conservatives."

We know that any use of the Bible and the Christian tradition is selective.

We understand that both the Bible and the tradition are many-sided, expressive of insights that arose over a long period of time in highly varied situations. The ideas we derive from these sources are not the only ones that can be found there. Our conclusions have no divine authority. We do not claim that our views are *the* Christian position. But we are conscientiously seeking to understand what is going on in our world and to clarify the relevance of our Christian faith and heritage to that world. We make our thinking as explicit as possible and invite those who do not agree with us to show us how to improve.

Progressive Christians Uniting is not simply a Christian think tank on social issues. We also work more directly on matters of faith. We have begun writing position papers on theological issues as well. We worship together and share our stories. We have held both large and small gatherings for worship and inspiration and also to mobilize for action. We have led in organizing a march for tolerance. We have had a program (PACENET) devoted to helping those who have been on welfare to enter the workforce, and we are now involved in trying to influence the process in Congress of reauthorization of Temporary Assistance to Needy Families (TANF). We hold workshops on current issues. We are active participants in the national antisweatshop campaign. We have held a major conference on reforming the prison system, and we are working to improve the implementation of California Proposition 36, designed to shift from a primarily punitive to a primarily therapeutic response to drug abuse. We follow legislation at the state level and organize to influence it. Nevertheless, we believe that nothing is more important for the revitalization of progressive Protestantism than regaining confidence in the way we bring faith to bear on the whole range of social issues.

All of the chapters in the main part of this book were first prepared as position papers of Progressive Christians Uniting. A few of these were written largely by one person. Some are the work of committees. Most have gone through many revisions. Most of these chapters, in an earlier version, were published locally by Pinch Publications in a book called *Speaking of Religion and Politics: The Progressive Church on Hot Topics.* They have been revised and updated for this book, and chapters on Social Security, global food security, and corporations have been added. All continue to be work in progress. Critical and constructive responses from readers are welcome.

The two other items in this book are of a different character. The first is the Confession of Faith, which follows this preface. Although there is great diversity among us in theology, and we each retain the freedom to state our own faith in our own way, the board of Progressive Christians Uniting found it possible to adopt this formulation of the faith we share. We offer it both in hopes that others will find it helpful and to make clear the Christian perspective from which all our work is done.

The second item is the appendix. Our organization came into being in 1995 at the same time that progressive Christians were organizing nationally and in other parts of the country. In part it came into being in response to the growing power of the religious right. We wanted to offer a different Christian voice. For us it has been important to understand the phenomenon of the religious right, and we think this is important for other Christians as well. We express our agreements and disagreements with this other Christian movement in several chapters, but we also offer, as an appendix, a history of this movement. We think both its supporters and its critics need a clearer view of how the religious right came into being and the forms that it has taken.

The book is for church people who want their faith to inform their thinking. When the whole of life and thought are unified in faith, there is an integrity and joy that we cannot otherwise know. The writers are progressive Christians who are seeking this kind of understanding. We commend the book to individual readers. There is no need for them to read the chapters in sequence. For example, although the chapters on the global economy are near the end, some may recognize their special importance and begin with them.

Still better will be the study of the topics treated here in classes and study groups. A group should select the topics that most interest its members. If members will spend an hour in reading and reflection before meeting, we are confident that shared discussion of the questions we offer will be fruitful for all.

We cannot think and act as Christians without information, and each chapter offers that. But our distinctive contribution lies in the sustained effort to learn from the Christian tradition and to bring that learning to bear on the issues we face today. We believe that discussion should focus on this. The proposed questions should encourage those who disagree with some of our conclusions to think about how *their* faith informs their conclusions.

The entire book belongs to Progressive Christians Uniting as a whole. Its board has discussed and approved all of its contents. Most of the detailed work has been done by the Reflection Committee, of which I am chair. Those who have been members of the Reflection Committee during the production of the book are William A. Beardslee, Gordon K. Douglass, Jane Dempsey Douglass, Barbara Fagan James, Philip N. James, Claire K. McDonald, Lee C. McDonald, Ward McAfee, James A. Sanders, and Carol Baker Tharp. Richard R. Bunce and Joyce Roebuck have taken part as staff members. In addition, many others have contributed to the formulation of the position papers, and among these the contributions of C. Dean Freudenberger, Paul Lewis, and

Jerry Stinson have been major. Of this whole group, the two who have written the most are the economist, Gordon Douglass, and the political historian and theorist, Lee McDonald.

We are grateful to Robert A. Vincent for assembling all the material and preparing it for publication.

JOHN B. COBB JR.
MARCH 2003

A Confession of Faith
Progressive Christians Uniting

We who come together in Progressive Christians Uniting confess that we join in this venture as a witness to our common Christian faith. We see much injustice around us, and we cannot be silent. We speak both through this statement of faith and through our common work. In both our confession of faith and our work together, we hope to give public voice in southern California to a progressive tradition of Christian faith that has recently been all but silenced by a new wave of conservatism.

We come from many Christian churches. It is not necessary to our work together that each of us states the Christian faith in precisely the same way or even that we take up all the theological debates of the centuries. Yet we cannot help but struggle over such timeless issues as the relation of God's grace to human responsibility.

There is much that we can say together about our Christian faith. We have been nurtured in Christian congregations by the preaching and teaching of the Word of God, by the sacraments, and by service together in the world. Whenever we hear the Bible read and explained, as God's Word to us, we are conscious that it belongs not just to our own confessional tradition but to the wider people of God. We share the first testament with the Jewish people and the whole Bible with all Christians. Whenever we participate in Baptism and the Lord's Supper, we are conscious that these sacraments declare our belonging to the one body of Christ, to the communion of saints of all times and places. Through Word and sacraments we have learned also that as the body of Christ we are called and empowered to serve the world God created, following the model of the ministry of Jesus Christ. And so we seek out others from the Christian family who share our concerns, from many traditions, to make a common witness. In so doing we both affirm the unity of Christ's church and seek to make its unity more visible to the world.

As heirs of the Reformation, we base our beliefs first of all on the teachings of the Bible. We respect its unique authority in the Christian community as conveying God's Word to God's people. Through the work of the Holy Spirit among us, the Bible still speaks God's Word to us as it has to believers of many generations. Yet we have varying perspectives on the Bible's relationship to other authorities, such as reason and experience, and we recognize that the biblical writers reflected the culture and thought-world of their own day and time. We want to bring to the study of Scripture and to our theological reflections upon it the best of modern biblical scholarship and minds open to the learning of our day: philosophy, science, history, the arts, the social sciences. Just as the Reformers' critical study of the Bible led them to challenge the teaching of the church at many points, so we also find that new insight into the meaning of the biblical text can lead us to challenge traditional teaching out of faithfulness to God's Word. Part of our ongoing common work must be theological reflection on our contemporary problems in the light of fresh reading of the Bible.

We believe that God's creative presence has always moved and is now moving towards a good world in which there would be harmony and justice among all aspects of the creation, a world which would by its very order praise God, its maker. We regret that some today would attempt to take us back to an older view of the world that denigrates the materiality of our existence, that too radically attributes evil to the flesh and good to the spirit. We affirm the biblical insistence that human beings are a totality of body and spirit that can be ruled either by evil or by the Holy Spirit. We affirm that all human beings are of the same family, sharing a common humanity, created equally in the image of God, and owing each other the love, care, and justice marking a healthy family. Increasingly we understand God's care for the whole creation, the interdependence of the human family and other parts of the creation, and the complexities of those relationships for the survival of us all; and we admire the beauty of our creator's work.

Nonetheless it is often hard to hear the praise of God in the disorder of our present world. We acknowledge with pain that our worship of God is often distorted by our preoccupation with our own interests. We acknowledge that the exploitation and injustice of human beings towards each other as well as towards the rest of the created world are not only threatening to the survival of our world but also are grievous sins against God, our creator. We also acknowledge that by denying that God has given us capacities for healing actions and by refusing to use those gifts to help restore justice and harmony in the creation, we sin grievously against God. Through the grace of our Lord Jesus Christ, we experience forgiveness for these sins and reconciliation with God. Through the grace of Christ, we trust that we can take up a new life of gratitude and praise of God. As a sign of this new life, we desire to worship God not only through liturgical acts, but also through our daily tasks and our life in the world. We will use our gifts and time and energy as an expression of Christian vocation; we will witness by practical engagement in the world to our commitment to make God's purpose and ruling of the world more visible.

The model for our ministry is the ministry of Jesus of Nazareth. He was Emmanuel, God with us, incarnating God's own love in human life for all to see, flesh of our flesh and bone of our bones. Jesus announced the presence of the reign of God by preaching good news to the poor and captives, teaching, eating with outcasts like the tax collector, talking publicly with women—even a prostitute, a ritually "unclean" woman, and a foreign woman—healing the sick, forgiving sinners, calling for repentance and belief in the gospel. The society in which he preached, caught up in a momentous culture clash with the occupying European power, could not bear his challenge to its religious, ethical, and social norms. Jesus, like prophets before him, was unjustly accused of blasphemy and sedition. He was crucified. Thus God in Jesus has experienced the worst of human suffering. God has also demonstrated in Jesus' resurrection that the power of sin and death has been overcome.

At Pentecost the Holy Spirit was poured out on the church, a sign that the reign of God has indeed begun. Disciples who had been frightened and disillusioned by the death of Jesus were empowered by grace to announce publicly God's reconciling work in the world in Jesus Christ. As followers of Jesus in the church, both ministers and lay people, we, too, are called, empowered, and energized for a public ministry in the name of Jesus Christ that reflects the love of God and will make the reign of God more visible, a reign of peace, love, and justice for all creation. The Holy Spirit gives us strength and courage to challenge the religious, ethical, and social norms of the society in which we live and work when they fall short of God's intention for the world. Our churches as well as our communities continually need to be reformed. We as Christians and our churches need to demonstrate for our contemporaries the radically inclusive love that Jesus embodied as we reach out with hospitality and loving service to women and men, children and older adults, people of different sexual orientations, people of different economic status, people of every race and ethnic community and nation.

All forms of injustice are to be challenged, and the various forms of injustice are interrelated. We in the Progressive Christians Uniting movement have especially embraced the call to work for economic justice. We see large numbers of our brothers and sisters here in southern California and around the world suffering from profound poverty, from hunger, from work under inhumane conditions, from homelessness, from lack of medical care, ignored or even persecuted by the judicial system, and badly served by overburdened social agencies. We know that these brothers and sisters are flesh of our flesh and bone of our bones whose cries we cannot ignore. They are not simply victims of corrupt individuals but also of corruptions of social and economic systems that are global in extent. From the Hebrew prophets and the ministry of Jesus, we have learned that God has a passionate concern for those who suffer injustice, that we should see the face of Christ himself in the faces of those who suffer, and that God judges harshly the refusal to come to their aid.

We recognize the spiritual danger of imagining that we can minister "to the poor"; we realize that the wealthy world of the North that we represent, regardless of our personal circumstances, has contributed mightily to the suffering of the poor, here and abroad. We ourselves are deeply implicated in the wrongs we seek to right. Rather, we struggle to learn how to stand with the poor and the marginalized in solidarity, respecting their dignity, learning from their wisdom, and working with them to challenge unjust structures so that the earth's bounty can be shared with all as God intends. As we do so, we often find new hope and courage from the hope and strength of those who suffer; we trust that we, too, will be changed and renewed and will find fresh understanding of our own humanity. We struggle to learn how society's false values and expectations can be changed and how new ways of living together justly can be developed.

We are also urgently concerned with the increasing evidence of damage to planet Earth, its nonhuman inhabitants, and its atmosphere as a result of human activity. We believe that God as creator has given worth to plants and animals and nonliving parts of the earth, even quite apart from their usefulness to human beings. We realize that acts of disrespect for the creation anywhere in the world have consequences for the whole creation because of the interrelation of all its constituent parts. We are among those in the countries of the North who are beginning to have some understanding of the global damage done by our own lifestyle, but we have not found the will or the capacity to make the more radical changes necessary to avoid increasing ecological disaster. Yet we trust that a sustainable lifestyle can be created that will also be rich in the abundance of God's gifts. Energizing the American Christian community to act on these concerns is part of our ministry. We also feel the urgency to help build networks of solidarity with concerned persons in the countries of the South, because effective global strategies for change must be just to all the human family.

As we struggle to open ourselves to the world, we will seek to engage ourselves with other issues as well, such as peacemaking. We know that our attempts in ministry towards restoration of a just order for all creation will be small steps, sometimes misguided, as we search for effective forms of ministry. Nonetheless we reject the idea that injustice to our brothers and sisters and to the planet earth and the suffering flowing from it are simply to be tolerated. We find hope for a new future in the conviction that in Jesus Christ the power of evil has been overcome. We call on our churches to join us in this witness to the presence of the reign of Christ among us.

Still we recognize that God's Spirit is at work more widely in the world, beyond the limits of the Christian community, creating a concern for justice in people of other religious faiths and in people who profess no faith. We give thanks for all those who share respect for human dignity and zeal for human rights, and we will seek to cooperate with them in our work and learn from them. As part of our concern for peace and justice, we will especially welcome and encourage dialogue with members of other religious faiths to foster mutual understanding and to find new ways of working together fruitfully for the benefit of the whole human family.

1

Religion and the Public Schools

The Harpers' oldest son was a second-string tight end on the high school varsity football team. The parents and the son both liked the coach, Sam Guard. He was a disciplinarian but also seemed to care for the personal well-being of each of his young athletes. Being fairly regular churchgoers, the Harpers were pleased to learn that coach Guard offered a prayer in the locker room before each game, especially since he didn't simply pray for victory, but that the team, win or lose, might play well, follow the rules, and respect the other team. He also included concern for injured players and ailing parents and siblings. They were consequently troubled to hear that a small group of Jewish parents objected to the prayers and at the next school board meeting were going to protest coach Guard's practice of praying. The Harpers' friends, Ed and Sue Righteous, called to say they were going to the school board meeting to defend the coach; but they did not have a son on the team, and they felt if the Harpers would attend and speak up in his defense, it would be very helpful. Would they do that?

I. INTRODUCTION

How should caring Christians respond to such a situation? There was a time in American history when prayers in public school raised few eyebrows. The separation between church and state written into the First Amendment of the U.S. Constitution was of course acknowledged by the courts and by citizens,

1

but hardly ever were public schools the scene of battle over what this meant. America was thought to be not just a Christian nation, but also a Protestant nation, as nineteenth-century anti-Catholic agitation seemed to suggest. The Supreme Court found no occasion even to mention Thomas Jefferson's oft-quoted phrase "the wall of separation between church and state" until 1879, when it cracked that wall a bit, finding that the principle of religious freedom could not protect Mormon polygamy from antipolygamy statutes. (In one 1890 case, a Mormon was jailed for saying he believed in polygamy, even though he was not a polygamist.)

Until 1897 the federal government actually paid Christian missionaries to work with and on Native American tribes. Presidents did—and still do—repeatedly invoke God in their speeches. In 1940 the Supreme Court said that school children who were Jehovah's Witnesses could be forced to salute the U.S. flag, even though the flag salute violated their religious beliefs. It was, in the students' view, "bowing down before idols" and forbidden by the Bible. This court action, however, launched such a wave of local persecution against the Witnesses that the Court reconsidered and reversed itself in 1943: school authorities could not legitimately require children to betray their own religious beliefs in symbolic exercises.

Today we are not necessarily a more secular nation, but we are certainly a more "multicultural" nation. Citizens vary widely in race, national origin, and religious belief. The estimated six million Muslims in the United States outnumber Presbyterians or Episcopalians. Buddhist and Hindu populations are growing. To recapture our sense of being a "Christian nation," as the Christian Coalition hopes to do, may be unrealistic. In any case, it would run counter to well-established interpretations of the Constitution. (Technically, the position of the Christian Coalition is that it wants not to suppress non-Christian religions, but to end what it calls the unfair persecution of Christians by "secular humanists.")

II. THE LAW

In 1948 the Supreme Court said that releasing public school students for religious instruction on school property was unconstitutional. In 1952 it held that releasing public school students for religious instruction off school property was constitutional. Since that time, there have been hundreds, perhaps thousands, of cases in state and federal courts affecting directly or indirectly the relationship between religion and public education.

We cannot even briefly summarize or do justice to the complex pattern of legal distinctions and rationales that have emerged out of these cases, and we will not try. But it is important for Christians responding to the question posed at the outset of this chapter to know enough constitutional law to be able to participate in the current debates on the issues outlined below. Even the avoidance of the courts may require some understanding of the law, for in our society conflicts between religions, or between religion and the secular, tend quickly to engage conflicts of legal understanding. As we shall see, the church has played, and will increasingly play, a significant role in maintaining religious liberty, and progressive Christians will want to be part of these efforts.

All of the case studies, examples, and policy issues we shall look at involve a sometimes delicate balance between avoiding any "establishment" of religion and avoiding any "prohibition" of the "free exercise" of religion, both of which are limitations imposed by the First Amendment of the U.S. Constitution, the first part of the so-called Bill of Rights. The text seems deceptively clear: "Congress shall make no law respecting the establishment of religion, nor prohibiting the free exercise thereof." Yet what seems to some like the protection of religious liberty will seem to others like the establishment of religion.

State-supported churches existed in several of the former colonies at the time the Constitution was written; so it has been claimed on the basis of a literal reading of the Constitution that the primary aim of the writers was to prevent the establishment of a national state church, though Jefferson and Madison, who helped write the Constitution, led the way to disestablishment in Virginia. After the Civil War, the Fourteenth Amendment imposed the restraints of "due process of law" and "equal protection of the laws" upon state governments, and in the twentieth century these terms came to mean that much of the Bill of Rights was a restraint upon state legislatures and local governments as well as upon the national Congress. In the 1930s a variety of local ordinances were enacted to restrict the proselytizing activity of Jehovah's Witnesses, but they were soon overturned by the Supreme Court as an interference with religious liberty.

School officials are obligated to be "neutral" with reference to religion. But what does neutrality mean? According to one view, neutrality means that government or school officials shall do nothing to aid religion. According to another view, neutrality means that officials shall do nothing to discriminate against religion. These views divide citizens as well as judges. Letting students out of school early so that they may receive religious instruction at church, temple, or mosque is certainly an aid to religion, but it does not discriminate against any particular religion. A recent episode in a Mississippi high school can illustrate discrimination. A Jewish student was denied the right to wear a star of David around his neck, although Christian students were allowed to wear crosses. The principal and superintendent argued that the star of David had been used as a gang symbol and the school board had forbidden the wearing of gang symbols. Jewish parents and the American Civil Liberties Union protested, and the school officials backed down. State aid for religion was not an issue here.

III. THE MAJOR CURRENT ISSUES

School Prayer

Is prayer ever appropriate in public schools? The courts have decided that teachers and administrators cannot lead students in prayer. On the other hand, with uneven success, some states and school districts have instituted periods of silence at the beginning of the school day. In 1981 Alabama amended an earlier statute to prescribe for schools a daily minute of silence "for meditation or voluntary prayer." But the Supreme Court struck it down, noting from the legislative record that the state senator who proposed the amendment clearly aimed to encourage prayer, which was an establishment of religion.

The lower courts, but not the Supreme Court, have ruled on a situation similar to the football fable that appeared at the start of this chapter. A coach-led prayer was deemed unconstitutional; a student-initiated, and student-led prayer was acceptable. The Harpers should offer sympathy and support for their Jewish neighbors; but will they?

The publication of a set of guidelines entitled "Religious Expression in the Public Schools" in 1995 by the U.S. Department of Education has helped significantly in guiding school officials as to what the law allows and forbids. Individual prayer and religious speech, such as voluntary grace before meals, is protected. But school endorsement of religious activity and teacher-led prayer are forbidden.

More contentious of late has been the issue of invocations and benedictions at school graduation ceremonies, notwithstanding a Supreme Court decision on this matter in 1992. The 5-4 split in the court and the eloquent but heated language on the dissenting side have served, if anything, to stimulate emotional responses. The opinions in the case represent views about religion and the American public that go well beyond legal technicalities and reflect positions each of us should think about.

Deborah Weisman was fourteen years old in 1989 when she graduated from Nathan Bishop Middle School in Providence, Rhode Island. She and her parents objected to prayers of invocation and benediction given by a Rabbi Gutterman, and eventually the case reached the Supreme Court. The rabbi, invited to participate by principal Robert E. Lee, had been given a set of guidelines prescribing, among other things, that the prayers should be "nonsectarian." Other court decisions had held that graduation ceremonies were not comparable to classroom situations, since the students were less obviously a "captive audience." Moreover, the Supreme Court itself in 1983 had said that opening and closing prayers before state legislatures did not violate the Constitution.

Justice Kennedy, writing for the majority of five, found that there was an element of coercion at the Bishop School graduation and that the principal had himself been involved in producing "a prayer to be used in a formal religious exercise which students, for all practical purposes, are obliged to attend." "[S]tate-created orthodoxy" was here set against "that sphere of inviolable conscience and belief which is the mark of a free people." Justices Blackmun and Souter, concurring with Kennedy, wished to add that coercion need not be proven to invalidate the prayer. Souter noted that Rabbi Gutterman's prayer included the admonition to "do justly, love mercy, and walk humbly" before God and that, ironically, these words from Micah 6:8 were taken from the King James Version of the Bible rather than from the Hebrew Scriptures. He thought this reflected an "official preference for the faith with the most votes," a deference that can only weaken rather than strengthen genuine faith. Souter, it might be noted, is a practicing Episcopalian, so he can hardly be accused of reaching his conclusion via the bias of secularism.

A caustic dissent written by Justice Scalia ridiculed Kennedy's position that there was implicit coercion in the graduation setting: "[I]nterior decorating is a rock-hard science compared to psychology practiced by amateurs." No one was forced to agree with the content of the prayers. Even in "this vulgar age" it is not too much to ask of students to sit in "respectful silence" if they do not agree with what is being said. In defense of the use of prayers Scalia appealed to American tradition. The majority opinion, he said, "lays waste a tradition that is as old as public school graduation ceremonies themselves." That opinion represents "the bulldozer of . . . social engineering." Established religion to our founders meant forced attendance at church, a privileged clergy, state taxation to support churches, civil penalties for the unchurched. There is nothing like that here, said Scalia. In the flag-salute cases children were threatened with expulsion if they did not salute the flag. There is nothing like that here. Scalia then traced the history of Thanksgiving proclamations and the tradition of public prayer that has meant so much to "our public culture." "To deprive our society of that important unifying mechanism in order to spare the nonbeliever what seems to me the minimal inconvenience of sitting in respectful nonparticipation is as senseless in policy as it is unsupported in law."[1] That Scalia is Catholic may or may not connect to his opinion but may be worthy of note.

On the legal status of student-led prayer in schools, a certain amount of confusion will most likely continue. In December 2001 the Supreme Court declined to take a case from the Eleventh Circuit Court of Appeals in Atlanta, which upheld a student-organized prayer at a Jacksonville, Florida, graduation, even though the lower court's opinion seemed at odds with a decision rendered by the Supreme Court in 2000 that overturned a student-led prayer at a football game in Texas.

Teaching about Religion

Can schools pay attention to the moral and spiritual development of children without stigmatizing minority religions? Can schools be neutral toward religion without encouraging secularism, that is, the idea that religion is not important? Can schools teach about religion without teaching religion? These are the questions that confront us as we deal with what our children ought to be taught.

We have already seen that releasing students for religious instruction away from school premises is acceptable under the law. Such programs usually operate well and to good effect, though of course there is always the danger of stigmatizing those who do or do not choose to participate, given the cliquishness of adolescent students. As distinct from released-time programs, attempts to teach about religion in the regular classroom have been trickier. State-required Bible reading has been declared unconstitutional. But teaching the moral, literary, and historical value of the Bible is desirable. Few teachers are well trained to teach this difficult subject in an objective manner. Those who do may lean over backwards in order not to offend any group, with the result that the course is lifeless. Dealing with the destructive things that have been done throughout history in the name of religion—Christian anti-Semitism, support for slavery, the Spanish imposition of Catholicism in Latin America, restrictions on women in some Muslim cultures, etc.—may be particularly difficult to deal with. Some teachers do, in fact, proselytize, in the classroom. Ironically, the parents who object that religion is not being taught in an objective manner are often the least objective in their own views. In one of the few significant court cases on this specific issue, a federal district court in Virginia held in 1970 that a Bible course in high school was suspect because students were allowed the option of being excused, suggesting that the course content might have some indoctrination in it. In a Michigan middle school in 2000 a teacher was suspended for three days because she loaned a book on the Wicca neopagan religion to a student (the student was writing a paper on herbs!).

Some parents have raised questions about religious music in schools, but a reasonable consensus has generally been reached in this area. For teaching purposes, the best music should be used. The history of Western music is suffused with Christian symbols, themes, and liturgy. There is no simple formula for what is appropriate music for school time use. Basically the criterion for, say, a high school glee club concert, is that if the music is chosen for its historical and musical significance, there is no problem. But the program itself should be secular and not religious, that is, a concert, not a service of worship. Public school choirs may sing in churches and synagogues, but not as part of a worship service. Some hymns may be inappropriate for a graduation ceremony. So far, the Supreme Court has declined to take cases involving school music.

Two subjects related to teaching have recently been the source of much contention: the teaching of evolution and schoolroom posting of the Ten Commandments. The educational significance of the evolution dispute is protracted and far-reaching. "Creationists" read the two creation stories in Genesis in a literal manner and believe that the scientific understanding of evolution contradicts the belief that God created biologic life once and for all. Some scientists and skeptical secularists, outraged at this abuse of scientific learning, put the logo of the Christian fish on their cars with "Darwin" replacing Christian symbols. Some Christians and Jews believe that a proper understanding of the six days of creation in Genesis is quite compatible with a scientific understanding of evolution, but that position seems to satisfy neither the scientists nor the creationists. What has happened is that outmoded nineteenth-century scientific theories based on more static notions of genera and species have become attached to and identified with what may be quite rich theological understandings, so that questioning the outmoded science is falsely taken by conservative and fearful Christians to be an attack on God. This confusion is one mark of the poverty of our society's teaching about religion.

The political exploitation of this confusion by the Christian right has made the situation worse. Concealing their curricular aims until after the election—a typical pattern—Christian Coalition supporters won a majority on the Vista, California, school board and attempted to impose a creationist curriculum, only to be later ejected by disgruntled voters in a special recall election. More recently, the Kansas Board of Education found itself split 5-5 on this issue. For obscure reasons, the creationists won over a doubter and by a 6-4 vote ordered the removal of evolution from the list of subjects to be tested at the secondary level, thereby providing grist for editorial and cartoon writers that embarrassed many Kansans.

More symptomatic than foundational is the recent dispute over public posting of the Ten Commandments, which also illustrates a willingness to make political hay out of religious conviction. Notwithstanding that the Supreme Court in 1980 declared such a practice unconstitutional, in 1999 the House of

Representatives approved 248-180 the Ten Commandments Defense Act. Sponsored by Robert B. Aderholt (R-Ala.) and added as an amendment to a juvenile justice bill, it declared that the states have the right to display the Ten Commandments in public places. President Clinton took the position that the amendment did not belong in the juvenile justice bill, and the Senate did not act on the proposal, a position that undoubtedly some of the House members who voted for it were counting on. Representatives are reluctant to vote "against religion" but quite often may count on Senate inaction to bail them out after a symbolic vote on a bad bill.

Among other problems, the Aderholt amendment did not address the question of how the Ten Commandments, or Decalogue, are to be defined. The version in Exodus 20 is different from the version in Deuteronomy 5. Jewish translations are different from Christian translations. Catholic translations are different from Protestant translations, and Protestants use several different translations. Congressman Jerrold Nadler (D-N.Y.), an opponent, asked in the floor debate whether communities with a Catholic, or Protestant, or Jewish majority could have their version posted for all; but he received no answer. Relevant to the issue of gun violence in schools is the distinction between "You shall not kill" and "You shall not murder" that appears in the Sixth (in some versions, the Fifth) Commandment. Robert Franklin, president of the Inter-denominational Theological Center in Atlanta, called the measure "well-intentioned but naive." Martin Marty in the *Christian Century* noted that in such legislative actions Muslims, Hindus, and Buddhists are left out of account. Moreover, Lutherans divide the anticoveting commandment into two. Further theological reflection along Lutheran lines, said Marty, raises the question of whether the law of the Hebrew Scriptures, reflecting primarily an angry God, should be set apart for public and student approval when divorced from the gracious God of the Gospels. The law without the gospel, Luther held, can make a person worse not better. "Of course," said Marty, "we Lutherans may be wrong about law and gospel. But we do, or should, or did have rights of conscience to persist in our error."[2]

The emotional and sometimes bizarre nature of school disputes involving religion is illustrated by a flap that occurred in May 2000 in the Willis school district, near Dallas, Texas. It was said that book covers containing the Ten Commandments on some students' books were ordered removed and thrown into a wastebasket. A teacher was later accused by irate parents of seizing the Bibles of two girls and throwing them in a wastebasket. A district investigation determined that both these allegations were untrue.

Both politics and religion, as subjects, are special in that teaching about them stirs deep emotions in the parents of students. Everyone has his or her own deep—or at least sensitive—feelings on these subjects and may not trust anyone else to teach the correct views to their children. The home schooling movement is one current reflection of this. Mathematics, chemistry, and ancient history are less problematic. Yet how can we call for the best education of our children if we exclude the best teaching about politics, science, and religion?

The Use of Facilities

A series of cases has established that students may organize religious activities in school facilities after hours, provided that the same facilities are open to other groups—groups, say, that express political or philosophic views—on an equal basis. Denial of such use is deemed a denial of religious liberty rather than a necessary avoidance of establishment. The protections of free speech as well as religious liberty apply to these situations. This position has been enshrined into federal law by 1984's Equal Access Law, which applies to any public school receiving federal aid. This is not to say that school facilities may not be inappropriately used, even when legally used. From the standpoint of school officials, local youth ministers may sometimes be overzealous in proselytizing on campus, or an outside substance-abuse lecturer may turn his after-hours presentation into religious exhortation.

Financial Aid and Vouchers

The post–World War II history of American public education shows that many state legislatures have tried in many ways to help parochial and other religious schools, with many such actions disallowed by the courts. Aid to private schools has been politically popular in certain areas because of the demographics; these actions also show the degree to which society has depended on private schools to educate a significant portion of its youth. State-supported school buses taking children to parochial schools was accepted in 1947 because it was deemed state support for children but not state support of religion. On the other hand, providing state-purchased textbooks, even on nonreligious subjects, was not accepted. It did not fit under the "child benefit theory." Yet later the Supreme Court approved a New York plan to "loan" textbooks to both public and parochial school students. The Court, in the famous case of Lemon v. Kurtzman in 1971, rejected a Rhode Island scheme to supplement the salaries of teachers of secular subjects in nonpublic schools, as well as a Pennsylvania plan to reimburse nonpublic schools for teachers' salaries and instructional materials in nonreligious subjects. This case produced the three-pronged "Lemon test," which has been followed by the courts ever since, though not without some qualms. Legitimate aid must: (1) have a secular purpose; (2) neither advance nor inhibit religion; (3) not foster "excessive government entanglement with religion." Under this test, grants for building repair, counseling, hearing and speech therapy services, indirect parental reimbursement and the like have been struck down. But educational tax deductions by parents of private-school children have been upheld.

What promises to bring us some fierce political battles in the future are school voucher plans. There are prominent and vigorous advocates on both sides. The nation's first statewide voucher program began in Florida in 1999, and challenging lawsuits continue to be filed. Opponents say that to give parents vouchers for tuition that may be used for either public or private schools will only strengthen elite private schools while weakening deteriorating public schools. They call public schools "the backbone of democracy," and say vouchers will be an encouragement for racial and religious fanatics to open their own private schools.

Opponents of vouchers contend that vouchers have racist overtones because there will be "white flight" and inner-city schools will suffer the most. Grants of voucher funds will not be enough to allow poor families to take advantage of nonpublic schools (Florida's grant is up to $3,389 per year; some other plans are much less than this). Comparisons of public and private school efficiency are defective because public schools must accept all children regardless of academic ability. Public schools are doing a far better job than critics acknowledge. Vouchers violate the constitutional separation of church and state.

By contrast, advocates of vouchers say that the competition for parent-controlled money such plans induce is necessary to turn around complacent public school systems. Catholic schools have been more effective educationally with less expenditure per pupil than public schools (to which argument opponents point out that teaching nuns may receive little or no salary). The opportunity to make basic educational choices will strengthen families. The racism charge is unfounded, for minority families will have the same chance to "spend" vouchers that other families have, and, besides, private schools are today in fact better racially integrated than public schools. Effective moral education is not possible in a religiously neutral, secular school. Neutrality breeds indifference.

Ronald J. Sider, president of Evangelicals for Social Action, has recently written in the *Christian Century*: "Biblical principles require what the United Nations' Universal Declaration of Human Rights (1948) stipulates: 'Parents have a prior right to choose the kind of education that shall be given to their children.'"[3] This leads him to a defense of a voucher system. But he thinks it should be tested in a five-year experiment that would put "several billion dollars" both in public schools as presently organized and in selective voucher systems, after which the nation could make up its mind on which path to follow. He thinks the constitutional problem, as well as the dangers of racial discrimination and religious sectarianism, can be met by a plan that would allow vouchers to be used only in schools that do not discriminate on the basis of race or religion. This would seem to beg the question of the religious content of the curriculum, which is independent of the religion of the student.

IV. DEFENDING RELIGIOUS LIBERTY

The general attitude of the mythical Harper family, represented above, is sufficiently common in the American public that political representatives have paid attention to their feelings. Being for religion, especially the Christian religion, is frequently taken to be a political advantage, though where a political constituency is religiously diverse, it is safer, from the representative's viewpoint, to be for religion in general without being too specific. Politicians contend with, and may be tempted to exploit, a massive amount of historical nostalgia about a past American community where everyone agreed on moral values and religious tenets, a community that probably never existed.

In early 1998, for the second time, Congressman Ernest Istook (R-Okla.) introduced a proposed constitutional amendment called the Religious Freedom Amendment (H.J. 78), which declared that while there shall not be any "official" United States religion, "the people's right to pray and to recognize their religious beliefs, heritage or traditions on public property shall not be infringed." The proposal further declared that while government shall not require any person to join in prayer or other religious activities, it shall not discriminate against religion "or deny equal access to a benefit on account of religion." Though this is sometimes referred to as the School Prayer Amendment, it is obvious that its implications go beyond the issue of school prayer. Legal scholars are not altogether sure what the implications of the last phrase may be; but a number of educational, church, and civil rights groups fear it would open the way to massive tax support of sectarian schools, through vouchers or by other means.

In the 105th Congress, 1995–96, Istook's measure did not even get to a committee vote; but in the 106th Congress his measure had the strong backing of the Republican House leadership, as well as the external support of groups like Pat Robertson's Christian Coalition and Gary Bauer's Family Research Council. On June 4, 1999, it passed the House 224-203, on a largely party-line vote, but this margin was insufficient for a constitutional amendment, which requires two-thirds support. The 52.4 percent support was actually less than the 59.7 percent support a similar proposal received in 1971. Since almost no one expected this measure to receive the necessary two-thirds vote in the House (let alone get the approval of three-fourths of the state legislatures, necessary for a constitutional amendment), many have called this effort "symbolic politics." The supporters wanted a colorful but painless (because ineffective) campaign issue for the 1998, and perhaps the 2000, election.

A serious game of judicial-congressional tag began in 1990 when the Supreme Court held that it was legitimate for Oregon to fire two Native American state employees for using peyote in a traditional ceremony. Congress is not usually sympathetic with drug use, but the rationale of the decision (Employment Division v. Smith) was such that many religious leaders from a wide spectrum of doctrinal positions became alarmed and began to pressure Congress for a remedy. The court, it appeared, would allow no religious exceptions to "generally applicable" laws, and that judicial assumption seemed to the petitioners a basic threat to religious liberty. Congress responded with the Religious Freedom Restoration Act (1993), which ordered that a state must show a "compelling interest" before a general and neutral law could be applied in such a way as to interfere with a central aspect of religious practice.

The Supreme Court gave its answer in 1997 when the town of Boerne, Texas, citing local historical zoning laws, refused to allow an overcrowded Catholic church to enlarge its sanctuary on its own land. This action was clearly forbidden by the Religious Freedom Restoration Act, but the Court found for the city of Boerne and declared the Religious Freedom Restoration Act unconstitutional, calling it an unjustified intrusion of Congress into the judicial process. Justice Kennedy, writing for a majority of six (out of nine) justices, said that the courts, not Congress, have the final authority to interpret the meaning of "free exercise of religion" as it appears in the Constitution. He added that there was no evidence that the city of Boerne was acting from motives of religious bigotry, and a cramped sanctuary is not a substantial threat to religious liberty. [City of Boerne v. P. F. Flores, Archbishop of San Antonio]

Many conservatives have supported the pro–states' rights movement that has characterized the court's decisions in recent years (often these decisions are 5-4). In this case, conservative as well as liberal religious leaders were united in deploring the Boerne decision, from Southern Baptists to Unitarians to Orthodox Jews. The U.S. Catholic Conference said the decision "has . . . made religion vulnerable to the whim of government." The lawyer representing the National Council of Churches called the decision the "Dred Scott decision" of church-state law. The American Jewish Congress called it "a huge blow to religious liberty."

As a result, Congress tried again in 1999. On July 15, 1999, the Religious Liberty Protection Act passed the House 306-118, with the support of an extensive coalition of religious leaders. The bill aimed to repeat the intent of the Religious Freedom Restoration Act of 1993, but with deletions that might make it acceptable to the Court, especially the deletion of direct legislative instructions to state governments, to which the Court objected. According to its sponsor, the bill aims not to repeal any of the protections stated in previous court decisions, but to specify in greater detail "protections available to people of faith who . . . face substantial burdens imposed by government on their religious practices." It would, however, once again require state and local governments to show a "compelling reason," such as health and safety, and to act "in the least restrictive manner" in order legally to infringe upon religious practices. But opponents feared that it might, for example, give landlords willing to invoke religious reasons the right to discriminate against tenants (e.g., interracial, unmarried, or gay couples) in ways that violate existing civil rights laws. Congressman Jerrold Nadler (D-N.Y.), who otherwise supported the bill, proposed an amendment he hoped would address this problem, but sponsor Charles Canady (R-Fla.) said the amendment would give religious protections "second-class status behind other civil rights" and the amendment was defeated 234-190, on a largely party-line vote. The remarks of one opponent of the amendment implied that a fear of gay rights was a reason to oppose it. The Senate has not yet voted on the bill.

In the meantime, Arizona, South Carolina, and Texas have enacted into law state versions of the Religious Freedom Restoration Act. These acts seem to have bipartisan appeal.

V. A CHRISTIAN PERSPECTIVE

Historical Background

As the discussion above has made clear, the complex process of determining what is permitted and what is forbidden in the public schools is largely settled in courts of law. This poses a problem for Christians because of the negative teachings of the New Testament with respect to Christians using the courts. It is, at best, a last resort (Matt. 5:25; Acts 19:38, Jas. 2:6). Our concern should not be who wins but how best to honor conscience (Rom. 2:15; 2 Cor. 1:12; 1 Tim. 3:9), to relieve suffering and oppression, to "comfort the afflicted and afflict the comfortable." Jesus, we know, asserted that *agapic* generosity transcended narrow legal justice (Matt. 5:40). He denounced the hypocrites who "have neglected the weightier matters of the law: justice and mercy and faith" (Matt. 23:23). The rich, we are told, benefit more from the courts than do the poor (Jas. 2:6).

Nevertheless, even in the New Testament, the courts play a positive role as well. Paul, Gaius, and Aristarchus may have been saved from a hostile mob in Ephesus by an appeal to the civil law (Acts 19:38). Christians should always be prepared to go beyond the civil law but need not disdain the civil law. We know that, even as some politicians exploit religious feelings for their own gain, many sincere religious convictions are at work in the complex patterns of political bargaining; ultimately it is for God to judge the purity of motives. Christians who enter the political arena, whether they stride in or tiptoe in, might keep in mind two of Jesus' sayings: "Beware of false prophets. . . . You will know them by their fruits" (Matt. 7:15–16) and "be wise as serpents and innocent as doves" (Matt. 10:16).

Even more than is the case with most of the other topics treated in this book, the situation in which we find ourselves with respect to religion and education is profoundly different from that reflected in the Bible. Any direct use of biblical teaching to resolve the issues we now face in our schools would distort more than it would help. We can be guided only by very general principles. We want freedom to keep alive and transmit to our children the Christian traditions in which we have found wisdom. That means that we do not want the culture to indoctrinate our children with alien ideas and values or to belittle the importance of religious teaching. But it equally means that we believe that members of other communities should have the same freedom that we have. The question is how public schools can foster freedom both for us and for others. This is a new set of issues growing out of the distinctive American experience.

In traditional societies, education was centrally a matter of transmitting the accumulated wisdom of the community to its children. This wisdom included information, of course, but at least equally, it was a matter of culture, values, and religion, usually not separated. The acculturation of children was largely unconscious. Schools might, or might not, play a role.

The Enlightenment of the seventeenth and eighteenth centuries changed this situation in three ways. First, it increased the importance of formal schooling. Second, it reduced cultural homogeneity by bringing toleration of religious diversity. Third, it introduced a new set of beliefs and values that competed with those of the religious traditions. It claimed objectivity and neutrality for its own position, especially in science, while relativizing the various traditional views. The American system of separation of church and state favored Enlightenment beliefs and values over those of particular religious traditions.

The tension was not acute as long as the norms for American culture were largely Anglo-Saxon Protestant. These norms could be merged with Enlightenment thinking, while viewing religious difference among Anglo-Saxon

Protestant denominations as of minor importance. In this context, public schools continued to transmit culturally accepted religious values.

Since World War II, however, other Christian groups, especially Catholics—as well as other religious communities, especially Jews—have become part of the American mainstream. They rightly oppose the use of the public schools to promote Anglo-Saxon Protestant values. The result is that a more secular form of Enlightenment teaching becomes the unifying factor in public education. The theory is now that the task of the public schools is to transmit neutral and objective information and values, whereas the churches, synagogues, mosques, and temples supplement these with their special teachings.

Conservative and Progressive Christian Response

Conservative members of several traditions find this unsatisfactory. The secular Enlightenment teaching, they believe, is far from neutral. It is, in fact, condescending, if not hostile, toward their central convictions. Also, the youth culture that dominates public schools is quite different from the traditional culture they want their children to imbibe. Some withdraw their children and either teach them at home or put them in private schools. They have the legal and moral right to do so.

A quite different problem arises when conservative Christians, under the leadership of such public figures as Jerry Falwell and Pat Robertson, celebrate the idea that we are and should be a "Christian nation." This has not won support from a majority of the population, and it has been discredited by law. Progressive Christians affirm the very important role that the Christian faith has played in shaping this nation and its culture but strongly oppose the attempt to reassert Christian hegemony today. This is partly because progressive Christians are more positive than others about some of the values of the Enlightenment. We believe our children should be taught what objective evidence supports without interference from religious dogma. We believe that our children's education is enriched by becoming acquainted with people of other cultures and religions. The Enlightenment values of tolerance and inclusiveness are important to us.

On the other hand, we share many of the criticisms made by conservatives. The secular form of the Enlightenment claims more objectivity and neutrality than it attains. Its worldview has become increasingly nontheistic, and it tends to underestimate the importance of religious traditions and ideas in history and in personal life. Its value system is thin, with the result that it has not prevented education from becoming preparation for employment in the market, rather than for service in society as a whole. Also, instead of transmitting adult values to youth, the schools too often allow an immature and even dangerous adolescent culture to dominate student life. The capacity of parents and of religious communities to counter these weaknesses appears to be declining.

We must take seriously a claim made by some who are often called conservative but are not always conservative in the conventional sense. They claim that our government should be neutral but is not. They claim that the schools as presently constituted are supportive of a "religion of secularism," paradoxical as that sounds. That is, they claim the schools actively oppose all forms of religious faith. There are two primary sources of evidence for this charge, anecdotes about teachers and school officials and a study of curricular materials. The latter is weightier than the former.

Perry Glanzer, a spokesman for James Dobson's Focus on the Family, Colorado Springs, Colorado, has written on *Religion in Public Schools: In Search of Fairness*.[4] He acknowledges that teacher-led prayer is and should be unconstitutional. But he thinks that teachers too often push a secularized view of the world and tend to demean religion. His evidence for this is largely anecdotal: a teacher refuses to accept a paper on Jesus for an open-ended essay assignment; a class valedictorian is ordered to remove a reference to her own faith in a valedictory speech. Many of the references he uses have been the subject of legal appeals. Among the millions of public school teachers, no doubt some are eager to put down religion and do so in a way that is not neutral (and therefore is not legal). There are probably just as many, unrecorded by Glanzer, who push a particular religious view unneutrally and illegally. Probably more typical is the teacher who, aware of the need to be neutral toward religion, leans over backward and gives the appearance of a secularist bias. In any case, because teachers are human, it should surprise no one that mistakes have been made and will be made in both directions.

A weightier argument arises from the study of textbooks. Warren Nord, cited by Glanzer, has recently written *Religion and American Education: Rethinking a National Dilemma*.[5] Nord studied a wide range of American school textbooks and concluded that in a largely unconscious, unintentional way they assume and promote a secular worldview. They treat with respect various competing "ideologies"—feminism, environmentalism, scientific naturalism—but do not include religion, and by that neglect create the impression that religion is not important and can be dispensed with or at best "tolerated." Glanzer feels that this scholarly study vindicates his position.

The *Phi Delta Kappan* gave Edd Doerr, executive director of Americans for Religious Liberty, Silver Springs, Maryland, the assignment of offering a rebuttal to Glanzer.[6] Doerr holds that the situation in most schools is not nearly as arid as Glanzer believes. The courts, he feels, have done a pretty good job of balancing the free exercise of religion and maintaining state neutrality. He thinks the 1984 Equal Access Law, allowing religious groups to meet in school facilities in noninstructional time, has worked well. The U.S. Department of Education 1995 guidelines entitled "Religious Expression in Public Schools" has, he says, been very helpful. "Official neutrality" has been respected, and most public schools have tried hard to respect and not denigrate religion.

The secularization of public education has been a major cause of the feeling of discrimination against religion. Progressive Christians recognize some justification to this feeling. We do believe that there are tendencies in recent Supreme Court decisions to subordinate religious freedom to other considerations in dangerous ways. We support the efforts of Congress to counter those tendencies.

On the other hand, before attempting to amend the Constitution so as to allow more room for prayers in school, as proposed by Rep. Istook, we should ask at least four questions: (1) whether the claims of religious persecution by government are sufficiently serious to justify a constitutional amendment; (2) whether all religions would be fairly and equally served by such an amendment; (3) whether the assumptions of the amendment's supporters run counter to the fact of religious pluralism that characterizes American society today; and (4) whether churches, temples, and mosques can cooperate with each other in opposing possible infringements of religious liberty in such a way that social harmony will be advanced and legal action unnecessary.

Progressive Christians for the most part judge that the best option is to continue to seek a balance between the concern to avoid favoring one group over another and genuinely appreciating and supporting the positive values of religious traditions as well as those of their critics. We agree with the critics, however, that underlying much of the instruction is a worldview that reflects a secular form of Enlightenment thinking, the "secular humanism" to which its critics so strongly object. This is a serious problem.

Implications for Four Current Issues

School Prayer

It may be difficult for Christians to oppose prayer in public schools, especially nonsectarian prayer, without appearing to oppose religion. But if we are sensitive to the diversity of religious feeling that may exist in any classroom, and if we are not enamored of watered-down and overgeneralized prayer designed to offend no one, then progressive Christians can oppose prayer in the classroom, quite apart from legal rulings against it. Even when the law is clear, we need to think about the best course of action apart from the law. We also, of course, ought to respect the law, even if we sometimes disagree with it. Christians have higher loyalties than the civil law; but we can also recognize that without civil law, the likely result is anarchy, a condition that benefits no one. It is now well established that teacher-led or teacher-organized prayer in the classroom is unconstitutional.

Less settled in law, and more difficult to judge, are questions about the place of invocations and benedictions at school graduation ceremonies. As Justice Scalia noted in his dissent in the Weisman case, religion has been an important part of a national sense of community. To banish it from community events related to the public schools seems questionable. On the other hand, Justice Souter is right that prayer tailored to satisfy the majority is diminished prayer.

Progressive Christians will be on both sides of this debate. We need not, indeed, cannot, reject a cherished tradition; but we are more apt to avoid a nostalgic and romantic view of tradition if we focus on the reality of the existing and impending multicultural society and work to turn it into a multicultural community. That will require extreme sensitivity to the diversity of religious beliefs and suggests a preference for a religiously neutral state quite apart from the constitutional and legal arguments for that point.

Teaching about Religion

Progressive Christians believe that knowledge about religions and their historical role in shaping culture is of great importance. This should be an integral part of education for all. Despite the difficulty of presenting this history in ways that are fair to all and offensive to none, the effort must be made.

We encourage greater attention to the teaching of world religions in the public schools, teaching that is sensitive, intelligent, informed, and responsible, relying on written materials that reflect these same qualities. Understanding another's religion not only increases tolerance for that religion but deepens the understanding of one's own faith, much as the study of a foreign language deepens the understanding of one's own language.

The currently controversial subject of the teaching of evolution and creationism is also one on which progressives are clear. We do not want the religious beliefs of particular communities to be taught under the guise of science. We affirm the freedom of scientists to follow the evidence wherever it leads them. Nevertheless, we are not happy with the current teaching of science insofar as it is bound up with a worldview that is mechanistic and reductionistic. Some contemporary scientists and philosophers are also critical of this eighteenth-century worldview and seek more ecological and organic ways of thinking about nature. Such ways of thinking are often more open to basic Christian concerns. Instead of having to choose between creationist and mechanistic models, progressive Christians can encourage the exploration of new ways of thinking about the creative and evolutionary process.

We are not sympathetic with the effort to introduce the Ten Commandments into the schools. Although in various forms Jews and Christians share them, the forms are various and there is no neutral form. In any case, they are not common to all religious traditions. We do not believe that posting them on walls will lead to greater virtue on the part of students.

The Use of Facilities

Progressive Christians support free speech and freedom of religious expression. Accordingly, we find the courts' decision to give religious groups equal access to school facilities commendable. We may question some of the theology espoused on such occasions (for example, in a Campus Crusade for Christ meeting) and still accept the occasion as a valid expression of religious liberty.

Financial Aid and Vouchers

Some of the most difficult issues arise here, especially with regard to vouchers. On the one hand, our support of pluralistic public schools makes us suspicious of the movement for vouchers. On the other hand, Sider's proposal for a five-year experiment seems reasonable. It is quite possible that the absence of spiritual values in the modern-day public school curriculum makes it impossible for meaningful moral education to take place in that setting and that American society is suffering as a result. Public schools often do address the positive values of tolerance in a multicultural society, but there is more to moral education than this. We should remember, however, that the most effective moral education is by example rather than by exhortation and that parents generally have more influence on the morals of their children than do teachers.

That progressive Christians are divided on the issue of vouchers makes the experimental character of Sider's proposal especially attractive. Much depends on the form of the particular voucher plan. The devil is in the details. We can agree that a massive infusion of public moneys is needed to benefit public education. California's reduction of class size to twenty students per classroom has had a conspicuously beneficial effect. Such expenditures, in our view, should certainly take precedence over tax cuts that benefit the rich more than the poor.

VI. WHAT WE CAN DO

- Christians can keep in close touch with what is happening in their local schools, especially with concerns that arise about religious practices.

They can support the schools in their efforts to be fair to all but call attention to times when this leads to favoring secular over religious values.

- Christians can develop relations with other religious groups (as well as other Christians) about school issues. Whenever possible, these groups should make joint proposals to the schools.
- Christians should be particularly sensitive to infringement of the religious freedom of minority groups and ready to support them in their struggles.
- Churches can have occasional classes or special speakers on church-state issues as they affect public schools, so as to remain current and be able to speak and act relevantly.
- Churches can invite those running for school board to explain their views on these issues.

Discussion Questions

1. To what extent do your personal beliefs about prayer in the public schools and the current restrictions on prayer in the public schools coincide?
2. Should the subject of religion be taught in public schools? Can it be taught without being objective and dull, on the one hand, or without proselytizing, on the other hand? How should teachers be trained for this role?
3. Are "released time" programs a good way of handling religious instruction?
4. Why are official relationships between public school officials and church officials often touchy? How can greater cooperation occur?
5. Is complete government neutrality toward religion possible?
6. Should religious liberty have preference over other civil liberties? Are there grounds for a new Religious Freedom Amendment to the Constitution?
7. What are the merits and the pitfalls of school-voucher proposals?
8. How does the Ten Commandments controversy reflect our multicultural society?
9. Can effective moral education occur in a religiously neutral educational environment?

To Learn More

The Yale law professor and Episcopalian Stephen L. Carter, in *The Culture of Disbelief: How American Law and Politics Trivialize Religious Devotion* (New York: Basic Books, 1993), argues that present American law and culture trivialize religion. Robert Audi and Nicholas Wolterstorff, *Religion in the Public Square* (Lanham, Md.: Rowman & Littlefield, 1997) is a debate concerning whether and how religion should have a greater role in public life. Warren Nord, *Religion and American Education* (Chapel Hill, N.C.: University of North Carolina Press, 1995) provides a good descriptive review of the field. Kern Alexander and M. David Alexander, *American Public School Law* (Belmont, Calif.: West/Wadsworth, 1998), chap. 5 details what the law says. Stanley Hauerwas and John Westerhoff, eds., *Schooling Christians* (Grand Rapids: Wm. B. Eerdmans, 1992), discusses the problem of teaching Christianity in the right way without interference. James T. Sears and James C. Cooper, eds., *Curriculum, Religion, and Public Education* (New York: Teachers College Press, 1998) provides a variety of points of view.

2

Basic Rights
for Our Children

A young man, aged eighteen, is suddenly "released from bondage and given a grant of freedom" when he graduates from high school in June and is sent forth by his foster family to live on his own. Los Angeles County will no longer pay his foster family to feed, clothe, and shelter him. Every year in Los Angeles about one thousand foster-care youths are emancipated from their homes with few skills, little money, and scant understanding of what it takes to survive. Many have spent the better part of their lives in foster homes, group homes, or residential centers. There is no slow march toward independence for these teenagers, no gradual loosening of the reins by watchful parents. And there is no home to go back to, no family to fall back on, should life on the outside prove too tough. Welfare workers say that almost half of the teenagers emancipated each year end up living on the streets.

I. INTRODUCTION

Douglas Sturm writes in his chapter "On the Suffering and Rights of Children: Toward a Theology of Childhood Liberation"[1] that "[c]hildren are among the most vulnerable and the most victimized of peoples. In part, children are victimized by their own immediate caretakers." He graphically describes the various methods of torture that are inflicted upon children worldwide and then asks us to focus on

[t]hose systemic conditions of our common life—economic, social, political—whose effects on the lives of children are at least equally violative of the meaning of childhood as direct physical abuse, if not more so. The lives of children are sharply delimited and irreparably damaged and degraded by structural forces which are susceptible to transformation, but sustained by those in positions of power.

Economic security, good health, safety, and the opportunity for education are some of the basic rights that we want for our children. Churches can address these public issues. Children are also subject to spiritual "poverty" in a society that stresses consumption and hedonistic values. Our children reflect these "values" in often-exaggerated ways. Our economic order encourages both overconsumption and envious cravings and habits of individual self-absorption that indoctrinate our children to define themselves as "consumers" first and foremost and that teach them that they are worthless unless they can flaunt specific product lines in their presentations of self. Part of the hope-lessness of the poor in the United States is defined by the overconsumption-ist norms that are commonly presented as ideal standards in a dynamically growing capitalist economy. The annual reports of UNICEF seem to recognize this while also stressing the suffering of children in real economic poverty.

The Children's Partnership in the year 2000 published the following statistics about American children:

- Children have replaced the elderly as the poorest age group, with poverty rates for children under age six twice as high as for adults and the elderly.
- Children who are poor are three times more likely to die in infancy, four times more likely to become pregnant as teenagers, and more likely to drop out of school than are their more affluent counterparts.
- Children spend an average of 4.4 hours each day in front of media screens (using television, videotapes, computers, and video games).
- Twelve percent of eighth-graders, 22 percent of tenth-graders, and 26 percent of twelfth-graders use illicit drugs.
- Thirty-nine percent of fourth-grade students do not read or write at grade level.
- Fifty percent of children never complete a single year of college.
- Three thousand children are added to the ranks of the uninsured each day.
- Five million school-age children are home alone after school each day.
- Roughly 50 percent of children in our nation's poorest schools are still not using information technology.
- Forty percent of parents do not feel good about their children's future.
- The percentage of voters more likely to be sympathetic to children's issues (adults of child-rearing age) is expected to decline over the next decade.
- Children between the ages of twelve and seventeen are nearly three times more likely than adults to be victims of violent crimes.

- The firearm-injury epidemic is ten times larger than the polio epidemic was in the first half of this century.
- Children witness more than 100,000 acts of violence on television by the time they complete elementary school and 200,000 acts of violence by the time they graduate from high school.
- Approximately five children die each day as a result of abuse or neglect.

II. THE IMPACT OF RECENT FEDERAL POLICIES ON CHILDREN

While few Americans disagree about the importance of improving the lot of the children who are the future of our nation, many support economic and political policies that actually worsen their condition. Between 1973 and 1990, while per capita gross national product (GNP) grew, the median income of families with children headed by persons under thirty years of age dropped by one-third! Child poverty in these families grew.

During the 1990s, the poverty rate decreased somewhat. Yet, for the poorest families, life got worse even in the economic boom period of the last half of the decade. From 1995 to 1999, approximately two million families with average incomes of about $7,500 annually lost 8 percent of their income.[2] This happened despite, and most likely because of, federal legislation enacted in 1996. Officially entitled the Public Responsibility and Work Opportunity Reconciliation Act and commonly called welfare reform, the legislation has succeeded in reducing caseloads dramatically. However, it has generally failed to lift families out of poverty.

The centerpiece of welfare reform is TANF (Temporary Assistance to Needy Families), which replaces AFDC (Aid to Families with Dependent Children). Studies are indicating that TANF adds to the instability of the poorest families due to a "work-first" emphasis that typically interrupts or delays education and training, leads to very low-wage, insecure employment, and lacks adequate support services and supplementary cash assistance.

Another prominent feature of TANF is time limits on eligibility for public assistance. The standard lifetime limit is five years, though states have latitude for shortening the limit even further, providing exemptions to some, and lengthening the limit in special circumstances. The limits inevitably will increase poverty, hunger, homelessness, and lack of child and health care for affected households. Even among families that have succeeded in meeting the established work requirements, fewer than 24 percent are receiving a level of pay sufficient to raise them above the poverty line for a family of three. This means that they cannot afford the supports necessary in order for parents to sustain their employment, such as child care and transportation. Single mothers may also be in need of more education and training.

The impact of these policies and practices is especially severe on families with children who are mentally and developmentally challenged, families with unanticipated health care crises, and victims of domestic violence. Nutrition, education, health, and family life are adversely affected. The needs generated by these conditions are too often treated as acceptable consequences by legislators and ignored by the churches.

The dismantling of federal oversight, such as statistical documentation of extent of need, and dispersal of responsibilities to the fifty states with differing programs has resulted in "disappearing"—some poor families have dropped out of assistance programs. Now failures and tragedies are hidden, and only the success stories of transitions from welfare to financial stability are visible. Many persons continue to be disadvantaged by institutional racism, and by prejudice based on ethnic origin, gender, and disability. The attempts of public, private, religious, and other nonprofit sectors to increase the provision of such supports, particularly child care, transportation and housing, have not kept pace with the needs. According to Second Harvest, the largest organization of food banks and soup kitchens in the United States, the number of persons depending upon these sources of food now exceeds 21 million per week.[3]

In the year 2000, the first comprehensive study of the effects of welfare reform on young children (done by University of California at Berkeley and Yale University researchers) suggests that poor children's lives do not improve when their mothers go to work. Welfare families are no better off than they were before the reform effort of the 1996 TANF bill. The study found that children in welfare families were generally being placed in low-quality childcare settings that were frequently unclean and relied heavily on television and videos to occupy their time. They were not read to. The mothers themselves showed a high incidence of depression. At least a quarter of the women appeared to be "socially isolated." While welfare mothers are now going to work in record numbers, California mothers in the study earned an average of just $7.47 per hour, well shy of the $12.50 or so it takes to be self-sufficient. And without Medi-Cal aid, food stamps, and a child care subsidy, their children's futures are questionable. Only half of the state's eligible mothers know about vouchers to pay for child care, or find convenient centers where they can use them.[4]

The Children's Defense Fund has found deepening poverty among the poorest families with children, as well as joblessness, inadequate wages, and inability to pay for food and shelter among a sizable minority of former welfare recipients. This report is based on the CDF's analyses of annual Census

Bureau survey data. Extreme poverty in this report is defined as family income below one-half of the federal poverty line—that is, below $6,401 a year (equivalent to $533 a month and $123 a week) for a three-person family or below $8,200 for a family of four. The report uses an inclusive definition of income that accounts for taxes and the value of certain noncash help (such as food stamps) as well as conventional sources of cash income counted in official government figures (such as wages and salaries, self-employment earnings, government benefit payments, child support, and dividends).

Senator Edward M. Kennedy of Massachusetts, along with Senators Specter, Leahy, Jeffords, Graham, Clinton, and Chaffee introduced the Nutrition Assistance for Working Families and Seniors Act on March 21, 2001. It is an attempt to reinforce the nation's core nutrition safety net, the Food Stamp Program. At the present time the application for food stamps is nineteen pages long. Senator Kennedy acknowledged that participation in the Food Stamp Program has declined 34 percent as a result of welfare reform, because it eliminated eligibility for legal immigrants. Households that endured hunger during 1999 included 4.9 million adults and 2.6 million children. A July 1999 General Accounting Office study concluded: "Children's participation in the Food Stamp Program has dropped more sharply than the number of children living in poverty, indicating a growing gap between need and assistance." Kennedy noted that while hunger and malnutrition are serious problems for people of all ages, their effects are particularly damaging to children. Hungry and underfed children are more likely to become anemic and to suffer from allergies, asthma, diarrhea, and infections. They are also more likely to have problems at school and difficulty in learning. When children arrive at school hungry, they cannot learn. Senator Kennedy's bill has been referred to the Senate Agriculture, Nutrition, and Forestry Committee, where it awaits action. Other bills on children's health, day-care standards, minimum wage, and welfare reforms are all pending in the U.S. Congress. However, they are delegated to committees at the time of writing.

After the bombing of the World Trade Center on September 11, 2001, persons who left public assistance for private-sector jobs suffered layoffs in the economic fallout. Some of the very areas that offered many welfare beneficiaries their first real jobs—service industries such as hotels, restaurants, airport concessions, and other travel-related fields, which during the boom of the 1990s soaked up workers with limited skills and experience—were the ones hardest hit in the aftermath of the terrorist attacks. In Washington, D.C., applications for welfare and other aid for the needy have increased by more than 50 percent since September 11. Some experts wonder whether their workplace experience has changed some of the former welfare beneficiaries, making them averse to accepting welfare again, and whether states will be willing to let their welfare rolls go up again.[5] These questions are yet to be answered. The well-being of many children is at stake.

There can be no solution to the problem of child poverty apart from changes in the economy that provide more jobs and better-paying jobs for young adults. Young adults have children, and children not only raised in poverty, but raised in poverty in the midst of affluence and overconsumption, can be very angry and destructive. They are expressing their spiritual poverty as well. Raising the minimum wage will help, but it will not by itself solve the problem of the growing gap between the rich and the poor families in which children are raised.

III. A CHRISTIAN PERSPECTIVE

Biblical Principles

All cultures and religions value children. Christianity is no exception. The child is cherished, both because the futures of person, family, and community lie in the children and because children are precious in their own right. The story of Ruth draws to an end with a celebrative statement, "A son has been born to Naomi" (Ruth 4:17). (The son was literally born to Ruth; Naomi was the grandmother.) The prophet Zechariah, looking to a better time, says, "And the streets of the city shall be full of boys and girls playing in its streets" (8:5). Jesus said, "Let the little children come to me; do not stop them; for it is to such as these that the kingdom of God belongs" (Mark 10:14).

Because the culture in both biblical and early-church times was dominated by the father, some wish to continue or reimpose this pattern today. This is impractical and neither genuinely biblical nor Christian. The patriarchal father was the head of not simply the nuclear family but of an extended tribe or clan that included relatives, servants, and (sometimes) slaves and was usually (like our own old-fashioned farm families) an economic work unit as well. The long period of adolescence that so marks family life today was not a part of that social organization. The extended family simply does not fit a mobile, industrialized, and urban society. We can, nevertheless, study the earlier model in order to identify and connect with the healing forces that, however imperfectly, were at work in it. We identify three:

The reality of interconnectedness. In contrast to the excessive individualism that so dominates our American imagination, we learn from Christian history that we depend on one another. We must support one another and take responsibility for one another if we are to survive and live fully. For children in earlier times, "social security" was provided by the extended family and the whole community as well as by their parents. The Bible repeatedly commanded that the community "take care of widows and orphans" (e.g., Exod. 22:22). In the absence of the extended family, children in need today must rely on society in the form of charity aid and various governmental agencies.

Valuing the child and the experience of the child. The life of the family was seen in the light of God's call. Children provide one of the basic images to convey this perspective. "Whoever welcomes one such child in my name welcomes me. If any of you put a stumbling block before one of these little ones who believe in me, it would be better for you if a great millstone were fastened around your neck and you were drowned in the depth of the sea" (Matt. 18:5–8). "Truly I tell you, unless you change and become like children, you will never enter the kingdom of heaven" (Matt. 18:3).

The simplicity and trust before God that is often difficult for adults to achieve can be learned from our young children. Possibly because they haven't yet developed a firm sense of past and future, they accept the infinite abundance of the present in complete trust. If we can see what is right beneath our feet, right under our noses, in this light, our fears filter away. This is like a treasure buried in a field, like a pearl of great price, and *a little child shall lead them.*

The God imagery found in Scripture. Among the most poignant images in the Bible is Jesus' comment as he considered Jerusalem: "How often have I desired to gather your children together as a hen gathers her brood under her wings!" (Matt. 23:37). The psalmist wrote, "As a father has compassion for his children, so the LORD has compassion for those who fear him" (Ps. 103:13). No one set of images is final, and for some persons, difficult childhood experience has made images of parental care unworkable. But for most, these images of persistent, noncoercive, compassionate, and loving parental care open an avenue of insight to the nature of God and provide guidance for our own conduct in relation not only to our own children but to all children.

Current Implications

The implications of these principles are well expressed in "The Covenant for God's Children" of the National Baptist Convention.

- Every child has the right to food, clothing, shelter, health care, and education. No child should be left out, regardless of the background, age, or status of his or her parents.
- Parents should be empowered to accept responsibility for caring for and supporting their children. Welfare reform must provide for services that will enable parents to care for their children, including medical care, child care, parenting training, mental health services, substance abuse treatment, counseling, and family-based services.

- Children need permanent homes and families. Welfare reform should increase the likelihood that children who cannot go home will be adopted. Welfare reform should include programs that reduce the financial burdens on families that adopt children who are hard to place or have special needs.
- Children need support from their extended families. Welfare reform should provide support for grandparents and other relatives who care for abused and neglected children.
- Churches should respond to and protect poor families and dependent children. Welfare reform should encourage community leadership and assist community institutions like churches and other religious organizations to support families. It should help people move from welfare to work based on their needs, not rigid regulations.
- Children have the right to be protected and raised in their own communities under safe, humane conditions that permit them to reach their full potential. Welfare reform proposals should not decrease the standard of care these children receive but should guarantee that children are safe.
- Young people leaving foster care need assistance to fulfill their potential to become responsible adults. Welfare reform should help them get jobs, housing, training, and higher education.
- Abused, battered, and neglected children need services in many areas, including health, mental health, and education. Welfare reform should encourage linkages among agencies that provide these systems.
- Children have the right to be supervised by competent and highly trained staff and cared for by loving and knowledgeable caregivers when under institutional care.

The Religious Right

Progressive Christians share with the religious right great concern for children and belief in the desirability of family as the context within which children are raised. Listen, for example, to Marian Wright Edelman:

> There is nobody in this country who believes more strongly than I that teens should postpone sexual activity, pregnancy and childbirth, that people shouldn't have children until they are ready to support them financially and emotionally, that parents should work to support their families, that children should be born within the bounds of marriage, and that children need two parents, although we must support and not stigmatize the often heroic efforts of single parents to raise children alone.[6]

However, progressive Christians are disturbed by the tendency of the religious right to suppose that these commitments are best expressed in depriving the children of teenage mothers of essential sustenance. The argument that these girls become mothers because of welfare is refuted by the facts.

Edelman points out that the rise and fall of teenage pregnancies is not correlated with the amount of government aid available.

> Teen births in this country actually declined fairly rapidly in the decades
> leading up to the mid-1980s. . . . They declined even during the short
> period when welfare was expanding. The teen birth rate started to rise
> again in the mid-1980s, but surely that was not caused by welfare
> changes—the rise occurred in a period when welfare benefits continued
> to shrink and rules changes made AFDC harder for teens to obtain.[7]

The real causes of teen pregnancy, Edelman goes on to say, are "hopelessness and lack of options—and a society with values so distorted [that it] lets
millions of its children grow up hopeless and undereducated."[8]

Two misconceptions contribute to the climate, encouraged by the religious
right, supporting legislation that punishes children for what are viewed as
parental failures: the notion of children as property and the notion that
poverty results from moral failure.

The notion of children as property. Both progressive Christians and the religious right affirm the sanctity of the family. Yet the patriarchal ideal of the religious right (which views children—and to an only slightly lesser degree
wives—as the property of the male head of the family and uses Scripture as
justification) does not allow for the outside intervention of others into the family unit. This model works only when each member stays in his or her "place,"
and "behaves" as he or she "should." Child abuse (particularly female child
abuse) under this system is rampant all over the world.

Sometimes the protection and nurture of children must be guarded by a
wider society outside the nuclear family. Our theology must affirm that children are a gift from God, not just to the nuclear family, but also to the wider
community. They are the heritage of a nation and the human family, not merely
of a couple. The willingness to allow children to suffer at the hands of their
caregivers or parents, for instance, cannot be condoned by a theology that
asserts human beings are stewards of the creation and children are worthy,
beloved creatures in their own right. A theology that emphasizes guardianship
of God's beloved children and not "ownership" of them can foster the acceptance of public policies that broaden the rights of persons outside the family to
care for children and intervene in their lives when necessary to protect them.

The notion that poverty results from moral failure. At times in the Scriptures being
poor is inextricably linked to God's judgment or the order of a universe in which
the rich and the poor each have a divinely set place. Therefore, the poverty of
children is seen as a curious birthright, a sharing in the sins of the parents.

In the speech at King/Drew Medical Center in Los Angeles in 1992 from
which we have been quoting, Marian Wright Edelman asked, "Why are our chil-

dren so poor?" and answered her own question, "Because their parents don't have enough income. I give this obvious answer because if you listened to the religious right, you would think that children are poor solely because their parents are acting immorally, because their values are perverse, because government help is ruining their lives, or because poverty is a natural consequence of our nation's diversity. . . . But in the first instance the cause of poverty is economics."[9]

People who are concerned about the nurture and rights of children must expressly put aside this view that parents' moral failure is an acceptable excuse for society's failing the children of the nation. Children, the most vulnerable members of society, should be placed above all else in our economic and educational priorities by society as a whole.

IV. WHAT WE CAN DO

Progressive Christians concerned about family and child welfare should support policies that would:

- Improve formulas concerning the provision of welfare assistance in addition to employment income for people leaving welfare, so that benefits do not drastically decline as income from employment increases.
- Increase the minimum wage so it will provide living wages for workers.
- Provide adequate pay and benefits, including full employee rights and protections to all who are employed.
- Provide education, training, and, when necessary, substance-abuse treatment to improve the employability of all potential workers.
- Provide child care, food stamps, health care, subsidized housing, and transportation support for those below the minimum income level.
- Increase the amount of child support that is passed through to the family from the government for those in poverty.
- Increase federal and state earned income tax credit.

We can engage in advocacy to take full advantage of new opportunities to promote the goals listed above and to oppose rules by states or local governments that restrict or oppress beneficiaries of TANF. We can celebrate program successes. One of these is the Head Start program, a government program that has approached the needs of young children holistically and effectively. It should be fully funded.

In addition to working for national and state policies that give all children a chance, we can support the efforts of the Children's Defense Fund and its ten suggestions:

1. Join the movement to Leave No Child Behind (this is a long-standing slogan of the Children's Defense Fund).

2. Educate yourself about children's needs and solutions to them. Then educate others.
3. See and hear the children around you. The most important thing in every child's life is a caring adult.
4. Volunteer to help children. You can mentor, tutor, be a Big Brother or Big Sister, or hold an abandoned baby at a local hospital.
5. Donate what you can to groups that serve children. Food, used clothing, kitchenware, computer equipment, and, of course, money can make a world of difference.
6. Consider becoming a foster parent or adopting a child.
7. Take a firsthand look at local children's problems and effective local solutions.
8. Speak out to the media and your local officials.
9. Work to make sure that every child gets a *healthy* start, a *head* start, a *fair* start and a *safe* start. To this we add a *moral* start.

To give every child a *healthy start* in life, we must

- ensure that, at a minimum, every child and pregnant woman has comprehensive health insurance coverage from a private or public source, and
- strengthen the delivery of health care so essential to children and pregnant women (including prenatal care, immunizations, and other preventive services), particularly among disadvantaged populations and within traditionally underserved neighborhoods and communities.

To give every child a *head start* in life, we must

- expand dramatically private and public efforts to support families with young children and bolster the parenting skills of new parents;
- take comprehensive steps to prevent teen pregnancy, including providing girls and boys with positive life options; and
- ensure the availability of high-quality child care, Head Start, and other early childhood development programs that promote the full development of children so that they enter school ready to learn while parents work to support their children.

To give every child a *fair start* in life, we must

- build a stronger economic foundation for families through job development and job creation efforts in depressed areas, as well as broader measures to ensure that jobs provide family-supporting wages and benefits, and
- ensure every child the quality education needed to become self-sufficient in the twenty-first-century economy.

To give every child a *safe start* in life, we must ensure that children have

- safe neighborhoods and safe schools,
- positive alternatives to the streets,

- positive interaction with caring adults, and
- protection from the guns that kill a child every two hours.

To give every child a *moral start* in life, we Christians must have

- private and public values that model respect for self and others,
- fairness and honesty in our neighborhoods, communities, workplaces, government, and at home, and
- a commitment to the Ten Commandments and the Sermon on the Mount in our daily life.

We can further affirm the United Nations Convention on the Rights of the Child. It took many months for the United Nations to agree on the term "rights" and to decide on the following:
Every child has the right

- to be loved
- to healthy food and medical care
- to protection from danger and cruelty
- to education and recreation
- to a name and to belong to a nation

Every child has the right

- to special help and care if he or she is handicapped
- to her or his own identity and to express his or her own culture, language, and religion
- to be cared for ahead of adults when there is a disaster

Every child has the right

- to live in a world without pollution
- to be free from discrimination of any kind
- to live in a society where there is peace and friendship among all peoples

This, not suffering, is what children deserve. However, the two nations that have not ratified the 1989 United Nations Convention on the Rights of the Child are the United States and Somalia. The Bush administration, like earlier U.S. administrations, argues that the treaty would supersede U.S. federal and state laws on sensitive issues. One of the main conflicts is over language. The United States wants to replace the term "reproductive health services" with "reproductive health care" because they fear that "services" includes abortion. The United States also wants to remove a clause providing special rehabilitation for girls who are war victims, fearing this could include birth control or abortion counseling for rape. Another issue may be the fact that the United States allows seventeen-year-olds to join the military, while the United Nations Convention specifies the age of eighteen as the lower limit.[10]

Each of us can covenant to work with our faith community to share with our children and adolescents by word and example a strong moral vision that builds inclusive, healing communities where no child will be left behind. To once again quote Douglas Sturm:

> The rights of children—to health care and education, to information and national identity, love and security, to economic and political power—are supportive of the life and growth of each individual child (within that child's particular cultural setting) and create a context through which the child's life contributes to the life of the community.[11]

Discussion Questions

1. Why is there so much public discussion of the needs of children, yet so much practical neglect of children?
2. What does it mean to "welcome" a child in the name of Christ? (Matt. 18:5–6) What are the social implications of this act? Should our personal aim be "to be like children" in the Christian faith?
3. Can you make an argument for sustaining the absolute authority of the father (patriarchy)? Against? Which are the most relevant present facts that speak to each argument? Does the religious right do a better job of acknowledging the underlying problem of the spiritual poverty of children today in its solutions?
4. Can the steady rise in the rate of divorce be reversed? What is good and what is bad about the relative ease with which divorces can be obtained? How does divorce affect children?
5. If we take the plight of poor children seriously, will we need to make basic changes in our economic and political system? Who is responsible for the poor in our society? How does the growing gap between the very rich and the very poor exacerbate the plight of poor children? Can government— local, state, and national—solve the problem? Or should individuals be responsible for their own circumstances?
6. What are the limits, dangers, and opportunities in the present welfare system?
7. Should the United States ratify the United Nations Convention on the Rights of the Child?

To Learn More

The Children's Defense Fund is perhaps the best resource for those interested in children's rights within the United States. Their website offers information and resources for researching national children's issues in greater depth. They publish *The State of America's Children Yearbook: A Report from the Children's Defense Fund* (Washington, D.C.: Ingram), which gives comprehensive, state-by-state annual data on family income, child health, children and families in crisis, child care and early childhood development, pregnancy, violence, and more. The founder of the Fund, Marian Wright Edelman, has written books on practical steps to help children, as well as devotional/inspirational literature reflecting her life work.

Douglas Sturm, a political scientist working from a Christian perspective, has written *Solidarity and Suffering: Toward a Politics of Relationality* (Albany, N.Y.: SUNY Press, 1998). The book includes a chapter on children's rights, basing these issues in his overall "politics of relationality." Sandra Nuñez and Trish Marx, *And Justice for All: The Legal Rights of Young People* (Brookfield, Conn.: Millbrook Press, 1997) provides historical background into young persons' legal rights at home, in the workplace, and at school, dealing with the controversy surrounding various laws, and suggests ways they are changing and being challenged. Sharon Stephens, ed., *Children and the Politics of Culture* (Princeton, N.J.: Princeton University Press, 1995) is a series of essays that explore the global dimensions of children at risk, the notion of children's rights, and the claim that every child has a right to cultural identity.

Web Resources:

www.childrensdefense.org —See above.

www.unicef.org —Official website for the United Nations Children's Fund. This site provides information on activities and programs internationally involving children. It also lists publications and current events involving children.

www.crin.org —This page has information about the state of children's rights at the international level. It is a source for other nongovernmental organizations (NGOs) doing work in children's issues, especially in the implementation of the Convention on the Rights of the Child.

http://pages.cthome.net/henry-helps/index.html —Lists good, well-organized resources (websites, materials, and organizations).

3

Reflections on Abortion

Susan, a thirteen-year-old girl, was often sexually abused and finally raped by her uncle; she became pregnant. Because the extended-family ties were very powerful, she was afraid to tell her parents what had happened. Furthermore, she knew that her parents had strong objections to abortion on religious grounds and believed they would never permit her to have an abortion. In her distress she called her older sister, a first-year college student. Her sister, torn by conflicting family and religious loyalties and uncertain what action she could legally take, nonetheless arranged for an abortion for Susan and accompanied her.

I. INTRODUCTION

Abortion is a deeply divisive public issue in American society today. Though a majority favors keeping abortion safe and legal, even these supporters are often uneasy about its moral justification. A vocal minority keeps the issue alive in the political process, attempting to end legal sanction for abortion.

Abortions have been induced for many centuries, often by practitioners of traditional medicine. In the past, medicines or procedures used to induce abortion were often as dangerous to the woman as to the fetus, and many physicians and religious people have condemned abortion as much to protect women as to protect the fetus. At times, when high rates of infant mortality have threatened the survival of family lines or even of whole societies, abortion was also seen as socially damaging.

Today the situation is very different. Overpopulation, with its threats of hunger and malnutrition as well as damage to the environment, is a major social problem of the twenty-first century. Around the world the rate of infant mortality is dropping, though unevenly; the rate remains higher in most of the countries of the South than in most of the countries of the North.

Furthermore, abortion performed with modern methods under hygienic conditions has become safe for women, particularly if performed within ten to twelve weeks of conception. In the U.S., 88 percent of abortions are performed before thirteen weeks; the percentage performed in the earliest weeks has been rising. Few abortions are performed after fifteen weeks.[1] For women who have a legal abortion, there is a mortality rate of about three out of every one hundred thousand women. This is a lower mortality rate than for those women who come to term and give birth to live babies. Among those having illegal abortions, however, the mortality rate rises sharply to between fifty and one hundred fifty per one hundred thousand women.[2] For teenagers, legal abortion is seven to nine times safer than childbirth.[3]

Still many moral questions divide Americans today concerning abortion. Is a fetus a human being? Is abortion murder? Who has the right to decide whether an abortion should take place? Does it matter morally at what stage of development the abortion takes place? What are the social consequences of abortion? These are familiar questions in the Christian tradition and in other cultures, but they are being answered in a new social and intellectual context.

II. CURRENT PRACTICE AROUND THE WORLD

Probably three-fourths of the world's population lives in countries where abortions can be legally obtained.[4] An estimated 52 million abortions were performed around the world in 1995. Approximately half of these were illegal, and 21 million of them were performed under unsafe conditions.

Countries differ widely in their laws related to providing abortion. In the Netherlands abortions are legal and performed free, but there is a five-day "thinking time" required if menstruation is more than sixteen days overdue. Abortions have been provided virtually on demand in Russia, where some women may have three to five abortions in their lifetime.[5]

It is estimated that the aggressive family-planning program in the People's Republic of China, which includes abortions, has reduced the number of births in that land between 1970 and 1990 by a total of 240 million. In a country that has a mere 7 percent of the world's arable land and must feed 22 percent of the world's population, the government's hope is to keep the population under 1.3 billion. Consequently it provides contraceptives free of charge and has until recently tried to regulate strictly who may become pregnant. No contraceptive is 100 percent effective, however, so the government provides hygienic abortions at no cost for those who become pregnant without official permission or who need to terminate a pregnancy for health reasons.[6] In spite of these strenuous efforts, however, China's population will probably not stabilize until it reaches approximately 1.7 billion people.

Wishing to have a sufficient number of soldiers, Japan made abortion illegal in 1930 but rescinded the law after World War II, when the government realized that further population growth was inimical to the national interest.[7] Currently abortion is a major element in Japan's population-stabilization program, especially since certain family-planning methods, such as oral contraceptives, have only recently been made available to Japanese women. There are some areas in Japan where it is estimated that for every live birth, there are one or more abortions.

In Latin America as a whole, where both the law and Catholic religion prohibit abortions, there is an average of one illegal abortion for every two live births, and in Uruguay three abortions to each live birth, according to Alice S. Rossi of the U.S. Public Health Service.[8] In Chile, where all abortion is prohibited, women who undergo abortions are prosecuted—usually after being reported by caregivers in the institutions where they were treated for complications.[9]

A Nepalese woman doctor recently stated that complications from illegal abortions accounted for more than half the maternal deaths in Kathmandu hospitals.[10] The law then forbade abortions, punishing them with prison terms of three years to life. Since March 2002, early abortions are permitted, and abortions at any time if there is danger to the woman's health or severe birth defects.[11]

In 1985, there were more than 3,700 women in Thailand who, having undergone illegally induced abortions, were admitted to 130 government hospitals. About 85 percent of them were married but too impoverished to take care of an additional child. This number does not count the women cared for in private hospitals or those who were secretly given an abortion in a government hospital to keep them from going to illegal clinics or those who suffered and died at home.[12] Laws regarding abortion in Thailand have become somewhat more lenient since that time.

Women are most likely to die from abortions in Africa, especially in east Africa. Though Kenyan law forbids abortions, many are performed in an unsafe manner. The law does permit abortions to be done exceptionally if the purpose is to save the mother's life and if it is done "in good faith and with reasonable care and skill." An organization known as Kisumu Medical and Educational Trust is teaching medical personnel how to complete failed abortions safely to preserve women's lives.[13]

In Ethiopia also, abortion is a crime. The jail sentence (three months to five years) takes into consideration mitigating factors, such as if this were the only way to avoid "grave and permanent danger to life or health."[14]

In the United States the number of abortions steadily declined from 1990 until 1995 but increased slightly in 1996. In 1997 it dropped by 3 percent to the lowest level since 1978. There were fewer than 1.2 million abortions in 1997. According to the Centers for Disease Control and Prevention, since 1995 there have been 20 abortions per 1,000 women aged 15–44, the lowest rate since 1975. This same rate held steady in 1997, the most recent year for which statistics are available.[15] It is not clear what has caused the decline since 1990. It is likely to be a combination of more couples using contraceptive methods than before (possibly including increased use of condoms to prevent AIDS), and abortion services becoming less available. The latter factor is stressed by Planned Parenthood Federation of America and the Alan Guttmacher Institute.[16] One reason for the decline in availability is continued violent intimidation of health-care providers at abortion clinics by abortion protesters. Another is that many doctors performing abortions are reaching retirement age and younger doctors have not been taught to do abortions in many standard medical training programs.[17] Still another reason is the proliferation of state restrictions on abortion.

III. SEEING ABORTION FROM VARIED PERSPECTIVES

A Biological Perspective

Several studies indicate that approximately 69 percent of all fertilized eggs are spontaneously aborted, usually in the first few weeks of pregnancy, and often before the mother realizes she is pregnant. This spontaneous abortion is a natural screening and usually indicates that there is a problem that would interfere with normal development of the fetus. Spontaneous abortions thus significantly reduce the number of babies that might be born with hereditary defects.

Prenatal testing often reveals the presence of serious genetic defects in fetuses at a later stage of development. If medical measures are taken to keep a fetus alive and bring it to birth in spite of serious defects, the damaging genetic load for the next generation is increased. From a biological point of view, the force of natural selection is diminished, thus significantly increasing the number of genetic disorders. Induced abortion in such cases can function in the way spontaneous abortions do.

On the other hand, if abortions are performed for other reasons, their effects may be negative from a biological perspective. This is especially true if parents select for one gender over the other. Now that parents can know the gender of the fetus early, this becomes a serious danger.

A Legal Perspective

It is only within the past 200 years in the Anglo-Saxon tradition that abortion has been restricted by law; for centuries prior to that time it had been a private, personal decision. The first known abortion laws in this tradition came in two cases in 1327 and 1348 in England that established the common-law right to terminate a pregnancy at any time. In 1803, for the first time, a statute restricting abortion was passed, making abortion a crime after "quickening," the time when the mother first feels the movements of the fetus.

Abortion is not mentioned in the U.S. Constitution. In 1812 the Massachusetts Supreme Court ruled that, with the woman's consent, abortion was legal before quickening. During the nineteenth century, abortion functioned as a means of birth control, but it was dangerous. At least partly out of concern about the inferior medical treatment offered by lay people, the recently formed American Medical Association acted in 1859 to condemn abortion. By the end of the century, through vigorous AMA lobbying of state legislatures, every state had made abortion a crime.[18]

Abortions did not cease, however. Prior to the 1973 Supreme Court decision in Roe v. Wade, which provided for legal abortion in all states, experts estimated that as many as one million illegal abortions took place in the U.S. each year.[19] They were provided both by doctors and by people without medical training. By the late 1960s safe abortion techniques were available, and within the AMA there was a campaign to liberalize abortion laws. Widespread public awareness of the births of children severely damaged in the womb by epidemics of German measles and by women taking thalidomide during pregnancy gave urgency to efforts to provide legal and safe abortions for women at risk.[20] The social context of antiabortion laws had changed radically.

In current United States law, a biological being becomes a human being at the moment of birth. Declaring in 1973 that abortion is a permissible medical procedure, the U.S. Supreme Court said, "The unborn have never been recognized in the law as persons in the whole sense."[21] There is a practical aspect to this, as pointed out by retired Supreme Court justice Tom Clark: The moment of birth is known. "[T]he law deals in reality not obscurity—the known rather than the unknown. When sperm meets egg, life may eventually form, but quite often it does not. The law does not deal in speculation."[22]

Nonetheless the Supreme Court ruling in Roe v. Wade distinguishes between the first trimester of pregnancy, when a woman is completely free to decide about abortion, the second trimester, when the state's right to regulate health care and protect fetal life may result in regulation of abortion, and the time after "viability," when the fetus could possibly live outside the womb, then thought to be after 24–28 weeks of gestation. After viability the state may protect the potential life of the fetus by prohibiting abortions not necessary to preserve the woman's life or health.[23]

In recent years state legislatures have increasingly used openings in the Roe v. Wade decision to restrict availability of abortion by requiring waiting periods, mandatory counseling, and parental permission for minors. These restrictions often delay abortion until the safe period has passed. As medically defined viability moves back towards conception through advanced technology, the available period for a woman's free decision to abort may be further shortened.

IV. PARTIES TO THE POLITICAL DEBATE

For the most part the political debate takes place between two parties. One calls itself "pro-life," the other "pro-choice." Often people are made to feel that these are the only options.

The Pro-Life Movement

Those who bear the label "pro-life" (sometimes called the "right-to-life movement") focus their main concern on the fetus. They stress that the fetus actually becomes a human being at conception. Any act intentionally done to prevent that biological entity from being born into the world is considered murder. They accent the right of the fetus more than the quality of life of the child that is to be born, and they subordinate the rights of the mother to the rights of the fetus.

The pro-life stance has led a few of its adherents to engage in extreme actions, such as the public harassment and even murder of doctors who provide abortions in family-planning clinics. There have also been many bombings of centers that not only provide abortions but also provide counseling to prevent teenage pregnancy, contraceptive services, prenatal and postnatal care for mothers.

The Pro-Choice Movement

Those in the pro-choice group focus on the right of the pregnant woman to decide what happens in her body. If she learns that the fetus cannot develop into a normal child, for example, this group feels she should be given the choice to bear the child or abort it. Among the principal factors this group would cite to justify abortion are rape, incest, congenital defects, and the mental and physical health of the woman. Pro-choice adherents believe that there is no particular point before birth at which it can be said that an embryo or fetus becomes a full human person. Rather, the fetus is in the process of becoming human.

V. A CHRISTIAN PERSPECTIVE

Biblical and Historical Teaching

While the biblical heritage must weigh heavily in any Christian ethical decision, the Bible provides no direct guidance about induced abortion. Nowhere in the Bible is abortion either forbidden or permitted. Some interpreters believe that the biblical traditions offer no guidance about abortion because the practice was too obviously wrong to need a rule about it. Since so many sexual and family questions are fully discussed in various parts of the Bible, however, it is much more probable that abortion was not mentioned because it was not specifically prohibited.

There is a reference to an accidental miscarriage. Exodus 21:22–24 discusses the case of a pregnant woman who is accidentally injured by a fight between two men and loses the fetus. The punishment is a fine to be determined by the judges, "what the woman's husband demands" and, if there is further harm, presumably to the woman, it shall be paid for by the rule of "life for life."

This text shows that the fetus was thought to have value, but that it was not regarded as a human person. That insight is a significant contribution to our present discussion. On the other hand, this passage, like most family law in the Bible, strongly weights the question towards the rights of the husband. The husband's loss is the focus. Modern interpreters must take into account the cultural traditions of the ancient Near East which shape this passage. Apart from its witness to the web of relationships surrounding decisions about the fetus, it offers no guidance in the typical contemporary context of a woman in trouble contemplating a therapeutic abortion.

One other type of biblical passage is often mentioned in connection with abortion. In Psalm 139:13 the psalmist praises God as the one who "knit me together in my mother's womb" and says, "Your eyes beheld my unformed substance." In Jeremiah 1:5 the prophet hears God speak: "Before I formed you in the womb I knew you, and before you were born I consecrated you."

These passages surely affirm that the growing life has value, and they express the profound faith that the whole course of one's existence is under the constant concern and guidance of God. But they do not deal with the question of whether the fetus is a human being. To the contrary, they affirm that God's concern reaches into the formative stages of human growth, precisely before one is a human being. They tell us that in any dealing whatever with reproductive questions, we are dealing with serious questions, but they do not tell us how to deal with such questions.

All Christians would look in a general way to the creation stories of Genesis, where humanity is created in the image of God, as a source of our profound reverence for all human life, and to God's blessing there of human reproductive capacities. Though such passages offer no specific guidance about abortion, they provide the context within which we must reflect on the value of the woman's life as well as that of all other persons caught up in the decision about abortion.

Though the Bible seems uninterested in abortion, many of the early church fathers condemned it, beginning in the second century, and some called it homicide. This period, beginning with the late second century, was the period when Roman law began to criminalize abortion, though Roman law did not characterize it as homicide at that time.[24]

Still another factor helping to explain how the new Christian concern about abortion developed is the way the Hebrew text of Exodus 21:22–24, discussed above, was received by Jews and then Christians in the Greek-speaking world. In the Greek Septuagint translation, the text says that if the "little child" [paidion] lost is imperfectly (i.e. not fully) formed, a penalty will be paid; if it is perfectly formed, the penalty is a life for a life. Here a decidedly Aristotelian distinction between the early and later stages of fetal development has been introduced. The influential first-century Jewish exegete Philo was much interested in this text, and his work came to be known to Christians; and of course the earliest Greek-speaking Christians used the Septuagint version of the Hebrew Scriptures. So quite early Christians began to distinguish between the lesser seriousness of abortion in the time before "ensoulment" (around forty days after conception for boys and eighty days for girls) and the greater seriousness after that time. Only after "ensoulment" (or "hominization"—becoming human) was abortion considered homicide.[25]

Differences in penalty for the two sorts of abortion can be seen consistently in the penitential practice and in the collections of canon law down to the nineteenth century.[26] With the exception of three years (1588–91) when Pope Sixtus V abolished the distinction, the lesser penalties for early abortion remained until Pope Pius IX. In 1869 he dropped the distinction concerning ensoulment and excommunicated all who had abortions.[27] Thus the new

Catholic teaching that *all* abortion is homicide corresponds in time with the period in America when the AMA was working to outlaw all abortion on medical grounds and must have reinforced that effort. Official contemporary Catholic teaching holds to this late-nineteenth-century position. In 1974 the Vatican's Sacred Congregation for the Doctrine of Faith stated that the fetus has human life from the moment of conception, even though it is not yet a full human being.[28]

The argument against abortion has been traditionally buttressed by the Catholic teaching that any act that intends to separate sexual union from procreation is sinful. Abortion voluntarily obtained indicates that the sexual partners did not enter into their union with an intent to procreate.[29] Some modern interpreters believe that this aspect of the church's teaching on abortion (as a "sin of sex" rather than a "sin of killing") is more significant than has usually been granted.[30]

Early Protestants did not make an issue of traditional teaching about abortion, though they believed abortion was wrong.[31] Nonetheless some of them were caught up in Renaissance rethinking of relevant aspects of traditional science. Medieval Christian thought was strongly shaped by the writings of Aristotle, who believed that the "seed" from which the fetus grew was given by the male, and the female merely nurtured the seed passively in her body. At the time of the Renaissance, there was much debate among the doctors about the physical nature of women. The new consensus of the Renaissance physicians by 1600 was that Aristotle had been wrong in assuming that the female contributed no "seed" to the creation of a child. Rather they now followed Galen, generally believed to have taught that women as well as men contributed seminal material to the formation of a fetus. Though some Protestant theologians, like Menno Simons and Melchior Hoffman, held to the older view, others, like the Reformed theologians John Calvin, John à Lasco, and Gellius Faber took the position of the Renaissance physicians in arguing against the traditional Aristotelian view.[32] The acknowledgment that women share in the biological "ownership" of the fetus would in more modern times have important influence in thinking about abortion. In other ways, too, Protestant theologians dropped Aristotelian assumptions about reproduction, like ensoulment at a later point in development than conception.

Current Church Teaching

Among Catholics in the United States there is deep division. Many in fact have abortions. There is an organization among active Catholics called "Catholics for a Free Choice." Its members believe that the opinions of church scholars and theologians have never been unanimous on abortion, and they want to debate the issue in an open forum.[33] Nevertheless, the official position of the church is strongly opposed to all abortions, Catholic hospitals refuse to perform abortions, and the American bishops have publicly supported efforts to overturn Roe v. Wade and make abortion illegal again.

Today most of the conservative and fundamentalist Protestant denominations stand with Catholicism in condemning all abortion. They were linked with the Christian Coalition's insistence that antiabortion language be used in the 1996 Republican platform, and many would be happy to see a constitutional amendment that would revoke the Supreme Court's Roe v. Wade decision. Christian Coalition "report cards" on candidates for election, featuring their views on abortion, have been distributed in many of these churches, and the issue remains important in contemporary political campaigns.

Most mainline Protestant denominations in recent years have come to affirm the right of a woman to choose abortion in difficult circumstances. As heirs of the Reformation, they have examined church traditions concerning abortion in the light of the Bible in its original Hebrew and Greek languages—and thus the Exodus 21:22–24 text in the original Hebrew version—and they have concluded that the Bible does not forbid abortion. Again as heirs of the Reformation, they have affirmed that the Gospel forbids making ecclesiastical laws that restrict Christian freedom and entangle consciences when the Bible does not require them. Though they do not promote abortion, they defend the freedom of women to make a responsible decision. Many denominational organizations, or divisions within them, are members of the Religious Coalition for Reproductive Rights.

The American Baptist Churches/USA have stated that in their tradition "the integrity of each person's conscience must be respected; therefore, we believe that abortion must be a matter of responsible, personal decision."[34] They, like other Protestants, refer to their commitment to the First Amendment guarantee of the free exercise of religion and the need for keeping abortions safe and legal.

Since the 1970s American Presbyterian General Assemblies have affirmed the pregnant woman's ability to reach a morally justifiable decision to abort, citing such circumstances as deformity of the fetus, conception from rape or incest, grave threats to the physical or mental health of the mother or child, or the socioeconomic condition of the family. They have also affirmed public legislation such as the 1993 Freedom of Choice Act to protect women's access to legal abortion.[35]

The United Methodist Church has said, "When an unacceptable pregnancy occurs, a family, and most of all the pregnant woman, is confronted with the need to make a difficult decision. We believe that continuance of a pregnancy which endangers the life or health of the mother, or poses other serious problems concerning the life, health, or mental capability of the child to be, is not a moral necessity. In such case, we believe the path of mature Christian judgment may indicate the advisability of abortion."[36]

The mainline churches also understand that women accepting the responsibility to make such difficult moral decisions need all the information that can help them make an informed choice. Christian women should be able to count on the support of their congregations, which can help to provide hope and courage to deal with daunting circumstances. And whatever they decide, they need acceptance and pastoral care.

A Progressive Christian View

As progressive Christians we affirm the effort of the mainline churches to preserve Roe v. Wade and retain for women the legal right to choose. However, with most mainline church members, we believe that it is also important, morally and theologically, to set the rights of the pregnant woman in a larger context, recognizing the valid interests not only of the father and other family members but also of the fetus and the wider society. We call our position "Pro–Human Family." The difficult moral question faced both by individuals and the body politic is how the right of the fertilized human ovum "is to be related to other rights, such as the right of the mother to make her own decision about whether to take on the enormous responsibility involved in giving birth to a child, the right of the father to share in such a decision, the rights of other children to have their interests considered, the right of society to expand or contract its population, the right of future generations to inherit a habitable world, the right of other animals to be fruitful and multiply."[37]

A pro–human family position emphatically does not promote abortion. Its goal is a situation in which the need for abortion will be very rare. But it recognizes that in our present, quite imperfect world there are times when safe abortions should be provided for women with special needs. Abortion is never a happy solution, but it is sometimes the least bad of those that are available. We hope that, increasingly, decisions about abortion will be made in light of the following four principles.

Respect life. Our faith calls us to respect all life, and especially all human life. This includes respect for the life potential of the fetus. The destruction of the developing human fetus should never be casual or considered inconsequential at any stage of development. Even though the fetus is still only a potential person, it is in the process of becoming a human being. Of course, respect for life calls also, and even more clearly, for respect for already fully developed human beings. It does not call for the sacrifice of mature human lives for the sake of the fetus.

Respect women. As Christians we know that both men and women are created in the image of God and equally loved by God. Unfortunately, we also know that in our tradition women have often, even usually, not been accorded equal status. Too often men have made the decisions with respect to women's lives and even with respect to their giving birth. Respect for women requires of us that they be accorded a fully equal place in society as a whole and primary responsibility to decide about what takes place in their bodies. Just as important is that we work together to create a society in which women will not be faced with the painful decision about abortion, a society in which they will not conceive unwanted children, on the one hand, and will not, on the other hand, be deterred from bearing wanted children because they have no homes, because they lack access to adequate health care, because they have no networks of personal support, or because they lack a faith which could provide hope and courage to meet the challenges of the future.

Respect for religious liberty. We believe that freedom to follow the dictates of one's own conscience is of inestimable importance. Any effort to coerce the conscience and limit personal freedom of citizens in this country through the power of public law in matters of human reproduction constitutes a serious threat to moral and religious liberty and threatens the freedom protected under the policy of separation of church and state. Christians should protect the freedom of health-care providers to offer needed reproductive services such as birth control and abortion. At the same time, we should respect the consciences of those doctors and nurses who believe that termination of a pregnancy is always morally wrong.

Respect the global human and nonhuman communities. Progressive Christians will nurture the capacity to see and address our personal problems in the context of the needs of our own society and all societies around the world. We will consider not only the short-term but also the long-term effects of our actions on humanity and on the sustainability of planet Earth. We will undertake to formulate population policies in light of this global concern and to set our thinking about issues of abortion in this widest context.

From these principles we make the following judgments about specific factors bearing on the decision about abortion. We do so first from the perspective of the fetus, then from the perspective of the woman, and finally from the perspective of society as a whole.

The fetus. The rhetoric of the pro-life group is overblown when it implies that with the fertilization of an ovum there is a human person. Nevertheless, its passionate commitment to the cause of the fetus is an important reminder that we are dealing with a potential human being. Christians should be gravely hesitant to destroy the rich potentialities embodied in a fetus. The opposition to abortion has strong grounds here. Nevertheless, even when we approach matters entirely from the perspective of the fetus, there are occasions when abortion may be indicated.

Today more than eighty genetic diseases and hundreds of chromosomal disorders can be diagnosed early in the pregnancy. There are cases in which it is known in advance that the baby can live only briefly and will require constant hospitalization. What life the infant would have may be one of pain. In some instances, even if a longer life can be expected, the anticipated disorder or deformity is so serious that an abortion may be the kindest act.

If neither parent will love the child or care for the child adequately, there can be unending calamity for both parents and child. Unwanted children always suffer. In extreme cases they are abused, battered, and even murdered. Two Swedish psychiatrists, Forssman and Thuwe, made a study of the long-term follow-up of more than a hundred children whose mothers had been refused abortions. Compared with the rest of the population, about twice as many of them were registered juvenile delinquents or had required psychiatric consultation or hospital treatment. More than three times as many of them had been in foster care or a children's home, and seven times as many were on public assistance after the age of sixteen.[38]

The woman. The rhetoric of the pro-choice group is disturbing when it implies that only the woman has rights with respect to the fate of a fetus. The fetus, on the one hand, and society as a whole, on the other, also have legitimate interests. At the same time, after so many centuries of patriarchal control over women, society now "has the duty to lean over backward to assist women who are seeking, psychologically and publicly, to take full responsibility for their lives. The decision as whether to bear or not to bear a child is so central to that responsibility that social interference should be muted."[39] A woman facing a decision about abortion needs to know that some women have long-term negative psychological effects after having an abortion. And those women who believe that abortion is morally wrong under all circumstances, even when carrying a fetus to term endangers their lives, should have their decisions fully respected. Nevertheless, there are a number of circumstances that count in favor of abortion, even though they should be weighed against others.

Victims of rape and incest are often justified in the refusal to bear the children of sexual predators. Girls of twelve or thirteen are often ill advised to become mothers. Not only is it relatively dangerous physically for them to bring the fetus to term, but also they are not psychologically or socially prepared to function as mothers. A woman who falls ill while pregnant or who suffers from severe chronic illness may be deemed by her doctor physically unable to bear a child. In some cases economic conditions are such that the woman simply cannot afford to have a child. When there are other children, the cost to them of an additional sibling becomes an important consideration.

Society. A concern for the welfare of global society now and in the future is a difficult concept for those of us living in the United States. It is particularly difficult to relate it to such intimately personal questions as abortion. Our culture tells us that our primary consideration is what is best for the individuals directly involved. But in the long run the well-being of individuals depends on that of society.

For most of human history, larger families served the interest of society. Women were discouraged from limiting family size. Today the social context has changed. The problem for the world as a whole is rapid population growth. Even relatively slow population growth, when combined with high per capita consumption of scarce resources, is a serious problem for the human family. (See chapters 16 and 14, "The Global Population Crisis" and "The Church and Environmentalism.") Accordingly, there is no longer justification, from the point of view of the real needs of society as a whole, for pressuring women to have unwanted children. Indeed, even wanted children can be a problem. If many parents want large families and act on that desire, in the end all suffer from overpopulation.

The conflict between individual choice and social need shows up in another way. Today in parts of Asia it is increasingly common for couples to abort female fetuses selectively. Influenced by cultural preferences for sons, yet needing small families, they use new technology to determine the sex of the fetus in order to assure birth of a son. What is perceived as good for the particular family *now* will *in the future* be damaging to society and to all the individuals who make it up, as the normal sex ratio of births is skewed.

If, despite the absence of benefit to society in requiring unwanted births, society refuses a woman access to an abortion, it should assume full responsibility for helping her and the child meet all the problems they will face. Unfortunately, in the United States there is more public pressure to outlaw abortion than to allot the money needed to take care of unwanted children. Some who show great concern for the unborn at the same time fail to hear the cries of babies who must bear, over a lifetime, the afflictions of being unwelcome in the hearts of their parents. These people sometimes seem to ignore the devastating effects of adolescent childbearing upon the mothers, the babies, the families, and society.[40]

One reason that the Japanese legalized abortion, according to LaFleur, was that it promotes their goal of making sure that all the children who are born are also *maximally wanted*.[41] The tangible benefits of this policy are suggested by UNICEF's statistics. Infant mortality in Japan is, along with that of Sweden and Finland, the world's lowest, while that of the United States rises yearly. Japanese literacy is 99 percent compared to 80 percent in the United States. The school dropout rate is only 6 percent compared to 30 percent here. Drug episodes and crimes of rape remain statistically very low.

VI. WHAT WE CAN DO

To reduce significantly the need for abortions in this country, let us work together to:

- Provide access for all women to the best contraceptive education and supplies possible, including "morning-after" medication, so that all children will be wanted children;
- Make a clear distinction between regular family planning and the option of abortion as a last resort;
- Educate young men and women to responsible and loving sexual life and parenthood;
- Provide support and counsel for women and men trying to accept the responsibilities of parenthood;
- Work to overcome inequities for women, especially by ensuring full educational opportunities and access to jobs that pay enough to support children;
- Confront the broader social problems that often lead to the need for abortion: lack of job training, less-than-living wages, homelessness or inadequate housing, lack of access to regular health care, unpaid maternity leaves;
- Make adoption more attractive and acceptable to women considering abortion.

To protect the health of women, we must insist that all abortions:

- Be done in a manner which is legal, safe, and respectful of the woman;
- Take place as early as possible in the pregnancy;
- Be available at a cost affordable to all in need.

To strengthen the social network, let us urge legislators to:

- Keep abortions safe and legal;
- Minimize regulations which will delay access to early abortions;
- Resist coercive pressures from those who wish to impose their own religiously motivated view opposing abortion on the whole society, and especially resist those who add antiabortion riders to unrelated and needed legislation;
- Resist denial of reproductive health services to community members when Catholic-owned health-care groups purchase community hospitals;
- Oppose efforts to restrict access by American physicians and their

patients to pharmaceutical products that can produce abortion and that have been proven safe and effective by standard testing methods;

- Ensure that low-income women in need of abortions have access through Medicaid or other programs;
- Keep perspective on the abortion issue by focusing effectively on the needs of children: affordable, high-quality daycare, education, housing, health care, proper nourishment, and parents not so overburdened by multiple jobs that they cannot care for their children;
- Be consistently generous in funding family-planning programs around the world, especially through the United States Agency for International Development (USAID) and the United Nations family-planning programs;
- Study and adopt a pro–human family stance.

To engage the medical community, let us urge doctors to:

- Find all possible ways to keep abortion as a medical procedure in the mainstream of medical practice;
- Support those of their colleagues who can in good conscience provide needed abortions;
- Assure that abortion, as a medical procedure, is included in the appropriate curricula of medical education.

To ensure meaningful dialogue with those who may take very different views regarding abortion, we must:

- Listen and ask questions, trying to create mutual understanding;
- Work to remove the inflammatory rhetoric of current public discourse about abortion, which fosters hatred and violence.

Discussion Questions

1. Reflect again on the story with which this chapter began. What do you suppose were the factors that led Susan to seek an abortion? What were the factors that her sister must have taken into account in making a decision to help Susan? In the light of the arguments made in this chapter, explain why you might or might not have made the same decisions as Susan and her sister.
2. What may be the effects on public policy regarding abortion if new pharmaceutical products permitting women to have abortions without surgery become widely available in America?
3. What are the laws concerning abortion in your state? Are there restrictions imposed? Are low-cost, safe abortions available to women with limited income?
4. How might your congregation act on the recommendations offered? Are there some with which you disagree?

To Learn More

Daniel A. Dombrowski and Robert Deltete, *A Brief, Liberal, Catholic Defense of Abortion* (Urbana and Chicago: University of Illinois Press, 2000) provides a scholarly critique of current Catholic teaching on abortion, showing what the authors see as its weaknesses and defending a Catholic pro-choice stance.

For books discussing the overall social framework of the abortion debate, see the following: Celeste Michelle Condit, *Decoding Abortion Rhetoric: Communicating Social Change* (Urbana and Chicago: University of Illinois Press, 1990) studies the rhetoric on both sides of the issue and its social function. Ted G. Jelen, ed., *Perspectives on the Politics of Abortion* (Westport, Conn.: Praeger, 1995) is a series of articles exploring the politics of abortion. Some articles attempt to reconceptualize pro-choice and to refocus on problems, such as child care, employment and compensation, that can make pregnancy a crisis. Eileen L. McDonagh, *Breaking the Abortion Deadlock: From Choice to Consent* (New York and Oxford: Oxford University Press, 1996) is an attempt to reframe arguments in favor of permitting abortion by moving from a "pro-choice" to a "pro-consent" to pregnancy. Axel I. Mundigo and Cynthia Indriso, *Abortion in the Developing World* (London and New York: World Health Organization, 1999) provide a collection of articles from different geographical areas around the world. The articles explore the relation between abortion and contraception, the quality of abortion care, adolescent sexuality, and implications of research for policy.

For historical and political perspectives, see Michele McKeegan, *Abortion Politics: Mutiny in the Ranks of the Right* (New York: Free Press [Macmillan], 1992), which discusses the history of the role of antiabortion stances in the politics of the right and recent emergence of pro-choice voices in that camp. See also Jean Schroedel, *Is the Fetus a Person? A Comparison of Policies across the Fifty States* (Ithaca, N.Y.: Cornell University Press, 2000). Rita J. Simon, *Abortion: Statutes, Policies, and Public Attitudes the World Over* (Westport, Conn.: Praeger, 1998) gives a comparative study of public policy in many nations.

Another Christian resource is the Religious Coalition for Reproductive Choice. They have an educational series on the abortion debate.

You can contact them at:

The Religious Coalition for Reproductive Choice
1025 Vermont Ave. NW, Suite 1130
Washington DC 20005
(202) 628-7700
info@rcrc.org
www.rcrc.org

4

Human Rights
and Civil Rights

* Article 38 of the Syrian Constitution guarantees free speech to its citizens. In 1992 Niza Nayyuf, journalist, human rights advocate, and leader of the Committee for the Defense of Democratic Freedoms and Human Rights, was arrested, tortured, and, after a trial deemed "grossly unfair" by Amnesty International, was sentenced to ten years in prison for "disseminating false information." With serious medical problems, he was refused medical treatment until he would disavow his political beliefs, which he refused to do. Thanks to an Amnesty International letter-writing campaign, he was released in 2001.

* In 1990 Dr. Saw Mra Aung, a physician, was elected to the Burmese Parliament as a representative of the Arakan League for Democracy, which speaks for a Buddhist ethnic minority. He was not allowed to take his seat (nor were members of the far larger National League for Democracy, which won 80 percent of the seats; the leader of the League has been in detention for years). Indeed, the military government of Burma, now called Myanmar, has prevented the parliament from meeting since then. In September 1998 Dr. Saw Mra Aung, now 81 and in poor health, was arrested and placed in detention.

* Recent studies in the United States have shown the degree to which local police departments participate in "racial profiling," stopping cars driven by African Americans simply because they are African Americans. The rationale is that in certain areas all "outsiders" are to be regarded as suspicious characters.

I. INTRODUCTION

The first two of these cases are but two of the hundreds compiled by Amnesty International, an organization headquartered in London that aims to reduce the abuse of human rights in the world by appealing directly to governments with large-scale letter-writing campaigns that focus on the plight of specific individuals. Its success led to a Nobel Peace Prize.

American church members will not be surprised by these reports and many similar reports that appear all over the world. Even those who are not regular newswatchers will be aware of wholesale murder, rape, and torture of innocent civilians in places like Rwanda, Kosovo, and East Timor. Since September 11, 2001, attention has been focused in a new way on depredations of human rights in Afghanistan under the Taliban. The world has often seemed an ugly place, so much so that when it comes to injustices abroad, Christians and non-Christians alike may be tempted to throw up their hands and say something like, "I'm just thankful I live in America. What can I do about the abuse of human rights in faraway places?"

The third case reminds us that human rights abuses, even if not as gross as the first two, also exist in the United States. Great progress has been made in the last fifty years to overcome the worst expressions of racial discrimination in America, but racial discrimination has not disappeared. Whenever we Americans are in danger of becoming complacent about historical and institutional racism, it is time to reflect that we were one of the last nations to abolish slavery; or to remember our generally unfeeling conquest of Native American tribes ("The only good Indian is a dead Indian"); or to recall the Japanese internment in World War II. While German bombs were falling on London, the British were giving German and Italian aliens individual judicial hearings. With the war still far away, the United States rounded up those of Japanese ancestry, citizens and aliens alike, and shipped them off to what amounted to concentration camps.

Recently, discussion of "hate crime" legislation has focused upon beatings and even murder of gay persons or those perceived to be gay. Such actions violate existing laws, but the attitudes of some Americans have been too easily tolerant of such behavior. We all claim to believe in free speech. But the record of what happens to "whistle-blowers" in government or business, those who dare to point out infractions of environmental laws or to call attention to deceptive practices, is not reassuring. Most of the time they are ignored, demoted, transferred, or harassed. Rarely are they rewarded. (The nongovernmental Government Accountability Project has documented many of these cases.)

The Southern Poverty Law Center, which began as an organization documenting civil rights abuses in the American South, has now expanded its scope and keeps records of hate crimes and hate group activity throughout the United States and, more recently, elsewhere. Its fall 2001 Intelligence Report lists scores of U.S. hate crime incidents for the second quarter of 2001. Typical reports are the firebombing of a gay and lesbian bar in Ventura, California; the vandalizing of a Muslim prayer room at Georgetown University; the beating of a black man in Lake Charles, Louisiana; a wooden cross burned on the lawn of a white woman with black children in Jamestown, Pennsylvania; an attack on a Pakistani teen in Brooklyn, New York; the burning of two crosses at a Portland, Oregon, Jewish cemetery; swastikas and "Heil Hitler" spray painted at a synagogue in Hammond, Indiana. The list goes on and on. This period also saw the sentencing to life imprisonment of Buford Furrow, the neo-Nazi Aryan Nations follower who murdered a Filipino American postal worker and wounded five people at a Jewish community center. Thanks to a stricter enforcement of hate crime laws and perhaps to a change in public opinion, the number of murders attributable strictly to racial or religious hatred has declined; but we know from lists like the above that racial hostility has not ended in our society and that building respect for differences and protecting basic rights are ongoing struggles.

In the first three weeks after the September 11, 2001, terrorist attack on New York and Washington, D.C., the FBI was called in to investigate 120 alleged hate crimes directed at people of Arab or Middle East extraction, and in some cases people of Indian or Latin American descent whom the attackers mistakenly assumed to be Arab. Several people were killed. The mailing of anthrax spores in the aftermath of September 11 led to four deaths. At this writing, authorities speculate that a lone domestic culprit may be responsible. Yet in consequence it was reported that during the anthrax scare the FBI received some six hundred phone calls a day from citizens worried about anthrax. Moreover, it seems often the case that acts of great malevolence stimulate, in response, further acts of malevolence at the expense of the innocent.

On the other side of the coin lies concern for governmental abuse of the rights of individuals. Without public hearings and without normal committee consideration, the U.S. Congress, after September 11, passed overwhelmingly the USA Patriot Act, which broadened the executive power of search and seizure under the Constitution and further limited the powers of judges in controlling search warrants, a constricting process that began with the antiterrorism and immigration "reform" legislation of 1996. Whereas wiretaps on telephones were formerly justified only in recording a suspect's conversation, now a suspect's conversations and later conversations of persons to whom he or she is talking may be tapped without a judge's approval. Moreover, under new electronic surveillance provisions, the seizing of e-mail communications, including files that may go well beyond the subject of the inquiry, is allowed. Amendments offered by civil rights supporters in both House and Senate that would provide some protection to nonsuspects were brushed aside. The electronic surveillance clauses fortunately have a sunset provision; Congress must reauthorize them in four years. But other clauses, including one that allows secret searches and seizures, that is, searches without informing home residents, are not covered by the sunset provision.

Of equal concern is the executive order issued by President Bush after September 11, without congressional input, that allows military trials of noncitizens, even if they are legal residents in the United States. (procedural rights in our Constitution apply to "persons" not just to citizens). The secretary of defense is empowered to set up military trials of those suspected of international terrorism. He or she sets the rules, including how many will serve on judging panels, what their qualifications are, and what the standards of proof and rules of evidence are. There is no judicial review. One of the few specific requirements in the order is that defendants may be found guilty by a two-thirds vote of the panel, even when the result may be life in prison or death. Yet under the Uniform Code of Military Justice, even military courts have heretofore required unanimity in capital cases, allowed appellate review, and honored constitutional protections against self-incrimination and double jeopardy, the right to an attorney, and so on. The executive order gives the secretary of defense the right to "transfer to a governmental authority control of any individual," which implies deportation without a trial is possible. All this is despite the specific constitutional clause that grants to Congress, not the president, authority "to make rules for the government and regulation" of the military forces.

In the two months after the September 11 attack 1,147 persons were arrested and detained without formal criminal charges being filed and often without being granted the right to have an attorney. Most were immigrants of Arab descent, and most were held in jails in the Southern District of New York. Only 182 were held by the Immigration and Naturalization Service. At least one person died in custody after thirty days, a person who had no apparent connection with the World Trade Center attack. How many were released and when were not made public. At least some were willingly giving information to the FBI prior to their arrest, which raises the question of why they were arrested, if information was the objective and no crime was alleged.

The foregoing suggests that a political climate of fear is likely to induce hasty action. It is also testament to the complexity and the difficulty of protecting individual rights in an age of multiculturalism, world tension, and interdependence.

II. THE DEVELOPMENT OF THE THEORY OF RIGHTS

Basic Rights

Fundamental to any right is a claim of value. Because human beings have value, they can claim rights. A right is a valid claim to some entitlement. At this point we find a basic contribution of Christian and Jewish faith to our thinking about rights. According to the Judeo-Christian tradition, human beings have value, and before God the inequalities that emerge in any society are erased; before God, all are of equal value. This does not mean exact equal status under all circumstances, or equality of possessions, or undifferentiated compensation. Equality is not sameness. It is quite the reverse. Equality of concern and respect can be seen as a prerequisite for discovering the uniqueness of each person. Seeing persons only through the lens of predetermined categories like income or education obscures their uniqueness and denies them their humanity.

Concern for human rights has been an important part of Western history, especially since the American and French Revolutions. The concern has become global and taken on new dimensions of meaning since World War II. The nations that had been allied in the war against Germany and Japan were aware of terrible abuses of human beings before and during that war. The post–World War II Nuremberg trials of war criminals had affirmed that there were acts, such as genocide, that must forever be renounced and prohibited. Accordingly, one of the first undertakings of the United Nations was to draft a Universal Declaration of Human Rights (UDHR). The UDHR was influenced not only by the Nuremberg Trials but also by the American Declaration of Independence (1776) and Bill of Rights (1791). With Eleanor Roosevelt as chair of the drafting committee, the UDHR was adopted in December 1948.

Article 1 of the United Nations' Universal Declaration of Human Rights (1948) may be taken as a primary text. It states: "All human beings are born free and equal in dignity and rights. They are endowed with reason and conscience and should act toward one another in a spirit of brotherhood." The articles that follow expound many rights: the "right to life, liberty and security of person" (Art. 3); the equal protection of the law (Art. 7); fair and public hearings before an independent and impartial tribunal (Art. 10); freedom of movement within a state (Art. 13); equal rights in marriage (Art. 16); the right to own property (Art. 17); freedom of "thought, conscience and religion" (Art. 18); freedom of expression (Art. 19); the right of assembly and association (Art. 20). The document condemns many practices: discrimination based on race, color, sex, language, religion, and national origin (Art. 2); slavery and "servitude" (Art. 4); torture and degrading punishment (Art. 5); arbitrary arrest, detention, and exile (Art. 9). The stories at the beginning of this chapter suggest that these standards are often violated. Nevertheless, the Declaration represents a consensus of hope. The seriousness of the United Nations commitment to human rights was expressed again in 1993 by the creation of the post of High Commissioner for Human Rights.

Rights and Duties

The corollary of the notion of rights is the concept of duty. If I have a legitimate right, you have a duty to respect that right. A moral right does not automatically translate into a legal or civil right (consider how long slavery was legal), but morality lies behind most civil rights. An argument can be made that America has become such a litigious society because an overemphasis on individual rights has weakened the sense of civic duty. People become impatient, uncooperative, and selfish. In a reversal of John F. Kennedy's oft-quoted words, they ask what their country can do for them, but not what they can do for their country. One should be cautious in making this observation, however. It is easy for those who are comfortable and well off to denounce rights claimants as selfish and grasping. What the rich see as good social order may appear as oppression to the poor. When the poor claim a moral and legal entitlement, it may look like troublemaking to the rich.

One of the outcomes of the terrible events of September 11, 2001, is awareness that in the face of large threats and dangers, the American people can and do put aside petty interests in order to help others, to contribute, and to share. The great paradox of war, including this new "war on terrorism," is that it can bring out the best and worst of people simultaneously.

Free Speech

There is a common but not very useful distinction between "civil rights," claims that ought to be honored, as with equal treatment, and "civil liberties," opportunities for action that ought to be protected. Free speech is a liberty, but it is also a right. A variation on the theme of equality is that one should be judged for actions not belief. The basis for criminal punishment should be harmful actions for which one can reasonably be held responsible, not what one believes. This principle owes much to the Christian idea that "God alone is the lord of conscience"; that is, God can know our inner being as no other person can. Therefore the direct insertion of someone else's belief into a person's conscience is literally impossible, and the attempt to do so coercively is a violation of the recipient's humanity and of the dignity to which people are entitled. Persons have not only the right but also the obligation to think for themselves. Immanuel Kant secularized this idea with his theory of moral autonomy. People should be treated as ends in themselves, not as mere means to someone else's end. This underlies the right to express one's views without fear of recrimination, as well as the right to privacy and to dignified respect. Even in our supposedly secular age, in which the religion of criminal defendants and witnesses is taken to be irrelevant, testimony in court is "sworn testimony" in which the witness holds up his or her hand and agrees to tell the truth, "so help me God."

The sanctity of the person and the right to hold unorthodox beliefs have not always been respected in our society. The loyalty oaths, "character assassination," and blacklisting of the 1950s gained the infamous label "McCarthyism." An earlier example was the treatment in the 1870s of a Utah Mormon who was convicted of violating the new antipolygamy laws because he said he believed in polygamy, even though he did not practice polygamy. Today we are accustomed to hearing appeals to celebrate diversity, but diversity in thought, even in academic settings, is in practice more often subtly discouraged than encouraged. Secular disdain for religious thinking is no less oppressive of the right to think for oneself than is fundamentalist suspicion of fresh theological reflection.

Criminal Law

In criminal trials, the same criteria of evidence should apply to all, regardless of race, gender, age, or nationality. These personal characteristics no doubt influence who we are, but they are characteristics we do not choose. (Part of the argument over whether sexual orientation should be added to this list of characteristics turns on whether sexual orientation is given or chosen.) The value of legal testimony should be judged by what the witness has seen or knows, rather than by the natural characteristics, the social status, or the power of the witness.

Fair judicial procedures are important, but by themselves they do not guarantee social justice: One example of injustice is the current practice of capital punishment in the United States. A disproportionate number of executed criminals are members of minority races. Criminologists find little support for the notion that capital punishment is a significant deterrent to crime, as is commonly argued. DNA evidence proving that many persons awaiting state execution have been wrongly convicted additionally calls capital punishment into disrepute. That we spend too much on prisons and too little on education, that prisons reinforce criminal tendencies rather than reform criminals, that nonviolent criminals and drug addicts are largely responsible for conditions of terrible overcrowding in our prisons—these may all be taken as evidence that just societies require more than sound procedural rights. (See chapter 7, "The Penal System.")

Social and Economic Needs and the Rights of Property

The portions of UN's Universal Declaration of Human Rights cited above reflect the United States' Bill of Rights, but the understanding of human rights in the UDHR is broader than the one that has been dominant in this country. Certain UDHR articles affirm rights of a different kind: social and economic rights. These include the right to social security (Art. 22), the right to work (Art. 23), the right to an adequate standard of living (Art. 25), and the right to an education (Art. 26). The UN Covenant on Economic, Social, and Cultural Rights (1966) goes into greater detail and holds that enough to eat, decent housing, and a minimum income should be regarded as basic human rights. The United States has not signed this Covenant because powerful American leaders view it as "socialistic." The premise of Western individualism, especially in the United States, is closely linked to the capitalistic assumption that individuals, not government, are responsible for economic well-being. Basic rights are seen as more procedural than material. Equality before the law is not seen as requiring government support for common physical needs. Freedom is seen as independent of one's income, even when, in fact, those with high incomes often benefit from the ministrations of high-priced lawyers who find convenient ways through the jungle of law. Critics of the "free enterprise" position say it grants too easily the freedom to starve. Or as Victor Hugo famously said, freedom has come to mean that some are free to live in fine houses and others are free to sleep under bridges.

In fact, of course, not all Americans subscribe to an ideology of complete individualism and minimal government. The current political debates over minimum-wage laws, or a national health-care system, or, indeed, the typical preoccupation of our political leaders of both parties with the state of the economy generally, suggest that the concern for human rights and the concern for material needs are not as separate as that ideology might suggest. "Socialism" is a scare word, even after the fall of the Soviet Empire; but material welfare cannot be divorced from political interests, only obscured by confusing terminology.

The rejection by the United States of the social rights proclaimed in the United Nations declaration is also connected with the near absolutization of property rights. Some business leaders fear that supporting economic and social rights is a threat to private property rights, since they can support the rights of workers against the rights of corporations. There is no doubt of the importance of property rights in a well-ordered society. There is wide agreement that people have a right to keep what they have earned through their own labor. However, there are real questions whether property rights actually function in contemporary society as a means of keeping what one has earned. Modern technological society generates wealth in ways that often seem quite arbitrary, judged by any standard of fair reward for honest effort. For example, the millions of dollars in compensation and stock options granted to corporate CEOs seem to bear very little relationship to corporate productivity. The right of property has often been invoked to justify a status quo of very unequal distributions of property, such that the right of property becomes a right of possessiveness rather than a right of fair reward.

The United States, the UN, and Global Human Rights

The Causes of Tension

The United Nations has for a long time been a whipping boy for political conservatives of a nationalist bent and for the religious right. Criticism persists even after Secretary-General Kofi Annan and the United Nations received the Nobel Peace Prize in 2001. The UN is alternately called corrupt, a threat to national sovereignty, and a voice for sentimental radicals. Some UN administrative staffs have been inflated and inefficient. But none of this justifies the reluctance of the U.S. Congress to support the work of the United Nations in extending and implementing agreements on human rights or to pay our dues to the UN. After years of delay, Congress has recently acknowledged reforms in progress and appropriated most of what we owe; but our account is still in arrears.

The ambivalence of the United States toward the development of an elaborate doctrine of global rights has contributed to these rocky relations between the United States and the United Nations. Americans have frequently accused the United Nations of hypocrisy because of General Assembly votes that contain idealistic language contrary to the actual behavior of the states that are voting. If such charges are directed only to the less developed countries, they overlook the power of the veto in the Security Council, carefully designed to protect the national sovereignty of the big powers.

Nevertheless, ill will toward the United Nations and suspicion of its work in the area of human rights has been intensified recently. On May 3, 2001, for the first time since the creation in 1946 of the 52-member UN Commission on Human Rights (the group that drafted the UDHR), the United States was not elected a member. This, plus the fact that Sudan was elected a member, has created much controversy.

The United States had campaigned overtly against the election of Sudan, with good reason. The Sudanese government has been guilty of monstrous human rights abuses. There has been civil war since 1983 between the Muslim north and the non-Muslim south, between the government's Popular

Defense Forces (PDF) and the opposing Sudanese People's Liberation Army (SPLA), exacerbated by years of famine. Government troops and roving militias have gang-raped and enslaved black women in slave raids on villages in southern Sudan. An estimated 100,000 people remain in bondage in northern Sudan. The anti-Christian government has bulldozed or burned thirty to fifty Christian churches, centers, and schools. The Nuba people are Muslim, but they are black and came from an area of toleration, where some intermarried with Christians. After they supported the SPLA, the government targeted them as the enemy, denying them food and humanitarian aid, forcing many to flee. According to Human Rights Watch, Sudan has had the largest internally displaced population in the world, around four million. The government set up "peace camps" in the Nuba hills; when the Nuba, desperate for food, came back to visit the camps, they were raped and conscripted for forced labor. Since 1989 two million Sudanese have been killed by war or starvation. U.S. Secretary of State Colin Powell has urged the Sudan government to stop aerial bombing of relief sites and hospitals and end restrictions on humanitarian aid. (Sudan has received $1.2 billion in various kinds of assistance from the United States since 1989.) President George W. Bush, responding to the National Council of Catholic Bishops and others, appointed Andrew Natsios as a special humanitarian coordinator to Sudan.

The press mistakenly portrayed the Commission on Human Rights vote as a choice of Sudan over the United States. The voting was not by paired choices, but it did reflect the complicated politics of the 54-member Economic and Social Council and the 189-member General Assembly. The voting was by secret ballot, so motives are obscure, but it is easy to see how charges of hypocrisy are sustained.

Political debates over these issues are crucially important in their own right, but they may have the side effect of concealing or muffling the important work the United Nations does in other areas of human rights and refugee relief, which includes not just handing out money (there isn't that much money), but in coordinating justice and relief efforts of churches and other nongovernmental organizations.

The U.S. Resistance to Global Human Rights

The ambivalence of Congress toward the work of the United Nations is manifest in relation to the development of international rights. Stemming from the UDHR, a number of treaties, called covenants or conventions, have been negotiated between nation-states. The United States has been a nonparticipant, or a reluctant participant, in most of these. President Carter signed the Covenant on Civil and Political Rights and the Covenant on Economic, Social, and Cultural Rights in 1977; but the Senate did not approve them at that time. In 1992 the Senate finally approved the Covenant on Civil and Political Rights, thus completing the process called "ratification." The Covenant on Economic, Social, and Cultural Rights has not been, and most likely will not be, approved by the Senate. Part of Congress's reluctance is based on opposition to UN family planning programs that do not appeal to domestic U.S. constituencies.

American ambivalence towards human rights is particularly clear with respect to the rights of women. By legislation, the post of Senior Advisor on International Women's Issues was created in the Department of State in 1994; but the Senate has not consented to the international Women's Convention, and the United States remains the only major country not to have ratified it.

Similarly, the House of Representatives has produced much support for a Freedom from Religious Persecution Act to protect American citizens abroad, but, as in many other areas, the United States does not join in treaties that would make such protections reciprocal. Some years after their origin, the Senate did consent to the convention on the elimination of racial discrimination and to the convention outlawing genocide. In 1994, ten years after its formulation, the Senate approved the Convention Against Torture and Other Cruel, Inhumane, or Degrading Treatment or Punishment, but it attached so many "reservations, understandings, or declarations" (RUDs) that the Netherlands has filed a legal complaint, alleging that the U.S. RUDs are incompatible with the basic purpose of the treaty. Only the United States and Somalia have not ratified the 1989 Convention on the Rights of the Child. Human rights leaders and others have expressed outrage at the American go-it-alone stance. As William Sloane Coffin has said, the United States should join the world if it expects to lead the world.

International Military and Political Action

In our day, the call of the oppressed is heard more clearly than ever before, due to the omnipresence of the television and video camera. It is harder to avert our eyes or pretend ignorance of distant wrongs. The negative side of this positive development is that we may become inured to suffering. Our new "realism" may harden our hearts. The international interventions in Bosnia, Kosovo, and East Timor, put together by big nation-states but sanctioned by the United Nations with the aim of restoring peace and good order, were opposed by Christian pacifists and others. Few hands remain clean in these matters. Yet such patterns of international cooperation scarcely existed in the nineteenth century.

Critics point out that such interventions, often too late to prevent the worst abuses, are driven by national self-interest more than by universal benevolence. Nevertheless they express a consensus that there are norms of human action whose violation the international community will not tolerate. The conviction of five Croatians for ethnic cleansing by the International War Crimes Tribunal in The Hague (formed in 1998) and the arrest and trial of the former Serbian president, Slobodan Milosevic, may prove to be of historic importance in the enforcement of human rights at the global level.

The terrorist attack on New York and the Pentagon once again raises the issue of whether crimes of international magnitude should be punished by nation-states or by international bodies. President Bush has declared that the pursuit of Osama bin Laden and his fellow conspirators requires a coalition of nation-states, and American diplomacy has worked to broaden the limits of such a coalition beyond our western European allies. At the same time the United States' support of the International Court of Justice and the War Crimes Tribunal has been highly qualified. The principle of sovereignty as a guarantor of existing power relations is not easily given up.

New Issues and New Directions

Although the relation of the United States to the United Nations has soured America's role in the development of rights theory, developments at home have opened up new questions about rights. We will look briefly at seven of these.

Affirmative Action

Affirmative action is an example of the difficulty of drawing an exact and abiding line between the theory of equal rights and the practice of equal rights. The Johnson administration sought to extend the Fourteenth Amendment's "equal protection of the laws" to women and minorities. The Civil Rights Acts of 1964 and 1965 and Johnson's War on Poverty applied the concept to programs like the Job Corps, Head Start, and food stamps. The aim was to shift the focus from desegregation to integration, to make a special effort to seek out women and minorities for jobs and benefits in areas where they had heretofore been discriminated against. Critics immediately attacked the idea as implying unfair "reverse discrimination" or unequal treatment for privileged categories of persons. They criticized the "quota system" and said minorities were receiving "preferential treatment" and that government was interfering with proper employer discretion. The rights of employers, they said, were being set against the rights of potential employees. Defenders of affirmative action said that the fear of "quotas" was a red herring; without a push in the right direction, women and minorities would, as in the past, simply be overlooked. Affirmative action involved the setting of "goals" not "quotas," and ending discrimination required such official encouragement.

The regents of the University of California not long ago terminated their affirmative-action program for the university, and some of the regents joined with other political leaders to sponsor a 1998 ballot proposition ending affirmative action for all public employees and public universities in the state. The proposition, ironically labeled the California Civil Rights Initiative, implied that white males were being discriminated against. Ward Connerly, a university regent who happens to be black, became a spokesman for the initiative, arguing that job discrimination against minorities and women was no longer a problem and that if he could become a successful businessman without government help, so could any other minority member. The initiative passed. Interestingly, polls showed that the measure won majority support when it was described as "against discrimination and preferential treatment," but when described as "outlawing affirmative action," opposition and support numbers were reversed. This is an example of the crucial significance of how words are used and the importance of mass communications in contemporary society.

Gender

The appearance of Elizabeth Dole as a presidential candidate and the small but significant increase in the number of women legislators and business CEOs are taken by some to mean that discrimination against women is a thing of the past. But there is a long way to go. Sexual harassment continues to be a troubling part of too many workplaces. The U.S. Equal Employment Opportunity Commission's suit against the Mitsubishi automobile plant in Illinois revealed what may be the most egregious visible case in recent history. Violence against women, traffic in women, and domestic bondage in Asia, Africa, and Latin America are tragically endemic. In the United States nine out of ten women who are murdered are killed by men known to them, and four out of five are murdered at home. A structure of male domination remains in place.

The rights of women were the central subject of the UN Conference on Women in Beijing in 1995. Its Platform for Action addressed twelve critical areas, including poverty, education, health, violence, and power sharing. It further called on governments to promote and protect all human rights of women and girls; to grant women equal rights to inheritance; and to treat perpetrators of rape in time of war as war criminals. As noted above, the United States remains one of only a handful of nations that have not ratified this agreement.

Sexual Orientation

Discrimination against gays in employment has declined significantly in recent years; but gay and lesbian couples are still typically denied rights of spousal inheritance, tax benefits, adoption, and family health benefits. The state of California has recently lifted its ban on gay adoptions and approved health insurance benefits for the partners of gay state employees; but this is not characteristic of all states. (For fuller discussion, see chapter 5, "Homosexuality and Same-Gender Unions.")

Group Rights

As suggested above, in the West basic human rights have usually been assumed to mean individual rights. But as societies become more multicultural and as the world becomes more interdependent, this assumption has been questioned more and more. We have come to see that the Western imperialist powers in Africa and Asia, for example, were not simply bringing freedom, democracy, and enlightenment to backward nations, but were—sometimes directly, sometimes indirectly—coercively uprooting native communal patterns. The two 1966 UN covenants spoke of the "self-determination of peoples" but conspicuously failed to define "peoples."

The tension between individual and group rights is unavoidable. There have been painfully wrenching Supreme Court cases in which the individual rights of children and family members come in direct conflict with Native American tribal rights. Pueblo tribal rules hold that the child of a Pueblo man who marries outside the tribe is Pueblo, while the child of a Pueblo woman who marries outside the tribe is not. This discrimination against women would seem to violate U.S. civil rights laws, but the courts have so far sided with the Pueblos. The rights of tribes with respect to particular pieces of land have also come into direct conflict with individual property rights as understood in U.S. law. This problem has worldwide counterparts.

Whenever in the wider political arena there is an attempt to balance individual and group claims, resentment and defensiveness are aroused as the tacit assumptions of two divergent cultures are brought into play. Loyalty to the group can strain individual rights as well as individual conscience, whether the group is a religious body, a business, a family, a labor union, a gang, or a sovereign nation-state.

Persons with Disabilities

After years of work, the Americans with Disabilities Act (ADA) was enacted in 1990, extending antibias protection to 43 million persons, including those who are blind, deaf, in a wheelchair, or developmentally disabled. The act has also been interpreted to protect people with chronic diseases, including asthma, epilepsy, cancer, and HIV infection. The law requires employers and public buildings to make "reasonable accommodations" to such persons.

This law was hailed as the most sweeping civil rights law since the 1960s. Many organizations have willingly or reluctantly complied with it, and a number of lawsuits resulted. In 1996, United Artists Entertainment announced the settlement of a lawsuit by agreeing to make theaters more accessible to persons with physical disabilities. The news is not as good for persons with developmental disabilities. A plausible assumption is that these persons' inability to be their own advocates has restricted the beneficial response. The organization People First has been addressing this concern by teaching these persons the skills of self-advocacy and standing with them while not presuming to speak for them.

A conservative U.S. Supreme Court has curtailed some of what ADA advocates hoped for. In 2000–2001 two disabled employees brought suit against the University of Alabama under the ADA. On a 5-4 vote the court found that Congress did not have the power to "abrogate the sovereign immunity" of the state in these circumstances, noting the Eleventh Amendment to the U.S. Constitution, which forbids suits against a state by citizens of another state. The minority felt that the Eleventh Amendment was irrelevant to this case and that the court has no right to "second-guess" the Congress, which had found ample evidence of state-sponsored discrimination. However, also in 2001, the court by an ample majority found that, under ADA, the Professional Golfers' Association had no right to forbid disabled golfer Casey Martin from using a golf cart in a golf tournament. Thirty-two disability-rights organizations supported Martin, in a case which the *Washington Post* headlined "Putting the Course before the Cart."

The Right to Die with Dignity

The right to die with dignity exists in tension with deep religious convictions about the sanctity of human life. Suicide is a sin in the eyes of many Christians. Only God, who gives life, should take life. In November 2001, U.S. Attorney General John Ashcroft issued a directive that had the aim of overruling Oregon's Death With Dignity initiative, passed twice by the voters of the state and replete with procedural safeguards. The directive ordered federal drug officials to prosecute doctors who prescribed possibly lethal drugs according to the new law. The Justice Department decision was immediately appealed, and a Federal District Court judge granted a restraining order on the directive. The issue of when an ovum and sperm, or embryo, or fetus become human has a counterpart in the issue of when an elderly dying patient ceases to be human. Is letting die different from killing? When is the relief of pain and suffering unjustified? Death in fact is often not dignified, and the language of rights is difficult to apply.

The Rights of Nature

Growing awareness of the ecological fragility of Earth has generated new understandings of rights. Although there are rights of economic development, there are also rights of being protected against exploitative economic development. Related to this are the rights of animal species to habitat and of individual animals to be treated humanely. (See chapter 14, "The Church and Environmentalism.")

III. A CHRISTIAN PERSPECTIVE

The idea of "rights" is not explicit in the Bible. Nevertheless, the proposition that the gross abuse of human rights is un-Christian seems obvious (even when Christians are coldly reminded of the Children's Crusades or the Spanish Inquisition). No one publicly opposes respect for human rights. Even notorious tyrants, shown to be responsible for such abuse, will declare their abiding respect for human rights. And that is part of the problem. With mere words, even the hallowed words of our worship, we seem helpless to engage, let alone overcome, the parade of injustice—jailings, torture, executions, denials of food and medicine, neglect of orphans—that the fully voiced power-holders and the wielders of the gun impose on the voiceless. Moreover, when the oppressed get weapons and decide to revolt, they can sometimes become as cruel as their former rulers, for which there are too many examples in Asia and Africa.

And yet we also know that with words humanity is governed and that the self-proclaimed mission of Christ and his followers is to "proclaim release to the captives and recovery of sight to the blind, to let the oppressed go free" (Luke 4:18). "There is no longer Jew or Greek, there is no longer slave or free, there is no longer male and female; for all of you are one in Christ Jesus" (Gal. 3:28). By emphasizing an otherworldly quality in these words, the elites of past times tried to make the words of Paul consistent with patriarchal hierarchies and slave societies. But attention to the way in which Jesus related to Samaritans, Gentiles, the woman at the well, and the poor and outcast generally, leads us to a different conclusion, namely, that all persons deserve, prima facie, equal concern and respect. Jesus, in the parable of the Good Samaritan, showed us the far reach of good neighborliness. In worship we sing, "In Christ there is no east or west."

The biblical and Christian traditions do not usually make the legal rights of people their central theme. But behind the secular legal language of rights is a way of understanding human beings that is deeply indebted to the religious traditions of the West. Before God, all human beings are of equal value and deserve equal concern and respect. As we noted above, the right to freedom of expression is closely tied to the Christian belief that God alone is the lord of conscience. Furthermore, the value of a person is not a separated, isolated value. Our lives are more valuable the more deeply they interact with others in local communities and with members of the wider human community. Genesis 1:26–27 tells us that all humankind is made in God's image.

Biblical and Christian faith is profoundly aware of the way in which power can be abused, and therefore aware of the need for a strong vision of justice, especially justice for those with little power in society. Progressive Christians see that the major gift of the vision of both Jesus and the Old Testament prophets lies in pressing ourselves and our society to create a stronger role for human rights here and abroad. We need to enable those all too easily excluded from the exercise of their rights to take part fully in the work of society. Says the Lord: "I will make justice the line, and righteousness the plummet" (Isa. 28:17).

Though the church defended slavery at various points in history, this runs counter to basic biblical themes. Moses said, "Slaves who have escaped to you from their owners shall not be given back to them. They shall reside with you, in your midst, in any place they choose in any one of your towns, wherever they please; you shall not oppress them" (Deut. 23:15–16). "You shall not deprive a resident alien or an orphan of justice.... Remember that you were a slave in Egypt and the LORD your God redeemed you" (Deut. 24:17–18). There is a heavy burden of responsibility here; but there is also hope, and the two go together: "If you remove the yoke from among you, the pointing of the finger, the speaking of evil, if you offer your food to the hungry and satisfy the needs of the afflicted, then your light shall rise in the darkness and your gloom be like the noonday" (Isa. 58:9–12). If we are not, strictly speaking, citizens of the world, all human beings are nevertheless our brothers and sisters. What the Bible calls "principalities and powers" have often been a threat to justice for individuals and oppressed groups. Yet, the call of religious folk to oppose such threats has been heard even in faraway places, and carries moral weight even when an adequate reform has been frustrated.

The question for Christians, therefore, is not so much whether to support the extension of rights as how to balance this with duties. Christians are called to be particularly concerned for the neighbor who is in need. That includes seeking the neighbor's rights. But in our society many are preoccupied with their own rights, with little concern for what happens to the rights of others as they gain their own. Too often, churches work for rights most vigorously when their institutional rights are at stake, and individual Christians seek their own rights with the same disregard for consequences as many other citizens.

In general the New Testament does not encourage us to make use of the legal system. In the Sermon on the Mount, Jesus urges his hearers to settle with their accusers before reaching the courts (Matt. 5:25). Paul encourages Christians to work out their problems within the church. Even today, the public struggle between Christians or church groups to enforce their rights against one another is far from edifying.

Despite these warnings, the reality of the present world calls on us to use political and legal means to expand the rights of the weak and oppressed as well as the right to act and worship as our faith requires.

Christians should support free speech even when what is said is offensive to us. Churches are respecting conscience when they encourage free discussions. We must demand the freedom to speak truth, even when it is unpopular, and we must recognize the right of others to speak what they regard as truth, even if we disagree. For us, the insight of Augustine is relevant here. Freedom can appear to be simply the opportunity to choose whatever one wants. But, said Augustine, a higher freedom is found in the character of those who have acquired the virtue of choosing well. God's good is higher than the satisfaction of our own subjective desires.

Issues of property rights are as difficult for Christians as for other people of good will. Jesus' parable of the Talents, among other things, assumes that enterprise is to be rewarded. His parable of the Field Workers, on the other hand, also suggests that the gifts of God go so far beyond what labor can produce that they are not to be equated with or measured by human effort. Although Christians generally affirm the right of private property even of the means of production, progressive Christians do not place this right above the right of workers to fair compensation or of hungry people to food. The right to own property legitimately acquired is one human right among others—not the one that trumps all the others.

Given this Christian perspective, we must be critical of the refusal of our government to ratify so many United Nations covenants, as well as of its general ambivalence toward the United Nations. The covenants derived from the UDHR have been supported by Christians in Asia, the Middle East, and Latin America who, observing the injustice and suffering imposed by oppressive military regimes, have augmented the saving of souls with the saving of lives. Catholic liberation theology in Latin America gave a new rationale for Christian identification with the problems of the poor and hence a keen sensitivity to the basic rights they were denied. North American Christians should join those in other parts of the world in giving vigorous support to the covenants derived from the UDHR.

Although Christians must always discourage war as an instrument of policy, we can more readily affirm the use of violence to protect human rights from extreme abuse than for most other purposes. We can celebrate the fact that increasingly nations appeal to the United Nations for sanctioning the use of military force for just purposes. We celebrate also the creation of international courts to try egregious violators of human rights. We know that the international court at Nuremberg was in part "victor's justice" (Russian and Allied war crimes were not tried) and that international courts today are not free of that tendency. But we believe they represent progress toward a world ruled by law. Without the precedent of Nuremberg, it is doubtful that the War Crimes Tribunal in The Hague would be considering the case of Serbian President Slobodan Milosevic or that the trials of those implicated in the terrible genocide in Rwanda in 1994 would be going forward as they are in Arusha, Tanzania, years after the event. We should encourage our own government to give fuller support to these courts. If those accused of the terrorist acts of September 11 could be tried in an international court, there would be more global confidence that justice was being done.

With respect to the new frontiers of thought on rights, we express our views on sexual orientation and the rights of nature in other chapters. With respect to the right to die, although Progressive Christians Uniting has not developed a position paper on this topic, our judgment on the basic issues is clear from the chapter on abortion (see chapter 3, "Reflections on Abortion"). Neither the right to die nor the duty to live is absolute. The central question may be how to maintain the capacity for a person to make self-affirming choices to the maximum degree, while not expending enormous sums of money and medical know-how merely to prolong life in an unwanted condition. Sensitivity to the emotional context of how and when to die should be one of the strengths of the Christian faith, and the churches can, through honest and sustained discussion, make a significant contribution to the understanding of this important social issue.

Despite the threat to individual rights involved in acknowledging group rights, we recognize that human rights are sometimes best protected in terms of group rights, and we support efforts to clarify and enforce these. The communal mentality of some tribes is probably closer to the attitudes of first-century Christians than many present-day churchgoers recognize. The best political strategy in dealing with culture conflicts is not to assert the superiority of our own "way of life" in a dogmatic way—however deeply we believe in its superiority—but rather to find in the statements of divergent group leaders common moral and political principles, principles to which all can reasonably be expected to subscribe.

For example, the principle of equality under law is now embedded in the UN's UDHR and the several related covenants. Many nations have signed on to these international agreements, even though their implementation leaves much to be desired. It is appropriate to call attention to the violation of a nation's (read group's) violation of its own professed standards of justice. The framework of the UDHR makes this possible and our Christian faith encourages us to support this process.

That the implementation of group rights is sometimes in tension with that of individual rights is clear with respect to affirmative action, and we know that our task is to find the right balance. However, it is our judgment that at present the reality of discrimination against groups warrants continued affirmative action in relation to those groups.

Society should go as far as possible to remove barriers to full participation by all its citizens; this is clearly a Christian mandate. Disabilities of various forms create some inherent limitations on such participation. But social attitudes and practices have added greatly to these barriers. Christians rejoice that much is now being done to reduce these unnecessary barriers. Christians also recognize that society, often led and taught by the church, has placed women at a severe disadvantage through most of history. Christian teaching has been overwhelmingly patriarchal. Implementing equal rights for women is clearly called for by the deeper Christian principle of justice. We rejoice that here too there has been significant progress, but we know that much remains to be done, especially at the level of male attitudes toward women. Christians have a particular responsibility to deal with the deep level of the male psyche that leads to so much sexual abuse and violence.

IV. WHAT WE CAN DO

The number of possible rights is infinite, and not all claims to rights are to be respected. As noted, many think that the litigious nature of America's present rights-claiming culture—in which the market is king, lawyers rule, and everything seems up for grabs—has weakened patterns of social civility and the sense of communal responsibility. Some persons think that the events of September 11 have changed these prevailing attitudes in the direction of a greater sense of communal responsibility; but only time will tell. The important thing is not the multiplication of rights but bringing justice to those who have been denied justice. It is a cliché to say we live in a rapidly changing and very complex world; this makes it very difficult to figure out how best to honor the rights of the most needful while hurting least the well-being of others. In such a situation, it is easy for the deprived to sound shrill, but even easier for the comfortable to delay acting. Vengeance and greed are unacceptable; but so are complacency and indifference. The church is in a unique position to steer a course between these poles. As citizens and as Christians we all have a continuing obligation to identify the worst injustices, to develop programs that remedy them, and to push authorities and the public to support such programs. In southern California, for example, Christians have created Clergy and Laity United for Economic Justice and have successfully supported labor organizing efforts and gained city support for a living wage.

Here are some examples of specific things a congregation can do:

- Write U.S senators in support of human rights treaties not yet approved.
- Give support for legal aid to an immigrant threatened with deportation for questionable reasons, or detained without a hearing.
- Campaign against racial profiling by local police.
- Support legislation, similar to Oregon's, that affirms the right to die with dignity in a manner that conforms to a terminal patient's wishes.
- Develop a Christian education program that examines the need for social, cultural, and economic rights as contrasted with the conventional praise for political and civil rights (the latter, of course, also need defending).
- Schedule a joint meeting with the United Nations Association to explain the often-misunderstood work of the United Nations in such human rights areas as refugee relief, world hunger, traffic in women, international labor standards.
- Support a pastor who gives expression to his or her Christian commitment by taking stands on "political" issues.
- Develop awareness of and appreciation for what church groups are already doing in the areas of human rights and civil rights.

Some denominations support officials who lobby for antipoverty legislation, develop programs to address the rights of immigrants, or have restorative justice programs to mitigate harsh or unjust treatment of prisoners. Others—especially, but not only, the peace churches (Brethren, Mennonites, and Quakers)—are concerned with refugees and other victims of war. Some interdenominational groups, such as Bread for the World, Habitat for Humanity, and World Vision, have done good work for the poor, unsheltered, and hungry around the world. Opportunities for rights-oriented congregational action at the local level remain abundant. Congregations can watch for and come to the aid of the voiceless whose rights have been ignored.

The extent of Christian-Jewish-Muslim cooperation after September 11 aimed to reduce anti-Muslim hostility has been heartening. Each congregation should have a committee on social justice, or a counterpart thereof, to look out for those who have been denied basic physical, psychological, and legal needs and call such needs to the attention of congregational members. Not all problems can be solved at once, but awareness and accurate information among people of good will is a starting place. As Martin Buber once said, "My need for bread is a material issue; but the need of others for bread is a spiritual issue."

Discussion Questions

1. How can we best use the Scriptures to shed light on current questions of human and civil rights? Which rights should Christians emphasize? How might the misuse of scriptural passages in the past to justify the execution of "witches" or the maintenance of human slavery inform our discernment in this matter?
2. What are the biblical roots of impartiality before the law and fairness before judges? Why did Jesus speak against resorting to the law courts?
3. How are refugees, aliens, and strangers to be regarded in the biblical perspective? What is the case for worrying about doing justice at home first?
4. Are some limits on individual freedom consistent with the gospel of Jesus?
5. What is the scriptural basis for regarding basic human needs—food, housing, and health care—as a right? When are rights an economic problem?
6. Is there a natural tension between the freedom of individual conscience and the power of the state? Does respect for persons mean, above all, respect for conscience? Is a "clear conscience" easy or difficult?
7. How can the Christian church help reduce the climate of fear, discontent, and isolation that leads to hate crimes?
8. Do my local congregation and my denomination pay enough attention to civil rights in the United States? To human rights abroad? Are they included in our understanding of Christian mission?
9. Do I know enough about the work of the United Nations in the area of human rights? Why is the United Nations so often criticized in America?
10. Does my congregation participate in Amnesty International letter-writing campaigns? Why or why not?
11. Does the pacifist alternative ("turn the other cheek") have an adequate hearing in my congregation and my denomination?

To Learn More

Maurice Cranston provides a good introduction to the topic in *What Are Human Rights* (New York: Basic Books, 1962). In *Taking Rights Seriously* (Cambridge, Mass.: Harvard University Press, 1978), Richard Dworkin defends an individualistic approach to rights. Louis Henkin deals with internationalization of rights in *The Rights of Man Today* (Boulder, Colo.: Westview Press, 1978). Carl Wellman evaluates new developments in the discussion of rights in *The Proliferation of Rights: Moral Progress or Empty Rhetoric?* (Boulder, Colo.: Westview Press, 1999).

Some quite recent books contribute to the understanding of particular issues. Michael W. McCann's *Rights at Work* (Chicago: University of Chicago Press, 1994) deals with the struggle for pay equity. What has happened in the area of race is surveyed in *The Unsteady March: The Rise and Decline of Racial Equality in America* (Chicago: University of Chicago Press, 1999) by Philip A.

Klinkner and Rogers M. Smith. Christian Davenport edited a book on governments' repression of their own people: *Paths to State Repression: Human Rights Violations and Contentious Politics* (Lanham, Md.: Rowman & Littlefield, 2000). A sharp critique of attempts to minimize the influence of organized religion in politics is found in Frank Guliuzza III, *Over the Wall: Protecting Religious Expression in the Public Square* (Albany: State University of New York Press, 2000). Amitai Etzioni has edited a special issue of the communitarian journal *The Responsive Community* (winter 2001–02) that deals with the issues raised since September 11.

5

Homosexuality and Same-Gender Unions

A young woman died of cancer in her early forties. She was a lawyer, and before her death she made sure that her partner for the last thirteen years had power of attorney and could carry out all her legal wishes and obligations after her death. However, the very first attempt at this was blocked by the mortuary where final arrangements were being made for her cremation and burial. When the papers were brought in for a signature, the mortuary representative would not recognize the power of attorney of a lesbian partner. "Her next of kin have to sign," he said. Her parents and sister were in the room, and her father signed the papers, but as far as they were concerned, the "next of kin" was their daughter's partner. "What would happen if we hadn't been here?" they asked. "Then we would have to wait for the coroner to make all these arrangements. It might take quite a while. The only other way would be if the deceased had come in before her death and signed for her own arrangements." The mortuary representative was obviously annoyed and disgusted with any same-sex partnership. It was a lesson to the family of the homophobia in society that did not allow even the most basic civil rights to gay and lesbian persons.

I. INTRODUCTION

During the last quarter of a century, we have experienced a sexual revolution. We have witnessed great changes in the cultural and religious understanding of sex roles, sexual behavior outside of heterosexual marriage, single-parent families, abortion rights, homosexuality, and the explicit ways in which all sexual matters are discussed. There is literally no aspect of human experience that remains untouched or unexamined by the sexual revolution. Despite all the moral ambiguities of this revolution, churches cannot avoid the effects of these changes on their congregations. Revolutions are frightening, and there is enormous resistance to these societal shifts. Today the issue of same-gender unions and the civil rights of same-gender partners is placed forcefully on the church's agenda. The question of the ordination of gay and lesbian persons is front and center in many mainline denominations as well. William Sloane Coffin was right when he said the issue of homosexuality is probably the most divisive issue in the American church since slavery.

According to James A. Nelson, who has written several books on sexuality, theology, and spirituality, we cannot say with any precision what causes homosexuality. It is likely an interaction of several factors, including genetic, hormonal, and environmental, but psychological and social influences alone probably cannot cause homosexuality. He writes that the genetic, hormonal, neurological predisposition toward homosexual, heterosexual, or bisexual orientation is present at birth for all people. But it takes the blending of various factors—and no one seems to be quite sure how—in the earliest years of a child's life to produce a lasting sexual orientation in that person. Once that is relatively fixed—and the research now says this is between two and five years of age—this sexual orientation cannot be changed permanently by therapy.

II. LEGAL CLIMATE TODAY

The legal benefits that married couples take for granted in society, which are the basis of patterns of family life as we know them, are denied to gay and lesbian persons in committed relationships. They do not have equal access to the civil status of marriage. They cannot:

- File joint tax returns
- Inherit each other's estates, except by will
- Share joint insurance policies
- Share benefits from annuities, pension plans, and Social Security
- Participate in health benefits, unless specifically written into a labor contract or under their terms of employment
- Jointly adopt children (California has recently made this easier by allowing social workers reviewing the home of a gay or lesbian couple to recommend adoption to a judge if it passes inspection.)
- Take family leave for bereavement or illness

- Have family rights in visiting one's sick or injured spouse in the hospital and making treatment decisions
- Make decisions for burial on the death of a partner
- Obtain wrongful-death benefits for a surviving partner and children
- Have the right to family reunification through immigration

The Supreme Court of the state of Hawaii in 1993 issued a presumptive ruling that unequal marriage rights for same-gender couples were unconstitutional under that state's law prohibiting discrimination based on sex. Though subsequent initiative and legislative action in Hawaii has reversed that decision, there are movements in Hawaii, Vermont, California, and some other states to give same-gender unions the same legal status as marriages between a man and a woman. The Constitution of the United States requires that each state give "full faith and credit" to the "public acts, records, and judicial proceedings of every other state" (Art. IV, Sec. l). This has always been interpreted to mean that a marriage legal in one state is legal in all states. In point of fact, at present not one of the fifty states calls same-gender partnerships "marriage," though on December 20, 1999, the Vermont Supreme Court held that "domestic partnerships" should carry the same legal protections as marriage.

California and Colorado voted down the right to same-sex marriages in the year 2000, at the same time that Vermont's House Judiciary Committee approved a bill that would recognize same-sex "civil unions." It has since passed and been signed into law. Nearly five hundred gay and lesbian couples were united in civil unions in the summer of 2000.

However, also in 2000 the United States Supreme Court decided that the Boy Scouts of America could prevent gay scoutmasters from serving. This decision has caused a firestorm in many cities and school districts that allow the Scouts to meet in their facilities. The schools had already been dealing with the question of Gay-Straight Alliances meeting after school. These clubs were designed as both support groups for gay students and, with the help of sympathetic straight students, a bulwark against homophobia. The Gay, Lesbian, Straight Teacher Network estimates there are about 700 GSAs nationwide, most of which were formed peacefully in the wake of the 1998 murder of Matthew Shepard.[1] The Scout decision by the U.S. Supreme Court seemed a step backward to many. In June 2001 Senator Jesse Helms proposed an amendment to President Bush's education legislation that would withhold federal funds from school districts that denied the use of their facilities to the Boy Scouts because of the organization's exclusion of homosexual leaders. Minutes later Senator Barbara Boxer proposed that all schools could open to a wide range of youth groups, including gay and lesbian student groups and the Boy Scouts. Both amendments also passed.[2]

The Pentagon in March 2001 broke the Bush administration's silence on gay persons in the military today, responding to an annual report on the "Don't Ask, Don't Tell, Don't Harass" policy started in the Clinton administration. The Pentagon spokesperson said that Defense Secretary Donald Rumsfeld is committed to issuing a Pentagon directive on harassment of homosexuals. According to the annual Conduct Unbecoming report by the service members Legal Defense Network, harassment of homosexuals was down in the armed services by 10 percent in 2000. Total violations of the Clinton policy—including asking about a service member's sexual orientation and talking to others about it—also declined slightly for the first time in the report's seven-year history. Still, death threats, assaults, and verbal gay and lesbian bashing continue almost unabated. The Anti-Harassment Action Plan resulted from a survey of 75,000 service members following the 1999 murder of Private Barry Winchell at Fort Campbell, Kentucky, after months of taunting about his sexual orientation.

In June 2001, however, the number of troops discharged from the U.S. military for homosexual conduct or for openly discussing their sexual orientation increased by 17 percent over the last year. Civil-rights groups charge that suspected gays and lesbians are often discriminated against and pressured to leave the military, despite Defense Department rules that forbid such harassment.[3]

The three largest automakers in the United States (DaimlerChrysler Corp., Ford Motor Co., and General Motors Corp.) announced that they will extend health-care benefits to same-sex domestic partners of their United States employees as "part of their commitment to diversity in the workplace."[4] At least ninety-four other Fortune 500 companies provide domestic-partner benefits. Many local and state governments are also giving their employees domestic partner benefits. A San Francisco law requires that companies doing business with the city offer the same employee benefits to domestic partners as to married couples. This law was upheld by a decision of the Ninth U.S. Circuit Court of Appeals in June 2001. This decision clears the way for similar laws in Los Angeles, Seattle, Berkeley, and San Mateo County.

On January 1, 2000, a new law took effect in California that allowed hundreds of gay and lesbian persons to begin registering as domestic partners. This law, AB26, affords some same-gender couples two benefits: hospital visitation rights and health insurance coverage for the dependents of government employees covered by CalPERS, the state retirement system.

The American Academy of Pediatrics endorsed homosexual adoption in February 2002, saying that same-sex couples can provide the loving, stable, emotionally healthy family life children need. They focused specifically on gaining legally protected parental rights for gay and lesbian "coparents" whose partners have children, but also said these rights could apply to same-sex couples who want to adopt a child together. Nine million U.S. children are estimated to have at least one homosexual parent. Nationwide about half the states allow second-parent homosexual adoption where one parent is already the legal parent, but a handful of states have prohibitive statutes.[5]

Legal maneuvering is an important method of social change. Still, many fear that any legitimizing of gay and lesbian unions would have adverse social consequences, such as encouraging what they believe to be immoral behavior, undermining the sanctity of the family, or sending young people the "wrong message" about the relationship between personal choice and sexual orientation. Legal prohibitions are seen as a kind of insurance policy or preemptive strike against the possibility of such legitimization. Some people arouse fear by alleging that "special rights" for gay and lesbian citizens go beyond the rights accorded other citizens.

Anna Quindlen, writing in *Newsweek*, says that change comes in small incremental ways when the world stops seeing differences as threatening. Instead, the differences become so ordinary that people begin to see bigotry in situations such as the Boy Scouts of America refusing gay leadership. "Straight men who were once Eagle Scouts sent back their badges. United Way chapters pulled their financial support. Cities and states that had passed laws prohibiting discrimination based on sexual orientation told Scout troops they could no longer use public facilities. Local Boy Scout councils asked the national group to reconsider its decision."[6]

But as we will see below, the mainline churches are still having difficult discussions over the ordination of gay, lesbian, and bisexual persons, and the blessing of same-sex couples.

III. CURRENT SITUATION IN THE CHURCHES

As 2003 opens, many mainline churches are splitting their national constituencies over the issues of ordination of gay, lesbian, and bisexual persons and the blessing of same-sex couples. The split reflects the division within society at large. In 1996 the Presbyterian Church added a section in their Book of Order that states, "Those who are called to office in the church are to lead a life in obedience to Scripture and in conformity to the historic confessional standards of the church. Among these standards is the requirement to live either in fidelity within the covenant of marriage between a man and a woman, or chastity in singleness." Amendment 01-A, approved by the General Assembly (national body) in July 2001, would have given presbyteries and sessions (regional and congregational bodies) the responsibility of judging who is called and fit to serve as a church officer. It would have nullified earlier actions of the General Assemblies that barred "self-affirming, practicing homosexuals" from service as ministers, elders, and deacons. However, this change was voted down by the presbyteries.

The United Methodist Church is officially opposed to ordination of gays and lesbians as well. On December 12, 2001, Bishop Elias Galvan of Seattle filed formal complaints against two openly gay United Methodist pastors asking that their ministerial standing be reviewed by the Judicial Council, the Supreme Court of the denomination. While one passage in the denominational Book of Discipline forbids the ordination and appointment of "self-avowed practicing homosexuals," another passage states that all clergy in good standing shall receive appointments. The court ruled that the passages are not contradictory. The outcome of a case reviewing the two ministers, who say they are practicing homosexuals but are in good standing, puts the church in an awkward position.

The Evangelical Lutheran Church in America will begin a study on homosexuality following an 899-115 vote in the 2001 churchwide assembly on August 13. The assembly action calls for a churchwide study on homosexuality and an action plan for implementation that will come before the 2005 ELCA churchwide assembly.

The 2.5 million–member Episcopal Church allows each diocese the option of whether to bless same-sex unions, as well as to appoint openly gay and lesbian clergy, but the General Convention (national) meeting in Denver in 2000 did not grant this authority as a general policy. The church had said in 1994 at its House of Bishops convention that it recognizes that the New Testament standard is a lifelong, monogamous, heterosexual union, but then four paragraphs later substituted the words "mature adults" for "man and woman." "We believe sexual relationships reach their fullest potential for good and minimize their capacity for ill when in the context of chaste, faithful, and committed lifelong unions between mature adults. There are those who believe this is as true for homosexual as for heterosexual relationships and that such relationships need and should receive the pastoral care of the church."[7]

Many individual congregations are choosing to ignore ecclesiastical restrictions both to ordain gay and lesbians and to bless unions of same-gender persons. The only major Christian denomination with a clear policy permitting the ordination of non-celibate gays and lesbians is the United Church of Christ.

IV. A CHRISTIAN PERSPECTIVE

Biblical References

Sexual issues are tearing our churches apart today as never before. The issue of homosexuality threatens to fracture whole denominations, as the issue of slavery did a hundred and fifty years ago. We naturally turn to the Bible for guidance but find ourselves mired in interpretive quicksand. Is the Bible able to speak to our confusion on this issue?

Despite a long tradition of using the following passages as showing that the Bible condemns homosexuality, these passages are now generally regarded by biblical scholars as making quite different points. They do not deal with unions between persons of the same gender:

- Genesis 19:1–29. The gang rape in Sodom is a case of ostensibly hetero-sexual males intent on humiliating strangers by treating them "like women," thus demasculinizing them. This passage demonstrates inhos-pitality, which was the sin of Sodom according to Jesus (Matt. 10:14–15; Luke 10:10–12)
- Judges 19–21. This brutal behavior, the same as in Genesis, has nothing to do with the problem of whether genuine love expressed between con-senting adults of the same gender is legitimate or not.
- Deuteronomy 23:17–18. This passage refers to a heterosexual male pros-titute involved in Canaanite fertility rites that had infiltrated Jewish wor-ship. The King James Version inaccurately labeled him a "sodomite."
- 1 Corinthians 6:9 and 1 Timothy 1:10. These passages refer to the "pas-sive" and "active" partners in homosexual relationships, or to homosex-ual and heterosexual male prostitutes. It is unclear whether the issue is homosexuality alone or promiscuity and "sex-for-hire."

There remain three passages in the Christian Old Testament that unequiv-ocally condemn homosexual behavior.

- Leviticus 18:22 states the principle: "You [masculine] shall not lie with a male as with a woman: it is an abomination."
- Leviticus 20:13 adds the penalty: "If a man lies with a male as with a woman, both of them have committed an abomination; they shall be put to death; their blood is upon them."
- Genesis 38:1–11 tells of God's displeasure at the spilling of semen for nonprocreative purpose.

All three passages reflect the Hebrew prescientific understanding that male semen contained the whole of nascent life. With no knowledge of eggs and ovulation, it was assumed that the woman provided only the incubating space. A tribe struggling to populate a country in which its people were outnumbered would value procreation highly, but such values are rendered questionable today in a world facing uncontrolled overpopulation.

In addition, when a man acted like a woman sexually, male dignity was com-promised. It was a degradation, not only in regard to himself, but for every other male. The patriarchalism of Hebrew culture shows its hand in the for-mulation of the commandment, since no similar stricture was formulated to forbid homosexual acts between females. Added to this is the repugnance heterosexuals tend to feel for acts and orientations foreign to them.

Old Testament texts have to be weighed against the New. Consequently, Paul's unambiguous condemnation of homosexual behavior in Romans 1: 26–27 must be noted.

> For this reason God gave them up to degrading passions. Their women exchanged natural intercourse for unnatural, and in the same way also the men, giving up natural intercourse with women, were consumed with passion for one another. Men committed shameless acts with men and received in their own persons the due penalty for their error.

Paul was unaware of the distinction between sexual orientation, over which one has little or no choice, and sexual behavior, over which one does have a choice. He seemed to assume that those whom he condemned were hetero sexuals who were acting contrary to nature, "leaving," "giving up," or "exchanging" their regular sexual orientation for that which was foreign to them. Paul knew nothing of the modern psychosexual understanding of homosexuals as persons whose orientation is fixed early in life, largely genetically. (The word "homosexual" did not come even into being until the nineteenth century.)

The relationships Paul describes are heavy with lust. They are not relationships between consenting adults who are committed to each other with faithfulness and integrity—something Paul simply could not envision. He did not know that homosexual behavior is manifested by a wide variety of species, especially (but not solely) under the pressure of overpopulation. This may be a quite natural mechanism for preserving species by preventing overpopulation. We cannot, of course, decide human ethical conduct solely on the basis of animal behavior or the human sciences, but Paul here is arguing from nature, as he himself says, and new knowledge of what is "natural" is therefore relevant to the case.

To disagree with biblical authors on questions of sexual mores is not new. There are many other sexual attitudes, practices, and restrictions that are normative in Scripture but that we no longer accept as normative:

- Sexual intercourse during the seven days of the menstrual period was prohibited. The woman was considered unclean at this time.
- The punishment of adultery was death by stoning. Adultery was defined by the marital status of the woman. A man could not commit adultery against his own wife, but only against another man by sexually using the other man's wife.
- A bride who was not a virgin was to be stoned to death.

- Nudity was considered reprehensible.
- Polygamy and concubinage were regularly practiced in Christian Old Testament times.
- The levirate marriage was practiced, in which a widow was to have intercourse with each of her dead husband's brothers until she bore him a male heir.
- The Christian Old Testament nowhere explicitly prohibits sexual relations between unmarried consenting heterosexual adults, as long as the woman's economic value (bride price) is not compromised—as long as she is not a virgin. Some early Christian communities needed proof of fertility (pregnancy) before marriage.
- Semen and menstrual blood rendered all who touched them unclean. Intercourse rendered one unclean until sundown; menstruation rendered the woman unclean for seven days.
- Social regulations regarding adultery, incest, rape, and prostitution are, in the Old Testament, determined largely by considerations of the males' property rights over women.
- Jews were supposed to practice endogamy—that is, marriage within the twelve tribes of Israel. This carried over to laws in the American South against interracial marriage.
- The law of Moses allowed for divorce. Jesus categorically forbids it. On the other hand, Jesus never mentions homosexuality. Yet we ordain divorced persons, and not homosexuals.
- The Christian Old Testament regarded celibacy as abnormal. Yet the Catholic Church has made it mandatory for priests and nuns. Some Christian ethicists demand celibacy of homosexuals, whether they have a vocation for celibacy or not.
- The Old and New Testaments both regarded slavery as normal and nowhere categorically condemned it. Part of that heritage was the use of female slaves, concubines, and captives as sexual toys, breeding machines, or involuntary wives by their male owners. Many American slave owners did the same and cited Scripture passages as their justification.

Progressive Theological Reflections

Walter Wink, to whom we are indebted for the above summary, says "that the crux of the matter is simply that the Bible has no sexual ethic. There is no biblical sex ethic. Instead, the Bible exhibits a variety of sexual mores, some of which changed over the thousand-year span of biblical history. Mores are unreflective customs accepted by a given community. Many of the practices that the Bible prohibits, we allow, and many that it allows, we prohibit."[8] He suggests that we critique the sexual mores of any given time by the love ethic exemplified by Jesus. Is it non-exploitative, does it not dominate, is it responsible, mutual, caring, and loving? He adds that Augustine already dealt with this in his inspired phrase, "Love God, and do as you please."[9]

To deny, repress, or hide one's sexuality is bad theology and bad psychology. The only healthy thing to do is to accept oneself and affirm one's sexuality. Without self-acceptance one cannot possibly live responsibly. But for gay and lesbian people this has been a gigantic struggle. They have frequently been told by their families that they don't belong to them, by the church that they are perverse and desperate sinners, by the medical profession that they are sick and abnormal, and by the Supreme Court of the land that they are criminals. Yet most gay and lesbian people have withstood this onslaught with health and stability and determination.

At the core of the Christian faith is the simple and profound assertion: God loves you just as you are. In the gospel the first and last word is grace. Grace means you do not have to become something different before you are loved by God. Grace is offered freely. You cannot buy it or learn it or deserve it. All you can do is receive it. That unconditional love and generous acceptance are not marginal to our religion; they are central to our belief. Grace is total acceptance. Our body's feelings, our body's erogenous dimensions, our fantasies, our masculinity and femininity, our heterosexuality, our homosexuality, our sexual irresponsibilities, as well as our yearnings for sexual integrity—all of these are graciously accepted by divine love.

It serves the common good of society when same-sex unions are legally accepted and when the church blesses these unions as holy before God. A stronger foundation is placed under the couple's commitment to fidelity, monogamy, and caring love. Social stability is enhanced.

George Regas, as pastor of All Saints Episcopal Church in Pasadena, blessed many same-gender unions. In a sermon he gave before retirement, he said the following about such unions:

> The Church's blessing of a same-gender union, where the couple is committed to a lifelong, faithful, monogamous, generous love, is the clearest symbol the church can offer that these children of God are fully accepted into the life of a congregation. It is an act of justice when the Church blesses the union of a gay or lesbian couple. When the Church says to gay and lesbian couples in the blessing that you and your love for each other are good and holy, God's radical grace liberates those couples from the prisons of self-hatred and contempt that gays and lesbians have ingested at the hands of a hostile society.[10]

Jesus demonstrated throughout his ministry that righteousness consisted of showing justice and mercy to those who experience it the least. He reached out to those who were marginal, rejected, stigmatized, powerless and suffering. Jesus said that when we offer justice and love to these, we do it to him.

V. WHAT WE CAN DO

- A change of heart takes place through personal encounters. Find ways to share life with gays and lesbians and let them tell their stories. Hear today's political rhetoric through their ears.
- Become good students on the issue of homosexuality. Read, reflect, and share what God's spirit is leading us to be and to do.
- Two generations ago, interfaith civil marriages were strongly discouraged and one generation ago interracial marriages were forbidden. The same arguments to prevent such civil unions are given today against same-gender couples. Positive experiences with such couples have changed attitudes. God calls us to stand on the frontiers of change and illuminate the new terrain with the light of the gospel.
- Be informed about legislation—city, state, and national—affecting the integrity, honor, and civil rights of homosexuals; and become strong advocates for justice and compassionate love.
- Forcefully urge your congregation to take an official position as an open and affirming church for gay men and lesbian women. Build networks of churches of inclusion.
- Work on the leadership of churches locally and nationally to do the following:

    a. Rather than condemn a "gay lifestyle," which implies promiscuity, understand that we do not endorse a lifestyle, but accept an orientation.
    b. See goodness in gays as they live faithfully the life God gave them.
    c. Take a strong position on gay civil rights.
    d. Become a church of radical inclusion.
    e. Bless same-gender unions when the partners in such unions are committed to lifelong, faithful, monogamous love. Support families that arise out of these unions.
    f. Apply the same standards to all persons when ordaining persons to the church's sacred ministry.
    g. Support legislation that gives legal status to same-gender couples.
    h. Advocate sex education for church youth groups, including studies of both sexual "activity" and sexual "orientation." Create an environment within the church in which it is all right to talk about sex.

- Link justice and kindness. The Hebrew prophet Micah proclaimed that righteousness has three requirements: to do justice, to love kindness, and to walk humbly with God (Mic. 6:8). The linking of justice with kindness by the prophet of old is no less urgent today.
- Challenge the political leadership to act courageously on their convictions and hold them accountable in the task of building a civil and just society. Illuminate the hypocrisy often found behind "family values" rhetoric against homosexuals. For example, a thrice-married Georgia congressman, Bob Barr, introduced the Defense of Marriage Act thus: "The flames of hedonism, the flames of narcissism, the flames of

self-centered morality are licking at the very foundation of our society and family unit."
- Seek out ways to be a personal witness to God's inclusive love, and locate networks of support where you can be an effective advocate for a public policy that includes gays and lesbians as equals in the totality of American life.

Discussion Questions

1. What is your experience with a gay or lesbian person? Do you know a same-gender couple or a family?
2. Do you believe the Bible is against homosexuality? Has this chapter changed your mind?
3. How does the way Jesus lived affect the question of homosexuality? Would his admonition to "love your neighbor as yourself" (Matt. 22:39) and "just as you did it to one of the least of these, . . . you did it to me" (Matt. 25:40) have a bearing on your attitude toward someone of a different sexual orientation?
4. Is it just to afford legal civil rights to same-gender partnerships, even though they are not allowed to marry? Is this "special rights"?
5. Do young persons in church need to talk about sexuality today? Can they distinguish between sexual "activity" and sexual "orientation"? Describe each. Is sexual orientation a "choice"?
6. Has science changed our view of homosexuality? If so, how?
7. Do homosexuals have something special to bring to the church? If so, should they be ordained as ministers and pastors?

To Learn More

Walter Wink, ed., *Homosexuality and Christian Faith: Questions of Conscience for the Churches* (Minneapolis: Fortress, 1999) presents short pieces from some of the nation's prominent church leaders who address the fundamental moral imperatives about homosexuality. James B. Nelson, *Embodiment: An Approach to Sexuality and Christian Theology* (Minneapolis: Fortress, 1994) looks at sexuality and the church in general, providing a chapter specifically on homosexuality. Another book, James B. Nelson and Sandra J. Longfellow, eds., *Sexuality and the Sacred: Sources for Theological Reflection* (Louisville, Ky.: Westminster John Knox, 1996) examines how sexuality is intended by God to be a dimension of our spirituality.

Respected psychologists examine the dimensions of race, ethnicity, gender, and sexual orientation in J. D. Goodchilds, ed., *Psychological Perspectives on Human Diversity in America* (Washington, D.C.: American Psychological Association, 1993). J. C. Gonsiorek and J. D. Weinrich, *Homosexuality: Research Implications for Public Policy* (Thousand Oaks, Calif.: Sage Publications, 1991) summarizes what science knows about homosexuality and its relevance for public policy.

Readers can also contact the following organizations for more information:

National Gay and Lesbian Task Force
1700 Kalorama Road NW
Washington, DC 20009-2624
(202) 332-6483
FAX (202) 332-0207
E-mail: ngltf@ngltf.org
Web: www.ngltf.org/

Parents and Friends of Lesbians and Gays
1012 14th Street NW, Suite 700
Washington, DC 20005
(202) 638-4200
E-mail: scalice@home.com
Web: www.backdoor.com/pflagsf/

Sexuality Information and Education Council of the United States
130 W. 42d Street, Suite 2500
New York, NY 10036
Phone: (212) 819-9770
Fax: (212) 819-9776
E-mail: siecus@siecus.org
Web: www.siecus.org

6

Is Social Security Really Broken?

Pierre Bradley found the requirement that he contribute substantially to Social Security an irritant and a burden. He did not need Social Security in order to be taken care of in retirement. On the other hand, he was very interested in building up his estate. He had long been a skilled investor, and he was sure that if he could keep the money he contributed to Social Security, he could add far more to that estate than he would ever get back from government payments. He strongly supported any move to give workers more control over the use of their Social Security taxes.

David Wilson had worked all his life at jobs that paid little more than the minimum wage. His wife had been similarly employed. They had managed a decent life and raised three children, but it had been hard, and there were no savings. Now as they approached retirement, they were relieved by the assurance that their income from Social Security would sustain them. It would not be easy to live on this, but life had never been easy. They would manage. They did not understand all the talk about allowing people to invest part of their contributions to Social Security. The stock market belonged to a world they had never understood. They were glad that their retirement income did not depend on anything like that.

I. INTRODUCTION

The system is broken. Unless we move boldly and quickly, the promise of Social Security to future retirees cannot be met without eventual resort to benefit cuts, tax increases or massive borrowing. The time to act is now.

> Initial staff report, President's Social Security
> Commission, July 19, 2001

Social Security emerged in 2000 as a critical issue in the presidential campaign. Governor George W. Bush wanted to let individuals invest a small part of their Social Security contributions in the stock market, where he thought they would earn a better return, and Vice President Al Gore wanted to keep the system largely intact with an infusion of general tax revenues. Now that George W. Bush is president, he has moved aggressively to implement his vision of reform with the appointment of a Social Security Commission whose members are understood to be already committed to some form of privatization of the Social Security system. This chapter assesses the Bush proposal and the wisdom of abandoning the noble commitment to social insurance that this country made in 1935 with adoption of the Social Security Act.

II. PAST, PRESENT, AND FUTURE

The Past

The Social Security Act of 1935 came into being during the Great Depression, a very different time from today. An omnibus piece of legislation that included many different types of social welfare programs, the act reflected values very different from the ones that we now associate with Social Security. For example, the original legislation placed a heavy emphasis on state, rather than federal, action. Twenty-eight states already ran what they called old-age pension programs in 1935, and Congress for some time before had been toying with the idea of providing partial federal funding for these state-run programs. Most states also had widows' pension laws. Each of these state programs featured means tests, since everyone anticipated that they would pay benefits only to people in financial need. As a consequence, the Social Security Act, now remembered as a program without means tests, included welfare with its accompanying means tests.

Furthermore, the social insurance programs—unemployment compensation and old-age insurance—were the least popular parts of the Social Security Act, and they came the closest to being turned down by Congress in 1935. Coverage under these programs was not universal, and the idea that the old-age insurance program should be self-financing, without contributions from general revenues, found few supporters. Nor was the provision of the modern program that protects benefits against inflation even discussed during the Great Depression.

In fact, the members of Congress found voting for old-age welfare assistance much easier than voting for old-age insurance—insurance that guaranteed benefits regardless of individual means. The social insurance programs featured payroll taxes that were unpopular with employers, and they required long start-up periods before they could gather enough funds to pay benefits. The other programs in the act channeled federal grants to the states, almost always a popular cause, for such purposes as public health services, aid to dependent children, and old-age welfare assistance. Unlike social insurance programs, they could begin almost as soon as the money started to flow. It was a minor miracle that Congress included in the act any social insurance programs.

It was not until the early 1950s that Social Security, as the old age insurance program came to be known, triumphed over old-age assistance. The program had broadened the range of its benefits to include family and survivors' benefits in 1939 and expanded its coverage and raised its average benefits in 1950. By 1954, after the Republican Eisenhower administration had endorsed the program, the goal of universal, compulsory coverage in a wage-related program that paid benefits as a matter of right and blended the values of adequacy and fairness in an acceptable way appeared to be within sight. Congress added an automatic cost-of-living adjustment (COLA) in 1972, greatly expanding Social Security benefit levels. Appendix A summarizes the nine social insurance principles now embodied in Social Security.

The Present

Social Security currently provides a minimum "foundation of protection" for retired workers and for workers and their families who face a loss of income due to disability or the death of a family wage earner. About 46 million people now receive Social Security benefits, and another 154 million people are working in jobs covered by Social Security insurance guarantees. Approximately 70 percent of beneficiaries are retirees and their family members. Disabled workers and their families comprise another 15 percent of beneficiaries. And about 15 percent of Social Security recipients are survivors, including nearly two million children.

During 2000, the average retirement benefit was $804 per month for an individual and $1,410 for a couple. A typical disabled worker with a spouse and children received $1,311, and a widow with two children got $1,680. While these amounts may seem small to a middle-class person, they provide a significant basis of economic security. Almost two-thirds of the typical retiree's income comes from Social Security, and for two-fifths of our elderly, Social Security provides more than 80 percent of their income. Low-income women are particularly at risk without Social Security.

All but about 5 percent of U.S. workers are covered by Social Security. Most of those who are not covered are government workers. The federal government, states, and many localities have alternative retirement systems that cover some or all of their employees. Most of these systems pay benefits to qualified employees who are disabled or retired because of age. Some also provide annuities for survivors.

Social Security is financed on a pay-as-you-go basis, meaning that the payroll taxes today's workers and their employers pay are used to finance the benefits provided today's beneficiaries and their families. Employees and employers in 2001 each pay 6.2 percent of wages, up to a maximum wage level of $80,400 annually.

At the present time, Social Security is taking in more in taxes than is paid out in benefits, and the excess funds are credited to Social Security's trust funds. The trust funds are financial accounts in the U.S. Treasury. Social Security premiums (the payroll taxes employees and employers pay) and other income are deposited in these accounts, and Social Security benefits are paid from them. The only purposes for which these trust funds can be used are to pay benefits and program administrative costs. The trust funds hold money not needed in the current year to pay benefits and administrative costs and, by law, invest it in interest-bearing securities that are guaranteed by the U.S. government. A market rate of interest is paid to the trust funds on the securities (6.9 percent in 2000), and when these securities reach maturity or are needed to pay benefits, the Treasury redeems them. In September 2001, the trust funds held about $1.2 trillion of these government securities, and the trust funds' trustees are predicting that the funds' securities are expected to continue growing until they reach $5 trillion in 2016. The earnings of U.S. Treasury securities held by the trust funds add another $60 billion to Social Security income for the year. The trust funds also receive the income taxes collected from higher-income recipients on a portion of their Social Security benefits.

During the 2000 presidential campaign, the public was introduced to a new metaphor: the Social Security "lockbox." Both candidates pledged that, if elected, they would place in a lockbox all the surplus moneys earned by Social Security, rather than allow them to be spent for other public purposes. What this really meant was never very clear to the public. The Social Security trustees are obligated by law to surrender any surplus of income over expenses to the U.S. Treasury in return for government securities. The trust funds, therefore, seemed more suited as a strongbox for securities than a lockbox for surplus cash. Then was the U.S. Treasury the likelier home for a lockbox, since it ended up with the surplus moneys? For years, the U.S. Treasury, as the government's fiscal agent, had simply spent the surplus moneys as directed by the administration and the Congress. This changed in 1998, when Congress and the Clinton administration agreed to use the excess moneys only to reduce the $3.5 trillion of national debt held by the public. Thus, as privately held government securities matured, the Treasury redeemed them, giving their former owners cash to spend or invest and reducing the government's debt. Given the popularity of this move, it probably is fair to assume that the lockbox Governor Bush and Vice President Gore invoked during the 2000 presidential campaign was little more than a pledge to continue using surplus moneys generated by the Social Security system to reduce the privately held debt.

Not anymore! As a result of the passage of the administration's tax plan, the rapidly deteriorating economy, and the "war on terrorism," recent budget projections show that the U.S. Treasury will have to tap the Social Security surplus to fund other programs throughout most of President Bush's first term. Enactment of recent proposals to reduce payroll tax rates as part of a stimulus package, moreover, would shorten the life of the surplus. If at some time in the future the Social Security trust funds must cash in some of their securities in order to supplement payroll tax revenues, the government will have to decide whether to make up the shortfall of payroll taxes with general revenue sources or income-tax receipts now going to fund other government programs, or by borrowing more money from private investors. The Treasury bonds held by the Social Security trust funds represent real obligations of the federal government, and a failure to redeem the bonds would constitute a default by the government on its obligations.

The Future

The trustees[1] of the Social Security trust funds are required by law to project program costs and income a full seventy-five years into the future, based on assumptions about economic growth, wage growth, inflation, unemployment, disability, fertility, immigration, and mortality—in short, about anything that affects population or the economy. Projections over such a long period of time are necessarily subject to a great deal of uncertainty. This is why the trust funds' trustees adjust projections annually and always include "low-cost," "intermediate cost," and "high-cost" projections of the future.

In their report issued in March 2001, the trustees project long-term economic growth of the Gross Domestic Product (GDP) under "low-cost" assumptions in the range of 2.2 to 2.4 percent annually, a rate of growth slightly below the long-term historical levels. They also project moderately longer life expectancies. Even so, these assumptions result in a forecast of full funding for anticipated program costs throughout the seventy-five-year period. Indeed, in 2075 the trust funds would hold more than five years' worth of benefits (compared to two years' worth today) and still be expanding.

Under "intermediate-cost" assumptions, economic growth falls sharply over the next decade and ranges from 1.7 to 1.6 percent annually from 2020 through 2075. This is only slightly more than half the rate of growth experienced in every decade since 1950. The trustees also predict that low average annual gains in productivity and relatively high levels of unemployment will prevail over the next century. Given the anticipated retirement of the baby-boomer cohort (people born between 1946 and 1964), a sluggish economy of this sort will drain the trust funds of accumulated surpluses by 2038, forcing cutbacks of benefits or sudden increases of taxes. The "high-cost" alternative assumes even slower rates of economic growth and much longer life spans. It forecasts exhaustion of the trust funds in 2030.

A careful look at the assumptions made by the trustees for their "intermediate-cost" projections leads us to conclude that some of their guesses are needlessly pessimistic about future costs. Consider, for example, that they expect life expectancy at birth to rise from 73.8 years to 80.9 years for men, and from 79.5 years to 85.0 years for women by 2075. Is that really plausible in an increasingly urban and infrastructure-starved society? Even at the slow rate of productivity and wage growth predicted by the trustees, moreover, workers will actually earn nearly 50 percent more after inflation in 2038 than they do today. Since Social Security benefits are based on earnings, the real value of benefits should rise by roughly equal amounts. This implies that even if the financing of benefits after 2038 is limited to what can be raised in payroll taxes, seniors will end up with real income higher than the typical retiree receives today.

Having constructed "high-cost" and "low-cost" projections to bracket their sense of what is probable, the trust funds' trustees prefer in their recent report to talk mostly about the "intermediate-cost" scenario. This is the projection that has been promoted by the Bush administration as the basis for major reforms of the Social Security system. The system is "broken," it says, because "it will go broke in 2038" without radical change.

The Congressional Budget Office (CBO), whose projections are usually accepted by both political parties when devising the federal budget, does not make 75-year projections. It does make forecasts for the next decade, however, and its expected rates of economic growth between 2003 and 2011 are about 3.1 percent, virtually twice the rate projected by the trust fund trustees over the next decade for the "intermediate-cost" scenario. Were it to be made a basis of an even "lower-cost" projection of the trust funds' solvency, the surplus would rise even more rapidly and continuously than in the "low-cost" projection.

This system is hardly "broken." There even is a school of thought that says Social Security should not have a separate budget, that Social Security receipts should be regarded simply as part of general revenue, and outlays as part of general expenditure. If that were the case, it is hard to see why people would get so worked up about 2016, when the Social Security surplus stops rising (according to the trustees' intermediate projection), or 2038, when the surplus disappears. Would anyone care if the payroll tax, which is only one of many taxes, collects less money than the government spends on retirement benefits, which are only one of many government expenses? Social Security benefits could be paid out of the general budget—a transfer of revenue that would clearly be justified if payroll tax receipts have meanwhile been used to pay off the national debt, releasing large sums that would otherwise have been consumed by interest payments.

We believe these conclusions to be reasonable and sound. Even so, the events of September 11 have cast doubt on so many expectations of our society that we no longer can be sure how "the war on terrorism" will affect the economy and the population, and therefore the solvency of the Social Security system. To be sure, the sudden increase in public expenditures and reductions in taxes proposed by the administration and Congress already are claiming portions of the Social Security surplus, and the deepening recession is bound to shrink the payroll-tax receipts that add to the surplus. Temporarily, at least, the "low-cost" projections look less rosy. But the American economy is resilient. We expect it to adjust to the new uncertainties reasonably quickly and to begin recovery in the near future, returning to the conditions that are closer to the "low-cost" than the "intermediate-cost" projections of the Social Security trustees.

III. TIME FOR A CHANGE?

Growing Interest in Change

For almost fifty years after Congress approved the Social Security Act of 1935, policy makers and the public seemed satisfied with the structure of the Federal Old-Age and Survivors Insurance Program. The fact that benefits were broadly shared and that tax rules were applied to everyone gave the system a patina of fairness. Few people quarreled with the notion that the government knew best how to manage the risks and rewards of a social-insurance system.

By 1990, however, interest began to develop in reforms that would depart from the one-size-fits-all design of the system, introducing elements of choice and giving participants in the system a say in how their promised social-insurance protections were managed or structured. Although these proposals differ widely in detail, all of them give participants more control over how at least a portion of the contributions they are required to make would be managed. Some plans would give workers partial control over who manages their personal retirement account, what assets are held by these accounts, how much is contributed to these accounts, and how fast balances can be withdrawn after retirement. Some plans would provide only modest discretion on these matters; even so, individual accounts would be considered owned by the workers. Just as with other assets owned by the workers, individual participants would assume some of the risks previously carried by the government.

There are at least four reasons why this surge of interest in reforming Social Security is happening now.

- Foremost among them is a growing sense among policy makers and the public that, as currently structured, Social Security is in trouble and that it cannot be saved this time by modest adjustments of its benefit structure or payroll-tax rates. On the contrary, more far-reaching structural changes are being called for as the nation faces retirement of the baby-boom generation and expected improvements in life expectancy. President Bush and his Social Security Commission are doing everything they can to convince us that the Social Security system is "broken" and that its salvation lies with the creation of individual accounts managed by the participants themselves. We do not believe these dire warnings are warranted.
- The last few years also have favored talk of reforming the Social Security system because the public has begun to learn about and use new retirement savings vehicles like individual retirement accounts (IRAs), 401(k) and 403(b) plans, and Keogh plans. As family assets have grown, knowledge of mutual funds also has multiplied, offering a seemingly endless set of choices about how to invest savings. The fact that small investors have been able recently to purchase and sell diversified portfolios of stocks and bonds without excessive transaction costs also is a tribute to the explosive growth of computer power and its dramatic reduction in the costs of processing information. Each of these institutional innovations has contributed to the search for reform.
- The relative prosperity of the 1990s no doubt also contributed significantly to the rush toward reforms of the Social Security system that would shift some of the risks of bad times to individual participants. Younger people especially lack memories about the adverse consequences of economic slowdowns, and only the elderly remember vividly the conditions of the Great Depression that led to a national commitment to guaranteed social insurance. The long expansion and the passage of time seem to have

dulled the people's appreciation for protection against the ravages of economic fluctuations. By the same token, the sunny economic climate of the
1990s and its accompanying inflation of stock prices may have convinced
many policy makers and participants that they could manage individual
accounts more successfully than the government. Few recall that the Dow
Jones average was lower in 1980 than in 1965. Perhaps its fall in the
months since October 2000 will have a more sobering effect.

- Nor is the American society as willing to comply with rules or customs
that seemed more important before, as during the Great Depression,
World War II, or the Cold-War years. We have become more tolerant of
diversity. We are not as ready to subscribe, as in 1935, to the notion that
a uniform structure of social insurance is desirable because it provides all
Americans with a common experience that helps to bind the nation
together. Even labor unions, the traditional champions of policies that
reinforce social solidarity, have lost some of their power and commitment. Without this constraining influence, social-insurance program
structures that offer choice to participants seem more desirable.

Bush's Privatization Proposal: An Analysis

President Bush has proposed allowing workers to divert part of their Social
Security payroll taxes into individual accounts. He also has said he would
maintain Social Security benefits for disabled workers and survivors, as well as
for both current retirees and workers nearing retirement, as they exist under
current law. Beyond this, neither he nor the Social Security Commission he
appointed has revealed in detail the other dimensions of the Bush administration's proposal. News accounts on November 30, 2001, report that the commission is toying with the idea of proposing multiple ways of creating private
accounts, each of which raises different policy issues, rather than choosing a
single recommendation.

In order to analyze the consequences of a proposal closest to President
Bush's original wishes, were it to be enacted, four widely respected specialists
in the field of Social Security[2] have made several basic assumptions that seem
to be in the spirit of the administration's thoughts. For example, they evaluate
the diversion of 2 percentage points of the current Social Security payroll tax
into individual accounts. In other words, an individual earning $30,000 would
be allowed to divert $600 a year (2 percent of $30,000) into a private account.
For purposes of analysis, these analysts also readily accept the assumptions on
which the "intermediate" projections of the Social Security trust funds'
trustees are based, since all of the president's comments clearly regard them as
appropriate. They take the administration at its word that it will not increase
payroll or other tax rates, and they assume—again to make analysis possible—

that non-Social Security expenditures (like defense and agricultural subsidies) will not be materially reduced. In the absence of more information from the administration, they also assume that all eligible workers will choose to contribute to individual accounts.

Under these assumptions, establishing individual accounts would have a substantial impact on the resources available to pay Social Security benefits. Individual accounts would receive 16 percent of current payroll tax revenue (2 percentage points of the 12.4 percent payroll tax rate) from the Social Security trust funds. According to Aaron and his colleagues, this means that benefits within the traditional Social Security program would have to be reduced by 32 percent for all workers under age fifty-five in 2002 (the year the plan was assumed to go into effect) just to avoid further deterioration in Social Security's financial condition (that is, to ensure that the trust funds are solvent through 2038). The reason they expect the benefits to be cut so much is the need *not* to cut benefits of retirees and workers within ten years of retiring. To extend solvency of the Social Security trust funds for fifty years, benefits would need to be cut by 37 percent; for seventy-five years, 41 percent. The earnings from individual accounts may or may not offset the effect of these benefit cuts.

If Social Security benefits were cut by the same percentage for all workers under the age of fifty-five, fifty-four-year-olds would have only about ten years to accumulate money in their individual accounts before retiring, whereas thirty-year-olds would have thirty-five years. As a result, older workers would experience much larger percentage reductions in their total retirement benefits (including income from the individual accounts) than would younger workers. Most individual account plans therefore phase in cuts in Social Security benefits in order to reduce the adverse effect on older workers. But if benefits are cut less for older workers (25 percent for fifty-five-year-olds), they must be cut more for younger workers (54 percent for twenty-five-year-olds) to achieve equivalent savings.

Supporters of individual accounts often respond that the earnings on individual accounts will easily make up the difference, producing an inflation-adjusted annuity at the time of retirement that yields substantially more retirement income, when combined with Social Security benefits, than is likely without individual accounts. This may or may not be true, depending on the skill of individual participants. Assume, for example, that workers invest their individual accounts by holding 60 percent of the account balance in the form of stocks and 40 percent in bonds, and that they earn on their investments a real (inflation-adjusted) return before administrative costs of 5.9 percent annually (based on the average return on equities from 1946 to 1995). If administrative costs on the individual accounts amount to forty basis points (or 0.4 per cent of the account balance) each year, the average return on individual accounts would be 5.5 percent.[3] If workers were allowed to invest in a broader array of financial assets, or to hold their accounts at a wider variety of financial providers, administrative costs could be substantially higher.[4]

When these earnings from individual accounts are combined with the (reduced) benefits of Social Security, total retirement income from both sources turns out to be *lower* than the income that would be received by the same participant under current Social Security legislation. The size of the shortfall varies by age, with the youngest and lowest-wage earners suffering the largest losses and the oldest and the highest-wage earners losing the least. Overall, the shortfall is about 20 percent.

Thus, in the absence of higher payroll tax rates or transfers of general revenue funds into the Social Security trust funds, and assuming (for the sake of argument) the accuracy of the trustee's "intermediate" projections, benefits will need to be cut significantly in order to assure solvency in the trust funds. The introduction of individual accounts into the system, moreover, will probably *reduce* benefits further rather than enhance total retirement income.

The above rates of return for individual accounts accord with historical stock market performance. Can we expect similar rates in the future? There is reason to believe that future returns on invested savings may be lower than in the past. Furthermore, even if average returns are sustained, large swings in returns over time can be expected.

Two factors suggest that stocks may yield less in the future than they have in the past. Despite recent drops in the market averages, stock prices remain at very high levels relative to corporate earnings. High price-earning ratios usually have been associated with lower market returns. Moreover, since growth of the labor force is expected to slow in the future to approximately zero, historical rates of return to capital in general and to stocks in particular may drop. These factors at least raise the possibility that investments in stocks and bonds may not yield as much in the future as they have in the past. If they do not, the income from individual accounts that was assumed above is too high.

Winners and Losers from Privatization

Rates of return also would vary greatly from year to year *and from individual to individual.* Privatization is attractive to financially sophisticated Americans who happen (by no coincidence) also to enjoy every other advantage in our society and who do not rely heavily on Social Security for their retirement income. But what about the less fortunate citizens, the ones who will need to live on their Social Security checks but who may not know the difference between a stock and a bond? Is freedom of choice such a blessing for them?

Will they understand the risks to which they may be exposed? When funds are invested in stocks and held to retirement, the accumulated balance at retirement is as volatile as the stock market, which not so infrequently moves up or down by 50 percent or more within a few years. The entire proposition that Social Security participants will come out ahead financially in a privatized system depends on their knowledge of and ability to manage investment risk and the costs of buying and selling. The devastating losses to their "defined-contribution" retirement accounts experienced recently by employees of the Enron Corporation are only one of many horror stories that can be told about the risks of private retirement accounts. The evidence on this subject is not encouraging.

Most privatization schemes work against the interests of lower-wage earners, women, minorities, the disabled, and survivors. The existing Social Security system is progressive in the sense it pays benefits to retirees who earned relatively low wages during working years a higher proportion of the premiums they paid into the system than it pays back to retirees who earned higher wages. This feature is especially important to women, who tend to earn less, work more intermittently, and live longer than men. Partially privatized systems, on the other hand, would not favor poorer people in this way, would not guarantee lifetime benefits for individual accounts, are unlikely to extend benefits to surviving spouses, and often do not protect private account balances from inflation.

Nor would the disabled and survivors fare well under partial privatization programs. Bear in mind that disabled workers, their families, and survivors of workers now constitute almost one-third of the beneficiaries under the current Social Security system. Were they to be granted individual accounts under a privatization plan, workers who become permanently disabled or die will have too short a time in which to build up an account balance adequate to supplement the (reduced) support they or their surviving family would receive from Social Security.

For similar reasons, minority participants in the Social Security system are more likely to suffer from partial privatization schemes. African Americans are only 12 percent of the population, but they make up 17 percent of Americans receiving Social Security disability benefits and 22 percent of all children receiving survivor benefits. Because privatization proposals would divert large amounts of money from the current system, it is unclear just how these survivor and disability benefits would continue to be financed. Most proposals to privatize also would weaken the progressivity of the system. Low-income minority individuals would earn interest and dividends (assuming a healthy stock market) only on their contributions to individual accounts, which would be based on their much lower wages. Even if low-income African Americans earned the same rate of return on their accounts as high-income earners, they would have very different portfolios because of the disparate nature of their salaries. The progressive nature of Social Security, combined with a cost-of-living adjustment that increases benefits every year, strengthens the safety net for minority individuals, who tend to be the most economically disadvantaged.

In short, the disadvantaged of our society—lower-wage workers, women, minorities, the disabled, and survivors—value the vital source of guaranteed support provided by the existing Social Security system. Essentially, privatization changes Social Security from a program of social insurance to one focused on personal gain. It may very well be possible for some clever or lucky individuals to achieve higher returns on savings, commensurate with the risks they take. Indeed, helping individuals accumulate wealth is not inherently bad policy. But Social Security's guaranteed benefits should not be sacrificed in the process.

IV. A CHRISTIAN PERSPECTIVE

Throughout history, the economic security of its members has been a concern in all societies. For the most part, this has been left to extended families. In some societies the lot of those who were not included in such families was tragic. Others, including Israel, made provisions. In the story of Ruth we read that those outside the family system were allowed to glean in the fields what was left by the reapers. The prophets repeatedly expressed concern for widows and orphans and for the poor. In Amos 2:6–7, God thunders in judgment against those who exploit the poor: "I will not revoke the punishment . . . [on those] who trample the head of the poor into the dust of the earth, and push the afflicted out of the way."

This concern was carried over and even intensified in the early church. It was the shared responsibility of the congregation to provide for the widows and orphans and the poor among its members. The widows, in exchange, took particular responsibilities in the church to care for others. The success of the church in providing security for its members was one factor in its growth.

When the church became established, it continued to play the role of caregiver to those who had no other support. How well it carried out this responsibility no doubt varied greatly from time to time and place to place, but that this was its task was not in doubt. The question arose only as nation-states came to prominence and subordinated churches, often taking their property away. Although churches never ceased seeking to serve the needy, some of the responsibilities that they had carried during the Middle Ages devolved on the nation-states of the modern world.

In the United States today many churches continue the tradition of ministering in various ways to the needy. But no church, and no combination of churches in today's increasingly secular world, can meet the needs of all those who are not cared for in families. In addition, cultural structures and attitudes have changed. The extended family has given way to the nuclear family. Some of these nuclear families cannot meet the needs of their members. Many of those individuals who are unable to support themselves do not want to be a burden on their children or relatives.

The Christian conviction remains that the basic needs of all, and especially of those who cannot care for themselves, must be met by the broader community. "[D]o not oppress the widow, the orphan, the alien, or the poor; and do not devise evil in your hearts against one another" (Zech. 7:10). But instead of attempting the futile task of accomplishing this through congregations, Christians now look to the state. We differ on exactly what policies and methods are best, but we share the commitment that the needy shall be cared for by some combination of private and public support.

From this perspective, we oppose the Bush administration's plan to carve out individual accounts from Social Security. It shortchanges the poor and the powerless. It aggravates disparities of income for participants. It adds risks and complexity to the system of economic security that many people prefer not to confront. And it alters the political dynamic that has sustained support for Social Security over the years. As special interests begin to identify with its various options, we already see the potential for fragmenting public support for the goals of the existing social-insurance program.

This does not mean that progressive Christians are inalterably opposed to the restructuring of Social Security in ways that increase participant choice and control over how they obtain their social-insurance protections. In theory, at least, structures that give participants choices have certain advantages. Far more than most other people, Americans have come to expect choices over what they buy and do. It is entirely possible that participants in the Social Security system, if given the ability to choose from among a number of different structures, would feel more satisfied with the nature of their protections. Also, a structure that offers participant choice may be less rigid and more capable of evolutionary change than one with a unitary structure. If properly designed, structures that offer choice may also be more efficient, in the sense they have the potential to deliver the social-insurance protections society deems essential at a reduced cost to the government. Alas, the search for more efficient structures usually ignores the economic security of those (usually the poor) who are unfamiliar with the risks and rewards of private investment decisions. At this stage of the public debate over Social Security, no structure that gives participants choices has come to our attention that we prefer over the existing unitary structure of benefits.

Nevertheless, our Christian perspective does suggest *proposals for government action* to strengthen the existing system:

Develop credible budgetary rules. It is time to establish some kind of conditional budgetary mechanism for the government that both addresses the long-term liabilities of Social Security and responds to short-term changes in macroeconomic conditions. The economy's sudden reversal reminds us that change can be both large and unpredictable, rendering budget projections quickly obsolete. Federal Reserve Chairman Alan Greenspan warned earlier this year that any long-term tax cut should be phased in and conditioned on the realization of long-term targets for the federal debt and for covering Social Security's liabilities. His warnings went unheeded.

Broaden the list of government securities the Social Security trust funds may hold. We agree with Chairman Alan Greenspan of the Federal Reserve System that the trust funds should not hold securities of private institutions for fear of influencing the securities markets. But we do believe that the balances in the trust funds could be recomposed to include government-issued securities that yield a higher rate of return than the nonnegotiable Treasury bonds they now are required to hold.

Remove the cap of $80,400 now limiting the amount of earned income subject to payroll tax. As the salaries of higher-income people rose in the 1990s, an increasing proportion of wage income escaped taxation. This made the payroll tax even more regressive and deprived the system of sufficient income to strengthen insurance guarantees for the least well-off workers.

Investigate means-testing of Social Security benefits. Under current law, up to 85 percent of Social Security benefits already are subject to federal income tax, depending on the level of total income. This percentage should be raised to 100 percent for high-income beneficiaries. In addition, a means test for Social Security benefits may need to be considered in light of new demands on government revenue. Since imposing a means test would fundamentally alter the principles and politics of social insurance (see Appendix A), it requires careful study.

Alter the formula used to calculate the benefits of retirees who earned relatively low wages when working. Despite its general popularity, Social Security rarely provides enough income for a comfortable retirement to those with little pension income or savings. Only 43 percent of senior households receive income from pensions, and retirees who earned relatively low wages rarely are able to save significant sums. Altering the benefit formula seems the easiest way to increase benefits and improve the quality of their retirement.

Increase elderly survivors' benefits. Lower-income widows and widowers are among the poorest participants in Social Security. Raising the benefit for the survivor of a married couple to 75 percent of their combined predeath benefit, with an income cap to limit the benefit for the highest-income recipients, would help them.

Reconsider the age of retirement with full benefits. Starting in 2003, the age at which participants may retire with full benefits will gradually rise from 65 to 67. Workers still will be able to retire with reduced benefits at 62, but their monthly benefits will be reduced even more. Raising the retirement age discriminates against workers with physically demanding jobs; workers, especially women, who entered the labor force later in life; older workers who tend to be fired first in downturns; and workers forced into retirement during mergers and reorganizations.

V. WHAT WE CAN DO

Christians concerned about the structure or adequacy of Social Security protections should challenge congregations and denominations to *witness to the need for social policy reforms.*

Inform ourselves. The first thing individual Christians can do is to seek the knowledge that better prepares us for action. This knowledge can be acquired in many ways; but as Christians, we want to be able to relate information about the need for economic security to our theological, biblical, and ethical understandings.

Organize a church study group. The church ought to be where we can learn more about being responsible stewards of economic life. If your congregation does not have a study group focusing on church and society issues, organize one and enlist your pastor and friends to join in your quest for new understandings. Study Social Security as its first venture.

Be a community of discernment. The faith community shouldn't pretend technical competence it does not uniquely possess. It can and should, however, engage in moral analysis of alternative Social Security systems, denounce their morally unacceptable outcomes, name the sin that is causing pain, and insist that more humane policies and systems be sought and implemented.

Encourage education for community action. Individual congregations need to bring together their theological reflections about economic security with education in community action for economic justice. Biblical and theological reflection is best oriented to active involvement in the world. Active learning best takes place when pastors and members of congregations carry out sustained, collaborative work on social issues.

Urge denominations to make a social policy witness. Most mainline Protestant denominations are equipped to express a stance and guide response to issues in the public order, like Social Security. The process that leads to their making a social policy witness involves careful exploration of biblical, theological, and ethical themes, as well as analysis of substantive issues and context. But *word* is rarely effective without a corresponding *deed.* Social policy implementation involves developing and managing church strategies and programs, the allocation of the resources needed to create the strategies, and the hard work that will make social policy fruitful in shaping the church and the public order. Now that Social Security reform has developed into a contentious political debate in the nation, it is essential that the church's views be heard.

Discussion Questions

1. How important is Social Security to your sense of economic security? Can you think of others who might answer this question very differently from you?
2. Given your personal situation, would you support the privatization of a portion of your Social Security premiums? Explain why. How do you feel about the plan(s) being proposed by the Bush administration?
3. Many members of your congregation receive Social Security benefits. How might they become involved in organizing a church study group to assess proposed changes in Social Security? How might such a group influence the outcome of current public policy discussions?
4. From a Christian perspective, assess the nine principles of social insurance contained in Appendix A.

To Learn More

For a quick introduction to proposed reforms of the Social Security system, browse the Web under "Social Security Reform." For more balanced views, see Henry Aaron and Robert Reischauer, *Countdown to Reform: The Great Social Security Debate* (New York: Century Foundation Press and Brookings, 1999), and Marilyn Watkins, *Social Security: A Success Story under Attack* (Economic Opportunity Institute, 2001). For sources that favor privatization, see works of the Heritage Foundation, and Sylvester Schieber and John Shoven, *The Real Deal: The History and Future of Social Security* (New Haven, Conn.: Yale University Press, 1999). *The 2001 Annual Report of the Board of Trustees* of the Social Security system spells out the assumptions leading to their three cost projections. Watch for the report of the Social Security Commission appointed by the president.

APPENDIX A

Nine Principles of Social Insurance[5]

- *Universal.* Social Security coverage has been gradually extended, to the point that 96 percent of jobs in paid employment are now covered.
- *Earned right.* Social Security is more than a statutory right. It is an *earned* right, with eligibility for benefits and the benefit rate based on an individual's past earnings.
- *Wage-related.* Social Security benefits are related to earnings, on the premise that one's standard of living while working is related to the benefit level needed to achieve income security in retirement. Under Social Security, higher-paid earners get higher benefits, but lower-paid earners get more back in benefits for what they pay in.
- *Contributory and self-financed.* Workers pay earmarked contributions from their wages into the system, giving contributors a moral claim on future benefits above and beyond statutory obligations. The fact the system is financed by dedicated taxes helps protect it from having to compete against other programs in the annual federal budget—an essential provision for a uniquely long-term program.
- *Redistributive.* Social Security pays at least a minimally adequate benefit to workers who are regularly covered and contributing, regardless of how low-paid they may be. This is accomplished through a redistributional formula that pays comparatively higher benefits to low-paid than to high-paid earners.
- *Not means-tested.* In contrast to welfare, eligibility for Social Security does not depend on the beneficiary's current income and assets, nor does the amount of the benefit. The absence of a means test allows Social Security to provide a stable role in anchoring a multitier retirement system in which private pensions and personal savings can be built on top of Social Security's basic, defined protection.
- *Wage-indexed.* Social Security is portable, following the worker from job to job, and the protection before retirement increases as wages rise.
- *Inflation-protected.* Once they begin, Social Security benefits are protected against inflation by periodic cost-of-living adjustments linked to the Consumer Price Index. Without COLAs, the real value of Social Security benefits would steadily erode over time, as is the case with unadjusted private pension benefits.
- *Compulsory.* Social Security compels all of us to contribute to our own future security. With a compulsory program, problems of adverse selection—that is, individuals deciding when and to what extent they want to participate, depending on whether their individual circumstances seem favorable—are avoided (as are the problems of obtaining adequate funding for a large safety-net program serving a constituency with limited political influence).

7

The Penal System

Jim Thompson was a slow learner. In happier circumstances he would have been diagnosed as having ADD and given special attention. But as it was, he acted out his frustration with school-work, angered his teachers, and dropped out of school as soon as it was legally possible to do so. His parents had not completed high school themselves and did not particularly care. He worked at Burger King for a while, but when some buddies suggested burglarizing a home whose occupants were away, he joined them. They were caught, and he was put in a crowded prison occupied primarily by older men. There were few opportunities for human contacts except with other prisoners, and many of these were abusive. In order to survive, he joined a gang there, and when he got out he established contact with members he had met in prison. That led to more crimes and to a longer stay in prison. Sometimes he wanted to escape this vicious circle, but he had no real contacts outside the gang and no marketable skills. In any case, employers did not favor ex-cons. He could see no other option, even though he knew his present course would probably mean returning to prison.

I. INTRODUCTION

The number of persons incarcerated in the United States in 2001 passed the two million mark, counting federal and state prisons and local jails. This is six times the number held in 1972, and a far higher percentage of the population than in any other major nation. Worldwide there are eight million prisoners. Thus, one-fourth of all the prisoners in the world are in U.S. prisons. We imprison at a rate four times that of Canada, five times that of Britain, six times that of Australia, and fourteen times that of Japan. The number of women in prison, most of whom are mothers, is five times what it was in 1980. Most states, including California, spend more on prisons than they do on higher education. The national outlay is $40 billion per year. California has built twenty-three new prisons since 1983, for a total of thirty-three.

An ironic fact is that this explosion in the number of prisons and prisoners has occurred in a period in which crime rates have been generally stable or falling. This is especially the case with reference to violent crimes, the crimes of which most people are rightly afraid. One study showed that 40 percent of the increase in number of prisoners is the result of a higher percentage of arrests leading to imprisonment. The other 60 percent is due to longer sentences. Many assume that the increase in the number of prisoners is the explanation for the decrease in crime. But the statistics are tricky, because the causal factors are very complex. A study ranking factors that affect rates of incarceration found that the number of crimes committed was eleventh in causal influence, behind such factors as the aggressiveness of the district attorney, the size of the police force, the level of public concern about crime. An example of how the crime rate and incarceration are almost independent of each other may be shown by comparing North and South Dakota. These two states are similar in size, population, urbanization, and economy. South Dakota has policies that put many times more people in prison than does North Dakota, yet the crime rate in each remains about the same.

Two policies have contributed dramatically to the apparent anomaly that the prison industry is booming while crime remains the same. The first is mandatory minimum sentences for drug possession. This policy has led to restrictions on judicial discretion and therefore has introduced a painful inflexibility into the criminal justice system. A further irony is that because the law allows the lowering of sentences for offenders who give "substantial assistance" in convicting other drug offenders, drug dealers (who can afford the best lawyers) have often been able to maneuver lower sentences for themselves by snitching on small-time users. The second policy is California's "three strikes" law, which gives offenders twenty-five years to life for a third felony. Most of the voters who supported the three-strikes initiative, which went into effect in March 1994, thought they were striking a blow against violent crime, or at least against major felonies. But a misdemeanor by a previously convicted felon is classified as a felony. Prison misbehavior can be considered a felony. Though not typical, defendants have been given twenty-five years to life for stealing a bicycle or stealing a slice of pizza. Twice as many persons have been imprisoned under three-strikes for possession of marijuana as for murder, rape, and kidnapping combined.

The prison crisis is in part an outgrowth of the discovery by politicians in the 1970s, after riots in Attica, San Quentin, and Soledad, that being "tough on crime" was a sure-fire way to win votes. Before this, Governor Reagan in California had signed an inmate's bill of rights, and Congress was moving toward supporting drug treatment rather than incarceration for nonviolent drug users. But the new "get tough" emphasis led to mandatory sentencing laws, a trend that was nationalized in President Nixon's War on Crime. The Sentencing Reform Act of 1984 virtually eliminated parole for federal crimes. The trend was also reflected in the reintroduction of the death penalty. The death penalty was on the way out when, in 1976, the U.S. Supreme Court reversed its previously held position that execution was usually prohibited as "cruel and unusual punishment" under the Constitution. Thereafter thirty-eight states began again to practice capital punishment, and the United States found itself in the company of China, Iran, Saudi Arabia and the Congo, the only four countries in the world to execute more people than does our nation.

II. PATTERNS OF THE PRISON SYSTEM

Racism

A clue as to why African Americans are far more likely than whites to end up in prison is found in the fact that they are arrested more often than whites for the same crime and are given sentences 20 percent longer than are whites convicted of the same crime. Racial minorities make up a majority of all inmates, and at least half of racial minority inmates are poor, functionally illiterate, and without adequate legal representation. Racial hate groups grow in prison, and, as a device of control, conflict between them has often been encouraged rather than discouraged by correctional officers. In California, Pelican Bay and Corcoran prisons have become notorious for gladiatorial fights between blacks and Hispanics. At Los Angeles County's Pitchess Detention Center, there were 150 recorded racially motivated fights between 1991 and 2000. Prison guards are mainly white.

Racial minorities, especially African Americans, frequently come from low-employment areas and are trapped in a vicious cycle of poverty, crime, and drug dependency. A 2000 study of 682 cases in which the death penalty was imposed found that 20 percent of those convicted were white, while 80 percent were minorities; of these, 75 percent were African American. The same study found that in cases in which U.S. attorneys sought the death penalty, 26 percent of the defendants were white, and 74 percent were of a racial minority. Two-thirds of all those incarcerated in 2000 in state prisons were African American men, out of less than 7 percent of the total population. Of state drug offenders, 79 percent come from racial minorities. Black males have a 29 percent chance of serving time in prison at some point in their lives, while white males have a 4 percent chance.

Given these figures, it is perhaps not surprising that racial profiling—for example, being stopped by police for DWB, driving while black—has become a civil rights and public relations problem for many local police departments. In Florida, 5 percent of all drivers are black or Hispanic, but they are 80 percent of those stopped and searched. The proportion of African Americans in the middle and upper classes has increased, but blacks of all classes have had the experience of being stopped by police merely on suspicion, while most middle-class whites have not had this experience.

Nonrehabilitation

The word "penitentiary," applied to American prisons, came from the Quaker notion that miscreants would be reformed if they could be penitent, and penitence would come from quiet solitude and reflection. Overcrowded prisons offer little stimulus to healthy reflection. There is solitude, but of the wrong kind, in "supermax" prisons. Prisoners in Security Housing Units (SHUs) are locked into tiny cells for twenty-three hours a day with scarcely any human contact. Meals are slid into the cells through narrow slits. If there is any therapy or psychological counseling at all, the therapist must sit outside the cell. At the very isolated, very modern, very expensive Pelican Bay prison in California, the SHU cell doors are solid steel with small holes drilled in them. The prisoner can see little other than the inside of the cell. For failure to slide the empty food tray back through the door, the prisoner may undergo "cell extraction" with stun guns and riot batons. In some cases noxious gases are pumped into the cell for the same purpose. The official rationale for such treatment is security for the guards—feces cannot be thrown at them. The unofficial rationale is that these prisoners deserve whatever they get. The result is that many SHU prisoners simply go mad. In the 1990s even the Pelican Bay medical officer conceded there were two hundred certifiable psychotics in residence, almost certainly an underestimate.

The level of psychological tension and potential violence for prisoners in supermax prisons (whether or not in SHUs) is very high. Recently in some prisons hardcover books have been denied prisoners because, it is said, they rip off the covers, shape them into a dagger, urinate on them until they calcify, then use them to stab guards. The "rules" for survival in these prisons are often bestial. A newcomer must become, according to some reports, attached to a big and muscular veteran prisoner who can intimidate and dominate other prisoners in order to prevent beatings and gang rapes of the newcomer. The price of this protection is exclusive homosexual favors, financial extortion, the sharing of drugs (access to illegal drugs is widespread), and other indignities. Perhaps 80 percent of prisoners in maximum-security prisons are gang affiliated. This too may involve a matter of survival. There have been cases in which a gang member is ordered by his gang leader to do a hit on a rival gang member. His dilemma is that if he follows orders, and succeeds in killing the rival, he will be caught by the authorities and given life. If he does not, his own gang will kill him. In such cases the prisoner may attack a guard, hoping to be sent off to an SHU with the possibility of a cooling off of gang hostility before he is returned to non-SHU cells.

Prison authorities have been conspicuously deficient in preventing rape and drug use in prisons. Some guards make money by selling drugs. Guards are still called correctional officers. As in many states, California's prison system is run by the state department of corrections, but correction or rehabilitation has been abandoned as a goal. The purpose of today's prisons is to punish. That goal was, in fact, written into California law in 1976 and signed by the supposedly liberal Governor Jerry Brown. Even the public has yielded to this development. A public opinion poll in 1970 found that 73 percent of Americans thought the primary purpose of prison was rehabilitation. A similar poll in 1995 found that only 26 percent did.

Family Ties

As of 2000, one and a half million children under eighteen in the U.S. have at least one parent in prison, a 60 percent increase since 1991. The increase in the number of women prisoners has been dramatic. In 1925, six of every hundred thousand American women were in prison. By 1998, the figure was fifty-seven of every hundred thousand. The increase, much of it in the last twenty years, is accounted for mostly by mandatory drug sentencing, an even larger factor for women than for men. Only a fourth of women have been convicted of violent crimes, and most of these were responding to spousal abuse. Sexual assault is not uncommon in women's prisons. In a recent period in California, five guards resigned and forty more were under investigation for sexual misconduct with women prisoners. Seventy-five percent of women prisoners have children. Some women in Valley State Prison for Women in central California have been punished by being put in SHU cells for affiliation with gangs through their connections with male family members. One quoted a guard as saying: "if they want to act like men, then they will be treated like men," suggesting an agenda other than simply maintaining prison order. SHUs for women have been the subject of protests by Amnesty International and an investigation by the United Nations program on violence against women.

Health care for prisoners has been poor for both sexes, and HIV/AIDS and hepatitis C among prisoners have achieved epidemic status. A class-action suit on behalf of 160,000 California inmates, filed in April 2001, alleged that the Department of Corrections is indifferent to the medical needs of inmates and that medical personnel are ill-trained and underfunded. There are examples of the nondiagnosis or misdiagnosis of major illnesses, including cancer, leading to premature death. These concerns have been the cause of great anguish for the families of prisoners, and women's groups have paid special attention to the health of women prisoners.

A few states have set up conjugal visits, allowing wives to spend the night with their prisoner husbands. A few more have encouraged family visitations by establishing picnic areas where wives and husbands and children can visit in relative privacy. There have been very few studies of the efficacy of these visitation programs, but most authorities agree that maintaining family connections is a basic factor in creating hope for rehabilitation. The split between the rural location of most prisons and the urban location of prisoners' families is one reason that only 20 percent of prisoners, on the average, ever have visitors.

Telephone calls are an important element in keeping families together. For many years telephone calls were highly restricted, but now, partly because telephone companies saw a neglected market and lobbied for them, almost all prisons have banks of pay phones. Inmates, being captive customers, are charged at the highest possible long-distance rate, and for authorizing this, corrections departments are given a kickback from the telephone company. The New York state Department of Corrections in 1997 received $21.2 million in telephone commissions, the California DOC received $17.6 million. (In California, MCI adds a $3 surcharge onto every call, of which the DOC gets 32 percent.)

White-Collar Crime

The growing incidence of white-collar crime reflects the extent to which our society focuses on making money and has so diminished an inner sense of social responsibility, weakened community bonds, and heightened individualism, that we have less sense of our obligations to others. Good business practice is often identified with making all the money one can, regardless of the consequences to others. When more money can be made outside the law, too often the question people ask is not whether this is moral, but whether they can get away with it. Unfortunately, skilled accountants and lawyers conceal much white-collar crime within the complexities of legitimate business. Much of it goes undetected. When detected, it is often not reported to police. When prosecuted, the perpetrators often have enough money to hire the best legal representation and avoid imprisonment. This is the other side of the coin, so to speak, that explains why half the prison population is illiterate and filled with the poor who have committed street crimes.

Guns

There has been a general increase in violence in our society. We have long been a violent society, to which the ready availability of guns and the heritage of slavery have contributed. But the theatrical presentations of the wild, wild West, which have been so central to the American tradition, routinely overstate the degree to which people were armed in the old West, and popular films and television dramas overstate the degree to which conflicts can be and are resolved with guns. Today in the United States there are around 200 million guns for a population of 280 million, and more Americans have been killed by privately owned guns since 1900 than have been killed in all American wars. Five children seventeen and younger die from guns every day in the United States. The debate over whether the Second Amendment constitutionally protects private gun ownership has become awash with mythological irrelevance. A majority of the public supports private gun ownership but opposes the right to own military assault weapons, which have generally been outlawed. Modest steps to tighten gun registration requirements have been taken, though the Federal Bureau of Alcohol, Tobacco and Firearms still grants licenses to virtually all who apply and the National Rifle Association remains a powerful political force. The Million Mom March on Washington in May 2000 made tighter gun controls and ending the prosecution of children as adults two of its primary goals.

Juvenile Crime

Out of frustration over the appearance of younger and younger criminals and school shootings, and perhaps from the mistaken view that harsh sentences are effective deterrents to crime, more than forty states have adopted laws that treat persons under eighteen as adults in cases involving certain crimes. Contrary to the impression that might be gained from local news sources, the homicide rate by juveniles in California fell by 50 percent in the 1990s. Yet California voters by a majority of 62 percent in March 2000 passed

Proposition 21, which allows offenders in certain crimes (including assault, hate crimes, and murder) age fourteen and above to be sent to state prison rather than to the Youth Authority. Moreover, the discretion once given to judges in this matter was handed over to district attorneys, prosecutors whose careers rest on the number of convictions they obtain.

Ninety percent of juveniles who go to prison for the most serious crimes are the children of teenage mothers. Fifty percent of the juveniles in California's ethnic gangs come from, in effect, no-parent families. The gang is their family. They may have been crack babies or may suffer from ADD (attention deficit disorder), or mental illness. They have often been abused by relatives or mothers' boyfriends. Eighty percent of juvenile drug cases now involve methamphetamine, which is cheap and relatively easy to get but affects the brain more permanently than other drugs, and creates a vicious circle of constant depression relieved only by more methamphetamine. Though not all are this badly off, it is still alarming that in Los Angeles County alone there are 23,000 juveniles under parole supervision and 60,000 juveniles in the foster-care system, with more who probably should be. Superior Court Juvenile Judge Martha Bellinger has said these children lack the three most basic of needs: someone to love, something to do, and something to look forward to.

One perhaps extreme example of warped justice applied to juveniles was the subject of a documentary film in 2000. Five Conejo Valley youths, ages fifteen to eighteen, in 1995 drove to an Agoura Hills home to buy or perhaps steal marijuana from another teenager. A fight broke out and the marijuana seller was stabbed, later dying from his wounds. Though only one boy did the stabbing, three were sentenced to life without possibility of parole. A fourth, because of his age, fifteen, was given twenty-five years to life. The fifth, who stayed in the car during the entire fight, was sentenced to eleven years in prison. Another case of some notoriety was the 1999 incident in Florida when Lionel Tate, then twelve years old, beat a six-year-old to death. The defense argument was that he was only "wrestling" in a manner seen on television. That defense was not persuasive. The prosecutor admitted the boy may not have intended to kill the girl, but felt it was more than an accident. He offered as a plea bargain incarceration for three years in a juvenile facility. The offer was rejected. The case went to trial and the boy received life in prison without the possibility of parole. William Schulz, executive director of Amnesty International USA, said, "Sentences like these violate international law—and common sense."

Treating juveniles as adults increases rather than decreases criminal behavior. Adult prisons to a greater degree than juvenile facilities are schools of crime. The juvenile system protects anonymity, but the adult system brands offenders, making employment after release difficult. This is not to say that the California Youth Authority prisons in Chino, Whittier, and Preston are models of rehabilitation. The state inspector general in May 2000 called them a "system in chaos." Among other things, critics called attention to metal cages resembling "dog kennels" used for discipline and staff encouraging gang fights.

III. THE PRISON INDUSTRY

Prison building has become big business. We have seen how telephone companies take advantage of captive users. Prison-construction specialists have convinced rural communities in California and Texas and Virginia, among other places, places where unemployment is high and the local economy is in decline, that a new prison will bring jobs and prosperity. The construction industry, food service vendors, the prison guards union, and local fathers join together to convince the legislature that a new prison is both necessary and desirable. This is acceptable to big cities, for unemployment is less of a problem there, and they are eager to export prisoners. Most California prisoners are in rural areas: Avenal, Blythe, Chowchilla, Coalinga ("Pleasant Valley" is the prison name), Corcoran, Delano, Ione, Mule Creek, Pelican Bay, Soledad, Susanville, Tehachapi, Tracy, Vacaville, Wasco. The hoped-for benefits to the small towns hardly ever materialize. Local stores do not get the food contracts. Guards are appointed on a statewide basis and are usually told to live some distance from the prison. Prison visitors may create weekend problems.

A recent trend is prisons run by private corporations. In 1983 there were none. By 2000 there were 150 private prisons in the United States, with heavy investment from Wall Street. The largest private prison manager is the Corrections Corporation of America, with headquarters in Nashville, which runs forty-six institutions in eleven states. The second largest is Wackenhut Corporation, which runs twenty-four institutions, including the largest, in Hobbs, New Mexico. Its board and top executives include two former CIA directors, a former secretary of defense, a former Marine Corps commander, and two retired Air Force generals, suggesting that the terminology the "prison-industrial complex," borrowed from the "military-industrial complex," may not be out of place. There is another parallel. President Eisenhower, who coined the phrase "military-industrial complex" in his famous farewell speech, was suggesting that a fictitious crisis, the "missile gap," was being used to justify big defense expenditures. Commentators are now suggesting that a fictitious crime wave is being used to justify big corrections budgets.

One appeal of private prisons is that by paying lower salaries for guards than under civil service, they can save money, but this often means raw and poorly trained guards. Since profit is the underlying motive, various other amenities may be trimmed, and talk of warehousing prisoners may be even more descriptive than it is in state-run prisons. At the same time, since these corporations are paid by the state or federal governments according to the number of prisoners, the pressure on the criminal justice system to keep the occupancy rate high is unremitting. Joseph T. Hallinan, a *Wall Street Journal* reporter, in his book *Going Up the River: Travels in a Prison Nation*, says:

> By building so many prisons so fast we have created a climate in which it is now in nearly everyone's interest to argue for prison terms that are longer, tougher, harsher. Because only through longer, tougher, harsher terms can the prison boom perpetuate itself. And self-perpetuation is where the money is. Americans have learned to profit from every kind of prison but an empty one, and this alone is incentive enough to keep prison populations growing.[1]

Prison Labor

The use of prison labor has both positive and negative aspects. With little or no funding for education or job training in prisons, any useful labor is beneficial, in that it gives inmates some functional purpose each day in an otherwise empty existence. It can improve morale and enhance self-confidence. In some cases it can mean a modest income and the acquisition of skills that may improve chances for employment on the outside. Inmates are generally glad for the chance to work. The negative aspect is that prison labor may be exploited for the benefit of external profit seekers. Congress in 1979 enacted the Prison Industries Enhancement Act (PIE), which exempts states from the ban on selling prison-made goods interstate, so long as "the prevailing wage" is paid. Prevailing wage is deceptive, since states may deduct 80 percent of the wage for room and board. Thirty states have laws permitting some use of prison labor by private industry. Mississippi and Texas have forced prisoners to work full-time for no pay. In Mississippi the prisoner who tried to organize opposition to this was thrown into solitary, where he may still be. In Oregon since 1994 prisoners have been required to work. They run computers and are telemarketing callers for private firms. They manufacture jeans for a Portland firm with the fetching label "Prison Blues." California airline reservations with TWA have been made (unknown to the caller) through prison telephone operators. AT&T has used Washington state inmates to pack and ship Microsoft software. In Ohio the United Auto Workers were able to get Honda to stop using prisoners to manufacture auto parts. In Illinois unions got Toys "R" Us to stop using prisoners for cleaning and stocking shelves. Eighty thousand inmates nationally have been so used. The California Prison Industry Authority, a semiautonomous, $153 million-a-year state agency, holds a virtual monopoly on state government supplies, including clothing, furniture, and meat cutting. Its 6,300 employee-prisoners are paid an average of $.55 an hour.

The Oregon system pays inmates market wages, but since employers cover no retirement, vacation, or health benefits and do not pay for Social Security, workers compensation, or Medicare, the payroll is 35 percent less than it otherwise would be. For obvious reasons, labor unions are adamantly opposed to the commercial use of prison labor, and labor leaders compare the U.S. use of prison labor with China's, which our government officially condemns. The exception is prison guard unions, which usually favor prison employment because it makes prisoners, from their standpoint, more docile. The California Correctional Peace Officers Association, one of the most powerful unions in the state, has 29,000 members, a $3 million Sacramento headquarters, and a shrewd leader in Don Novey. It contributed more dollars to the 1998 election than any other group in the state, $5.3 million, and counts Governor Davis as an ally. Compared to other states, California guards are well paid, but this is related to the fact that the California prisoner-to-guard ratio is the highest in the nation. If the guards do not complain about this burdensome ratio, their wives do, for it makes the job more hazardous.

The movement for using prison labor more commercially is complex and confused; but it goes forward. Ronald Reagan's attorney general, Edwin Meese, is now chair of the Enterprise Prison Institute, whose purpose is to encourage wider use of prison labor. One critic calls this "correctional Keynesianism," that is, a scheme whereby taxpayer money is used as an investment to benefit corporate enterprise.

The Crisis In Summary

The ongoing prison-industrial complex, building more and more prisons and adopting policies that continue to fill them to overflowing, constitutes a crisis. The situation is sustained by a flawed argument and an untested assumption: if the crime rate is down, it must be because we have so many prisons; if the crime rate is up, it's proof we need more prisons. It has produced a permanent underclass, largely of racial minorities, and has generated fear and hopelessness. We seem to be in a downward spiral.

Simply locking away all who commit nonviolent crimes is self-defeating for these reasons:

1. It is extremely expensive. It costs the state somewhere about $30,000 per year to incarcerate one prisoner. A fraction of this amount spent on crime

prevention, drug treatment, and job training would be far more beneficial to society.
2. It denies the humanity of both perpetrator and victim. Justice based only on revenge and punishment is justice unfulfilled. Restorative justice is a higher and more humane goal. (See below.)
3. It does not reduce the rate of crime. In the long run, it may increase the rate of crime. Prisons as they presently exist do not reform criminals but breed criminals.

IV. A CHRISTIAN PERSPECTIVE

Prisoners in the Bible

Christians agree with virtually all citizens that crime reduction is desirable. They also side with those who favor preventative measures over punitive ones whenever possible. Christian reflection on these matters begins with what the Bible has to say.

The people of the Bible knew well what it means to be put in prison. From the story of Joseph (Gen. 39) to the time of Paul (Acts 16:19–34; 23:35; 2 Cor. 11:23), many biblical characters experienced imprisonment. The prison systems were, of course, very different from ours, and nothing like the massive numbers of prisoners we accept was known in the ancient world. Imprisonment was often for political reasons: offending a ruler, losing a war, incurring debt, and being regarded as politically dangerous. Punishment and not reformation was the motive. (See Samson in Judg. 16:21.)

The writers of the Bible were often sympathetic toward those who were in prison. Like Peter (Acts 12:5) and Paul in the book of Acts, the people with whom the biblical stories deal often belonged to minorities that more privileged members of society looked down upon. Visiting prisoners was an important witness to achieve solidarity with them (Matt. 25:36, 44). The transforming work of God would include "release of the captives" (Luke 4:18, quoting Isa. 61:1).

While the Bible frequently speaks of prisoners, it does not give much direct guidance about how to deal with the enormous network of present-day prisons that are supposed to punish wrongdoing, keep criminals from continuing their destructive patterns, and set them on a better path. Still, there is much we can learn from the biblical tradition.

- *Prisoners are people like ourselves.* Both the Jewish Bible and the Christian New Testament work against our tendency to separate ourselves from others, including criminals, and, in effect, to think of them as less human than we are. Correspondingly, we need to take responsibility for what goes on in prisons, since people like us are involved. That's why the author of Hebrews (13:3) wrote, "Remember those who are in prison, as though you were in prison with them."

- *We belong together with the whole community.* The Bible warns us not to isolate ourselves in supposedly safe environments so that we will not be threatened by the disorders of the society in which we live. Our aim in the justice system should be not simply to protect ourselves but to work for the good of the whole community.

- *People can change.* Though the prisons of the ancient Near East were not meant to be places of rehabilitation, the biblical witness that people can change, that the healing forces which come from God can transform even badly damaged people, should set us on a determined course of learning how to build both a prison system and a social environment that will enable the healing of broken lives.

The idea of putting tens of thousands of nonviolent people in prison, where they may be turned into violent persons, seems contrary to the foregoing beliefs. Biblical faith should help us reach out in community with others, including those who have taken a wrong path, and to help them turn around. Imprisonment will be a necessary step for some, but we should find other ways to deal with most nonviolent crimes. (See chapter 8, "The War on Drugs.")

Punishment and Forgiveness

This need not imply that the idea of punishment is to be rejected altogether. For many Christians this idea is central to justice; they believe that if someone injures another, the injurer should be injured in some comparable way—"an eye for an eye and a tooth for a tooth." But to replace private vengeance, which can easily escalate into private feuds that would bring social chaos, the state is given this responsibility. We feel that the law can be more objective than injured parties are able to be, so we shift responsibility for justice to society as a whole through its legal institutions.

The Jewish Scriptures place considerable emphasis on justice in this punitive sense, although they strongly sound the note of mercy as well. Many Christians appeal to these Scriptures on the subject of justice.

On the other hand, for many Christians, Jesus' opposition to this kind of justice complicates matters. Jesus, stressing the alternative Jewish theme of mercy, calls for repeated and unlimited forgiveness and returning good for evil. These Christians may give reasons for imprisonment other than punishment, such as protecting society through the reduction of crime. Or they may cite the practical maxim of Gandhi (who was not Christian but was much influenced by the New Testament): "If everyone followed the rule 'an eye for an eye' the world would soon be blind." Yet they may confine forgiveness and "turning the other cheek" to individual behavior, and yield to punishment as the rule of the state.

Other Christians who do not think the rationale of punishment for punishment's sake is persuasive will rely on the need for imprisonment as a protection for society. The weakness of this argument is that in many cases the crime is not a crime against the whole society and is unlikely to be repeated. Certain crimes of passion, for example, a man killing his wife, are unlikely to be repeated, for the circumstances are unrepeatable. Imprisoning such a murderer will not reduce crime, and the culprit is not a threat to society. Yet most of us still feel there should be punishment. Requiring a price for a crime can be a way of affirming the dignity and responsibility of the offender. A too easy forgiveness seems to ignore the crime and not take the offender seriously as a responsible human being. Sometimes the criminal wants to pay his or her "debt to society."

Though forgiveness is central to the Christian message, it is difficult to imagine forgiveness on a societywide scale because two conditions attach to meaningful forgiveness: First, only the injured party is in a position to forgive; to forgive for another person is presumptuous. Second, the offender must be aware of and acknowledge the offense, otherwise the forgiveness is wholly internal and communally empty. Perhaps the closest the world has come in recent years to communal forgiveness is in the Truth and Reconciliation Commission of South Africa, by which those offended against under apartheid get to tell their stories in public and the offenders, if they confess their crimes in public, receive amnesty.

Forgiving attitudes are not easy to achieve. L. Gregory Jones, dean of the Duke University Divinity School, like many of us is "haunted" by how unforgiving so many American Christians seem to be, how quickly they look away when a state execution occurs, how unwilling they are to admit their own complicity in a justice system that dehumanizes prisoners, lawyers, and prison officials alike. Churches, he says, have been generally "unwilling to interact with recently paroled ex-convicts."[2]

There is a place for punishment, and there is a need to protect society; but if as Christians we recognize prisoners as fellow human beings, then punishment will have a secondary role. The goals of reducing crime and redeeming prisoners, though different in name, will often lead to the same proposals. Indeed, reducing the number of people inclined to criminal behavior is by far the best way to reduce the amount of crime. That is done through the investment of time and effort and public and private funds in the task of raising loved and respected children in stable families who are part of healthy communities. There are aberrant and psychopathic personalities who, quite apart from material incentives, find crime tempting and exciting; but they are a minor part of the crime problem, contrary to what simplistic and violent popular films may suggest.

V. WHAT WE CAN DO

None of us as individuals can change the whole system; but all of us can contribute to a change of climate. Christians can point out that the "tough on crime" rhetoric that wins votes has led us in the wrong direction. There is a growing recognition that heavy-handed, wholesale incarceration driven by desire for vengeance does not work and is racially biased. As church members, citizens, and voters, we have the power to make a difference.

Christians in all the institutions of society should address the problem of crime. Without changes in the economic system, for example, efforts in other areas can only stem the tide of decay. That topic requires extensive and separate discussion. Even within our present economic system, however, there are possible steps that Christians should support.

Efforts at crime prevention should begin with prenatal care. Children born with attention deficit disorder (ADD), fetal alcohol syndrome, low birth weight, oxygen deficiency, malnutrition, and a host of other preventable ills are more likely to offend the system and spend time in prison than those with a healthy start.

Good parenting combined with community support can direct most children away from gross antisocial behavior. If the educational system aims to serve the whole person for the whole of his or her life and not just train youth to compete in the marketplace, it can help parents learn to nurture their children and provide additional positive nurture within the context of schools.

Alternative schools can be developed to work with troubled and "at risk" children. Teachers can identify children needing special attention. A wisely guided community will direct substantial resources to working with these children. Specially trained counselors can help.

Community policing has in many places worked to reduce crime. Community policing is an attempt to get police involved in the life of the community prior to outbreaks of violent acts. The symbol of this policy has in some places been police on bicycles rather than in police cars, for people can and do talk more easily and more casually to police on bicycles. This can help build a respect for police and a stronger sense of citizen responsibility for reporting potential or actual crimes. Another mark of such activity has been the establishment of Neighborhood Watch groups, where neighbors get together periodically and talk about safety issues.

Police have a difficult and stressful job. If they are called in only as a last resort to cope with life-threatening situations, they cannot be expected to appear convivial and may only appear threatening. If it is financially possible to have enough police officers, their mere presence may deter crime, as well as build linkages with responsible citizens. The recent Rampart Division scandals in the Los Angeles Police Department, like those in other large cities, show that a minority of police can themselves fall into criminal behavior such as planting evidence, taking bribes, selling drugs, and using excessive force. One of the reforms instituted by Chief Bernard Parks to improve the situation was to strengthen community-police partnerships by assigning nine senior officers to specific field areas where in the past there had only been one. The aim was to increase police accountability and institutionalize community policing. In the ghettos of large cities there are still too many places where police are seen as an alien force to be hated and feared. The citizens do not cooperate with the police, and the police respond with contempt for the citizens. As long as citizens possess weapons, police must be trained in paramilitary ways; but training should include other dimensions as well.

Victim participation and reconciliation is difficult but almost always worth a try. This is one aim of the "restorative justice" movement. In Oregon, when two teenage boys threw rocks from an overpass at cars on a freeway, they were apprehended and brought together with those whose cars had been hit. They were confronted with the consequences of their thoughtless maliciousness. An agreement was reached for them to recompense those they had injured by working for them. As a result, it seemed unlikely that the boys would be drawn into further criminal behavior. At present this kind of resolution is most common where juveniles are involved; however, it need not be so limited. In Japan the system allows victims to play a role in decisions about what happens to the criminal. There may be cultural factors that make this work better in Japan than in the United States, but the approach deserves further experimentation.

Too often victims of crime are injured twice, once by the offenders, and again by police, defense lawyers, and the press, who require the victims to tell their story repeatedly, even if it is a humiliating one. In 1994 the American Bar Association passed a resolution urging every level of government to incorporate "victim-offender mediation/dialogue programs into their criminal justice processes." Victims should confront offenders only when they wish to do so, which is often the case. Often victims want to know why they have been victimized. Even with adults, if the crime is not major, they may prefer some measure of restitution to the cold impersonality of court proceedings. When they have participated in shaping the outcome, the victims find it easier to move on, and the perpetrator is less likely to repeat. Victim-offender reconciliation programs have a role to play even when the offender is imprisoned. In California, the family of a woman killed by a drunk driver was devastated and furious, but they were persuaded to talk to the alcoholic offender, a woman who was now in prison. There was no change in the sentence, but the family began to work with the offender so that a change in her life might in some way compensate for the loss of life. There was, according to observers, a gain for both the offender and the victims.

Mandatory sentencing laws should be changed, returning discretion in sentencing to judges, where it belongs.

The death penalty should be abolished. There are strong religious reasons against the taking of human life. Beyond that, the administration of the death penalty has been unjust and inefficient. There is little evidence that the fear of the death penalty is a deterrent to murder, as many assume. Most murders are acts of irrational passion; indeed, most murderers are persons known by the victim. The length of time convicted murderers spend on death row is inordinate, and legal appeals tie up the courts for years. Of 5,760 death sentences meted out between 1973 and 1995, on appeal 2,370 were thrown out due to serious error. As noted above, a significantly higher percentage of blacks who have been convicted of murder are given the death sentence than of convicted whites. Recently the use of DNA tests has revealed the extent to which innocent persons may be executed; eighty-seven persons were freed from death row on this basis by June 2000. The evidence on executing the innocent became so compelling to Illinois Governor George Ryan that in January 2003 he commuted the sentences of 167 condemned inmates.

Prisons must be changed. The young and first-time offenders should not be housed with hardened criminals. Continuing relations with family members and others who support constructive lifestyles should be encouraged. There should be more chaplains, psychologists, therapists, and social workers serving in prisons. There should be better medical diagnosis and treatment. Mental illness should be recognized earlier and treated. Opportunities for education and job training should be increased. Gang-based conflict should be actively discouraged, not encouraged. Vigorous steps to stop homosexual rape should be taken. Addictive drugs should be kept out of prisons and drug treatment programs instituted (some reports say 80 percent of prisoners have or have had drug problems). Guards should not use racial epithets. Guards should be carefully selected to screen out the sadists and carefully trained to treat prisoners with basic respect. The ratio of guards to prisoners should be increased. There should be more prison camps and fewer maximum-security prisons. SHUs as they presently operate should be eliminated. There should be transition programs for prisoners about to be released, so that they are not abruptly tossed out on the street with no prospects other than to return to crime. There should be more halfway houses. Parole and probation should be better funded and expanded. Prison labor should be rewarded with pay relative to the work skills required, and there should be reasonable opportunities to spend, save, and invest.

All of this sounds reasonable and obvious, but given the climate of popular opinion on crime and the general indifference of the public as to what goes on in prisons, none of these changes will be easy to achieve. In 1980 a blue-ribbon commission of fifteen persons including three sheriffs, a prison chaplain, two judges, a deputy warden, a former chief of the U.S. Courts Division of Probation, and other distinguished citizens, all appointed by the Joint Rules Committee of the California state legislature, studied the prison situation and made twenty recommendations, a number of which are replicated above. Twenty-one years later almost none of their recommendations have been put into effect, and the condition of prisons and prisoners is worse than it was in 1980.

Discussion Questions

1. Are there biblical themes relevant to crime and punishment that have been missed in this discussion? How would they affect your judgment about present policies in America?
2. Do you agree that Christians should acknowledge a role for punishment as such in response to crime? If so, should it be larger or smaller than what is recommended in this chapter?
3. Do you agree that the most meaningful sense of forgiveness must be at a personal level? Why or why not?
4. Can Christians support the present level of imprisonment in the United States? On what basis?
5. How can churches best connect to former prisoners and to their need for employment and support?

To Learn More

The statistics on crime and prisons in this chapter were derived from The U.S. Department of Justice, *Annual Report on Crime*; The Justice Policy Institute, New York (www.cjcj.org); The Interfaith Network for Human Rights, Chicago (www.amnestyusa.org/interfaith); The Criminal Justice Consortium, Oakland, Calif., *Facts for 2002* (www.idiom.com/mcjc); the news columns of the *Los Angeles Times*, the *New York Times*, and works listed below, especially Hallinan.

Articles and books that will provide a general overview of the current prison situation and instances of abuse include Sasha Abramsky, "When They Get Out," *Atlantic Monthly*, June 1999; Hugo Adam Bedau, ed., *The Death Penalty in America: Current Controversies* (Oxford: Oxford University Press, 1997); Alexander Cockburn, "California's Gulag on Trial," *Nation*, Nov. 22, 1999;

Joseph D. Davey, *The Politics of Prison Expansion* (Westport, Conn.: Praeger, 1998); Gerald Austin McHugh, *Christian Faith and Criminal Justice* (New York: Paulist Press, 1978); Christian Parenti, *Lockdown America: Police and Prisons in the Age of Crisis* (New York: Verso, 1999); Jeffrey H. Reiman, *The Rich Get Richer and the Poor Get Prison*, 5th ed. (Boston: Allyn & Bacon, 1997); Eric Schlosser, "The Prison-Industrial Complex," *Atlantic Monthly*, Dec. 1998; Franklin E. Zimring and Gordon Hawkins, *Incapacitation: Penal Confinement and the Restraint of Crime* (Oxford: Oxford University Press, 1995).

Several authors have provided stories of their experiences with prisons and the prison system. The book by Helen Prejean, *Dead Man Walking: An Eyewitness Account of the Death Penalty in the United States* (New York: Random House, 1993), has been turned into a movie and had popular success. Other books and articles include Todd Bigelow, "Taking Jesus to Jail," *Los Angeles Times Magazine*, Apr. 16, 2000; Ted Conover, "Guarding Sing Sing," *New Yorker*, Apr. 3, 2000; Ted Conover, *Newjack: Guarding Sing Sing* (New York: Random House, 2000); Joseph T. Hallinan, *Going Up the River: Travels in a Prison Nation* (New York: Random House, 2001); and the special issue on prisons of *Yes! A Journal of Positive Futures*, no. 15, fall 2000.

For those who are currently in prison ministry or who would like to know more about it, there are several good resources available: Jane Ann Lewen, *Cell Block Services* (United Methodist Jail Ministries, Indianapolis, phone 1-317-293-4660); Henry Covert, *Ministry to the Incarcerate* (Chicago: Loyola Press, 1995); Virginia Mackey, *Restorative Justice* (Presbyterian Church (U.S.A.), 1992, phone 1-800-524-2612); Richard A. Symes, *As Though You Were in Prison with Them: A Resource for Prison Ministry* (Presbyterian Church (U.S.A.), 2000, phone 1-800-524-2612).

8

The War on Drugs

James Callahan is Euro-American. He was in college in the early '70s. Several of his friends were enthusiastic about LSD and persuaded him to try it. His experience was fairly positive. A couple of times he tried other drugs. In general he was careful to experiment only on weekends, when he had no responsibilities; but the drugs themselves affected his judgment, and once he drove his car while under the influence and had an accident. The police guessed the cause of the accident and arrested him. His parents were shocked, but they persuaded the judge that they could handle matters. They made him promise to quit and talk to a counselor. He did stop using drugs for several years. Since then he has used marijuana from time to time but very discreetly. He prefers its effects to those of alcohol, and he has had no further trouble.

Robert Carlson is African American. He was raised by a mom who worked hard but could barely make ends meet. His father was in prison much of the time. His mother tried hard to steer him away from trouble with the law, and most of the time he obeyed her. But she was often away from home, and he wanted the approval of older boys in the neighborhood. They gave him alcohol and drugs, and he began to get into trouble and give up on school. In due course he was arrested for possession and sentenced to prison. The social pressures in prison made him contemptuous of his mother's values and the "justice" system in general. Released, he began mugging to support his habit and was returned to prison. He is out now but has spent eight years in jail or prison. Another conviction and the three-strike law will ensure that he will spend much of the remainder of his life there.

I. INTRODUCTION

What Are "Drugs" and How Are They Used?

Drugs in the broad sense are part of the lives of almost all of us. Doctors prescribe them regularly for all sorts of ills. The War on Drugs is not an attack on drugs in general; what is commonly meant by the drugs we make war on is addictive drugs. Actually, however, the most widely used addictive drugs are alcohol and tobacco, which are legal. These are still the drugs that do the most harm, in the sense that more people are addicted to them than to any other drugs. Alcohol causes the most accidents. Tobacco shortens more lives.

In the late nineteenth and early twentieth century there was a war on alcohol that culminated in Prohibition in 1920. Making the production and sale of alcohol illegal went against the culture of many Americans, and the crime of bootlegging was widespread. Public opinion turned against the attempt to change drinking habits, and Prohibition was repealed in 1933. There are still laws against public drunkenness, underage drinking, and driving while under the influence. Some local jurisdictions have more limits on the sale of alcoholic beverages, but the widespread use of alcohol is now socially and legally accepted.

The history of tobacco use is quite different. Although some churches discouraged smoking, it was socially accepted until quite recently. As awareness of its effects on health grew, campaigns against tobacco use gained strength. There have been almost no proposals to outlaw its use, but warning labels have been put on cigarette packages and in advertising, and there are more and more smoke-free zones. Tobacco companies have recently been forced to pay huge sums to states to compensate for the cost of medical care to victims of their products.

The current War on Drugs, waged by a succession of Republican and Democratic administrations, is directed against psychoactive drugs, which are listed in great detail in national legislation. The law must be updated repeatedly to keep up with new chemical formulations, and, in fact, it is not able to keep up fully. "Uppers" like the methamphetamine Ecstasy come into fashion and appeal to young thrill seekers, and "downers" like barbiturates appeal to the overstressed. But the major enemies have been around for a long time: marijuana, LSD, cocaine, morphine, and heroin.

These drugs have been used in four ways: first, medically, to alleviate suffering; second, to achieve religious or pseudoreligious experiences, seeking to explore dimensions of reality not accessible in ordinary experience; third, recreationally, by those seeking to enjoy unusual, serene, or exhilarating experiences; and fourth, by addicts who require regular doses to avoid the acute suffering brought about physiologically by withdrawal. The addict often goes through continuing cycles of depression and exhilaration.

The medical use of drugs such as morphine to relieve pain is fully accepted by society, even though it can lead to addiction. Currently the medical use of marijuana is highly controversial; it has been approved by the voters of California in a ballot initiative but is still forbidden by federal legislation. The religious use of drugs, under well-controlled conditions, does relatively little damage, but this can be used as a spurious justification for recreational use. In a famous Oregon case two Native American state employees were fired and denied workers compensation because they had used peyote in a Native American religious ceremony. The United States Supreme Court held in 1990, by a 5-4 vote, that "sincere religious beliefs" were involved and that under the constitutional obligation of government to be neutral in regard to religion, the state of Oregon was in error. In this case, religious leaders of almost all major denominations supported the Native Americans, not necessarily because they supported religious drug use but because they feared that a decision in the opposite direction would pose a governmental threat to religious freedom in general.

Recreational use of drugs can sometimes be harmless, but it can lead to bizarre and destructive behavior. It can also lead to addiction, which is an argument relied upon in justifying the War on Drugs. The sense of urgency in attacking this use of drugs increases as parents discover that their children are being encouraged to experiment with drugs at school, on playgrounds, and sometimes in their children's friends' homes. If the drug problem were limited to a few adult addicts, it is doubtful that it would have generated the widespread social concern that it has. There is a social consensus: a climate that encourages children to indulge in drugs is unacceptable; addiction to drugs is a social evil; society has an interest in protecting its children from the temptation to experiment. The debate is about the most effective method of achieving the agreed-upon end. The method adopted by the official War on Drugs is prohibition.

II. THE WAR ON DRUGS AND ITS FAILURE

Richard Nixon declared the War on Drugs during his 1968 campaign. It was politically popular. President Nixon himself implemented the war, primarily through creating drug-treatment programs, including the use of methadone as a medically approved substitute for heroin. These were positive steps in aiding drug users to kick their habits. But over time, the military name of the campaign seemed increasingly to be reflected in its methods. Ronald Reagan's favorite shibboleth was that government should not be involved in people's lives, but he encouraged government involvement in the War on Drugs through legal and military activity and diverted funds from treatment to interdiction. Under George Bush's drug czar, William Bennett, the use of drugs was viewed not as sickness but as immorality; those who use drugs were simply to be punished. Bill Clinton restored some attention to treatment, but overall he continued the policies of his predecessors on a still larger scale under drug czar General Barry McCaffrey. President George W. Bush has continued the War on Drugs and between $35 billion and $40 billion of federal and state taxpayer money per year is spent in its cause. (In 1980 the figure was around $2 billion.) Under President Nixon, 60 percent of drug funds went to treatment. In 2000 the figure was 18 percent. McCaffrey resigned at the end of the Clinton administration. As of 2002, President Bush had not replaced McCaffrey. The Office of National Drug Control Policy was being headed by Acting Director Edward H. Jurith, and more press attention was given to the Drug Enforcement Agency with the appointment of Asa Hutchinson, ex-Congressman from Arkansas, as its administrator. Hutchinson, in an interview, continued the language of the War on Drugs but conceded the need to move in the direction of rehabilitation.

Under McCaffrey twice as much was spent on advertising as on after-school programs. According to McCaffrey "60 percent of all the drugs that enter the United States start or pass through Colombia." This was said in defense of a policy of airborne fumigation of coca crops, which has been blamed for the deforestation of 700,000 acres of Andes forest lands and the washing of toxic chemicals into rivers and ground water, killing fish and wildlife. The EPA has, for domestic use, required warning labels on these chemicals, and even some of the manufacturers, such as Dow Chemical and Eli Lilly, have warned against their widespread use in Colombia and Peru. Yet fumigation and widespread attempts at interdiction continued.

A recent official report of the White House Office of National Drug Control Policy stated the "National anti-drug policy is working." But the conclusion is highly questionable. The report itself cited budget increases in funds for drug control, mentioned a decline in cocaine production in Peru and Bolivia but did not mention Colombia, and cited surveys showing that the percentage of twelfth-graders admitting to marijuana use has leveled off at around 25 percent, none of which would seem to add up to success.

The popularity of the 2000 film *Traffic* suggests the public may be aware of another reality. In the film Michael Douglas plays the role of the U.S. drug czar, whose own daughter becomes embroiled with drugs. U.S. and Mexican officials are outmaneuvered by drug smugglers. When the drug czar calls for fresh ideas and new thinking from government officials, he is met with stony silence.

We have been able to win some battles, but not the War on Drugs. The United States has become entangled in a civil war in Colombia. The special forces we have trained there have killed hundreds of persons connected with drug cartels, including their leaders. This has been at great cost of money and lives. But the destruction of particular drug cartels does not end the production of drugs or their entry into the United States. Today production in Colombia is partly controlled by left-wing rebel forces that have gained increased power through the wealth this brings them. The government of Colombia is more threatened than ever and seeks increasing support from us in its war against the now imposing rebel army. By contrast, the cost of military helicopters used in Colombia would provide treatment for around 200,000 substance abusers in the United States.

We devote extensive resources to the interdiction of supplies at the border. We make many arrests and capture large quantities of drugs. But the amount that enters the country has increased. The statistics for 1998 showed that 545 metric tons of cocaine reached the United States. As a result the price on the street has gone down. As is shown in the chapter on the prison system, we have imprisoned hundreds of thousands of persons on the charges of possession and use of illegal drugs; but the use has not gone down. Forbidden drugs are available for a price even in prison, and a large proportion of prisoners continue to have a drug or alcohol problem. In part because of overcrowding and in part because of the abandonment of rehabilitation as a goal, in-prison treatment programs have been sharply reduced. The National Criminal Justice Commission report in 1996 stated that three out of four men in California prisons had a history of drug use, but only 10 percent were involved in drug treatment programs, and only 1 percent received comprehensive and adequate treatment as defined by the National Institutes of Health. Treatment in prison has declined further since then.

All of this suggests that huge expenditures for prohibition and punishment have failed; the alternative of drug treatment, using resources for reducing demand more than for cutting off supply, has not yet been given a fair try.

III. POSSIBLE ALTERNATIVES

Drug Courts and Proposition 36: A Hopeful Turn?

Despite the grim record noted above, there is some cause for hope. Florida and then Arizona by initiative in the 1990s began a system of special drug courts, in which judges could send nonviolent drug offenders to treatment programs rather than to prison. The judge monitors the offenders' progress through regular reports and courtroom appearances. Failure to adhere to guidelines results in a prison sentence. By 1998 Arizona reported savings of $2.5 million in the costs of incarceration. Three out of five completed the three-month program, and three out of four of these remained drug-free. Colorado has experimented with a similar program.

California created its first drug courts in 1998 with the help of a federal grant of $300,000 for a pilot program. The California legislature is now funding the program at $18 million a year, which is a modest amount considering the magnitude of the problem. Only 2 percent of possible participants have been covered by the drug courts. But drug courts have sharply reduced the recidivism rate, at an annual cost of $900 to $1,600 per participant, compared to an average of $24,000 per prisoner for regular incarceration in California.

Of greater significance is the initiative vote by the California electorate in November 2000, by a 61 percent majority, to enact the Substance Abuse and Crime Prevention Act, more popularly known as Proposition 36. It allocates $120 million annually to support a variety of rehabilitation programs for nonviolent drug offenders. In a rough sense, it turns all criminal courts into drug courts, effective July 1, 2001. One estimate is that 37,000 offenders will be diverted from the California correctional system into community-based programs. Some funds are set aside for family counseling, job training, and literacy schooling, so that addicts, once clean, can get jobs. Though some police officials have doubts about the workability of Proposition 36, across the nation 59 percent of police chiefs believe that drug offenders should be treated rather than incarcerated. Domestic violence is a vexing problem for police to handle and drugs or alcohol are implicated in many domestic violence situations. There is some hope that, in the long run, drug treatment programs can reduce the number of domestic violence cases. Some drug court judges feared their discretion might be limited under Proposition 36; but under the new law they can still prescribe the terms of probation and decide when an offender has violated those rules and should be sentenced under preexisting laws.

The success of Proposition 36 will depend on how all sorts of "niggling details" (as one reporter put it) are handled in fifty-eight different counties. There are different projections of numbers based on how police, district attorneys, judges, treatment centers, and addicts themselves respond. Many fear existing treatment centers will be overwhelmed. But one district attorney was quoted as saying that so many drug offenders, even first-timers, have other offenses in connection with their offense (including resisting arrest) that the numbers will not be as great as some have expected.

Two weeks into the new program Los Angeles County Public Defender

Mike Judge said of the transition, "So far, it's been fairly quiet." Others say it will be "a slowly cresting wave" that will "build over time." Los Angeles County has about 40 percent of the state's eligible drug cases. A Sacramento drug treatment program director has pointed out that drug counselors are already in short supply and there are already waiting lists for participation in existing drug programs. In Sacramento three existing drug programs were selected by the state Department of Alcohol and Drug Programs to handle Proposition 36 outpatient cases. It is not yet clear what the outpatient to inpatient ratio can be. Sacramento County has projected an increase of 37.5 percent, or 2,100 additional slots, in the demand for drug treatment as a result of Proposition 36. One of the three existing programs in that county projects seeing 700 patients a year, 150 at a time.

The NIMBY ("Not in My Back Yard") phenomenon has hurt efforts to expand drug-treatment facilities. Placer County tried to expand a treatment center for women. Three hundred people showed up at the board of supervisors in protest, and the plan was killed. In Gardena, near central Los Angeles, in June 2001, neighbors organized a campaign against setting up a 125-bed treatment center in a building that had been vacant. The city council, despite the passage of Proposition 36, rejected it. There are too many similar examples of "good citizens" unwilling to run any risks for the sake of helping those in need. Some say this grassroots attitude will mean outpatient treatment will have to be more successful than it has been.

The Lindesmith Center (in 2002 renamed The Drug Alliance), which studies drug-policy questions, on June 27, 2001, issued a report card with letter grades on how well eleven (of fifty-eight) California counties were prepared for implementing Proposition 36 (as of that date a few counties had not yet applied for Prop. 36 funds). The criteria were how much of the money granted by the state went to treatment as opposed to routine probation department or police operations, how much community involvement there was in setting up new programs, how supportive boards of supervisors were, the number of available existing treatment centers, and so forth. As might be expected, the grades ranged from A to F. On the overall grade, only San Francisco County received an A and only San Bernardino County an F. Los Angeles County was B minus.

Some of the disputes that have already arisen reflect the different orientation of prosecutors and defense attorneys, including public defenders. For example, prosecutors often want very detailed health records of offenders to be made a part of the record before the decision is made whether to send them to prison or a treatment center. To give the offender a better chance at a fresh start through a treatment center, the public defenders tend to favor a more restricted disclosure process. The role of the probation department has been a source of contention in some counties. There is concern that probation departments, chronically underfunded and overworked, may siphon off some Proposition 36 funds for other, standard operations. As mentioned above, what constitutes "resisting arrest" may become a bone of contention. If drug offenders are uncooperative at the time of the initial arrest for possession and are charged with resisting arrest, this becomes a separate criminal offense that will remove the offender from the possibility of treatment under the new law. Whether the possession of "drug paraphernalia" constitutes a separate offense is also in question.

Appeals to higher courts have already been made over differing interpretations of the sometimes-ambiguous initiative. For example, one Superior Court judge held that an offender arrested before July 1 but not sentenced before July 1 qualified for Proposition 36 diversion; another Superior Court judge held that such an offender did not qualify. California Governor Gray Davis opposed Proposition 36 and has followed a hands-off approach since its passage, despite the fact that the proposition is supposed to save $1.5 billion in incarceration costs over five years, and that California's prior rate of drug defendant incarceration—115 per 100,000 population—is twice the national average. One expert said it will be the year 2003 before most of these issues are settled and the success of the program can be fairly evaluated.

The European Experience

Switzerland has an estimated 33,000 heroin addicts. The government there has adopted a "harm reduction" strategy. The pilot programs in Zurich and Bern, begun in 1994, feature clinics to which addicts come every day to receive "heroin maintenance" injections of pharmaceutical heroin. The typical patient is a thirty-three-year-old man who has been on heroin for thirteen years and has made ten previous efforts to stop. Half of the patients have been in psychiatric hospitals, almost half have tried to commit suicide, and many suffer severe depression. Many Swiss are uncomfortable that the government seems to be abandoning the goal of total abstinence from drugs. But the program has undeniably produced social benefits. Crime has dropped sharply. The use of cocaine (which has more unpredictable effects than heroin) has fallen significantly. The HIV/AIDS rate is down, since unsterile needles are a major cause of HIV/AIDS and the clinics use sterile needles. By being stabilized under medical supervision, two-thirds of the patients have been able, as they were not before, to keep productive jobs. The dropout rate has been relatively low, and two-thirds of those who do drop out are either abstinent or go into an alternative methadone program. The doctor in charge of the Bern program has said that when addicts try abstinence on their own and lapse, as they often do, there is a big risk of overdosing, whereas medically controlled doses of heroin can be tolerated for long periods.

Like the Swiss government, the government of the Netherlands has begun to see drugs as a public health problem more than a crime problem. The Ministry of Health tests Ecstasy tablets and issues public warnings when they contain especially dangerous substances like strychnine, as they often do. Smoking marijuana in Amsterdam coffee shops is still illegal; but prosecutors decline to prosecute, provided shops adhere to strict limitations as to the amount permitted on the premises at one time (18 ounces).

Portugal in July 2001 adopted a policy that authorities distinguish from the Swiss and Netherlands experiments, though in some ways it is similar. Criminal penalties are kept on the books but are enforced by incarceration against sellers not users. Users may be punished with fines and community service but not with prison. Vitalino Canas, Portugal's drug policy czar, told an American reporter: "We're trying a sort of third way between the hard approach you have in the United States and the soft approach some countries have, like Holland. . . . We think drug users are not the criminals but are the victims of a crime and should be helped like other victims of crimes."[1] Possession of more than ten "daily doses" is taken as ipso facto evidence that one is a dealer. Addicts who have more than this amount still risk prison. Drug trafficking remains punishable by up to twenty-five years imprisonment. Before this policy was adopted, police had been reluctant to arrest young Ecstasy or hashish users, knowing that if the offender went to prison he or she would most likely come out using not hashish (marijuana) but heroin. Both England and France have been trying pilot programs allowing police to be more tolerant and use more discretion in arresting drug users.

The United States is, of course, a very different nation, with different geographical and cultural conditions from these nations. But the question nevertheless irresistibly presents itself: can Americans begin to see the problem of drugs more as a public health problem and less as a problem of crime? Is decriminalization without legalization possible?

IV. A CHRISTIAN PERSPECTIVE

Biblical Teaching

We cannot find explicit answers in the Bible to most of today's social problems. The problems faced by ancient Israel and in early Christian communities were different from those we face today. The Bible says nothing about marijuana or heroin or cocaine. Nevertheless, biblical teaching is relevant to our topic. The most direct and practical teaching has to do with wine. We learn that there were sects that gave up the drinking of wine. Apparently John the Baptist abstained. But in the Bible as a whole, drinking wine is taken for granted. Certainly Jesus drank wine, and this played a significant role in the Last Supper, in memory of which the church has celebrated the Eucharist. Paul thought that a little wine was good for digestion. In the Bible there is no direct justification for the prohibition of alcohol. On the other hand, it is clearly recognized that wine can be abused. Drunkenness is strongly and uniformly disapproved, although it does not seem to have been a major social problem. Without automobiles and freeways, drunk driving was less of a hazard.

Somewhat more broadly, Jesus and Paul both direct attention away from detailed rules about eating and drinking that were so much a part of the Jewish tradition. Paul says that food offered to idols before being placed on the table is not really affected by that ceremony. There is nothing inherently wrong with eating it. The believer's concern should be for the effect of this eating on others, in this case, less mature believers who still see such eating as participation in religious practices from which they are trying to free themselves. In a somewhat similar way, Jesus points out that what comes out of the mouth—what we say—is far more important than what we eat and drink. Of course, if imbibing something leads us to harm others, it becomes important.

Still more broadly, we can consider the mode of consciousness encouraged by the Bible. This can best be done in contrast to those cults that were based on mind-altering experiences. For example, the oracles of Apollo at Delphi went into trances in order to get their divine messages. In some of the mystery religions, people engaged in mind-altering practices. In Indian religions special forms of meditation lead to a change of mental state. In the Bible there is very little of this. Dreams are important at a few points: Joseph's success in interpreting a dream gained him leadership in Egypt, and another Joseph learned in a dream of the danger to Jesus in Bethlehem.

Saul first banished witches and then consulted one. She went into a trance. There is no explicit condemnation of this activity, but the prior banishing of witches implies suspicion on the part of Israel. More important, there are indications that those who are called "false" prophets may have employed mind-altering methods, but the "true" prophets are not depicted as doing so. God's call to them and communication with them seems to have occurred without dreams or trances. Paul speaks (2 Cor. 12:1–4) in passing of having been caught up into the third heaven. Presumably he refers to an altered state of consciousness, some kind of mystical experience. But what is remarkable is how little he makes of it or encourages others to seek it. Jesus apparently spent long hours in prayer alone, but when he teaches others how to pray, he does not describe the methods and techniques of meditation. He simply offers what we know as the Lord's Prayer.

Biblical teaching, in other words, is exoteric rather than esoteric; it addresses ordinary people in their ordinary mode of consciousness. It does not deny the possibility of extraordinary experience or deny that something of value might be learned thereby. But it does not regard the extraordinary experience as superior. In short, it does not reject altered states of consciousness on principle, but it does not encourage them. It encourages us to face our problems in the everyday social world, trusting in God, rather than seeking release through special states of consciousness.

Theological Reflection

In these respects, Christian theology has been largely continuous with biblical teaching. Mysticism has played a somewhat larger role in Christian history than in the Bible and has been more important among Catholics than among Protestants, but mainstream teaching has never viewed it as the central path of faith. Christian life is played out in the realm of ordinary experience.

For most of Christian history, as in the Bible, moderate drinking of alcohol was taken for granted while drunkenness was condemned. Alcohol became controversial among Christians only with the rise of distilled liquors that were much more potent than wine and beer. Tobacco was introduced into Europe from the New World, but it was not generally perceived as an issue to be addressed by the church. Other drugs began to be used in Christendom in the eighteenth and nineteenth centuries. Standard Christian teaching with regard to such matters was moderation or temperance.

This teaching became controversial in the United States when the abuse of alcohol became a widespread social problem, especially on the frontier. Drinking alcohol came to be associated with the saloon rather than the home. Many men wasted their income on alcohol and then returned home to abuse wives and children. Many Protestant churches began to side with the women who protested against saloon culture. Since drinking was so closely associated with saloons, the opposition to saloons became a call for abstinence, and the call for individual abstinence became a call to prohibit the sale of alcohol altogether. Large numbers of Protestant churches in the United States campaigned for Prohibition, and from 1920 to 1933, through the Eighteenth Amendment to the Constitution, their position was the law of the land.

The problems with Prohibition, however, taught the churches a lesson. The effective teaching of most old-line Protestant churches with regard to alcohol now is the traditional Christian one of accepting its use and opposing its abuse. The churches are also clearer now than earlier that it is a mistake to try to legislate the moral teachings of one segment of Christianity in a pluralistic society. They oppose what appear to them to be efforts by Roman Catholics and some Protestants to do this on other issues, such as abortion.

During the same period some churches also encouraged abstinence from tobacco. This was not nearly as intense a campaign as that against alcohol. But in some denominations those seeking ordination were required to vow not to smoke. Ironically, this legalism was widely abandoned about the time that the damage of smoking to health was becoming widely known and led to restrictions on smoking and suits against tobacco companies. From all this, the churches have been largely aloof.

The rise of the drug culture in the sixties and seventies aroused alarm in the churches as in much of the culture. Churches made pronouncements, but the drug culture did not evoke any major movement or fresh theological reflection. The reaction of church members was part of the general cultural response. A few Christians were interested in the religious experiences to which hallucinogens were supposed to lead, but this had little influence in Christian teaching, either favorable or unfavorable. Far more were appalled at what the drug culture was doing to young people and worked to end it.

Whereas the earlier prohibition of alcohol was led by the Protestant churches, the current prohibition of drugs has not been. After the failure of the earlier prohibition, some church leaders are skeptical of this one. On the other hand, most Protestants recognize the enormous harm that drugs can do. Since almost all organized religious groups share the opposition to drug abuse, legislation against it does not involve imposing the views of one on others. And for many Christians the best response to a social evil is still to use the power of the state to outlaw it.

V. OPTIONS FOR PROGRESSIVE PROTESTANTS

Protestants are opposed to the abuse of drugs but are not necessarily committed to prohibition as the best means of countering such abuse. The failure of the prohibition of alcohol has taught us that simply prohibiting by law what we think harms people may not work. On the other hand, the earlier failure was in part because Prohibition was imposed on Catholics, Jews, and many others who did not agree with the policy. The condemnation of the abuse of drugs is today so widespread that we can be open to fresh considerations and be guided by practical results. As noted above, the War on Drugs has failed. It is time to reconsider.

There are three general choices now available. The first is to pursue the current War on Drugs with greater and greater intensity. Both political parties seem to believe that this is what the American people want; so other alternatives are little discussed. But there is no evidence that intensification of present patterns will result in anything other than more militarization, frustration, and suffering. The Colombia story is becoming well known. Increased effort at interdiction seems simply to generate more channels of transportation. Doubling the rate of arrests or the severity of the punishment of users is unlikely to reduce the number of pushers or users. Progressive Protestants should withdraw support from these failed policies.

The second alternative is to end the prohibition of addictive drugs the way we ended the prohibition of alcohol. The parallels between the two are considerable. The prohibition of alcohol did not make it unavailable, but it did create crime "families" that became wealthy and powerful and contributed to the corruption of many politicians, police, and judges. The same can be said of the prohibition of drugs. Enforcing the law against alcohol consumed a disproportionate part of police efforts, as does the current prohibition of drugs. However, complete legalization could well lead to a social climate that subtly or not so subtly encourages drug taking, especially among children and teenagers. Despite laws against underage drinking, alcohol is widely advertised and is sold in supermarkets; so determined or rebellious children have ready access to it. A comparable situation with respect to cocaine and heroin is hard to accept.

The third alternative is decriminalization without legalization. Supporters of the War on Drugs use "legalization" as a scare word, implying the abandonment of restrictions on drug use and consequent chaos, which progressive Protestants certainly do not favor. But the authority of the law can be used to regulate, control, and treat drug users without turning them into ordinary criminals. That is the aim of measures such as Proposition 36. At present a certain segment of drug users are turned into ordinary criminals in their desperate search for money to get a fix. As the Swiss experiment shows, state-controlled drug clinics can sharply reduce such crime. The high prices for drugs that are generated by the efforts at interdiction are another causal factor in breeding criminal activity, on both the demand and the supply side. That is, dealers get in the game because they know they can get very high prices for what they sell; and users steal because that is the only way they can pay the high prices.

Progressive Christians see promise in this third way, but it is no simple solution. Piecemeal changes, improvements that can be made on an ad hoc basis, and adjustments that take account of varying local conditions would seem to be the only way to go.

VI. WHAT WE CAN DO

The War on Drugs is widely perceived to have a moral underpinning and the support of the Christian community. For this reason, it is particularly important that Christians speak up in declaring it a failure. We must make clear that opposing the use of addictive drugs does not entail prohibition, that the cost of prohibition is outrageously high, and that giving all responsibility to the legal system can lead to much injustice.

We can support the growing movement to frame the problem of drugs as a public health issue more than as a criminal issue. There are, and no doubt always will be, disagreements about exactly what changes should be made; but the main problem is that politicians, who live by public opinion polls more than by scientific data, still suppose that a War on Drugs and being tough on drug users will win votes. We can do much to change that impression. It is time that we were hearing sermons on the issue of drugs and engaging congregations in discussion of the subject. We should encourage experimentation by the states and careful monitoring of the results. We should oppose the present tendency of the federal government to preempt the area of drugs and interfere with experimentation by the states.

Changing public opinion and the law is only one role for the churches. Churches must meet many dimensions of human need. Important among these is the needs of addicts themselves. Congregations already provide space and support for addicts who are willing to seek release from their addictions; Alcoholics Anonymous is the most famous program of this sort, but far from the only one. It may be possible for some churches themselves to develop and provide treatment centers.

The most important role for churches is in the area of prevention. This involves, as a supplement to what public schools can do, the education of youth and, even more, the education of parents, giving them help in dealing with their children. Prevention also involves calling people to a full and meaningful life from which they will have no need to escape into illusion.

Once we have recognized the harm done by both the use of drugs and the War on Drugs, we can commit ourselves to study and support policies that reduce this harm. Eight steps commend themselves to progressive Christians.

Make treatment centers available to all who want help. Studies show that the most successful programs are those that include, in addition to therapy sessions and chemical treatment, assistance to addicts in stabilizing their lives and finding work. This would be expensive, but less expensive than throwing people in prison. The annual cost of keeping a person in prison is around $25,000. Outpatient drug treatment for the same period costs around $1,800, and one 140-day residential treatment program cost in 1998 $6,800.

Give those convicted of drug use the choice between prison and drug treatment. This is the aim of both drug courts and the Proposition 36 program in California. It is widely believed, however, that the $120 million a year appropriated for Proposition 36 will not be sufficient to make this choice available to all who need it.

Distinguish among drugs the ones that are least harmful and treat them differently. Marijuana is the most popular of the illegal drugs and the least harmful. Marijuana is not harmless. Some studies suggest that long-term use can do psychological and mental damage; but the harm is less severe than comparable long-term use of alcohol. Most use of marijuana is occasional, and it is not addictive, as heroin or cocaine are. One percent of the population uses it regularly, and some of these people develop a psychological dependence on it. Some of these seek treatment, and others are forced into treatment by employers. The severity of laws against marijuana is justified only by the idea that it is a gateway drug, leading the user to harder drugs, but there is no evidence that this necessarily occurs.

Do away with mandatory sentencing. Judges need to have discretion in sentencing so that the special circumstances of each offender can be taken into account. One study showed that in the United States the average sentence for marijuana possession was about the same, fifty months, as the actual time served for murder and kidnapping. Giving judges more discretion is one of the effects of drug courts and Proposition 36 legislation, but federal mandatory sentencing guidelines remain untouched. (See chapter 7, "The Penal System.")

Change what happens in prison. At present most of those who serve prison terms are less able to avoid crime and drug addiction afterward than they were before going to prison. Recidivism is high. At a minimum, prisons should provide drug therapy programs for those who need it and want it. Progress in therapy should be a factor in considering probation. Ideally, the whole prison system should make rehabilitation central to its purpose.

Recognize the complexity of addiction. There are many genetic, physiological, psychological, and sociological factors that enter into addictive personalities. No single or simple program will eliminate the problem of addiction. Not all addicts are drug addicts. But treating drug addiction as a medical problem will eliminate much criminal activity and will also allow many to live fairly stable and normal lives.

Eliminate racism. The enforcement of U.S. drug policy has been permeated with racism. Longer sentences have been imposed on users of crack cocaine, who have tended to be economically disadvantaged African Americans, than on users of powder cocaine, who have tended to be middle- and upper-class whites. There is no physiological difference between the two substances. A

Human Rights Watch study found that while drug use is a problem in all racial groups, blacks and Latinos were far more likely to be arrested and prosecuted and given long sentences for drug offenses. Blacks constitute 13 percent of all drug users, but 35 percent of those arrested for drug possession, 55 percent of persons convicted, and 75 percent of people sent to prison. Racism in this area has a long history. The first antiopium laws were directed against Chinese immigrants. The first antimarijuana laws were enacted in response to fears about Mexican immigrants.

Change the socioeconomic conditions that lead to the abuse of drugs. This may be the most important, but also the most difficult to implement. Much drug use is a means of escape, for a time, from intolerable family, societal, or work conditions. Abused, neglected, and abandoned children often find escape through drugs appealing. In some neighborhoods, pushing drugs on others may be seen as an easy source of income otherwise unimaginable. The drug culture tends to thrive where family ties are weak or frazzled. A healthy society offers everyone tangible hope for the future. Those with self-confidence and hope for the future are much less likely to be trapped by drug use.

Discussion Questions

1. What relation do you see between the current prohibition of addictive drugs and the earlier prohibition of alcohol?
2. What Christian teachings guide your approach to a sound drug policy? How can they best be explained to non-Christians?
3. Do you see flaws in the programs described above under the heading "European Experience"?
4. What experience have you had with addictions in your own family or with relatives, friends, or coworkers? Why is it difficult to share these experiences within the confines of a Christian community?
5. How far should the church go in support of specific legislation addressing the problems of addictive drugs?

To Learn More

Books dealing with the political issues of drugs and American culture include Dan Baum, *Smoke and Mirrors: The War on Drugs and the Politics of Failure* (Boston: Little, Brown, 1996); James P. Gray, *Why Our Drug Laws Have Failed and What We Can Do about It* (Philadelphia: Temple University Press, 2001); Kevin Jack Riley, *Snow Job? The War Against International Cocaine Trafficking* (Somerset, N.J.: Transaction Publishers, 1996).

Historical discussions about the drug issues include Mike Gray, *Drug Crazy: How We Got into This Mess and How We Can Get Out* (New York:

Random House, 1998) and David F. Musto, *The American Disease: Origins of Narcotic Control* (Oxford: Oxford University Press, 1999).

Two books dealing with the personal issues of drug abuse are Julian Cohen and James Kay, *Taking Drugs Seriously: A Parent's Guide to Young People's Drug Use* (London: Thorsons, 1994) and Maralys Wills and Mike Carona, *Save My Son* (Center City, Minn.: Hazeldon, 2000).

Progressive Christians Uniting has a study guide entitled "Prisons, Drug Abuse, and Treatment in California" intended for use in Christian adult education classes. It is applicable to other states. Contact Progressive Christians Uniting for copies.

281 S. Thomas Street
Suite 502
Pomona, CA 91766

www.progressivechristiansuniting.org

Web Resources:
Campaign for New Drug Policies— www.drugreform.org
Institute for Policy Studies— www.ips-dc.org
Lindesmith Center/Drug Policy Foundation— www.lindesmith.org
Proposition 36— www.prop36.org
White House Office of Drug Policy— www.whitehousedrugpolicy.gov

9

The Immigration Dilemma

Sung Kim is a Korean immigrant. He was able to come to the United States after his parents' death, because his sister had come earlier as a GI bride, and the immigration service allowed him to join her. Life in Korea had been very difficult under successive military regimes that ruthlessly limited the aspirations of workers. It was not easy in the United States either, but Kim worked very hard in his sister's restaurant, saved some money, and started his own restaurant. He is now a successful businessman, still working hard and living frugally, but married, raising a family, supporting a church, seeking citizenship, and clearly contributing to the American economy.

James Richardson is an African American who dropped out of high school after two years. He has no marketable skills. He wants to make his own way and is willing to take minimum-wage unskilled jobs. He resists pressures to supplement his income through illegal activities. Although he fathered a child, he can contribute nothing to her support. He keeps hoping that he can move up the ladder enough to help the child's mother. But even minimum-wage jobs are hard to keep, partly because undocumented immigrants are willing to work for less. He is often unemployed. He resents the constant inflow of new people as undercutting his chances of a decent future.

I. INTRODUCTION

Throughout history, the world's people have always been on the move, migrating from one location to another. People leave their homes for many reasons: they may not be able to support themselves or their families; crops may have failed, so that there is not enough food; the environment may no longer sustain settlement; war or persecution may have disrupted life; a group of people may simply want a better life for themselves and their children.

If history is an account of migrating people, current global realities point to ever increasing migrations. Virtually all of the demographic, political, and economic trends shaping the world's future point to more, not less, forced migration of people. Swelling populations, growing inequality, mounting violence, and degraded environments will inevitably push more and more people from their home communities. This means that it is urgent to clarify the policies dealing with migration and immigrants.

Generally we use two different terms for those who are on the move. People who seek admission to another country because of a well-founded fear of persecution if they return to their home country are usually called refugees. Typically they fear harm because of their race, religion, nationality, political opinion, or membership in a particular group. At the start of 2001, the number of refugees "of concern" to the United Nations High Commissioner for Refugees (UNHCR) was 21.8 million, or one out of every 275 persons on Earth. This compares with a somewhat higher figure of 26.1 million in 1996. The highest number of refugees is in Africa, followed closely by Asia and Europe.

A second group of migrants, referred to as immigrants, take up residence in another country for other reasons, often economic. Globally, according to the United Nations Population Fund, currently twenty million people are on the run from drought or other environmental problems, and more than sixty million people are economic migrants seeking a better life or survival. All these migrants amount to about 2 percent of the world population.

Another important distinction is between those who seek a permanent new home and those who hope to return to their homes when conditions allow or when they have made sufficient money. In general, those who hope to return remain in a neighboring country, for example, migrant workers from Mexico in the United States. Those who seek to make a permanent change, on the other hand, may look elsewhere for their future home, for example, Indian and Filipino engineers in the U.S. high-tech industries.

However, dividing people into clear-cut categories of refugees and immigrants is becoming more and more difficult. The U.S. government, for example, has tended to regard anyone coming from a Communist country as a refugee, but persons in greater personal danger coming from countries with which we are allied rarely receive that status. Are those fleeing grinding poverty and starvation really immigrants, or do they also deserve the title refugee? Is their emigration really "voluntary"? How do we classify people fleeing countries where poverty is closely linked with a repressive political system? Increasingly discussions of immigration and refugee assistance will need to deal with all the world's migrants.

II. CURRENT MIGRATIONS

Worldwide Problems

The most massive problems of migration are in parts of the world—Pakistan, Burundi, Thailand, Bosnia—that seem distant to Americans. The Burmese-Thai border is an example. Burma (currently called Myanmar by the illegal junta ruling the country) is an example of how a ruthless and repressive government can cause massive emigration. In 2001 there were 135,000 people from Burma living in refugee camps on the Thai side of the border. They had to flee from fighting around their homes brought about by the reign of terror imposed by the military. There are also an estimated one million displaced Burmese living illegally throughout Thailand.

The Thai government does not feel that it can accept responsibility for an increasing number of refugees. In a recent report the Human Rights Watch/Asia shows that many of the refugees already in camps in Thailand, as well as others who are trying to flee into Thailand, are being forced back into Burma. For many of them, this means persecution and even death. It is hard to see any happy solution to this problem without the replacement of the present Burmese junta by Daw Aung San Suu Kyi, whose party won over 80 percent of the vote in 1990.

Almost anywhere that immigrants arrive in large numbers, they encounter hostility. In Turkey there is anger toward refugees from Iran, Iraq, and North Africa. Tamils driven out of Sri Lanka are rejected in England. Moroccans are seen as a problem in Italy. There have been anti-immigrant riots in Germany and attacks on hostels for asylum seekers in Switzerland. One European in three believes there are too many people of another nationality or race in his or her country. It is apparent that as the need to seek refuge increases, the difficulty of finding hospitality will increase.

We must particularly admire poor countries that, with very few resources, nevertheless provide a place of refuge for huge numbers. For example, Malawi, with a population of less than ten million, worked with the United Nations to care for more than 700,000 Mozambicans for more than a decade before a peace settlement allowed them to begin voluntary repatriation in 1993.

Immigration into the United States

Statistics such as these remind us that the United States' record in refugee resettlement is not especially impressive. It ranks behind Sweden, Canada, Australia, and Denmark in terms of per capita resettlement. Those who complain that this country carries too much of the burden should be reminded of this fact, especially in relation to our resources and the enormity of the global problem. We should be reminded also of the importance of supporting the United Nations in its worldwide work with refugees.

Even so, this nation has been created by immigration, and debates about the number and sources of immigrants now play a major role in national political life. This has not always been the case. Without much public debate about the merits of accepting more migrants, the level of immigration into the United States slowly began to rise during the mid-1960s, accelerated in the 1970s, and soared in the 1980s; significant statutory, judicial, and administrative actions taken during the 1980s approbated a near-record level of annual entries in the 1990s. Unless these policies are reversed by specific policy interventions, mass immigration is likely to remain a significant feature of the U.S. economy and society.

Is this a good thing? As American citizens and Christians, we need to seek answers to this question. Which ethical perspectives should we bring to bear on this policy question? Should the U.S. become more or less restrictive in its admissions? Who will be admitted and who will be turned away?

While it would be useful to frame these questions in more global than national terms, this book is primarily devoted to our Christian responsibilities for U.S. policies. Therefore, the remainder of this chapter will focus primarily on the policies governing immigration into this country and on their implication for those affected by them.

Roughly 675,000 immigrants enter the United States each year as legal permanent residents. Most of these are admitted for family unification or employment-related purposes. Another 120,000 people are annually admitted to the United States as refugees fleeing political persecution.

The U.S. Immigration and Naturalization Service (INS) estimates that approximately 275,000 undocumented immigrants enter the United States and stay each year. Because they are undocumented, it is difficult to obtain accurate numbers. Contrary to widespread impressions, almost half of those do not sneak across the border but rather arrive legally and stay beyond the expiration of their visas. Approximately one-half of the undocumented immigrants are from Mexico. Estimates of the total number of undocumented immigrants range widely, from 5.4 million to more than 11 million. California accounts for 40 percent of the total.

III. THE HISTORY AND PATTERNS OF IMMIGRATION INTO THE UNITED STATES

If we go back far enough in time, all human inhabitants everywhere outside of some region in Africa are immigrants. Nevertheless, it is best to view the first humans to arrive in an area as the natives or indigenous people, with those who come later as immigrants. Sometimes immigrants enter a country, mix with the indigenous people and jointly constitute the primary population of a region. At other times, immigrants and indigenous people share the territory without much mixing. At still other times, immigrants conquer and enslave the indigenous people or even exterminate them.

Several patterns of immigration are to be found in the New World. In some places, the indigenous people were conquered, ruled, and exploited by the immigrant minority. In some of these places, there was considerable intermixture of populations as well. In other places, the immigrants displaced or even exterminated the indigenous people, sometimes intentionally, sometimes not.

In the United States the indigenous population was pushed back, decimated, and limited to reservations where they could hardly support themselves. Currently the vast majority of the population consists of immigrants. (If we consider the indigenous people to constitute their own nations, then we may say that the U.S. as a nation is composed almost entirely of immigrants.) As we celebrate our immigrant history, we should be mindful of its effects on Native Americans.

Successive waves of European immigrants to these shores added to the security of those immigrants who had already arrived. They contributed to their economic prosperity and expanded the "settled" areas, that is, those from which Native Americans were driven out. Some of these settlers came by choice; others were indentured servants and debtors who were rather rapidly assimilated into the new immigrant societies. But Africans brought as slaves remained slaves, as did their children, including those of mixed race, for many generations. Even when they were freed, they remained largely segregated until very recently.

Since the immigration with which we are currently concerned is of persons who want to come, our focus will be on the history of voluntary immigration, but we cannot understand the current scene without remembering the centuries-long history of black slavery, as well as the way in which immigrants displaced the native peoples from their land.

Earliest American History

Immigration was among the issues behind the war for independence. The colonists wanted rapid growth of population, whereas the English king discouraged this. Accordingly, one of the grievances against King George listed in the Declaration of Independence concerned the right of people to migrate. The king "has endeavoured to prevent the population of these states, for that purpose obstructing the laws of Naturalization of Foreigners, refusing to pass others to encourage their migration hither."

James Wilson rose at the Constitutional Convention of 1787 to speak in favor of open immigration, noting that almost all the general officers of the Pennsylvania line in the U.S. Revolutionary Army were foreigners. Although the British dominated the early settlement of the American colonies, the Germans were close behind. In 1795, George Washington asked God "to render the country more and more a safe and propitious asylum for the unfortunate of other countries."

But from the beginning the United States has had ambivalent feelings about immigrants. George Washington also favored restricting government service to native-born persons. And in a letter to John Adams in 1794 he wrote: "My opinion with respect to immigration is, that except of useful mechanics and some particular description of men and professions, there is no use of encouragement."[1]

People have recognized that immigration has been critical for American economic progress at various points in our history, but there has also been a great deal of anger, and outright xenophobia, toward immigrants. Benjamin Franklin himself noted: "Americans hailed newcomers to its shores as the bulwark of democracy, however, in times of crisis it has also used the foreign born as a scapegoat for unsolved social problems."

Immigration and Ethnicity

Although most Americans in the nineteenth century favored immigration because it added to national power, speeded up the exploitation of new lands, and provided labor for established business and agriculture, there was also opposition. Some of this was based on ethnicity. Indeed, more and more Americans began to call for a monolithic society with an Anglo-Saxon identity, where everyone would speak the same language, profess the same religion, and be similar in manners and customs. Members of the nativist Know-

Nothing party opposed Irish and German immigration, saying that this did not fit the American mosaic.

Various states attempted to restrict the influx of immigrants and passed laws especially against the return of refugees after the Revolutionary War or attempting to prevent European nations from settling their criminals in the United States. But eventually the U.S. Supreme Court held state laws on immigration to be unconstitutional.

Toward the end of the nineteenth century, immigration shifted from Ireland and Germany to eastern and southern Europe and included many Jews. Also, total numbers increased drastically. Whereas the average number of immigrants during the period of continental expansion (1820–79) had been 162,000 per year, from 1880 to 1924 it was 584,000. Assimilation became more difficult, and earlier immigrants became increasingly resentful of newer ones.

As cities such as New York became more crowded and more "foreign," reactions against immigration escalated. One New York writer illustrated the worst of this when he said, "The floodgates are open. The dam is washed away. The sewer is choked. The scum of immigration is viscerating upon our shores." Nevertheless, during this same period a Jewish writer, Israel Zangwill, coined the phrase "melting pot" to describe America, and Americans responded enthusiastically to Emma Lazarus's poem with its questionable interpretation of the Statue of Liberty as welcoming immigrants: "Give me your tired, your poor."

Restriction of immigration explicitly based on ethnicity was directed only against Asians. After the Taiping Rebellion in China in 1848, some 300,000 Chinese came to the United States. After they had helped America build its railroads and harvest its fields, in 1882 the Chinese Exclusion Act was passed. In 1907–8 Japan entered into a gentlemen's agreement with the U.S. government: the United States agreed not to exclude Japanese immigrants by law, while Japan agreed not to issue passports to any who wished to come here.

These racist actions against Asians were defended because of another effect of immigration. New immigrants are typically a threat to the economic advancement of earlier ones. As the earlier arrivers begin to establish themselves and gain higher wages, new immigrants come who are willing to work for less. It is more difficult to organize labor unions when there is a steady influx of workers who are desperate for jobs. When the economy is expanding rapidly, the problem is minor, but in hard times, it is more serious. Ethnic conflict has often been triggered and intensified by the economic interests of earlier immigrants.

Ethnic diversity in this country was increased greatly by the annexation of half of Mexico by the Treaty of Guadalupe Hidalgo in 1848. Even today a majority of the Chicano population in the United States results from this annexation, rather than from subsequent immigration. It is ironic that these earlier immigrants into what is now the United States are often treated by later arrivals from Europe as if they had less right to full citizenship and participation. The current push for English-only ignores the fact that this 1848 treaty guaranteed Mexicans in the ceded territory the right to their own language and culture.

This treaty also illustrates the arbitrary character of many borders, especially those drawn by imperial powers in Africa, which ignored both geography and the affiliations of the native people. The intention in this treaty was for the United States to annex Alta California, leaving Baja California to Mexico. Mexico regarded San Diego as part of Baja California, but the United States forced on Mexico its interpretation of the boundary as running south of San Diego. The resultant boundary is related to no natural barrier and is extremely easy to cross. In considering the right of Mexicans to cross the border drawn by this treaty, we need to remember the circumstances of its creation.

The absorption of this large Mexican population into the United States led to tensions with the increasingly predominant Anglo-Saxon population. In the latter half of the nineteenth century, Mexican culture had the misfortune of being identified in the Anglo-Saxon mind with both Catholicism and revolution. This gave sentiments of racial superiority even greater impact. The nativist heritage is one that continues to play itself out today in new and varied forms.

The End of Unlimited Immigration

Despite the growing prejudice against new arrivals, the borders were completely open to Europeans until 1875. Even then, restrictions were not placed on total numbers or on nations of origin. The intent was to prevent the immigration of those who were "undesirable." Convicts and prostitutes were excluded in 1875; in 1882 exclusion was extended to "lunatics, idiots or any person unable to take care of himself or herself without becoming a public charge." In 1891 paupers, polygamists, and those with loathsome or dangerous diseases were barred. In 1903, epileptics, beggars and anarchists were added to the list. In 1906 it was required that immigrants speak English. The process of restricting immigration in this way continued until 1918.

Far more important than these "qualitative" restrictions on immigration was a changing climate among American voters. Throughout the nineteenth century, despite ethnic prejudices exacerbated by economic concerns on the part of workers, the dominant segment of the American people wanted immigration in order to increase the power of the nation, complete the westward expansion, and provide labor for infant industries. But by the end of the century the population sufficed to give the nation international status, the frontier was gone, and the labor force seemed sufficient. Additional population had to be absorbed in already settled areas. Since most of those who now wanted to come were ethnically different from the majority who were already here, ethnic and racist elements gained ground in the opposition to continued large-scale immigration.

The result of this change in national attitude toward immigration was quantitative restriction favoring the ethnicities that had been longer established in the country. In 1921 the 1910 census was selected as the basis for establishing quotas on new immigrants. It allowed annual immigration from each nation of up to 3 percent of the population from that country already settled in the United States in 1910. This gave large quotas to northern European countries, while drastically reducing immigration from eastern and southern Europe. To intensify the latter effects, legislation in 1924 shifted the base to the 1890 census and reduced the percentage to 2 percent. Still more restrictive policies were enacted in 1929.

Hostility toward immigration, along with anti-Jewish prejudices, led to horrible consequences during the 1930s and '40s. In 1939 Congress defeated a bill that would have rescued 20,000 refugee children from Germany, on the grounds that the admission of the children would have exceeded the German quota. This decision was made even though American families were prepared to sponsor the individual children.

World War II led to some changes in the direction of flexibility. In 1945 and 1950 laws were passed that waived visa requirements for spouses of American military personnel. And in 1948 the Displaced Persons Act enabled 400,000 refugees from Europe to enter the United States.

This did not reflect a basic change of attitude. In 1952, the quota system was reaffirmed, along with a preference system for distributing visas within each country's allotment. This law passed over the veto of President Truman, who wanted a more humane immigration policy. He said, "The quota system is long out of date and it discriminates, deliberately and intentionally, against many of the peoples of the world."

During the 1960s Americans became embarrassed about the overtly racist character of their laws, including those governing immigration. A commission appointed by Truman produced a proposal to end the national quota system, and this change was eventually embodied in legislation in 1965. This legislation did not, however, move in the direction of the unlimited number of immigrants that had characterized the United States prior to 1921. Instead, it set an annual ceiling of 120,000 immigrants for the western hemisphere and 170,000 for the eastern hemisphere. This policy was revised in 1976 and 1978 to eliminate the hemispheric quotas as well. The effect of these changes was to increase immigration from Asia, southern Europe, and Latin America.

In place of quotas a new system of preference categories was established, in order to favor those held to be most desirable as immigrants. Three groups were to receive preference. First, the new law put an emphasis on family reunification, so those with immediate family already in the United States went to the top of the list. Second, there were provisions for labor needs, which meant a priority for "members of the professions and those with exceptional abilities in the sciences and the arts." Third, those with demonstrable reason to seek refuge from war or political persecution were to be welcomed.

Since 1965 legal immigration has been based primarily on the family reunification policy, which gives preference not only to spouses and minor children, but also to adult sons and daughters and parents of adult immigrants, as well as brothers and sisters. If a member of a family gained a foothold in this country, he or she could begin a chain of immigration, also called "network immigration." Limits have been raised several times, reaching 675,000 in 1990. Between 1965 and 1989, immigration was approximately 500,000 a year. Since 1990 annual immigration—both documented and undocumented—has averaged more than a million.

Because a major amount of immigration has taken place outside the law, an effort was made in 1986 to deal with this problem. The Immigration Reform and Control Act gave amnesty to about three million undocumented residents who had lived in the United States prior to 1982 (or 1986 for agricultural workers). This offer of amnesty recognized the difficulty of identifying and deporting a large number of undocumented persons, and it helped to protect them against abuses by employers who sought to take advantage of their vulnerability. To deter further illegal immigration, the act also penalized employers who knowingly hired undocumented workers. At best, this part of the act provided a mechanism to discourage illegal immigration that could work in tandem with immigration controls at the border.

But in fact the employer sanctions have not been vigorously enforced, and some employers are prepared to take the risk of occasional fines in order to hire workers cheaply. Those employers who try to obey are easily deceived by readily available counterfeit documents. Worse, the law has had the effect of discouraging other employers from hiring persons who they suppose *may* be undocumented because of their ethnicity.

Then in 1996 the Congress passed and the president signed the Illegal Immigration Reform and Responsibility Act. Earlier drafts of this legislation had called for major reductions in the number of new legal immigrants. In its final form, however, the act focused primarily on measures that removed from undocumented persons most of their rights of judicial appeal of administrative actions by the INS. The Welfare Reform Act of 1996 also made alien status the basis for denial of access to key government services and programs. The desire to limit freedom of entry is obviously a powerful political force in America.

In the short term immigration restrictions were tightened still more for security reasons after the events of September 11, 2001. Until those attacks, the forces for liberalizing immigration had gained new strength as two new presidents in the United States and Mexico set ambitious goals that might allow undocumented immigrants to work legally in the United States and guest workers to migrate freely and openly into America. Then, too, organized labor began seeing new immigrants less as a threat to American jobs than as a potential source of new members. The Catholic church also supported legalization for the rapidly growing number of Hispanic migrants. Reform seemed finally on the way. Then suddenly, the nation found itself faced with a "war" on terrorism that inevitably would restrict movement across borders.

IV. OBJECTIONS TO LARGE-SCALE IMMIGRATION

Beginning in the late 1960s a new perspective on immigration began to emerge. This was rooted in concern about global overpopulation and overconsumption, which have come to be seen as threatening to the life-support system of the planet. Although the primary focus is global, its supporters believe that stabilization of population must occur in each region. (See chapter 16, "The Global Population Crisis.")

It is sometimes supposed that overconsumption is the problem of the affluent countries and overpopulation that of the poorer ones. However, thoughtful leaders recognize that increasing population in the affluent countries is a greater threat to the future of the earth than increasing population in poorer countries. The impact of each nation on planetary resources is its population times its per capita consumption. Hence, population increase in the United States is a particularly serious matter, and citizens of the United States concerned for the future of the whole earth have a particular responsibility to stabilize population here, as well as to stop the increase of per capita consumption.

Among industrialized nations the United States is unusual in its continued population growth. This is not due, for the most part, to an excessive number of children born to those who were born in the United States. The major source of population growth among native-born Americans is unwanted pregnancies among teenage girls exploited by older men, and we should support efforts to reduce these. But it is growth in the number of immigrants and their descendants that will account for as much as 90 percent of the growth of the U.S. population in the new century.

This chapter has noted three types of objection to continued large-scale immigration. First, there are concerns about the threat to the dominant Anglo culture from the large number of immigrants from Asia and Latin America. People worry that their culture will be overwhelmed by persons of a different color or a different language. These concerns often have racist overtones. Second, people are nervous about the economic impact of more immigrants, who may steal their jobs. It is difficult to raise working standards, moreover, when new immigrants are ready to work under almost any conditions. Third, it is impossible to stabilize population as long as a million immigrants enter the country each year and bring with them the desire to have larger families.

There is yet another source of the current opposition. People worry that immigrants will swamp social services such as education, health, and welfare. In the 1980s many Americans became convinced that they paid too much in taxes and that governmental programs should be cut back. The programs they especially opposed were the ones that guaranteed all residents some minimum of economic well-being, health care, and education. Many came to believe that these welfare programs encouraged laziness and irresponsibility and were particularly resentful of immigrants who may have been attracted to this country by these programs and taken advantage of them. These concerns about saving tax dollars were manifest especially in the proposed Personal Responsibility Act, which was part of the Republican Contract with America. It would have withdrawn the safety net from virtually all immigrants. This bill excluded immigrants from sixty different governmental programs. Whereas in the past legal immigrants have been viewed as future citizens, they were here viewed as a burden on the state without the right to assistance. Elements of this "personal responsibility" proposal were included in the new welfare legislation, as noted above, although much of their implementation was left to the states.

Much of the public opposition to the current level of immigration is directed against undocumented immigrants. Many who do not wish to penalize legal immigrants nevertheless believe that the nation should control its borders. California Proposition 187, which passed with 59 percent support, required that teachers, doctors, social workers, and police check the immigration status of all who seek access to public education and health services and denied most services to those without legal documents. The California Supreme Court found several of its requirements unconstitutional, delaying implementation of this proposition.

V. A CHRISTIAN PERSPECTIVE

Reflection on the Biblical Material

The clearest teaching of the Christian faith is that we should love God and one another. Our actions should stem from this love. This involves total concern for the total welfare of all through space and time.

The Bible spells out some of the implications of such love in relation to strangers in our midst. We are told that soon after the Hebrew slaves escaped Egyptian oppression and formed a new nation, they spoke of the need to welcome immigrants in their new community: "You shall not wrong or oppress a resident alien." (Exod. 22:21)

When they developed their law code, hospitality was put at its core. Thus we read, "When an alien resides with you in your land, you shall not oppress the alien. The alien who resides with you shall be to you as the citizen among you; you shall love the alien as yourself, for you were aliens in the land of Egypt" (Lev. 19:33–34).

The law code went beyond that mandate to spell out practical dimensions of how people should care for foreigners. For instance, "When you reap the harvest of your land, you shall not reap to the very edges of your field, or gather the gleanings of your harvest" (Lev. 19:9). Further practical specification is given: "Every third year you shall bring out the full tithe of your produce for that year, and store it within your towns; the Levites, because they have no allotment or inheritance with you, as well as the resident aliens, the orphans, and the widows in your towns, may come and eat their fill so that the LORD your God may bless you in all the work that you undertake" (Deut. 14:28).

Our concern to welcome foreigners is not only because they are the neighbors we are called to love but also because they bring us blessing. We need to welcome strangers into our midst if we are to grow and move forward in our journeys of learning and faith. We never know in what form we will find God.

There are biblical stories of God coming in the form of the stranger. Abraham and Sarah receive strangers with kind hospitality, only to discover those strangers came with glad tidings from God. A widow offered food and shelter to a stranger, Elijah, who turned out to be a voice from God. And in the New Testament we have the story of Jesus' disciples offering welcoming hospitality to a stranger they met on the way to Emmaus, only to discover the Risen Christ. In Hebrews the point is made explicit: "Do not neglect to show hospitality to strangers, for by doing that some have entertained angels without knowing it" (13:2).

Sorting Out the Current Issues in Christian Perspective

There are three groups of immigrants to be considered:

- *Refugees.* In the past the United States has generally made admission easy for refugees from Communist countries but quite difficult for those who flee repressive regimes that our government supports. The sanctuary movement undertook to work for the latter persons. We are convinced that this is required by our commitment to the gospel. Our refugee policy should never be an instrument of international policy, but it should offer a safe haven to those who truly need it.
- *Legal immigrants.* Their needs for education, medical care, and economic well-being are the same as those of citizens. It is our hope and expectation that they, or their children, will become citizens. Although it is reasonable that the commitments made by their sponsors be enforced, we cannot countenance discrimination against them.
- *Illegal or undocumented immigrants.* Christians can agree that such persons are children of God to be respected no less than anyone else. We can also agree that denying them health care and denying education to their children are unacceptable policies.

Love calls us to treat the strangers in our midst with hospitality and to care for their needs. But immigration policy poses more difficult questions for the Christian. The fact that we express love quite personally and directly to those who have come to our communities does not necessarily mean that we should encourage massive immigration. Can our faith give us guidance on this?

Our concern should be for the well-being of all who are involved. In most instances, people who have to leave their homes in other countries and must make the difficult adjustments required by our society experience separation. In addition, their home nations lose their contributions. The effects on the society into which they migrate are mixed.

Christians are called to examine the conditions that cause people to emigrate from their homes. In most instances it is better to change conditions in those countries from which would-be immigrants come, so as to enable them to stay, than for them to migrate. We must acknowledge that some of our government's policies in Latin America have driven many from their homes who would have preferred to remain. The low-intensity warfare against peasant populations by Latin American governments has been supported by the United States. We should certainly admit refugees who are victims of this warfare, but even more clearly we should do what we can to change the policies of our government, and especially the often-destructive role of the CIA.

The United States is working with the World Bank and other governments of industrial nations to impose the neoliberal economic system of a global market on Third World nations. The resulting economic disruptions sometimes lead to heavy pressure on some segments of society to emigrate. Defenders of the neoliberal paradigm argue that in the long run these policies will bring a prosperity that will solve the problem. Critics believe that the application of this paradigm permanently divides the rich and the poor and that in some instances the poor will continue to be under increasing pressure to emigrate. Many Christians believe that major redirection of the global economy is needed. (See chapter 12, "Globalization of Economic Life.")

If we work wisely and effectively to improve the economic possibilities in other countries, the desire to immigrate into this country ought to decline. The difficult question is by how much the pressure to admit all those who want to enter would then be eased. But as long as many do wish to enter, chiefly for economic reasons, we must reflect as Christians as to how to respond. Here Christians differ.

A Theological Debate about Borders

Some argue for a world without borders on the grounds that the earth belongs to God, and all its resources should be available to all its people. As people move freely to whatever part of the world they wish, there will be increasing intermingling of cultures. This will be enriching to all. From this vision they conclude that all restriction on immigration into the United States should be abandoned. They see its basic motive as selfish hoarding of our resources. From these premises one should also conclude that all the earth's resources should be held by a world government for the use of all, since national boundaries are by no means the only obstacle to access to resources. Apart from such other changes, freedom of a poor Mexican to cross into the United States may be more the freedom to work for U.S. agribusiness or sweatshops than equal access to economic resources. (See chapter 11, "Responding to Sweatshops.")

The underlying view of human beings in this argument is individualistic and universalistic. That is, the ideal world is a single community composed of all the individuals who make it up. Although diversity of individuals is prized, existing communities of people—familial, ethnic, and religious—play no role except to contribute individuals to the new pluralism.

There is much in the biblical heritage that leads in this direction. Primitive Christianity, especially, cut against established community identities, calling people into the new reality, the church where there was neither Jew nor Gentile, neither male nor female, neither slave nor free. Extending this ideal for the church to the whole world, the goal can now be depicted as a world that has abolished all antecedent identities in the new one, which is enriched by all the diversities brought into it but also transcends them all.

Nevertheless, many Christians experience problems with this vision. Not all people want to give up their special ties to those who share their ethnicity and religious culture. Jews and Native Americans are among the most vociferous objectors, but ethnic and religious ties are important to most people. To condemn all of this because we Christians have a different set of values may not express Christian love. Imposing our ideal for the church on the public life of the world is likely to be felt by others as Christian imperialism.

An alternative Christian vision, which allows for continuing diversity of peoples and cultures, is the world as a community of communities, each of which in turn is a community of communities. This requires that each of the subcommunities has concern for the common good of all, as well as for the good of its own people. But it recognizes the contribution to the common good of the special caring that people have for their own families and for the larger communities of which these are a part.

Communities require some kind of boundaries. Not all of these are geographical, and even those that are geographical may be quite porous. But the elimination of borders is not part of this vision. Within a community, people accept a responsibility for each other that is more immediate and practical than the responsibility they take for humanity as a whole. They require structures in order to exercise this responsibility. Some of these communities require political governments; these cannot function without geographical borders.

The issue in this Christian perspective is not whether borders are acceptable but what decisions are to be made about restrictions on movement across them. Should capital, goods, and people move freely across them, or should the governments involved control these movements? In the past the United States has welcomed capital and labor while restricting goods. At present the tendency is toward ever-freer movement of capital and goods but restricted movement of people. Are these acceptable policies? Decisions should be made for the sake of the national community, but also with the common good of the whole world in view.

The emphasis on all the earth as belonging to all its people, on the other hand, supports continuing policies of free movement of capital and goods, while adding that of free movement of people. Other Christians believe that this global market concentrates wealth—and therefore also power—in fewer and fewer hands, destroys urgently needed human communities, and leads to radically unsustainable practices. They favor restrictions on the movement of capital, goods, and people, so as to strengthen the ability of people in national and subnational communities to participate in shaping their own destinies. These are issues for further discussion among Christians.

Clearly, in wrestling with these questions, the Christian should be guided by love. This has a double character and expression. Love functions as an immediate response to the one who is present, especially the one who is in greatest need. Love also functions to guide reflection about the wide range of consequences of every action over time and space. Sometimes acting spontaneously to satisfy the expressed desire of another individual may work against the common good viewed over time. Many of the most difficult decisions facing the Christian are occasioned by this tension.

If the emphasis is placed on the immediate expression of love to the individual before us, it is difficult indeed to justify refusing entrance to this country to one who will personally benefit by it. If the emphasis is placed on concern for the whole community over time and throughout the world, arguments can be made for three positions:

- Admit into our country any who want to come.
- Continue to restrict immigration, perhaps more than at present, and to do what can humanely be done to limit it to legal channels.
- Restrict immigration, but consider some particular arguments against closing the border with Mexico.

Supporters of each of these positions confront their distinct problems. Those who support open borders must propose ways of dealing with the disruptions that would result and alleviating the hardships these disruptions would cause. They should also respond to the concerns about total population and environment. Finally, they should clarify the full implications of the principle that the earth is the Lord's for the economic system that should accompany open borders.

Arguments for Restricting Borders

Those who defend restricting immigration need to show that, despite the apparent cruelty of this policy in relation to individuals who are denied admittance, it is beneficial to our own country and at least compatible with the common good of the whole world. Hence we must review, from a Christian perspective, the reasons that have led to favoring such restrictions.

The first argument is that people need a relatively homogeneous society and that the ethnic diversity of immigrants threatens homogeneity. This argument may make sense for some societies, such as Japan. But the United States has a different history and should continue to engage in a different experiment, that of a truly multiethnic nation. We do not know whether this experiment will succeed, but we do know that a monolithic Euro-American society can only be oppressive to many of the nation's inhabitants. A Christian may at most argue that immigration should be so controlled that the increase of diversity should be gradual, so that society can adjust successfully.

The second argument is that the rapid influx of new workers limits the improvement of conditions for workers already here, whereas restrictions on immigration make improvement possible. According to Roy Beck, the reduced rates of immigration from 1925 to 1965 had the effect of tightening labor markets. "Sweatshops virtually disappeared, black Americans finally got the chance to enter the industrial economy in major numbers, and most Americans eventually achieved a middle-class economic status during this era."[2] Of course, such changes have multiple causes, and Beck cannot demonstrate how much of the improvement was due to reduced immigration. But there can be little doubt that while the increasing availability of cheap labor often benefits employers and consumers, it impedes efforts to raise standards for workers.

The third argument stems from global consideration of the population-consumption problem. This was spelled out above. As long as countries are able to export surplus population, they are not likely to be motivated enough to work for population stability by other means, and the global population explosion will not be checked. Furthermore, the increased population of high-consumption countries such as the United States is a far more serious problem for the planet than that of low-consumption countries.

This is an important point. On the other hand, Christians cannot be satisfied to deal with this problem simply by denying other countries a safety valve for their excessive population growth. This should be accompanied by assisting these countries to provide a livelihood for their own people and by supporting their efforts to improve birth control practices. We should also make sincere efforts to reduce our own consumption and shift from our present national quest for endless growth to a goal of sufficiency and a sustainable life system. (See chapter 16, "The Global Population Crisis.") Apart from this larger pattern of effort, keeping out those who seek to solve acute economic problems by entering the United States takes on the character of selfishness that its opponents ascribe to it.

A fourth argument has considerable political importance but cannot be decisive for Christians: that immigrants are costly to taxpayers. Others reply that, overall, they at least pay their way in taxes. Nationally they pay their way through federal taxes, but taxes paid by them to some states, such as California, fall short of their cost to those states. If so, then special assistance from the federal treasury to those states may be in order. But Christians will not support either free immigration or restrictions on such grounds, unless the problem looms far larger than is now the case. We support instead paying what taxes are needed to meet the basic needs of all the inhabitants of our nation.

What Means of Enforcement Can Christians Support?

Those Christians who adopt the systemic expression of love and also find the arguments for restricting immigration persuasive must face the question of what these restrictions should be. Do they support present law and enforcement procedures? Do they support the Jordan Commission's[3] proposals to reduce immigration by one-third to one-half? Or do they have their own policy proposals to make? At present we commend the Jordan Commission's report as the most balanced and humane proposal now realistically before us as a nation.

Setting limits for legal entry into the country and defining priorities is relatively easy. Much more difficult is preventing persons from entering the country without documents or staying on when visas expire. At present most of the attention is focused on the former task although, as noted earlier, more than half the now undocumented residents have entered the country legally.

While immigration issues are not specific to any one country, border control seems to focus on the Mexican border. Efforts to stop the flow of would-be, undocumented immigrants across that border fail to achieve their objective, and intensified efforts add more to suffering than to effective enforcement. Although Christians who think in systemic terms cannot but acquiesce in the imposition of some suffering in pursuit of the common good, they must oppose policies that increase suffering with little compensatory gain to the common good. In short, the militarization of the border is not an acceptable strategy of enforcement.

The Immigration Reform and Control Act of 1986, which curtailed the possibility of employment and granted amnesty to those who had already settled here, was a far more appropriate approach than the militarization of the border. If work were not available, the number who would try to enter would decline sharply. This too would inflict hardship on some, both the would-be workers and those who now employ them, but it would be much less inhumane than what is now happening at the border. Furthermore, it would discourage both those overstaying their visas and those crossing the border without documents. Attempts to prevent border crossing by force could be greatly reduced if not eliminated altogether.

Thus far this policy has not worked, for the reasons cited above. More serious efforts to enforce it are possible, and these would be preferable to the militarization of the border. But the more basic problem is that efforts to reduce the "pull" factor while leaving the "push" factor untouched are never likely to suffice. When conditions in Latin America are sufficiently miserable for political or economic reasons, the difficulty of obtaining work in the United States will not stop the effort to enter. Any effort to enforce employer sanction should be accompanied by heightened efforts to address the problems that lead people to leave their homes in other countries.

Some have proposed that all of us carry identification that would indicate whether we have the right to work in this country. This would have to take a form that is difficult to counterfeit. Others regard this as an appalling infringement on individual rights. However, in a culture in which we are accustomed to carrying various sorts of identification, this would not be a terrible hardship. If the payment of this price by all of us would enable the nation to enforce its laws with much less violence, we should consider it seriously.

On the other hand, if we judge that the price of enforcing the law, by whatever means, exceeds the benefits, then we should accept the fact that for practical purposes we have an open border with Mexico. Remembering that much of the West was settled earlier by Mexicans and then taken from Mexico largely by force, we might consider that Mexicans have a particular right to enter freely. The resources we now use to control immigration across this border could then be shifted to assimilating the increased number of immigrants and easing the economic hardship of those adversely affected by this immigration. This need not mean that we open ourselves to unlimited immigration from all sources.

Where Does This Leave Us?

We should not expect all Christians to agree on this issue. Some will continue to work for restrictions on immigration, and others will seek to ease or remove them. Both approaches benefit some and hurt others. We should be particularly concerned for those who are hurt. Whatever policy we adopt, we should keep in mind the global problem of excessive pressure on the life-support system of Earth and do what we can to slow the growth of both population and per capita consumption by the affluent.

We share commitment to welcoming the strangers who are in our midst, learning from them, and working to create a multiethnic society in which all have a place of integrity and full participation. Depending on our judgment, some of us may decide that this welcome will not extend to employment of those who circumvent our laws. But we will strongly oppose the denial of education and health care to their children.

This discussion illustrates the difficulty of arriving at a shared Christian view on some issues. Even when we agree that we want to act out of love for all, we may differ as to whether this places our treatment of the needy individual above systemic considerations of the common good. We may differ in our judgment of the importance of local communities in relation to the global one. We may also differ in our assessment of the amount of evil necessarily inflicted in the process of enforcing our laws.

We may also disagree in our visions of the common good. In this case, we may disagree in our judgments of the seriousness of the ecological crisis and in our evaluations of the currently dominant neoliberal global economy. That requires additional study and reflection.

But there is much on which Christians agree. We can agree that our immigration policies should express love for the people of the countries from which immigrants come, for those already in this country, especially the poor, and for immigrants and would-be immigrants themselves. We can agree that we should work toward a world in which no one is forced to emigrate because of political injustice, economic desperation, or ecological degradation. This means that we cannot be complacent about the enormous disruptions all around the world—political, economic and ecological—that threaten only to become greater in this new century and that force tens of millions of people to leave their homelands and seek resettlement in other countries that are ill-equipped to provide for them. Nor can we be complacent about the harshness with which refugees and immigrants are often treated in the lands into which they move, including our own.

VI. WHAT WE CAN DO

We should become increasingly informed and concerned about what is happening in the countries from which people want to emigrate in large numbers. Especially when policies promoted by our own government are responsible for their desire to leave their homes, we should demand change in those policies. We should support all those who are working wisely to improve conditions in those countries so that people can find fulfilling lives in their own nations.

We can agree that those who enter this country legally should be helped to adjust to life here and treated respectfully and appreciatively, first as guests and then as fellow citizens. And we can agree that the means we use to prevent others from entering the country outside the law or remaining when their visas expire should be humane ones that respect the human rights of those whose presence in our country we disallow.

Congregations can pay attention to the difficulties faced by recent immigrants in their communities. Sometimes they can provide tutoring in English or arrange for assistance in dealing with the Immigration and Naturalization Service and other government agencies.

Many congregations share their buildings with congregations made up of immigrants who want services in their own languages. This provides opportunities for other expressions of friendship and support.

In the aftermath of September 11, 2001, immigrants from Muslim countries often suffer harassment. Churches can express solidarity with them and undertake to learn more of their faith and culture.

Discussion Questions

1. Does the Christian faith justify restricting immigration into our country?
2. If so, what criteria should Christians support for selecting those whom we admit?
3. If not, what is our responsibility to those already here who may be disadvantaged by the inflow of new people?
4. Is concern about population growth a legitimate Christian consideration in determining immigration policy?

To Learn More

Heaven's Door: Immigration Policy and the American Economy by George Borjas (Princeton, N.J.: Princeton University Press, 1999) is the best introduction to the economics of immigration. See also Roy Beck's *The Case against Immigration* (New York: W. W. Norton, 1996). *The Handbook of International Migration: The American Experience*, edited by Charles Hirschman and others (New York: Russell Sage Foundation, 1999) is the best introduction to noneconomic aspects of migration to the United States. See also the two-part series on "Who Should Get In?" in *New York Review of Books*, Nov. 19 and Dec. 20, 2001. The only book-length introduction to the Christian ethics of immigration policy is Dana Wilbanks' *Re-Creating America: The Ethics of U.S. Immigration and Refugee Policy in a Christian Perspective* (Nashville: Abingdon Press, in cooperation with the Churches' Center for Theology and Public Policy, 1996).

10

Do Corporations Serve the Human Family?

James Hinton was an effective CEO of a medium-sized public corporation specializing in kitchen equipment. He was also a committed Christian and he tried to bring his faith to bear in the way he ran the company. As a result of his fairness and real concern for those who worked for him, the company had high morale and strong worker loyalty. Suppliers and retailers were glad to do business with it. Because he insisted that wherever his factories were located, management would be good citizens and environmentally responsible, the public relations of the company were excellent. He had also established a good record of profitability.

Nevertheless, he was under pressure from his stockholders. Competitors had increased their profits faster than he had. Some of his major stockholders were pressing him to close unionized factories in the United States and move production to Mexico. They also urged that new technology justified reducing middle management positions. Taking such steps would increase profits and raise the price of the stock.

Hinton had bent to the new realities. He had persuaded unions to moderate their demands because of the danger that factories would be closed if costs rose further. He had stopped replacing middle management who retired. But he resisted closing factories on which whole communities depended and laying off managers who had worked faithfully for the company for years. The human costs were simply too high.

Now he knew there was a good chance that he would be replaced. To most of his stockholders, higher profits and stock prices were more important than what happened to employees. He decided he would stand his ground and be voted out, if that was his destiny, with his principles intact. Sadly, he reflected, his good conscience would not help his employees.

I. INTRODUCTION

The opening story illustrates a profound tension. Corporate leadership consists of all kinds of people, many of them persons of conscience concerned for the good of humanity and the future of Earth. But the present global corporate system exerts pressures rooted in other concerns. Many corporations submit to these pressures and commit themselves to little else than the bottom line. A few resist in various ways. The behavior of corporations and the system that presses them in a negative direction play a large role in determining the future of humanity.

Indeed, many argue that corporations have become the most important institutions in the world. Of the hundred largest economies in the world, half are nations and half are corporations. The role of corporations in the United States is enormous. Incorporated businesses account for well over two-thirds of the U.S. economy's privately produced income. In manufacturing, transportation, public utilities, and finance, corporations do almost all of the nation's business. In trade and construction, they do about half the total business.

Corporations exercise vast influence on public policy. Through their control of the media, they largely shape our knowledge of, and opinions about, what is going on in the world. Tens of millions of people work for them and have their lives profoundly shaped by the internal policies of corporations. Most middle-class Americans have investments in corporations, and we collectively put pressure on these corporations to maximize profits and growth, even at the cost of other values. It is past time for Christians to study and appraise these institutions, both their role in the larger society and their effect on the lives of those who work in them.

Two other chapters in this book deal with closely related topics. One is on globalization and the other on the sweatshops that flourish in a global economy. This chapter focuses instead on corporations as institutions in their relationship to the wider society and to their employees.

Part 2 of this chapter surveys the history of the corporation and its rise to dominance. It distinguishes two types of corporations in today's world and notes their different social roles. The "stakeholder" corporation is widespread in Japan and Europe, but the dominant American form is the "stockholder" corporation. Part 2 concludes with comments on the strengths and weaknesses of stockholder corporations and the appropriate role of government.

Part 3 focuses on the internal organization of the stockholder corporation and its effects on its employees. At present these corporations still tend to value things above people, but some farsighted managers are finding ways in which the relative value can be shifted to the benefit of employees. National legislation can encourage this shift.

Part 4 identifies and applies some Christian commitments that are relevant to evaluating corporations. Part 5 then proposes actions that Christians might take. Some of these actions can be taken now by corporate leaders; others require changes in national and international policies.

II. THE ROLE OF THE CORPORATION IN SOCIETY

History of the Corporation

The modern corporation is a descendant of the joint-stock trading companies that emerged to finance the seaborne empires of England and Holland in the seventeenth century. The British East India Company and the Hudson's Bay Company are examples. They had the practical appeal of limited liability for shareholders and a guarantee of "perpetual succession" beyond the lifetime of a single owner. Not until the nineteenth century were corporations much involved with industrial manufacturing. In the United States in 1800 there were only 335 profit-seeking corporations, and nearly all of these had been incorporated in the previous decade. Most of these were formed for the construction of turnpikes, bridges, and canals and for the establishment of banks, insurance companies, and fire brigades. The first American corporation involved in large-scale manufacturing was a textile firm, the Boston Manufacturing Company, established in Waltham, Massachusetts, in 1813. By 1830 it had only seventy-six stockholders.

The rise of a market economy and what was called the industrial revolution was a development of great complexity of which the appearance of the corporation was one facet. The decline of feudal obligations, the growth of natural science, new inventions, and the movement of people from farm to cities all played a part. Gradually, over centuries, there occurred what Sir Henry Maine called a movement from the feudal "status society" to the modern "contract society." In subtle ways the lust for money, condemned by Christians as greed, became less of a sin, and the striving of aristocratic nobles for glory and honor became less of a virtue. A number of eighteenth-century thinkers encouraged "innocent" moneymaking and commerce as a practical diversion from the war-making tendencies of nationalist rulers. The movement toward individualism, often associated with the Reformation and the Renaissance, was a backdrop for the invention of the corporation.

In 1776, the year of the Declaration of Independence, Adam Smith published his *Wealth of Nations*. His notion of an "invisible hand" guiding and protecting self-regulating markets is still quoted (and misquoted) against arguments for government regulation of markets and corporations, notwithstanding that today's corporations are vastly different from the joint-stock companies of Smith's day. Indeed, Adam Smith thought the business corporation had no significant future.

The U.S. Constitution (1787) is silent on corporations; but the U.S. Supreme Court gave a great boost to the position of corporations in American society, beginning in the 1870s and 1880s, sometimes quoting Adam Smith in its opinions. It developed this support in a somewhat ironic way.

The Fourteenth Amendment was adopted in 1868 to protect the rights of those freed from slavery by the Thirteenth Amendment (1865). It said, among other things, that no state shall "deprive any person of life, liberty, or property, without due process of law." The amendment proved to be of little help to black citizens, but the Court defined "persons" to include corporations, and under its doctrine of "substantive due process," the liberty and property of corporations were significantly protected from state regulation. Business corporations, even monopolies, flourished.

Entering the twentieth century, progressives challenged the new order of corporate dominance. Many Christians were convinced that Christian values were violated by the new dominance of corporate moneymaking, influence, and power, and through the Social Gospel movement, they supported progressive causes. New federal legislation, most notably in the area of railroad regulation and pure food and drug laws, was enacted. Yet the Supreme Court continued to serve as a corporation veto voice over needed social reforms involving the exploitation of both adult and child labor.

Ultimately, the negative social conditions fostered during this era of corporate dominance brought the era itself to a close. Workers could not afford to purchase all of the goods being produced by the corporate engine. Limitations in consumer purchasing power contributed as much to the Great Depression as did the crash of an unregulated stock market.

From its earliest beginnings, the labor movement in the United States existed primarily to improve the economic condition of workers, rather than to engage in class struggle to alter the form of government or to promote socialism. While its success in winning higher wages, shorter hours, more vacations, easier work rules, and fringe benefits such as pensions and health insurance was very limited until the 1930s, its goal of "business unionism" rarely wavered. American unions thus were the opposite of labor movements in many foreign countries, where unions have come to run major political parties, like Britain's Labour party, and have waged the class struggle for major political reforms. Even so, American labor organizations like the American Federation of Labor (AFL), founded in 1881, and the Congress of Industrial Organizations (CIO), formed in 1935, were influential proponents of legislative reforms (especially the Wagner Act of 1935) and helped change government attitudes toward labor and management.

Franklin Roosevelt's New Deal of the 1930s reshuffled America's economic rules. The federal government, previously the enemy of collective bargaining, became its greatest advocate. New regulations were established over the stock market, banking, and virtually every other corporate enterprise. Big Government, as well as an emerging Big Labor, effectively became countervailing forces to Big Business. Roosevelt also forced a showdown with the U.S. Supreme Court that resulted in the latter surrendering its procorporate role. By the mid-twentieth century, it appeared that the ugly aspects of corporate capitalism had at last found a solution in government regulation.

Following World War II, the industrialized world lay in ruins except for the United States, whose economy came to dominate global markets as never before. In order to recreate a healthy world economy, the United States helped defeated enemies get back on their feet. Their recovery was aided by the fact that many of their old, obsolete factories had been destroyed in the war, so that their rebuilt industries were state of the art. In this postwar world the United States steadily moved toward global free trade. Over the decades, as the economies of Japan and Europe recovered, American corporations once more encountered serious foreign competition. In this changing scene, the multinational corporation also emerged as having distinct competitive advantages. It owed allegiance to no nation but primarily to the goal of maximizing profits, which often led to establishing operations where wages are low and governmental regulations weak. In this new global market, governmental countervailing forces were less effective.

Within the United States pressures to deregulate the economy increased. Labor unions were weakened. The economic downturn following the end of the Cold War pushed the United States further in the direction of reversing trends in place since the New Deal. The logic of Adam Smith was used to justify the painful dislocations wrought by the new global free market. Worldwide, gross exploitation of labor and the environment began to occur in ways reminiscent of America in the late nineteenth and early twentieth centuries.

A century ago, there were calls for government to become a countervailing force to corporate power. Today, given the lack of any meaningful world government, there is no comparable expectation, although organizations like the International Labor Organization (ILO) provide some pressure for change. In the absence of global governmental organizations, only national governments can protect workers' rights and the environment and meet the needs of those disinherited by dynamic economic changes that treat human beings as just another expendable commodity. Corporations may be expected to counter by pleading the necessity to remain competitive in the unregulated global market.

Today corporations have taken on lives of their own, with their own goals, objectives, and values, which often govern their behavior more than the people who run them. The drive for corporate profit, market share, growth, and power is now a concern worldwide. "Globalization" is the term applied—often pejoratively—to this new situation. Multinationals are corporations that coordinate their activities with a large number of related entities throughout the world, produce in many places with a complex network of suppliers and customers, and are involved in many different kinds of transactions internationally. They are growing in power and influence at the expense of individuals and governments around the world.

Many of the world's most successful multinational corporations—whether Japanese, European, or American—are engaged in a fundamental shift in corporate organizational strategy. Each is downsizing, trimming its in-house operations down to its core "competencies," and contracting with other, mostly smaller firms to do much of its manufacturing, often in lower-wage countries. The corporations thereby save money and undermine the bargaining power of workers.

As technological change has become more deeply science-based, more corporations have come to realize they no longer are capable of generating all the research and development of new products needed to remain competitive. These pressures have pushed firms into cooperative research and development ventures even with their competitors. Complex networks of business alliances have multiplied so rapidly and pervasively that the system has come to be called "alliance capitalism."

Stakeholder and Stockholder Capitalism

Given the importance of corporations for all sectors of society, we should consider the groups that have an especially large stake in their ways of functioning. The major stakeholders, in addition to stockholders and managers, are employees, customers, suppliers, neighbors, and society as a whole as represented by government. In Europe and Japan the form of economy that has developed around corporations is called *stakeholder* capitalism. Obviously, corporations have a commitment to those who have invested money in them, but in this system they are understood to have responsibilities to their other stakeholders as well.

Where this system prevails, corporations are expected to promote social harmony. Europe also places a high premium on social welfare. High profits have been assigned less importance than economic stability. Moreover, European and Japanese policies are intended to limit hostile and foreign takeovers.

Where stakeholder capitalism prevails, largely as a result of the activity of strong unions, there is an excellent public safety net for employees. Corporations have much less freedom to dismiss employees, those who are dismissed are buoyed up by unemployment insurance as long as four years at up to 90 percent of their last wages, and a great deal of retraining is available. Critics of stakeholder capitalism argue that this system cannot compete in the global market. Yet in at least four European countries—Austria, the Netherlands, Ireland, and Denmark—the economy is growing faster than in the United States, unemployment is lower, and exports are increasing.

A fundamentally different understanding of the corporation and its role in society underlies the *stockholder* capitalism of America. Here a firm's fundamental purpose is to make profits for its investors or shareholders. The firm has minimal legal obligations to employees and/or to the communities in which its facilities are located. Moreover, in the United States, a business corporation is regarded as a commodity that is bought and sold like any other commodity, without regard for the social consequences of such transactions. Waves of leveraged buyouts and corporate takeovers in the 1980s and 1990s were extreme examples of this mentality.

Even in stockholder capitalism the question of stakeholders is important. In this case the controlling stakeholders are the executives and managers, together with the major stockholders. These people make the major decisions. These corporate stakeholders must take some account of other stakeholders, especially as these are represented by government regulations and taxes. In general, corporations have seen regulatory bodies as restricting their freedom and have worked for deregulation.

On the other hand, corporations do appreciate the immediate benefits they can gain from government policies. Accordingly corporations have sought to make governmental interests consonant with their own by supplying much of the money and strategy used in election campaigns. If the candidate receives millions in money and services from General Motors, then he or she will think twice before supporting legislation opposed by General Motors. Further, knowing that members of Congress are usually understaffed, corporations provide lobbyists and experts who perform many essential services for legislators, such as providing detailed analysis of provisions of a bill and drafting new legislation—with the corporation's interest uppermost in their minds. "He who pays the piper calls the tune." Few public interest organizations can afford to provide comparable resources.

Corporations know that government expenditures in infrastructure and education are important for their well-being. Some economists believe that it was large public sector investments in the late 1940s and 1950s—in roads, infrastructure, education, research and development, and so forth—that built the foundation for our great success of the past decade. Unfortunately, corporations in general have not sufficiently recognized their long-term interest in such investments. The problem is that their payoff is realized in decades, not years, whereas corporations typically aim at profits in the short term and try to divert public expenditures into areas providing benefits sooner.

Corporations have become highly sophisticated in assessing the power of stakeholder groups and in resisting actions against corporate interests. Employees are major stakeholders. In the United States, corporations have seen organized labor—unions—as restricting corporate freedom of action with respect to wages, safety issues, and so on. As a group, they have worked to prevent the organization of unions and to weaken them, once organized. In the past quarter century they have been remarkably successful.

If we broaden the definition of the stake in corporations, then many types of stakeholders emerge who are less visible. Humanity as a whole has a huge stake in the way corporations in the aggregate shape society. At present, the forces at work in our economic system tend to divide people into categories: those who benefit from its workings, an elite who can sell skills that are highly valued in the market; a much larger group who "serve" the economy in humdrum jobs that offer few chances of personal growth and little more than a basic remuneration; and the vast "underclass," sometimes called the "disposable people." The latter include those in the United States, perhaps 20 percent of the population, who live below the poverty line, and the millions in the countries of the South who live in destitution.

These poor and destitute people have an enormous stake in corporate policies that hurt them—through actions that limit governments' ability to help them, through worsening of their natural environment and exploitation of their natural resources, and through exploiting them as cheap labor. The poor have potential power in their numbers, but they can exercise it only if they work together. Today there are populist movements in many countries that undertake to gain power through solidarity.

Planet Earth is a stakeholder. Its life-giving resources are being depleted, and those who seek short-term exploitation rather than long-term compatibility with Earth are despoiling it. From the perspective of humanity as a whole, the failure of most corporations to take this stakeholder into account may be their most important failure.

Environmental policy is an area of continuous struggle. Environmental organizations have become effective spokespersons for Earth and have had some success in influencing corporate action through public opinion and governmental regulations. There are intense struggles all over the world, often against corporations, for the preservation of parts of the environment. In order to blunt the effects of pressures from the environmental movement, many corporations engage in sophisticated, but misleading, public relations and use their power to influence government policy in ways that enable unsustainable use of resources to continue. Earth continues to suffer from the corporate quest for quick profits.

We have written about these tensions between stockholder capitalism and its nonstockholding stakeholders in terms of dominant trends. In general, the effort to serve stockholders by increasing profits trumps concerns for humanity as a whole, the poor, and the natural environment. But this need not be the whole story and in fact is not. As corporations, including stockholder corporations, become more dominant in the world, more of their leaders are reflecting about their responsibility.

Many corporate leaders want limits placed on the freedom to exploit people. Many have policies against the use of child labor, for example. Many commit themselves to conforming to the laws of their host countries around the world, paying the prevailing wage, and observing health and safety regulations. One difficulty is that they contract out most of their production, and although they require their contractors to commit to observing the rules, there has been little success in enforcing them. Nevertheless, many corporations make sincere efforts to avoid the worst abuses of the system. Some corporate leaders are responding positively to pressures by consumers to have their factories monitored by local nongovernmental organizations.

Genuine environmental concerns may play a still larger role in emerging corporate policy. Several leading corporations, including Royal Dutch Shell and Ford, have withdrawn from the organization they helped to set up to oppose efforts to slow global warming. Many are genuinely trying to reduce pollution and to use resources more efficiently. For example, the Mirant Corporation of Atlanta has committed $50 million over ten years to monitor and reduce greenhouse gases in its production of power.

There are important efforts to show that environmental responsibility need not conflict with corporate interests. The Rocky Mountain Institute, established by Amory and Hunter Lovins, has long been a leader in encouraging corporations to recognize that their profits need not depend on unsustainable exploitation of resources. For example, it persuaded a number of electric utilities that encouraging the use of more efficient appliances, thus slowing the increase of usage of electricity, actually improved profits. Today it promotes what it calls "natural capitalism" on a broader basis, and many companies are interested. This entails the recognition that whereas in the past labor was scarce and natural resources plentiful, it is now natural resources that are in short supply. In the future, the Lovinses argue, profits will be made by those who economize in their use of these resources.

Some privately owned corporations have made dramatic adjustments for the sake of Earth. Ray C. Anderson, founder and chairman of Interface, Inc., has led his company, which manufactures carpet tiles, to emphasize recycling in such a way as to be environmentally sustainable. He has shown that this does not prevent the company from operating profitably.

Strengths of Corporations

Corporations serve the public in many ways. They have been the driving force in the development of new products and services that have led to a steady improvement in the quality of life over the past two centuries. They have increased the amount of capital available for investment. They have provided millions of jobs and a comfortable retirement for many, employees and investors alike.

Four strengths of corporations deserve to be noted.

Economies of scale. In many industries, economies of scale have been realized from the use of automated tools and interchangeable parts, the breakdown of complex processes into simple repetitive operations, the specialization of function and division of labor, and the use of computer-aided design, production, or analysis. Harvesting these economies of scale often requires relatively large entities making relatively large investments.

Ability to raise capital from a large number of investors. The large investment required to realize these economies of scale is rarely possible for individual proprietors. Corporations, selling shares of stock, can raise the large sums required. This is possible because of the legal separation between ownership and responsibility for the company's operations. Thus risk and reward are limited by the size of the investment by the stockholder. Further, the corporation's continuity is largely unaffected by its ownership, because shares are easily transferred from one person to another and most shareholders are not involved in governance.

Global perspective. The larger corporations are often multinational. The chapter on globalization indicates that there are problems resulting from this. But there are also strengths. Freeing themselves from parochial perspectives, the leaders of large corporations can think in global terms about both the present and the future. Their global interests often favor international cooperation and peace rather than ethnic and national rivalries.

Transcending social prejudices. Precisely because corporations value people for their ability as workers, they sometimes lead in overcoming social prejudices. In South Africa transnational corporations sometimes led in breaking down apartheid policies. Today in the United States some corporations treat their gay and lesbian employees more justly than do most churches and government agencies, providing them medical insurance coverage and family benefits for their partners.

Weaknesses of Corporations

Short-term perspective. Corporations must show quarterly performance improvements or their investors may abandon them. They pay lip service to long-range planning, but often it is an academic exercise with little influence on the company's day-to-day behavior. Most firms seek to exploit limited resources in the short term, trusting future generations to find alternatives.

The short-term perspective and the failure to invest for the long term derive from personal considerations as well. Many executives and managers are in their positions of power and influence for a very short time—perhaps three to five years—and are unwilling to make investment decisions whose payoff will occur after they have left their positions.

Adversarial relationships. While most evident in the justice system, adversarial relationships also characterize relations between management and labor and underlie competition in the marketplace. Efforts to curb corporate freedom of action for the public good are also adversarial in nature, represented in agencies like the Securities and Exchange Commission (SEC), the Financial Accounting Standards Board (FASB), the Federal Reserve, and the Internal Revenue Service (IRS). Adversarial relationships pit one side against the other, when working together may produce a better outcome for both sides.

Of course, not all corporate relations are adversarial. The alliance capitalism mentioned earlier shows that corporations can cooperate with one another. However, they do so in order to compete more effectively against other corporations, and the alliances often make corporations stronger in their adversarial relations with governments.

Focus on individualism; deification of the market. In the United States most people support the freedom of the individual (person or corporation) to pursue his or her own interests in as unfettered a manner as possible. "Each to his own and the devil take the hindmost." The other side of that belief in individual freedom—responsibility to the community and especially to those at the bottom—is all too often ignored. Many Americans also believe that "the market"—the "invisible hand"—will correctly synthesize a proper "public interest" from the self-interest of millions of individuals. This attitude is prominent in corporate boardrooms. During an interview for the presidency of a university, one of the authors of this chapter was roundly criticized by a trustee—a developer—for taking any other view of the "public interest" than the result of all self-interests. Many economic thinkers recognize the need for some regulation to assure the proper operation of markets.

Displacement of costs. There are two ways in which corporations displace costs onto society. Cities perceive benefits in having large corporations located there, and corporations can take advantage of this to gain subsidies and tax breaks from governments. Examples include the building of a stadium, the provision of tax breaks for the owners of a sports team, and similar incentives to attract corporate headquarters. We recently saw such a competition when Boeing decided to move from Seattle. In such cases, costs of doing business are shifted from corporations to taxpayers.

The other practice of cost displacement involves the almost universal practice of externalizing costs. At present, the cost of producing a product is figured on the costs of the raw materials and labor that go into it, plus its share of capital investments and overhead. The cost does not include depletion of the raw materials, the product's effects upon the environment, its disposal, and the effect upon people of producing and using the product. Life-cycle costing is a way of taking all of these additional factors into consideration. The price of the product has to be higher, but the taxes that would be based on these costs to society would be used to ameliorate the long-term negative effects. This would be a realistic way of making a corporation's activities pay their own way.

Contribution to income gap. In the past few decades the gap between the rich and the poor in the United States has grown greater. Stockholder corporations have led in creating this gap. The widening of the gap accelerated in the late '90s. In 1995 the average corporate CEO received compensation 141 times as great as the average factory worker. By 1999 that ratio had increased to 475–1.

Governmental Responsibility for Corporations

Because of stockholder capitalism's reduced emphasis on the good of the whole community, the public safety net for the down and out has been seriously damaged, unions have been seriously weakened, environmental deterioration continues at a rapid pace, and corporations can do just about as they please. Even in this economy, however, government has responsibility for the common good. Although corporations have increasingly influenced government in the exercise of its powers, government agencies still affect corporations extensively. The Securities and Exchange Commission regulates the stock market. The Justice Department enforces antitrust laws. Many laws designed to protect health and safety and the environment restrict what corporations can do.

In principle, governments have a still more fundamental role in relation to corporations. Governments charter them. They have the legal power to modify or revoke those charters when corporate actions work against the common good. They are reluctant to do so because the charters lead to benefits for the governments as well as for investors in the corporations. Further, if one state revokes a charter, the corporation will find another that will grant it. Many of America's largest corporations are chartered in Delaware because, among the fifty states, Delaware places the fewest restrictions on them. Under globalization, it may be possible for a corporation chartered in the United States to become chartered in another country if the other country offers fewer restrictions. On the other hand, a multinational corporation chartered in the United States has far more access to the corridors of power than does one chartered outside the First World.

III. CORPORATIONS' TREATMENT OF EMPLOYEES

Dehumanizing Pressures in Corporate Life

Once they have established the corporation's mission, senior executives have two primary responsibilities. They allocate resources, and they oversee the employees to make sure that resources are efficiently used. Their success is normally measured by the amount of corporate profit. Where labor is expensive, as in the United States, corporations invest in physical capital to reduce the amount of labor needed. One result is that employees are often treated simply as means to corporate ends, rather than as persons whose well-being is important in itself. This can lead to acute insecurity at all levels of employment.

At the top, the senior executive level, the expectation is leadership of the corporation so that its profits, market share, value, and power increase. If the corporation fails to grow by these measures, the executive is likely to be out the door. Our opening story was of the struggle of a socially concerned executive in face of these pressures. In the real world, the chances are that he would lose his job, as did Kay R. Whitmore of Eastman Kodak in 1993. His directors wanted massive layoffs to improve profit margins; Whitmore strove to moderate these demands.

At the bottom, the unskilled level, a human being's only value to the large, stockholder-owned corporation is his or her physical labor. As machines replace this physical labor, the value of unskilled employees is further reduced, and they are often deprived of their ability to earn a living.

In the middle, at the highly skilled level, the situation is different. In today's competitive high-tech world, the technical genius is king. Who would have expected a "techie" like Bill Gates to become the richest human? Persons who can conceive new technical ideas on which the corporation can build are valued highly. They help set the strategic direction of a corporation. These people include executives and managers, marketing superstars, research and development people, internal consultants, and many of the technical geniuses who can see beyond the advancing frontier to the products and services of the future. They invent and design the product, and they also design the manufacturing system to produce it and its marketing system.

However, in this world of rapid technological progress, today's skills are often without value tomorrow. Only those who can keep up with advancing technology continue to be useful. Even highly skilled employees are subordinate to the corporation's need to move forward. Their career success depends on the answer to the question "What have you done for me *lately*?"

As corporations downsize and trim costs to maximize profits, the use of temporary employees has escalated. Temps receive from the corporation no long-term commitment or fringe benefits and often work on a part-time basis. Workers from agencies for temporary employment are overwhelmingly women.

In addition to insecurity, many employees suffer from discrimination. Despite important exceptions, corporate culture in the United States reflects, and sometimes exacerbates, the sexism and racism of the wider society. Women and persons from minority backgrounds remain badly underrepresented in the boardroom and in the upper echelons of management. The "glass ceiling" has not disappeared. Despite laws against sexual harassment and broad social agreement that it is unacceptable, such harassment continues to be widespread. Similarly, more or less overt racism often makes life within the corporation uncomfortable for persons from ethnic minorities, despite laws intended to end discrimination.

Hostile takeovers are an additional source of suffering. Socially responsible corporations are a popular target for such takeovers. A sad example is the takeover of Pacific Lumber Company by Charles Hurwitz. Pacific Lumber, a family-owned company, was highly responsible ecologically and committed to the well-being of its employees. Hurwitz saw that profits could be made by changing those policies and proceeded to do so.

Humanizing Developments within Corporations

Nevertheless, many corporate leaders are committed to humanizing their relations with employees. Most corporations have officers in charge of human resources, and their number and status is increasing. Our opening story was about a concerned and committed CEO. The story recognized the strength of the pressures against which he worked. The outcome was left uncertain. In fact, corporations differ greatly in the way they treat their employees. Some view themselves as living organisms, and management develops systems to support their people's idealism and creativity so that they may cocreate their enterprises.

Thirty years ago, retired AT&T executive Robert Greenleaf wrote a pamphlet, *The Servant as Leader*, to show how executives could contribute to a more caring society. He defined a servant leader as one who "makes sure that other people's highest priority needs are being served" so that they "become healthier, wiser, freer, more autonomous, more likely themselves to become servants." The servant leader also asks, "What is the effect on the least privileged in society?" Greenleaf's work has been influential. In 2001 several hundred corporate executives attended the Greenleaf Center's annual conference to share their experience, challenges, and successes in implementing servant leadership.

Interest in servant leadership, with its impressive concern for a variety of stakeholders, is greatest where those in position to influence policy are personally involved in the working of the corporation. For the most part, this occurs in smaller, privately owned corporations, although middle management in large publicly owned corporations also shows great interest. The personal commitment of CEOs and managers can make a large difference in the lives of people working for corporations within the parameters that now exist. It is possible to resist dehumanizing pressures and to develop business practices that are both humane and profitable.

The following sections will spell out further both the dehumanizing pressures operative in corporations and the ways in which concerned executives and managers can counter these pressures. The next pair of sections shows the dehumanizing effects of valuing machines above people and how this tendency is being countered. The third pair of sections deals with the negative aspects of the current scene, which is dominated by information technology, and possible humanizing responses.

Machines vs. People

The industrial revolution has been turning people into machines. Machines began to do far more physical work than people and became very expensive.

Accordingly, management sought ways to optimize the value of the machine at the expense of persons. Since people are adaptable and machines are not, people were asked to work the way the machine worked best, whether it was good for them or not. This culminated in the 1920s in the "scientific management" of Frederick Taylor.[1] Jobs were broken down into simple tasks. These were often automated, and when they were not, the person performing the job behaved much like a machine. This accelerated the de-skilling and dehumanization of people by industry begun early in the industrial revolution.

Taylor's theory of "scientific management" has affected the way corporations think about people and things, which influences the way they act. An important illustration is the way the Financial Accounting Standards Board (FASB) sets the accounting rules used by American business.[2] The FASB's rules count "things" (e.g., buildings, capital equipment, machine tools) as assets and expenditures for them as investments. Conversely, expenditures for people are expenses, not investments. The largest single expense for most organizations is payroll, that is, people.

This system operates according to these unwritten rules of business:

- Maximize the effective use of assets through investment.
- Minimize expenses by keeping them low.

Among other things, this means:

- Acquire useful things.
- Squeeze people out.

A recent study by Walker Information Inc. showed that three-fourths of all employees in the United States do not want to be with their present employers two years from now. Gary Kaplan of Kaplan and Associates commented that "we have communicated to the labor market this concept that people are expendable, that people are not much different from office supplies."

This dehumanization of production is especially manifest when a corporate farm in the Third World replaces peasant farmers with agricultural machinery. Not only do the individuals who are displaced suffer personally, but the local economy also suffers. The corporation profits rise, although the social and political costs may eventually reduce the profits.

Affirming People

Squeezing people out is called downsizing. There has been a great deal of this in recent years, but the widespread assumption that it increases profits is a doubtful one. We cannot replace the contributions that people make to corporations.

John Seely Brown tells of some studies done by anthropologists that illustrate the importance of people to the corporation.[3] What they found was that:

- There are policies and procedures that govern work processes.
- When workers were interviewed about the work processes, they described what they did in terms that matched the policies and procedures.
- When workers were observed doing their jobs, however, what they did bore only a superficial relationship to the policies and procedures and to what they said they did. There were uncountable departures that were made necessary by little quirks in the situations they faced.

In other words, workers adapted as needed in order to make sure the job got done well. Machines cannot do this.

Some corporations take advantage of the knowledge and wisdom embodied in their workers. For example, when Boeing was in danger of losing a crucial contract because of problems with its plane, management turned to workers for advice and help. The result was an improved product and a successful contract renewal.

During the last business recovery, many large corporations downsized in order to improve their profits and stock prices by "removing the fat." This strategy is seldom successful in the long term. Most already profitable businesses that downsized to further improve profits found the improvement short-lived. This is easy to understand. Once everyone is used 100 percent, a company has very little ability to take on new profit-making opportunities. The only way they can take on a new opportunity is by hiring and training new people, which is very costly and reduces the potential for added profits. Worse, if everyone is used 100 percent and anything goes wrong, customer service deteriorates. Poor customer service means decreased sales, which immediately leads to decreased profits.

There are, of course, times when loss of business forces a corporation to downsize. Some of the layoffs of the airline industry after September 11 were no doubt necessary. Yet corporations need to think more carefully about their responses to short-term reversals. Often the people laid off are in such programs as research and planning, which do not contribute to immediate profits. Companies that find a way to keep their people in a downturn often gain a significant competitive advantage that carries them to great heights when business enters an upswing.

Hallmark is an example.[4] Hallmark commits to keeping its people, but it doesn't promise them that they'll be able to stay in the job they feel they're best suited for. They shift people into marketing and sales, redoubling their efforts in those areas in order to gain back the business lost. Hallmark holds that bad economic times are a management problem and should not be solved on the backs of employees. Once the company is back on a growth path, people can go back to the jobs they want, but many find that the exposure they had during the hard times opened their eyes to new possibilities.

It is possible to think of people as investments rather than simply expenses. The idea of "human capital" already exists, applied chiefly to those persons with special skills who are most difficult to replace. But it has relevance to the entire labor force. It would not be impossible to include this idea in accounting.

Indeed, efforts have been made from time to time to implement human resource accounting (HRA). In HRA, transaction data are collected to show the "relationships" of these transactions to people—employees, customers, and so forth. Using HRA, for example, the cost of retaining and training an employee is far less than the cost of replacing him or her and training the replacement. This approach places investment value on people as well as on machines and buildings. Using HRA it is possible to obtain a value for the total human resource of a business and to measure the fluctuations in this value over time. Unfortunately, FASB has not accepted human resource accounting.

Dehumanizing Pressures in the Information Age

One great strength of the corporation is its contribution to the productivity of labor. The high standard of living enjoyed by most Americans is the result of many factors, but the growth of real wages as industrial productivity has improved is certainly one of them. Yet the quest for improved productivity has often contributed to the dehumanization of workers. To understand this phenomenon better and to show that, at least in the present situation, this dehumanization can be mitigated, we must consider the question of productivity more closely.

The industrial revolution brought productivity tools to the production process. The sewing machine made it possible for textile workers to produce much more per hour of labor. The development of power tools since that time has accelerated, evolving in the past two centuries to the giant five-axis lathes of the aerospace industry and the computer-aided tools used in nearly every business function today. The evolution of these tools carried with it changes in the way employees are used. Those experienced in the "old ways" lost economic power while those who knew the "new ways" gained it. Those cycles have shortened over the years with the acceleration of technological change. In agriculture and manufacturing, the introduction of power tools occurred steadily over at least two centuries, and the organizational and management changes and training they required have become routine.

Today the most important new power tools, which we call collectively "information technology," are designed to enhance the intellect. The current focus is on improving the productivity of management and services, but this has proved to be slower than expected. Investments in information technology have been high over the past few decades, but the expected productivity increases have been slow to appear. This is in part because we have not understood until recently how to make organizational and management changes and provide appropriate training in those sectors.

Why has work in the administrative and services areas been hard to understand? There is little question regarding the value of products versus the investment of labor, tools, and materials employed. But what is the value of a letter, a report, a meeting, or a telephone call? In fact, greater "productivity" at one level may induce lower "productivity" at a higher, more expensive one. For example, if a report usually produced once a month is now, with the help of information technology, produced weekly, then the reading time required of the supervisor quadruples.

There is another effect as well. Consider the engineering arena. Engineers used to draw designs by hand, and each redraw was started from scratch. With computer-aided design (CAD), the initial drawing is easier and quicker; but even if it weren't, the revisions need not be drawn from scratch. Only the changes need be redrawn. Theoretically, this means that designs should be completed more quickly—most experts estimate about four times as quickly. Why aren't they? Because engineers are often perfectionists. They aren't content to leave the design at the stage they would when drawing everything from scratch. Now that revisions are so easy, they want to fix little things that they'd have left alone before. So, instead of producing designs four times faster, they often take as much time as if they were done by hand—but the designs are much better!

Producing letters and reports has often been subject to the same effect—the search for a better result instead of a faster one. Letters that might once have been retyped once are now retyped twenty times; spreadsheets are done over and over. The effect is now understood and better managed, and office productivity is now increasing.

Information technology has many other effects. For example, access to information is much faster and easier today than it was five years ago. In large organizations, this has meant that today a manager can often keep track of ten or twenty people, while before he or she could keep track of only five or six. This has reduced the size of the bureaucracies that large organizations inevitably require. The productivity factor has also reduced the size of the workforce being managed. This is one cause of downsizing. These two effects have also made easier the merging of large organizations in order to take advantage of economies of scale.

The faster movement of information has led to an accelerating pace of business—indeed, of most aspects of life. The introduction of the computer, far from increasing our leisure and freeing us for more reflective pursuits, has multiplied the pressure on us to produce, increasing stress in the workplace and even at home as it improves productivity. Few can get by these days with a 40-hour workweek, and in many families both mother and father have jobs. People at the bottom of the economic pile often must take several jobs just to make ends meet. And those without skills are harder pressed to find jobs.

Thus the net effect of pressure to increase productivity in a corporation often is to squeeze people, not to enhance them; not to help them realize *their* potential and therefore help the corporation realize *its* potential; not to cooperate, but to compete to stay employed. Recall the lemon theory of management: you squeeze them until they're dry, then you throw them away.

The introduction of new information-based tools is hardest for people from backgrounds that have kept them from developing even rudimentary skills. Retraining often does not help much if they lack such basic skills as reading and figuring. Information technology has been especially hard on these people because it has displaced so many unskilled jobs.

The conventional wisdom says that the new tools create more jobs than they displace, and this may happen with information technology. But we still have to deal with those who cannot become qualified for the new jobs, or for whom the new jobs come long after their old jobs have been eliminated. The size of the problem is larger than before, and the level of people displaced is higher.

Another negative effect of the pressure for productivity is that such pressure tends to drive out the ability to reflect. Many advances over the years have come because people have been able to sit back, relax, and think about what they were doing and how to do it better. Some institutions promote reflection. The university, for example, provides a sabbatical for its faculty—a year of study and reflection every seventh year of employment. Productivity might improve faster if corporations provided comparable opportunities.

Humane Response to the Information Age

The beneficial possibilities for workers in the information age can be understood better by considering how the changes new technology requires are implemented. Increasing productivity usually means introducing a new technology into an organization. This takes time and resources. The new technology usually requires changes in the procedures for accomplishing a particular business objective—manufacturing a product, for example. It may also require changes in the organization's business processes, its structure, and its management practices.

Workers who will use the new technology and its procedures must often be reorganized and then trained in the use of the innovations. They then learn by experience, beginning the learning curve that most companies rely on to keep ahead of their competition. As people learn the new way, adjustments that facilitate it become apparent. These changes have to be made and the workers retrained, and then they must learn again by experience. This implementation life cycle occurs whether the new technology is for research, development, manufacturing, marketing, service delivery, or administration.

Corporate policies can foster different stages in the implementation life cycle. In the *initiation* phase, policies encourage experimentation with the new technology and with the organization and management practices that support it. As use of the technology grows within the corporation, *contagion* sets in and usage skyrockets. At this stage, corporate policies to bring the implementation under *control* are instituted. As the technology spreads further, policies designed to integrate the new technology into the regular operations of the company are introduced. This assures that implementation across the organization is coordinated and that the parts of the organization work together effectively. Once procedural *integration* is well under way, the corporation may need to make changes in its *information management* policies to assure that information is coordinated and shared by all parts of the organization. When all of this is working smoothly, the company is said to be mature in its use of the technology.

Organizations differ in the effectiveness with which they use each generation of productivity tools. In some organizations people are excited to learn new ways to do their jobs, learn quickly, and share their knowledge with each other. In other organizations the opposite is true. The former are often called "learning organizations."

One of the most important issues today is husbanding and using the knowledge and experience that exists in a corporation. In recent advertisements, Hewlett-Packard (HP) laments, "If only HP knew what HP knows . . ." Many corporations are using information technology to collect and organize what they learn—in the research lab, in the financial world, at customer locations, and so forth—and to make this information available to everyone in the corporation who can make use of it. Learning organizations do this well, and the information store they develop is called "intellectual capital."

Another way to build intellectual capital is to develop expert systems or other artificial intelligence technology to capture the experience of an employee and make it available to others. In a sense, this is "enminding" the intellectual labor of an employee in a machine just as older technology "embodied" his physical labor in a machine. This can bring gains to the corporation at the expense of the employee. However, it need not do so. It can provide the employee with tools for more creative work.

Arie de Geus, former strategic planner for Royal Dutch Shell, once said, "I have come to believe that the only sustainable competitive advantage is the ability to learn faster than your competitors."[5] He was referring to *strategic* learning by the corporation, but those organizations that can learn to manage and share their information and know-how and to make effective use of new tools and techniques also have a significant advantage on the strategic front.

In order for an organization to learn, its people must learn and must share their learning with each other. This has to be true at all levels for maximum effectiveness. All of the people must learn to work together cooperatively, not competitively, to make the organization into an evolving organism whose parts are interdependent. An organization that creates such an environment and invests in education and training is making a long-term commitment to people—but to their employees as a body, not to any individual employee. Although the working environment is improved, no individual employee has increased job security.

The more we learn about the use of the new computer/communications-based productivity tools, the more we learn that restructuring of business processes, changes in organization and management practices, and skill in executing the technology implementation life cycle are critical. We also learn that breaking jobs into little tasks, as Taylor recommended, is often counterproductive, and that we need to give people more responsibility and control over their work. Although productivity improvements continue to displace many workers, corporations at the leading edge of the new technologies are often becoming much more people-friendly.

IV. A CHRISTIAN PERSPECTIVE

The corporations that so profoundly shape our lives today emerged only in the eighteenth century, but they have evolved dramatically since then. Obviously the Bible and the church tradition do not address directly the issues that they raise for us. Nevertheless, Christians informed by this tradition bring a distinctive perspective to bear in current reflection about them.

Affirming material well-being. Although some Christians have juxtaposed the life of the spirit and concern for physical well-being, Jesus contrasted himself with the asceticism of John the Baptist on this point. As Christians we believe that enjoyment of food and drink is good. We hope to provide enough of the world's good things for all. Insofar as corporations help achieve this goal, Christians affirm them.

Affirming knowledge. Although some Christians have feared knowledge as a threat to faith, most have experienced faith as encouraging a quest for knowledge. Theology is often described as faith seeking understanding. Wherever Christians have gone they have established schools. The Christian conviction that the God we worship formed the heavens and the earth led believers to develop science in early modern times as a source of knowledge of God and God's world. Insofar as corporations contribute to the continued expansion of knowledge and its dissemination among all people, we affirm them.

Affirming technology. Although we all recognize that knowledge can be used destructively and that some technology is used in ways that are harmful to human beings and other creatures of God, Christians believe that human beings are authorized to shape the world as necessary to meet our needs. Accordingly, Christians support the advance of technology, so important to corporations, insofar as it enables us to meet human needs more effectively.

Affirming persons over things. Jesus taught that the Sabbath is made for human beings, not human beings for the Sabbath. All the more, this is true of physical things. Corporations should value people over things and order their activities accordingly. This applies both to their internal operations and to recognizing the importance of various stakeholders outside the corporation.

Care for the earth. We Christians have been slow to recognize that our modern way of life is degrading the Lord's earth. We have been awakened to this realization chiefly by scientists. Now that we are awakened, we must call on all our fellow human beings to work with us toward a sustainable use of Earth's resources. Since most of these resources are now controlled by corporations, the policies they adopt in this regard are of utmost importance to all of us.

The condemnation of greed. Through most of Christian history, Christians regarded greed as a major sin. It was assumed that individuals who took more than their share impoverished others. There were always greedy people who amassed fortunes, but they were not admired. In the eighteenth century it was discovered that seeking private wealth through industrialization increased the wealth of society as a whole. Individual and corporate greed seemed to benefit, rather than harm, others. The church's opposition to greed was muted. Today we see that the pollution and exhaustion of resources motivated by greed threatens the health of Earth. The traditional objection to greed has become relevant again. Most corporations are preoccupied with the "bottom line" and, therefore, subject to this critique.

The preferential option for the poor. Catholic liberation theologians have reminded us that the Bible encourages us to view historical events from the vantage point of the poor. As corporate dominance leaves global poverty unalleviated, Christians must work to counter this dominance.

Responsibility rather than fate. Many people, including many Christians, have supposed that the order of society is simply given, but the prophetic tradition derived from Israel teaches otherwise. Human choices, responding to God's call, play a large role. The present situation of corporate dominance, in which many Christian values and principles are ignored or violated, is the result of human choices. We are called to reassess these choices and make new ones.

V. WHAT WE CAN DO

As an Individual

Recognize that we are part of the problem. We invest our money to obtain the highest possible return; we purchase products we want with little regard for the process that produces them, the conditions under which the people who carry out that process work, or the source of the raw materials used in it; we follow the values and goals of our work group, our supervisor, or our corporation with very little thought. Rarely do we compare our actions against the values we hold dear. We should become much more deliberate in applying our values to these and other actions we take every day.

Encourage consumer action. We can promote consumer action. Shoppers can learn to choose products that have been produced in socially responsible ways. Information is readily available about companies that have adopted sensible codes of conduct guaranteeing that their products are made under acceptable standards. Such codes of conduct must have a monitoring system that is transparent and sufficiently independent of the companies to be credible.

Promote the common good. As citizens, individual Christians can be stewards of public life. We can assume leadership positions, support sensible government programs, and confront policies and leaders when necessary. Individuals can support the Partnership for Trust in Government, a project of the Ford Foundation and the Council for Excellence in Government, an alliance of twenty-two nongovernmental organizations from industry, labor, the nonprofit sectors, and the media that are committed to restoring a healthy balance between skepticism and public trust in government.

As a Congregation

Be a community of discernment. The faith community shouldn't pretend technical competence it does not uniquely possess. It can and should, however, engage in moral analysis of laws and economic systems, denounce their morally unacceptable outcomes, name the sin that is causing pain, and insist that more humane policies and systems be sought and implemented. That is an authentic prophetic task of the community of faith in economic life, regardless of the extent or organization of markets.

Broaden adult education programs. Nor should the church shy away from mastering the technical competence needed to understand the workings of stakeholder and stockholder capitalism. The churches of America are full of people with knowledge about economic life and its institutions. They should be recruited to develop adult education materials and social-witness policies to accord with the church's social teachings.

Encourage education for community action. Individual congregations need also to bring together their theological reflections about economic life with education in community action for economic justice. Biblical and theological reflection is best oriented to active involvement in the world. Active learning best takes place when pastors and members of congregations carry out sustained, collaborative work on social issues.

Celebrate good corporate behavior. Congregations also may work through their denominations and ecumenical bodies to identify good corporate behavior. The Presbyterian Church (U.S.A.) recently gave awards to Motorola, for putting a stop to its production of parts used to make land mines, and to Starbucks Coffee, for adopting a code of conduct for suppliers that requires evidence of adequate wages and human rights for workers.

Link investment decisions to mission policies. Congregations that own invested assets need to consider carefully the social responsibility of the policies of those corporations. Congregations and denominations can form partnerships with the Interfaith Center on Corporate Responsibility (ICCR) in New York, which monitors corporate actions on social issues and coordinates the filing of proxy resolutions decrying inappropriate conduct by particular corporations. ICCR and its church partners, for example, have supported resolutions on water pollution and toxic chemical wastes associated with paper production; working conditions and environmental and health hazards associated with foreign-owned factories in Mexico; exploitation of child and slave labor in Third World countries, particularly in clothing manufacture; discriminatory lending patterns in low-income and minority neighborhoods by banks and mortgage companies; pay equity and equal employment opportunity; arms sales to foreign governments; and exorbitant executive pay unrelated to company performance.

As Consumers, Stockholders, Employees, and Executives

Promote "servant leadership." Not all corporations are alike, and some are freer than others to deviate from the strictures of globalization. By and large, it is large multinational organizations that have exerted the most influence on the design and operation of the neoliberal global economic system now in place, so it is likely they have the least incentive, yet greater opportunity, to act differently. Although the bottom line is important to all corporations, there is considerable room for concerned leaders to adopt more humane policies. We commend the practice of servant leadership as developed by the Greenleaf Institute.

Develop codes of conduct. Some companies that once refused to acknowledge their responsibility for factory conditions in other countries now have undertaken more serious internal monitoring of the factories they buy from, and several companies have begun experimenting with different forms of external monitoring using local human rights groups. Still other companies, made aware of serious violations in the factories of their suppliers, work with the contractors to improve conditions, rather than exposing the local community to the trauma of plant closings and heightened unemployment.

Improve employment security. The existing economic system is taking away from workers the economic security they previously enjoyed with long-term employers and is replacing it with a new kind of job contract that weakens loyalties and shifts responsibility for staying employable primarily to the workers themselves. In an increasingly turbulent labor market, more and more employers are discriminating against older workers, workers hired on a contingent basis, and workers unwilling or unable to assume the costs of developing new job skills. Conscientious corporate leaders can resist these tendencies.

Despite the limits placed on corporate leaders by the competitive situation, some of them continue to provide their employees good wages, decent fringe benefits, challenging work assignments, and, where necessary, training opportunities to build new skills. Many companies also follow practices that reward long-term employees with greater job security, better benefits, and better severance packages when severance is necessary. We applaud these efforts to restore a greater sense of security to their workers.

Avoid environmental damage. Motivated in part by the desire to avoid adverse publicity, corporations today are trying harder to appear sensitive to the environmental consequences of many production processes. None wishes to be known as a polluter. Yet the costs of processing hazardous and solid waste are often high, tempting corporations to risk being caught in order to save money. Corporate leaders who care about the environment should seek ways to ameliorate the damage their operations create with the application of new technologies.

Recognize the timescales involved. Sustainability upon planet Earth requires considering effects that may occur far beyond the five-year time frame usually involved in corporate strategic planning. Many effects will not show up for thirty years or a hundred years. For some actions consideration of the eons of geologic time is necessary. The first law of the Iroquois had it right: "In our every deliberation, we must consider the impact on the next seven generations."

Support wise governmental regulation. Corporate executives and boards often work to reduce governmental involvement in the marketplace, assuming that business thrives when least regulated. However, lack of common rules for all firms puts pressure on each to lower standards. Corporations that want to act more responsibly should propose and encourage government regulations that would encourage such behavior.

As Citizens Attempting to Influence Government

Take charter power more seriously. State governments should take their charter power more seriously. If states cannot exercise effective control over corporations, then the federal government should charter them. Perhaps there should be a global chartering organization. Whatever mechanism is found, balance should be restored between freedom of corporate action and the ability of government, acting for the people as a whole, to serve the common good.

Investigate needed structural reforms. In stockholder capitalism, the leaders of most major corporations sit at the top of an authoritarian organization structure that gives them authority over economic resources greater than those of most countries. The law, the financial incentives of their compensation packages, and the board of directors all tell them that this power is to be used almost exclusively to increase shareholder return. The stockholders, moreover, typically are kept unaware of the actions taken in their name for their exclusive benefit and are shielded from any liability for the consequences of those actions. Does this not imply the need for appropriate public authorities to consider seriously proposals to reform the organizational structure of publicly traded, limited-liability corporations in America? Is it time for the government to consider limiting the size of corporations, stripping them of some of their special rights and privileges, and finding ways to vest partial ownership in the employees, community members, customers, and suppliers?

Investigate the Financial Accounting Standards Board. It is hard to question the need for accounting standards. As stated in the FASB mission statement, "Accounting standards are essential to the efficient functioning of the economy because decisions about the allocation of resources rely heavily on credible, concise, and understandable financial information." But are the standards proposed by the FASB the best guide to the allocation of resources by business entities? Until 2002 it resisted counting the stock options given to executives as expenses, even though they clearly are employee costs and some accounting firms are insisting that their clients count them as operating costs. Now it is at least giving serious consideration to this change. The Securities and Exchange Commission of the federal government has statutory authority to establish financial accounting and reporting standards for publicly held companies. However, the SEC's policy has been to rely on the private sector—that is to say, the FASB—for this function "to the extent that the private sector demonstrates ability to fulfill the responsibility in the public interest." The leadership of the FASB is drawn from public accounting firms, representatives of large corporations, and major associations of preparers. We note with interest the absence of representatives of the public interest. Armed with legislation to establish a new accounting oversight board, the Securities and Exchange Commission should immediately launch an investigation of the FASB's ability to be stewards of the public interest. The investigation should be broadly based and consider issues such as human resource accounting, life cycle costing, and cost exporting.

Invest in research and development, infrastructure, and human capital. In the 1970s, when Americans were putting in place the investments in highways, airports, safer cities, and so forth, that would eventually pay off in the 1990s, federal investment in these activities averaged better than 2.5 percent of gross domestic product (GDP). The percentage shrank dramatically during the 1980s under the Reagan and Bush administrations, and it continued to decline under Clinton and the Republican-dominated Congress in the 1990s. By 2001, it was down to less than 1.5 percent of GDP. Similarly, the federal role in financing education and supporting worker retraining and relocation has lagged. To use unexpectedly high levels of federal revenue to finance huge tax cuts or to needlessly reduce the public debt is poor stewardship, since many of these funds have a much higher use correcting vast underinvestments in the very grounding of healthy economies.

Encourage corporate best-practice policies. Governments can reward corporations that adopt best practices. For example, governments can encourage corporations to contribute to a portable pension plan, invest at least 2 percent of their payroll in the education and training of their employees, and subscribe to a health plan covering all employees who have been with the firm at least three months. Companies can also be encouraged to offer some form of profit sharing and to work harder at compliance with health and safety standards. They can also participate in national apprenticeship and school-to-work programs and place more of the R and D expenditures domestically.

Review tax and other legislation affecting corporate costs. Market forces do not ordinarily reflect all the social and environmental costs of economic activity. The true costs of production include not only the usually reported costs of a business, but also the costs of externalities that damage the environment and may lead to countervailing public expenditures for, say, health-care and cleanup costs. If producers were encouraged through various economic incentives to count all costs as costs of production, they would search harder for more efficient ways of organizing production. Then too they no doubt would set prices at levels more commensurate with total costs, goading consumers into more environmentally sensitive decisions about what and how much to buy.

Enforce antitrust policies. For the last century, public policies have attempted to contain monopoly and curb corporate abuses of market power in two ways: by prohibiting certain kinds of business conduct, and by curbing market structures that are thought to lead to anticompetitive abuses. In recent years, the enforcement of antitrust laws has weakened, in part because many people have become skeptical of the ability of government to improve the performance of large multinational enterprises. While it is true that the intrinsic rivalry of very large firms, particularly those involved with rapidly changing technologies, has made enforcement of the laws more difficult, these facts do not excuse the government from enforcing the law.

Establish fair trade based on labor rights and standards. What is needed is the creation of a *fair trade* regime and a new global economic architecture analogous to what the leading nations of the world developed at the end of World War II. Instead, we are getting a further devolution of power from individual governments to the private sector and growing international economic chaos. One way to counter this trend is for the World Trade Organization to adopt something stronger than existing protections (against slavery, forced labor, the suppression of unions, and the exploitation of child labor) without undermining the incentive for multinationals to invest in developing nations. It should include some form of international labor rights and some form of international standards regarding minimum wages, hours of work, health and safety, and benefits. Meanwhile, labor leaders must continue to push for labor-rights-and-standards language in new bilateral and regional trade compacts.

Discussion Questions

1. What are the major barriers to social responsibility on the part of corporations? Are these barriers economic, psychological, or just habit? Can these barriers be overcome?
2. What positive contributions are corporations making to your life and the life of your community?
3. How do corporations with which you are familiar treat their employees?
4. How effective is the safety net for those who lose their jobs through corporate downsizing? How sensitive are corporations to their needs?
5. Collect statements given by corporate leaders in annual reports, press releases, the media, and so forth. Do they contain a concern for the poor? How do they propose to deal with the poor?

6. Has automation affected you or someone you know? Describe what happened; how the person dealt with it; what resources were available to help them, and the outcome.
7. Interview corporate leaders; ask about their employee policies and social responsibility activities. Develop an interview guide to help in this project. Write the results as a report, then abstract it as an opinion piece for your local newspaper.

To Learn More

Detailed discussion of management issues discussed in this paper can be found in three books. John Seely Brown and Paul Duguld, in *The Social Life of Information* (Boston: Harvard Business School Press, 2000), discuss the need for human interaction with information in order to gain the most value from it. Peter Senge, *The Fifth Discipline: The Art and Practice of the Learning Organization* (New York: Currency/Bantam Doubleday Dell Publishing Group, 1990) is the seminal book on a learning organization. Robert K. Greenleaf, who died in 1990, has been a powerful voice in the dialogue to reshape management and leadership practices. He developed a theory of servant leadership as an executive at AT&T. The center he founded eventually became the Robert K. Greenleaf Center, located in Indianapolis, Indiana. His ideas can be found in *The Servant As Leader* (Indianapolis: Robert K. Greenleaf Center, 1991). An example of a business seeking to be environmentally responsible is Interface Inc. The CEO, Ray C. Anderson, describes the transformation of company practice in *Mid-Course Correction: Toward a Sustainable Enterprise: The Interface Model* (Atlanta: Peregrinzella Press, 1998).

The discussion of the wider economic context is highly relevant to the actual and desirable functioning of corporations. Barry Bluestone and Harrison Bennett, *Growing Prosperity: The Battle for Growth with Equity in the Twenty-first Century* (Boston: Houghton Mifflin Co., 2000) describes the typical Wall Street approach to growth based upon balanced budgets, free trade, flexible labor markets, and vigilant monetary policy and then proposes an alternative based upon public investment and productivity growth through organizational learning. Herman E. Daly and John B. Cobb Jr., *For the Common Good: Redirecting the Economy toward Community, the Environment, and a Sustainable Future* (Boston: Beacon Press, 1994) provides an excellent alternative set of principles to those of mainstream economic theory. David C. Korten, *When Corporations Rule the World*, 2d ed. (West Hartford, Conn.: Kumarian Press, and San Francisco: Berrett-Koehler Publishers, 2001) provides a comprehensive discussion of the effect corporations have had around the world on people who are not part of the power elite and gives recommendations for improving society's ability to help these people take care of themselves. Ronald Schettkat, "How Bad Are Welfare-State Institutions for Economic Development? The Amazing Vitality of the European Tigers" (*Challenge* 44 (2001): 1, 35–55) shows that the recent successes of the economies of Austria, the Netherlands, Ireland, and Denmark, which surpass those of the United States in certain respects, occur in part because of, not in spite of, the ways they protect their working populations.

11

Responding to Sweatshops

Out in the Pacific Ocean, on a chain of fourteen islands known as the U.S. Commonwealth of the Northern Mariana Islands, a $1 billion garment industry has been booming since the 1980s. Carmencita "Chie" Abad was an accounting clerk in the Philippines when she paid a recruiter $2,000 so she could work in a garment factory there. Abad said she anticipated it would be a good job—after all, it's the United States—but instead she said she toiled 84 to 100 hours a week for $2.15 an hour in a dust-filled factory that makes clothes for the Gap. The Chinese workers there have it worse, she said. They're forced to live in barracks with no running water and no air conditioning in a climate that's hotter than Houston.

I. INTRODUCTION

In the nineteenth century, industrial firms that lacked the nerve or resources to improve their products or processes often chose to compete by contracting out production. The profits of the contractors were the difference between the amount of their contract and their expenses, consisting chiefly of what they paid their workers. Because they paid minimal wages for excessive hours in unsanitary conditions, their profits were said to be "sweated" from the workers.

The term "sweatshop" has been given a more official definition for the late twentieth century by the General Accounting Office (GAO). A sweatshop is an establishment that is a chronic or a multiple violator of labor law. Specifically, it occurs when "an employer . . . violates more than one federal or state labor law governing minimum wage and overtime, child labor, industrial homework, occupational safety and health, workers' compensation, or industry registration."

From a worker's point of view, employment in a sweatshop may be the only job available; even so, it is likely to subject him or her to low wages, physical abuse, coercive regulations, unsafe working conditions, and the trauma of living in unpleasant and unfriendly circumstances—whether the factory is in Los Angeles or China's Guangdong Province. This is exploitation, plain and simple.

II. THE RECENT RETURN OF SWEATSHOPS

In the industrialized world, conditions of manufacturing employment improved gradually in the nineteenth and twentieth centuries. Several factors were involved. First, improved productivity and growing prosperity created a context in which extreme exploitation of labor was not required or accepted. Second, workers organized to demand better conditions. Third, public opinion supported labor sufficiently to lead to legislation implementing many of its demands. Fourth, the fear of Communist influence in labor unions reduced opposition to improving the conditions of labor on the part of industrialists and investors in the First World.

By the 1960s, factory labor in the industrialized nations was generally well paid, and conditions of labor were reasonably good. This raised the price of goods but also the demand for them. Poor working conditions continued in agriculture, in domestic service, and in other areas where unionization was lacking and enforcement of government regulations was difficult. But sweatshops in the original meaning largely disappeared. They are still rare in most of the long-industrialized nations.

However, sweatshops as defined by the GAO have returned in force to the United States, especially in the apparel and footwear industries. Once again, sweating is occurring primarily in mature industries where innovations are fewer. Even more strikingly, conditions similar to those that first gave rise to the name are now a dominant factor in factories in the industrializing nations of Latin America and Asia. Most of these factories work under contract for large retail chains or for their agents in the industrial countries. In these countries the application of the GAO definition is problematic because there are often few laws against low pay, long hours, employment of children, and unsanitary working conditions.

Why Sweatshops Have Returned—The Global Economy

As the costs of transportation and communication plummeted after World War II, the opportunity for greater commerce across national borders rose dramatically. This globalization of the potential for commerce also was encouraged by the readiness of national governments to lower barriers to international trade and capital movements—to be sure, sometimes as a condition of assistance from the International Monetary Fund and the World Bank. Consequently, trade among nations multiplied more rapidly than production, and monetary transfers grew even faster than trade.

This boom in international transactions was accompanied by dramatic changes in the ways private enterprises do business. Western firms grew in size, made investments abroad, built alliances with other businesses throughout the world, and set up complex networks of producing and financing stages on a truly global scale. In the absence of effective international controls, these transnational corporations (TNCs) were free to locate production and finance wherever it suited them best and to engage in practices forbidden at home. What had been "international" trade—trade largely controlled by governments at their national borders—gradually became "transnational" trade, influenced primarily by private corporate decisions. This freedom of movement also weakened the ability of host governments to impose stringent standards for environmental and labor practices.

As competitive pressures mounted with globalization, many firms were forced to seek new ways to reduce costs and to search for wider markets. Some chose to build factories abroad, where labor or resources could be gotten at lower prices. In the apparel industry, for example, a typical worker in the United States earns $8.52 per hour, compared to one in China earning $.23, El Salvador $.59, Pakistan $.26, Dominican Republic $.69, and the Philippines $.76.[1] Others, such as large retail firms like Wal-Mart, Sears Roebuck, and Nike, typically bought their merchandise from vendors who contracted with them to supply so many dresses, shoes, or toys that met specific design and quality standards. They, in turn, subcontracted the actual manufacture of garments and toys to many relatively small independently owned factories. Since these TNCs, unlike those that produce durable goods, invest little or nothing in the factories where their goods are made, they are freer to cancel contracts with their vendors when demand is slack or when cheaper sources of supply can be found, often in yet another country.

This outsourcing of production has permitted large retailers to expand rapidly and to book substantial profits. For many developing countries, like Mexico, Honduras, Indonesia, and India, it also has meant a significant rise in factory employment. In China alone, the number of employees working in factories with limited-duration contracts from Western firms exceeded 19.5 million in 1996. No doubt this figure is considerably higher today.

But foreign direct investing (FDI) and subcontracting also have brought to these countries considerable uncertainty and a troubling inequality. The uncertainty is primarily the product of competitive market forces and the serious transfer of power over the economy from national governments to transnational corporations. Globalization means that the TNCs compete with each other for low-cost sources of supply, and the vendors that make their goods then compete for the contracts by submitting the lowest possible bids. To make a profit, they must find subcontractors who will work their employees long and hard for very low wages. Hence much of current practice is a global replica of the nineteenth-century system that gave rise to "sweating."

This so-called "race to the bottom" has added to the number of people earning factory wages in several developing countries, but at very substantial cost. The cost is only in part the low wages, child labor, intimidation, and unsafe working conditions found in so many sweatshops. It is also the dislocations to common life as contracts wax and wane and workers are forced in and out of the labor force as competition dictates. And it is the social costs, illustrated so vividly in the Asian crisis, that suddenly mount when investments are withdrawn, incomes fall, and government safety nets fail.

Why Sweatshops Have Returned to the United States

The global economy is an important factor in the return of sweatshops to the United States as well. With the reduction of tariffs and other barriers, it is cheaper to produce many labor-intensive goods abroad and ship them back into the United States than to produce them in this country. Accordingly, many formerly well-paying industries have moved their production overseas in order to reduce costs. Even when they continue to produce in the United States, they outsource much of their production to foreign contractors who pay lower wages. The threat of plant closing and job loss has a chilling effect on workers and substantially weakens their bargaining position. Thus, there has been downward pressure on U.S. wages for unskilled and less-skilled positions. The poorest fifth of the American people has grown steadily poorer despite the great increase in the nation's wealth.

Yet another of globalization's legacies has been the flood of migrants seeking employment in factories of countries far from their homes. For some employers in the United States, the availability of large numbers of immigrants from Mexico, Guatemala, El Salvador, Haiti, and other developing countries has provided opportunity to profit from sweating. Although much of the garment industry has been moved outside the country, there are advantages to retailers in having some productive facilities inside the country. Easy access, quick turnaround, and special circumstances help to explain why. But none of these advantages is sufficient to allow for good wages to those who work in the industry.

One may ask why the workers and the authorities allow sweatshop conditions, which involve violation of state and federal regulations, to occur. The workers are generally immigrants accustomed to low wages and more concerned to have *some* work than about its quality. Many of them are undocumented, fear deportation, and are, therefore, in no position to protest. The authorities also know that enforcement of standards may lead to decisions that transfer operations to another country, reducing the employment base at home and further aggravating the trade deficit. Both state and federal governments have reduced their inspection staffs as the problem has grown in magnitude. Apparently the judgment has been made that it is better to keep these sweatshops in the United States than to drive them out.

In California over the past ten years, on the other hand, the legislature has on three occasions passed laws to counteract sweatshops. Although the legislation was twice vetoed, on September 29, 1999, Governor Davis signed legislation that holds retailers and manufacturers responsible for the practices of their contractors. In the three-year period the law has been in effect, we are finding out just how difficult it is to see that this new law is responsibly enforced, given a shortage of inspectors and the resistance and political influence of companies who wish to be exempt from its provisions.

Los Angeles is now the sweatshop capital of the United States. More than five thousand sweatshops dot the city. Garment manufacturing is the largest manufacturing industry in Los Angeles, and the economics of this industry make sweatshop conditions almost inevitable. Only one-third of southern California's registered garment factories comply with federal minimum wage and overtime laws, and well over 90 percent of garment factories within the region violate health and safety laws, according to the California state Department of Occupational Safety and Health. We seem forced to choose between sweatshops and the loss of this employment opportunity for poor immigrants.

III. CORPORATE RESPONSES

With some justification, corporations disclaim responsibility for the existence of sweatshops. They are ruled by the global system as much as are workers and consumers, and they can survive only as they adopt the practices encouraged by the system. Many of them have affirmed policies to the effect that all their production should conform to the laws applicable where their goods are produced. Their policy is also to pay standard wages in these locales. They explain these policies to their vendors—and they, in turn, to their subcontractors—and require their commitment to abide by them.

Indeed, under prodding from the White House, a unique task force of apparel companies and nongovernmental human rights organizations in April 1997 issued a Workplace Code of Conduct and Principles of Monitoring that set as its objective to eliminate forced labor, child labor, harassment or abuse of workers, unsafe working conditions, excessive hours of work, and below-minimum wages. Subsequent negotiations led to pledges by most major retailers not to do business with companies overseas that use forced labor or require employees to work more than sixty hours a week. Companies will also prohibit hiring children younger than fifteen except in countries where fourteen-year-olds can work legally. The agreement, by what now is known as the Fair Labor Association (FLA), also commits the companies to pay the minimum wage required by local laws.

The negotiations did not result, however, in pledges by companies to pay a sustainable living wage to workers or to institute credible independent monitoring systems of working conditions in contractor factories. For these reasons, the Interfaith Center for Corporate Responsibility, a coalition of 275 Protestant, Roman Catholic, and Jewish faith groups and agencies, withdrew its support of the agreements, even as other human rights groups endorsed them. United Students Against Sweatshops also criticized the agreement and was instrumental in forming the Workers Rights Consortium as an alternative to FLA.

While initiatives of this sort advance the campaign against sweatshops, there are three reasons why they are likely to be ineffective. First, local laws and customs may be such that they do not inhibit extreme exploitation of workers. Second, the system of seeking the lowest bid possible often forces contractors to bid less than would be required to avoid violation of these policies. Even so, retailers do not acknowledge any legal liability for infractions committed by their vendors or subcontractors. All they can do is to encourage compliance, they say, or withdraw from the contracts wedding them to particular vendors or contractors. Third, most corporations are more interested in succeeding in relation to their competitors than in ensuring that their contractors in fact abide by the rules. Although some inspect the factories with which they contract and assure their customers that they do so, there is little indication that these in-house inspections have much effect in changing the real conditions of labor.

Nevertheless, existing corporate policies probably do deter the use of child labor and prison labor. Although they do not lead to reasonable pay or hours of work, they may inhibit contractors from physical and sexual abuse of workers.

Furthermore, although the bottom line is important to all corporations, there is much room within them for concerned leaders to adopt more humane policies.

A few retailers, moreover, have adopted helpful reforms easily transferable to other situations. Some companies that once refused to acknowledge their responsibility for factory conditions elsewhere now have undertaken more serious internal monitoring of the factories they buy from, and several companies have begun experimenting with different forms of external monitoring using local human rights groups. Still other companies, made aware of serious violations in the factories of their suppliers, work with the contractors to improve conditions rather than exposing the local community to the trauma of plant closings and heightened unemployment. These experiences show that conscientious leaders in corporations, despite the limits placed on them by the competitive situation, still have freedom to make better and worse choices.

The problem is not so much that there are no people of goodwill in leading positions in TNCs. The problem is that the steps needed to mitigate current abuses would tend to make a corporation globally noncompetitive. When economies were primarily national, it was possible to establish national laws applying to all competitors that ended extreme abuses. As long as competition was chiefly with competitors bound to those laws, the system worked. But there is no authority in position to raise standards globally, and it is difficult for corporate executives to take truly effective initiatives as long as their competitors do not.

Sweatshops are not an abuse of the current global economic system but its natural and inevitable expression. Global competition to produce goods cheaply requires those practices that bring about sweatshops. Nothing in the system or its effects works against this consequence. If sweatshops are to be reduced or eliminated globally, a different system is required.

The change in public opinion that would be most significant would be one that no longer supported the global market controlled by unregulated TNCs. This would be a reversal of the long shift of public moral support away from government regulation and in favor of large corporations rather than small businesses. Such a reversal would make possible the gradual institution of standards favorable to workers and to the environment country by country, while restricting capital flight from countries that raised these standards.

IV. A MORAL ARGUMENT FOR THE SYSTEM

Although few would deny that the global economy is now causing widespread exploitation of workers, many oppose significant restrictions on its functioning. Some of these, no doubt, do so out of self-interest, since the system has proved extremely profitable for investors. But many support the system on moral grounds.

Their argument can be stated quite simply. There are still enormous unmet economic wants in the world. These can best be met by economic growth, that is, by increasing the production of goods and services. The most efficient means of increasing production is the free market, and the larger the market, the more efficiently resources can be allocated.

When challenged with regard to the enormous suffering of the poor accompanying this global system, defenders point out that in the earlier stages of European industrialization, the poor suffered. But, they insist, as industrialization advanced, the poor benefited. We must accept temporary sacrifice for the sake of long-term prosperity.

A more contemporary version of this argument concerns what normally happens to the distribution of income in late-developing countries as they grow. Recent empirical evidence confirms the fact that the gap between rich and poor widens at the early stages of development. By the time developing countries graduate from the class of nations the World Bank calls low-income countries to the class of lower middle-income, the distribution of income has stabilized. Thereafter, as nations move from lower-middle to upper-middle, they tend to experience a narrowing of the gap between rich and poor. Thus, the argument goes, one need not depend on European history to show that the poor (eventually) will benefit from development. Alas, the data on which this argument is based are more than a decade old—old enough not to have captured any changes wrought by a rising tide of private capital.

V. A CHRISTIAN PERSPECTIVE

Personal and Structural Emphases

All Christians care what happens to other people and especially to the weak, the poor and the oppressed. The biblical teaching is too clear to allow for indifference. None of us can be complacent in the face of massive suffering. But for many Christians, the systemic issues are outside the sphere of consideration; for them, the focus is on personal morality. This can express itself in several ways.

Some Christians emphasize personal morality in the workplace. They urge that workers be treated humanely and with respect for their persons. Workers, in turn, should serve their employers honestly and well. They ask also that those who are able respond to the needs of their neighbors in charitable ways.

Some Christians are inclined to judge harshly those who benefit from this system. They point to the enormous profits made by corporations and the stratospheric level of the compensations of their CEOs. Appalled by the contrast between these salaries and the wages of the workers, they condemn these CEOs personally, along with the investors who also profit.

Some Christians, distressed by their recognition of how as consumers they participate in the system, try to buy selectively from companies less involved in it. Or they undertake to withdraw in part from the consumption-oriented system by living more frugally.

There is validity in all these responses. Personal morality is needed in factories as it is needed everywhere else. For many people caught in the system, this is the most that they can offer. For workers, there is considerable difference in the quality of life according to the moral character of those for whom and with whom they work.

Uncritical defense of an exploitative system from which one profits personally is morally reprehensible, even if the impersonal system, more than personal decisions, determines its exploitative nature. Most investors and CEOs are far less concerned about the suffering from which they profit than Christian sensitivity would require. Even if greater concern would not change the system, it might moderate its effects significantly.

For Christians to focus on their own involvement in the system is also eminently appropriate. We are to remove the logs from our own eyes before undertaking to remove the specks from the eyes of others (Matt. 7:5). The whole system is geared to the benefit of consumers, and we are all part of it. To condemn others while not recognizing our own participation would be hypocritical.

Progressive Christians participate in all these responses, but we add another dimension. We understand that systems are often more determinative of what happens to people than the moral decisions of those functioning within them. Often the systems seem so far beyond our capacity to affect that the types of responses listed above exhaust the possibilities for us as well. At the time of the writing of the New Testament, few of the hearers of the gospel were in position to challenge the injustices in the Roman imperial system that governed their lives. We get little guidance there as to how to deal with such systems.

On the other hand, the Hebrew prophets were less removed from the sources of power and more willing to criticize the system and the policies that implemented it. Again and again when we recognize the systemic character of the evil with which we struggle, we look to them for inspiration. In Ephesians 6:12 (KJV) there is a recognition that our struggle is not against flesh and blood but against "principalities" and "powers." The New Revised Standard Version speaks of "rulers" and "authorities." Both are clear that these are not simply human beings. There is no analysis of such powers, but there is, at least, the assertion that we are to struggle against them.

For many centuries Christian teaching has led to ideas about changing the system. In the period of the Reformation, peasants stimulated by Christian ideas rose in revolt against the nobility, demanding a more egalitarian system. Some of the forces behind Cromwell had similarly radical ideas. But these efforts failed. To most people, in the West as elsewhere, the basic social, political, and economic order seemed simply given. Usually it was sanctioned by the church and held to be established by God.

The systems under which we live are not simply given; they are ultimately human creations depending on the consent of those they govern. People in the West came to recognize these truths only in the eighteenth century. Our Declaration of Independence, a definitive statement of these truths, formed the rationale for the successful American Revolution. These ideas then inspired the French Revolution and, in the early nineteenth century, the Latin American insurrections against Spanish colonial rule.

In the nineteenth century we fought a Civil War in this country, one of whose purposes and effects was to end the slave system of the South. In that century there were also many proposals for changing the system of industrial production to reduce the exploitation of workers. Of these proposals Marxism became the most influential.

Surprisingly, the extraordinary transformation of the international economy in recent decades has received little comment from those who should have been concerned about it. History shows that human beings can change the basic socio-political-economic system that rules our lives—but often at a very high cost. The fact that an existing system is bad does not mean that the system that replaces it will necessarily be better. Change can be for the better or for the worse.

Progressive Christians are called to examine and evaluate the system under which they live. If we find it unjust, we must ask whether a less unjust system is possible and whether the price of change is too high. We need also to distinguish our righteous anger about what a system is doing to people from our attitude toward those who defend the system and profit from it.

Many Christians judge that our proper role is to mitigate the evils of the present system, rather than attempt to change it. This may be because they believe that fundamental change is not desirable, not possible, or too costly. They support efforts to end the worst abuses of the global economy, such as child labor and the use of prisoners to undercut wages. They encourage more self-policing by transnational corporations. They sometimes look with hope to such international bodies as the United Nations, the International Labor Organization, and the World Trade Organization to regulate global labor practices.

Progressive Christians believe that this response is inadequate. We see little prospect for basic improvement of the lot of the poor through such approaches. We believe that more radical changes are possible and that the cost of change is likely to be less than that of continuing the present system. We recognize that the present system expresses the dominance of a "spirituality" of consumerism throughout the world. We must work at once to change the system and the value system that supports it.

A Christian Case for Changing the System

To those who believe that economic growth is the only way in which the urgent material needs of the poor can be met and that their present suffering is a necessary precursor of a better world, we present the case for radical change.

Economic growth is not well correlated with the reduction of poverty unless its rate is very high and it is accompanied with policies that favor poor people. Countries that have developed programs to help the poor have sometimes succeeded even when their economic growth is very low. Others whose growth has been rapid sometimes have seen the lot of the poor deteriorate. Economic growth rarely has reduced poverty except when it has been accompanied by policies specifically directed to benefit the poor. It has, on the other hand, often enriched those with capital.

The current global system makes effective organization of labor virtually impossible. If workers demand better conditions in one location, investment is simply shifted elsewhere. The situation is similar with respect to legislation. An industrializing nation that raises wages for its people is apt to experience capital flight. The argument that undirected growth will lead to markedly different results for labor depends largely on the analogy with what happened in industrialized countries in the twentieth century. But the improvement of the lot of workers there depended extensively on labor organizations and supportive legislation.

Globalization has reversed the trend toward the improvement of the condition of many workers in the United States. Today we have continuing growth in the United States, but because of competitive pressures, technological innovation, and market-oriented governance systems, the economic situation of unskilled and semiskilled workers is growing worse. The notion that economic growth by itself benefits the poor, without labor unions or supportive legislation, has little historical support.

It is sometimes argued that when there is sufficient economic growth, labor will become globally scarce and wages will rise. *But this would require a rate of growth that would exhaust resources and render the environment uninhabitable.*

Limits of this kind are already appearing in China, where rivers alternatively flood and run dry at enormous economic cost. Long before labor becomes scarce, the costs of "development" greatly exceed its benefits. The poor, of course, pay these costs most heavily. *If we truly want to benefit the poor, we must find some other way than the overall increase of economic activity to do so.*

Placing our faith in the endless increase of wealth is profoundly contradictory to the biblical message. Jesus himself said that we cannot serve both God and wealth (Matt. 6:24). Christians cannot affirm a world organized for the increase of wealth. The biblical message about the poor consistently calls for solidarity with them and their just treatment in the here and now. It does not support the faith that the increased wealth of the rich will eventually trickle down to the poor.

To Christians who believe that the globalized economy is an expression of irreversible technological changes and is, in any case, so fully entrenched that it will inevitably dominate the future, making protest and objections irrelevant, we present the case for an alternative.

While it is true that the powers and principalities that rule this world are indeed powerful, and the common people weak, *the powers and principalities draw much of their strength from the moral support of those who believe in them.* In the past generation these have been legion, including many Christians. These sincere supporters dominate the university, the media, and the government at all levels, as well as the corporations. Without this moral support, the immense changes effected in the past two decades could not have occurred.

This moral support is weakening. More and more people all over the world are finding that the promises of the global market are not fulfilled, even where it is most successful. Today the moral voice of humanity speaks much more clearly through the Non-Governmental Organizations (NGOs), which now meet regularly concurrent with United Nations summits, than through the representatives of governments and TNCs. Many of the NGOs are indigenous to countries that have suffered most from the prevailing system.

The NGOs are calling for radical change and proposing an alternative vision of bottom-up development. The idea of microlending, for example, has captured the moral imagination of many. Research shows that education for girls and targeting the poorest of the poor are crucial components of successful microlending programs. As Christians it is not difficult to recognize that *this bottom-up proposal is far closer to biblical thinking than the dominant present system.* It corresponds to the actual practice of church-related programs that have usually taken the form of community development oriented to meeting the needs of local people, rather than industrial development oriented to the enlargement of the global market. Church groups are among the NGOs and have contributed to the emerging vision of a different kind of world.

Perhaps the most fundamental need of this new vision is clarity on how the overall macroeconomy would function. By focusing exclusively on bottom-up approaches to development, progressive *Christians have not yet come to grips with the difficulties of designing a new whole from the sum of its parts.* That is the famously elusive "third way" that cries out for careful research and analysis.

Opposing further steps in the globalization of the world's economies also has some chance of success in the near future. Congress first refused to give the administration fast-track for negotiating an extension of NAFTA throughout Latin America and for the Multilateral Agreement on Investment (MAI). It was only in the fog of a "war on terrorism" that Congress narrowly changed its mind to authorize fast-track. The massive protests against starting another round of bargaining at the World Trade Organization (WTO) in Seattle in November 1999, and at subsequent meetings of the IMF, World Bank, the World Economic Forum, and other groups, indicate that we are far from alone in our concerns. None of these actions signal an end of globalization or even the failure of these proposals, but it does indicate that *public opinion is far more wary of the continuing extension of the dominant system than it was a few years ago.* To be sure, the withdrawal of moral support from the present system will not lead to its immediate collapse. The institutions that support it and the TNCs that now rule the world are far too well entrenched and too powerful to be so easily dislodged. No doubt the system will give way only as its internal contradictions weaken it dramatically.

But that is far from impossible. There has been much concern recently that the financial problems of southeast Asia, Russia, Brazil, and Argentina would spread throughout the global economy and cause massive disruption. That has been avoided thus far. But the forces that caused these problems have not been tamed. They are built into the system. To change them would be to change the system. *Instead of viewing the global economy as an invincible inevitability, people should see its fragility. The question is not so much whether it will come to an end but how much of human civilization will survive that end.*

To those who fear the cost of the change, we offer this encouragement:

There will certainly be a price. An enormous price has been paid already for the recent shift from an international market to a global economy: greater inequality, weaker governments, fragmented safety nets. Is it any wonder then to suppose that the costs of still more globalization will be even higher, as the power to control private interests wanes and the capacity to help the "losers" weakens further? And if that is so, *can the costs of changing the entire system possibly be as large?*

Bottom-up programs are already in place and gaining increasing support. The World Bank, for example, although still strongly committed to the existing system, recognizes the importance and value of microlending. It is obvious that top-down development does not reach hundreds of millions of the poor, so that those who care about the poor are having to build a new and different economy among the poor.

Even in Europe, because of the high unemployment there, a new bottom-up economy is developing among the unemployed. *It is possible to work for the expansion of these local economies even in the context of the dominant global top-down one.* This reduces the suffering brought about by the present economy and paves the way for transition.

VI. WHAT WE CAN DO

Act faithfully within the current corporate structure. Christians in positions of leadership in corporations cannot change the system, but they can still take steps that benefit workers.

An example is the work of a devout Christian, D. Dean Kays, who managed the redesign and completion of the King Abdul Azziz International Airport at Jeddah in Saudi Arabia. His employer was the Ralph M. Parsons Company. Kays observed that workers on this project were very inefficient. He also noted that they ate poorly at noon, when they were required to provide their own food. He found that sanitary conditions in their camp were poor and that sickness was frequent.

As a Christian, Kays wanted to improve the lot of the workers, who had been brought in from other countries, and who sent most of their pay back to their families. But he could not ask Parsons to reduce its profits for this purpose. Hence, he had to convince Parsons and others involved that improvements in the food and living conditions of the workers would lead to greater labor productivity and thereby recover the additional costs. He was successful in doing so, crediting God with guiding him through the maze of actions and conversations through which he persuaded those involved.

The workers were bused back to their camp at noon and provided with a nutritious meal without charge. Their living conditions were improved, and, as a result of those changes, their health and productivity also improved. Some of these higher standards carried over into future Saudi contracts and practices. Without cost to the employers, thousands of lives have been bettered because of the compassion and effectiveness of one executive.

Redouble individual efforts to live frugally and generously. The preceding section emphasized the withdrawal of moral support from the currently dominant global system. This is a goal toward which Christians can contribute. Christians must lead the way to a basic reconception of the "good life," one that is less materialistic and more frugal. We can withdraw our personal moral support from the whole religion of consumerism. We can also encourage others to do so.

Encourage congregations to talk about sweatshops. Many Protestant church members do not realize that many of the goods they routinely purchase are produced in intolerable conditions of exploitation. There will be no change of basic policies until the morally sensitive public becomes concerned and articulate. Social action committees, adult education groups, and special programs of awareness are essential to this educational task. This book can be distributed widely and used for discussion groups in churches. Sweatshop Watch publishes a helpful quarterly newsletter.

Promote consumer action. Shoppers can learn to choose products that have been produced in socially responsible ways. Information is readily available from Co-op America and other organizations about companies that have adopted sensible codes of conduct guaranteeing that their products are made under acceptable standards. Such Codes of Conduct are crucial and must have a monitoring system that is transparent and sufficiently independent of the companies. Consumers also can learn to ask retail stores if their products were manufactured without sweatshop or child labor, and how they know it.

Support campaigns that target poor company performance. For several years, for example, the People of Faith Network has called for Wal-Mart, the world's largest retailer, to improve conditions for its "vendor partner" factory workers, and to hire independent monitors to report on factory conditions. Co-op America maintains a Ladder of Labor Responsibility that lists the "bottom rung" companies in several product categories.

Congratulate college students for leading the way. Efforts targeted on specific markets are most likely to be successful. For example, students on many college and university campuses have demanded accountability by the manufacturers of athletic equipment and school sweatshirts sold to campus constituencies. Not since concerns over South Africa's apartheid policies reached a height in the mid-1980s have so many students been galvanized by a social issue beyond their university gates. As a result of the student campaign, Nike released the names and locations of factories in Indonesia where their shoes are manufactured. The Workers Rights Consortium, which student activists helped organize, works with NGOs overseas to review conditions at factories making apparel carrying college logos. Its code of conduct includes many of the same provisions as the FLA's code, but it is much broader and includes additional protections for women and specific safety and health codes that must be followed. It also calls for a "living wage." Requiring companies publicly to disclose the names and locations of the factories making their products is a better method of assuring compliance with fair labor standards than depending on company codes of conduct. Then consumers and human rights groups can make direct links with employees to hear their concerns.

Promote responsible church purchasing. Thus far we are not aware of a comparable effort directed at church purchases. It may be possible to learn, for example, where choir robes and hymnbooks are produced and under what circumstances and to get enough churches to commit themselves to responsible purchasing to affect these industries, should it prove that current production is in unacceptable contexts.

Encourage visits to sweatshops. Several groups organize group tours of areas in Los Angeles, New York, and abroad where sweatshops can be experienced firsthand. In Los Angeles, the Garment Worker Center coordinates visits by church groups. Borderlinks in Tucson, Arizona, offers educational programs that introduce participants to Mexican maquiladoras in the context of a broader view of problems at the border.

Take legislative action. As more people and institutions become concerned about sweatshops with greater understanding, it is becoming possible to make them a serious political issue at state and national levels. Recent action in California is encouraging. So, too, would be more adequate funding in the state for enforcement and tough penalties for violations of labor standards. A U.S. administration genuinely concerned about these matters could make a difference. For example, the Corporate Code of Conduct Act (H.R. 4596), before Congress at the time of writing, would require all U.S.-based corporations with more than twenty employees abroad to enact a code of conduct that would apply to its "subsidiaries, subcontractors, affiliates, joint ventures, partners or licensees." Were it to receive support from the current administration—an unlikely possibility—then legislative action modifying the present global economic system might be possible.

Discussion Questions

1. Los Angeles County is the "sweatshop capitol of America." Why is this such an important part of the local economy?
2. Many of the garment factories that supply giant American retailers like Wal-Mart and Nike are located in countries like Honduras, Bangladesh, and China, where costs of production are much lower than in the United States. These factories employ hundreds of thousands of workers, mostly younger women, who otherwise might not have found remunerative work. From a Christian perspective, isn't this a good thing? What else needs to be considered?
3. This chapter reviews a number of responses by Christians to the evils of sweatshops—responses all the way from justifying them temporarily, in the hope economic growth will eventually eliminate them, to radical

changes in the structure of the global economy. Where does your faith understanding place you on this continuum?

To Learn More

For historical background of U.S. sweatshops, see Leon Stein, *Out of the Sweatshop* (New York: New York Times Book Co., 1977). The best contemporary account of "the sweatshop capital of America" is Edna Banocich's *Behind the Label: Inequality in the Los Angeles Apparel Industry* (Berkeley: University of California Press, 2000). Attempts by human rights activists to joust with world markets are chronicled by Kimberly Ann Elliott in *Whitehats or Don Quixotes: Human Rights Vigilantes in the Global Economy* (Cambridge, Mass.: National Bureau of Economic Research, 2001). See also the guides for consumer action by Co-op America, *National Green Pages* (Washington, D.C.: Co-Op America, annually). For offshore production, see Khosrow Falenni, ed., *The Maquiladora Industry: Economic Solution or Problem?* (New York: Praeger, 1990) and Leslie Sklair, *Assembling for Development: The Maquila Industry in Mexico and the U.S.* (San Diego, Calif.: UCSD, Center for U.S.-Mexican Studies, 1993). See also Louie Mariam, *Immigrant Women Workers Take on the Global Factory* (Cambridge, Mass.: South End Press, 2001).

12

The Globalization
of Economic Life

Mary Jo stood contentedly in her front yard, as firmly planted in Middle America as any of the cornstalks out back. "I wouldn't invest in Asia," she said, shaking her head decisively. A fifty-nine-year-old secretary with big, sparkling eyes, a plaid shirt and no pretensions, she added, "Investing in Asia frightens me."

Yet Mary Jo, who has never traveled outside the United States, is in fact invested in Asia and all over the world, although she does not know it. After retiring in April from her job as a secretary with the state government, she has relied on a pension fund that has large investments abroad, giving her indirect ownership of stocks in Indonesia and Russia and Brazil. And the cash she tucked away in an A. G. Edwards money market account was funneled to big banks, which helped build elegant hotels and office towers from Argentina to Vietnam.

Meanwhile, sitting on the ground beside her hut, Bangon chopped up wild plants for lunch and pondered a wrenching question: What does her four-year-old daughter need more, food or a mother? A gentle woman whose soft face is framed by thick black hair, she explained that the family cannot afford both. As a result of the Asian financial crisis, her husband has lost his job as a construction worker, and so the family earns only a trickle of cash through odd jobs in this tiny village in northeast Thailand. That money can be used to buy rice and milk for the little girl, Saiyamon, who has become anemic and malnourished. Or Bangon can try to save the tattered small-denomination bills to pay for a stomach operation that she needs to save her own life.[1]

213

I. INTRODUCTION

In its broadest sense, globalization refers to the rapid growth of linkages and interconnections between nations and social communities that make up the present world system. While this world system involves many aspects of society, its *economic* dimension—the erasing of national borders to allow the free flow of goods and money—is the subject of this chapter. As economic globalization occurs, decisions and activities taking place in one part of the world have more and more consequences for people and communities elsewhere in the world.

Economic globalization takes many forms. It may involve trade between individuals or businesses in one country with those in another. Globalization of this sort is as old as recorded history. Ancient coastal tribes traded with those in the mountains and deserts, each gaining prized goods they could not otherwise have enjoyed. Today we take for granted the fact that much of what we consume or use originated elsewhere, often in a strange foreign land.

Or businesses may decide to produce their products not only at home but also in other countries, either to evade the tariffs or quotas of countries where they wish to sell their products or to cut their costs of production by, say, hiring cheaper labor. Then globalization involves the bundling together of financial capital, technology and other strategic inputs in order to transfer them as direct foreign investment (hereafter, direct investment) in another country.

Direct investment implies *control* over the assets transferred abroad. Foreign investments that don't involve control are called foreign portfolio equity investments (hereafter, portfolio investment). They are more likely to be made by financial institutions or investors like pension funds, insurance companies, or investment trusts, which are interested only in a return on their investments commensurate with the risks they are taking. If returns fall or risks rise, portfolio investment is much less dependable than direct investment as a source of longer-term finance for a country's development.

The activities of transnational corporations are a still deeper form of globalization. They coordinate their activities with many entities throughout the world, producing in many places with complex networks of production and finance. This form of globalization has recently been named "alliance capitalism," in order to stress the growing importance of strategic alliances between business entities, as businesses search for ways to protect their competitive advantages and global market positions. (See chapter 10, "Do Corporations Serve the Human Family?")

Governments also compete for economic advantage globally. They often support private research and development activities, finance worker retraining, protect the environment, and promote interfirm alliances. When governments decide it is in their interest to cooperate rather than compete, they may form supranational organizations, like the International Monetary Fund (IMF) and the World Trade Organization (WTO) or less formal regional bodies, in order to achieve shared objectives, for example, stable macroeconomic conditions, more growth through trade, and "market-friendly" economies.

II. ECONOMIC GLOBALIZATION

Recent Acceleration

Rapid growth of trade. Since World War II, trade between nations of goods and services has grown much faster than world economic output, primarily for three reasons. First, rapid improvements in transportation and communications have made it easier and cheaper to reach new markets. The cost of a three-minute telephone call between New York and London, for example, has fallen from $55 (in 2001 dollars) in 1950 to $1 today. Second, successive rounds of tariff negotiations have virtually eliminated border barriers among developed countries, and many less developed countries have unilaterally reduced their tariffs and quotas, even without prodding from the IMF or World Bank. Third, processing trade—trade that involves goods whose components cross borders more than once before reaching final buyers—has expanded rapidly. A Ford F-150 truck is assembled from parts originating in at least forty-five countries. Trade is widespread for almost all nations, and its importance is rising virtually everywhere. A quick review of the labels in one's clothing is a good reminder of the pervasiveness of trade.

Trade between nations also has been transformed in recent years, from transactions over which national governments exercise significant control—*international* trade, if you will—to a form of globalized trade engineered and managed by large, dominant transnational corporations—*transnational* trade. Well over one-third of all U.S. imports and exports, for example, takes place between the divisions and subsidiaries of the same company. This distinction is important for the reason that it signals a transfer of power and control away from national governments that, for all their failures, can be influenced by the general public. Transnational corporations, on the other hand, are set up to serve only their stockholders.

Even faster growth of foreign direct investment. By latest count, there are at least 39,000 transnational corporations owning production facilities outside

their home country. Direct investments by these large firms, which are growing more than twice as fast as trade, are probably the best indicators of the
growth of deep cross-border economic integration. In fact, worldwide sales of
the foreign subsidiaries of transnational enterprises now exceed the value of
all internationally traded goods.

Most direct investment decision makers are in the leading industrial countries, although investment decisions by firms in developing countries like
South Korea, Taiwan, and Brazil are increasing quite rapidly. The hundred
largest transnational corporations (excluding those in banking and finance) are
estimated to control about one-third of the assets held by transnational corporations abroad.

Foreign direct investment also is a primary means of transferring technology across borders. In this case, the technology is transferred *within* the firm,
where it becomes part of the investing firm's significant and continuing financial stake in the success of a foreign affiliate. It too has been growing rapidly—
by some measures even faster than trade—but its growth has been
concentrated in a relatively few large firms with strong technological and
brand-name assets.

The flood of portfolio investment across borders. Encouraged by "market-
friendly" policies of developing countries—policies often imposed on debtor
nations by the IMF—individual investors, pension plans, and mutual funds
increased their stakes fivefold in the stocks and bonds of Third World companies in the early 1990s. Such rapid growth contrasted sharply with the experience of the 1980s when investments in stocks were rare.

Around 1997, stock equity investors suddenly began to reassess the risks
of their exposure, and the Asian financial crisis was born. In retrospect, the
flow of portfolio investments was too fast to be absorbed into productive
activities. It created bubbles in stock and real estate prices and encouraged
luxury consumption that gave the illusion of prosperity unrelated to real
increases in productivity. The quicker portfolio investments flowed into
Thailand, Malaysia, Indonesia, South Korea, and Hong Kong, the quicker
money was sucked out of the productive sector to join the speculation. When
investors finally sensed their risk, they rushed to pull their money out.
Hence, the flood of portfolio investments reversed direction by the end of
1997, ushering in severe recessions in many countries, from which none has
fully recovered.

The proliferation of business alliances. Cross-border agreements between firms
based in different countries have become increasingly important complements
to traditional trade and direct investment activities, with the range of such
agreements growing ever wider. Their rapid growth since about 1985 is
explained by the fact that technological changes are becoming more deeply

science-based and that in some fields—notably information technology—few (if any) large firms are any longer capable of generating all the research needed to remain competitive. Thus, many transnational corporations have been driven to sharing knowledge about new technologies, production processes, and distribution techniques. A flurry of mergers and acquisitions in the late 1990s boosted direct investment flows substantially, despite a slowdown in global economic activity.

The Institutions of Globalization

As transnational trade and investment soared in the 1990s, so too did the regulatory machinery for assuring their continued growth. During this period, the World Trade Organization emerged as the dominant arbiter of trade; the IMF was transformed into a bank of last resort; the IMF and the World Bank sorted out their respective roles in deeply indebted countries; the Organization for Economic Cooperation and Development (OECD) negotiated a Multilateral Agreement on Investment (MAI) designed to restrict a nation's ability to regulate foreign investment; and the sophistication of business alliances between dominant corporate players metastasized throughout the multinational business community.

There is little doubt that these bodies exert enormous influence over the societies and economies of peoples everywhere. Because their design and coordinated management accords with the so-called Washington Consensus described below, they are best described as proponents of trade and investment as a means of encouraging the growth of markets throughout the world. Their stated aim is "prosperity broadly shared." Whether or not these institutions deliberately favor economic over other human aspirations, their preoccupation with economic ends has been widely criticized as "an ideology ordering our thought and action," to the detriment of other individual and social purposes. Alternatives to the institutional design of the Washington Consensus are summarized in part 5.

The Consequences of Globalization

This summary of the spread of economic globalization—and of its sponsorship by the Washington Consensus—suggests why it has grown so rapidly. The first reason is the pressure felt by business firms from customers and competitors continually to innovate and upgrade what they produce. As firms discover the limits of their own core competencies, they are recognizing the need to combine their skills with those of other firms, often in other countries, in new forms of "alliance capitalism."

The second reason is the spread of market-oriented policies by national governments and regional authorities. In the last ten years thirty countries have given up central planning, and a hundred others have liberalized their policies governing trade, foreign exchange, and/or capital transfers. The privatization of state enterprises in many countries and the relaxation of government regulations have added incentives for cross-border integration, both within transnational corporations and between independent firms or groups.

There is no doubt that the expansion of international trade, direct and portfolio investments, and networks of business alliances have benefited many people. The political changes and technological advances of the 1990s provided a stronger basis for economic growth than at any other time since the mid-1940s. This was because a globally integrated economy can lead to a better division of labor between countries, it is argued, allowing low-wage countries to specialize in labor-intensive tasks while high-wage countries use workers in more productive ways. It allowed firms to exploit bigger economies of scale. And with globalization, capital can be shifted to whatever country offers the most productive investment opportunities, rather than being trapped at home financing projects with poor returns.

But globalization also has its costs, which must be weighed along with its benefits in order to assess its true consequences.

Heightened inequality. Competitive pressures and more market-oriented policies create pockets of unemployment not easily corrected in the short run. The structural changes causing unemployment tend to exaggerate the differences between those with the education, skills, and mobility to flourish in an unfettered world market—such as the owners of capital, highly skilled workers, and many professionals—and those without such attributes. Globalization has a way of eroding the bargaining power of groups that cannot move, leading to greater instability in their earnings and hours worked. The apparent "losers," unlike the highly skilled "winners," are made increasingly anxious about their place in an integrated world economy, whether they are blue-collar workers in New England textile factories or subsistence farmers in Mindanao.

The best evidence of this is found in growing income inequalities. The gap between rich and poor countries has long been the major source of inequality among people of the world. Somewhat surprisingly, this gap has closed slightly over the past couple of decades. Income distribution within countries, on the other hand, has widened rapidly, and this has had a deleterious effect on many parts of the world. Almost everywhere in the West, despite "social safety nets," the youngest, poorest, and least educated are significantly worse off than their counterparts were twenty years ago. Many poor countries also are becoming *less* egalitarian in the face of globalization. The rural poor, especially the smallholders and the landless of Asia and Latin America, are being ruthlessly dispossessed and displaced.

What forms of globalization are responsible for these disruptive changes in the markets for workers? Many people blame the changes in more developed countries on competition from low-wage countries. Most economists, however, blame the losses of lower-skilled workers on technological changes (e.g., computerization) that are biased against the demand for low-skilled labor.

While both of these reasons no doubt have contributed to the widening of income gaps within countries, the much larger reason appears to be the dramatic policy changes, described as liberalization, that commenced at the end of the 1970s. In the richer countries, these changes included a move from macroeconomic policies that tried to control the levels of aggregate demand (Keynesian policies) toward ones that tried to control money supplies (monetarist policies), and a shift from state-provided welfare toward pay-as-you-go social services. At the same time, the public provision of basic services such as water and electricity, frequently at subsidized prices, has been replaced by privatized providers at "economic" prices; industrial interventionism and labor protection have given way to laissez-faire; and tax systems whose major purpose was to correct inequalities have been transformed into systems mainly intended to promote incentives and economic efficiency.

There were parallel changes for developing countries, where policy was subject to the same paradigmatic shifts, largely as a result of the influence of the richer countries, most directly through conditions imposed by the IMF and the World Bank. When in the 1980s many developing countries no longer could generate sufficient income to meet their debt obligations, they were faced with the choice of retreating into complete economic isolation or seizing the lifeline thrown them by the IMF and the World Bank—a lifeline composed of "stabilization" and "structural adjustment" loans available only if they agreed to far-reaching and "market-friendly" changes in national economic policies.

These stabilization and structural adjustment programs took scarce economic resources away from other possible uses by poor countries. Consider, for example, the costs of implementing Western financial codes and standards, one of many requirements to be met. Here the choice for countries starved for development was between training more bank auditors and accountants in order to meet the standards of financial liberalization and using these resources, say, to hire more secondary-school teachers or boost spending levels for the primary education of girls. These decisions seem to hit the poor the hardest, with the urban working class particularly at risk.

Conflicts over social priorities. Globalization also creates conflicts between governments over domestic social priorities and the social institutions that embody them. Indeed, it is precisely the convergence of the policies just mentioned that has forced countries into what Thomas Friedman calls a "golden straitjacket" but others call a "toxic straitjacket"—a standardization of policies worldwide that vastly narrows the ability of single countries to honor their more unique political and cultural preferences. In Friedman's terms, "your economy grows but your politics shrink." Deviate too far from the new globalization rules, and a country soon will see its investors stampede away, its interest rates rise, and its stock market prices fall.

Put another way, the argument against unrestricted global freedom of trade and movements of financial capital is not primarily an economic one. Rather, it is that the economy should serve the needs of society, not society the imperatives of the market. There is not much doubt that free markets are the most economically efficient type of capitalism. For most economists that ends the matter. Yet what so-called "social market economies" do—like those of Japan and most of Europe—is in no sense irrational. In those countries, policies to maintain social cohesion are just as important as efficiency in the allocation of scarce resources.

Consider, for example, the struggle the European Community has had over the harmonization of policies on employment, welfare, immigration, and competition in order to create a common market and a common currency and to remain internationally competitive. In Japan, large corporations have started to dismantle the postwar practice of providing lifetime employment, one of Japan's most distinctive social institutions, in order to adapt to the pressures of globalization. In South Korea, labor unions have taken to the streets to protest the government's relaxation of firing restrictions. And Latin American countries are competing with each other to liberalize trade, deregulate their economies, and privatize public enterprises.

Efforts by developed countries in North America and Europe to "harmonize" labor standards are motivated only in part by the fear in developed countries of losing jobs to workers earning much less in developing countries. International labor standards have become a point of contention in trade disputes not only for economic reasons, but also because low wages and weak safety standards abroad violate the human rights of workers. The United States and others are finding it increasingly difficult to negotiate worker protections for the charters of multinational institutions like the World Trade Organization. The failure of the WTO meeting in Seattle in December 1999 was more the result of this policy straitjacket than of the protests in the streets.

Disagreements also are rising over the environmental consequences of globalization. Because pollution is generated most often by industrialization, the countries that are soon becoming the most industrialized, like China,

Brazil, Indonesia, and India, are the likeliest sources of future global pollution. They are unlikely to throttle back their industrial plans in order to protect the environment, as some in the United States and Europe have suggested. That would raise their costs and erase their competitive advantage. Arguments in Kyoto at the December 1997 Summit on Global Climate Change vividly illustrate the political tensions wrought by globalization. (See chapter 14, "The Church and Environmentalism.")

Fragmented safety nets. The so-called invisible hand of the market is acceptable to most people only if the losers from market forces are compensated by the winners. A central function of government has been to assist in this transfer by helping the losers to adjust to change—usually by means of unemployment compensation, severance payments, and adjustment assistance. In essence, governments have used their fiscal powers to insulate domestic groups from excessive market risks, particularly those originating in international transactions. This is the way governments have maintained domestic political support for liberalizing trade and finance throughout the postwar period.

But recently, the idea of giving support to the losers has come under withering attack. Employers no longer grant job security, partly for competitive reasons and also because they are more mobile and less dependent on the goodwill of local workforces. Governments are less able to help the losers because in a world of heightened financial mobility the slightest hint of raising taxes leads to capital flight. Moreover, the ideological onslaught against the welfare state has paralyzed many governments and made them unable to respond to the domestic needs of a more internationally competitive economy.

Accordingly, at the very time increased integration into the world economy has raised the need of governments to redistribute tax revenues or implement generous social programs in order to protect the vast majority of the population that remains internationally immobile, governments find themselves less able to raise taxes. The heightened mobility of financial capital has led to competition among nations to attract foreign investment, and a key tool of competition is to offer a relatively low-tax environment. Tax competition, in turn, threatens to undermine the individual and corporate income taxes. The United States and other affluent countries have responded, first, by shifting the tax burden from (mobile) capital to (less mobile) labor, and second, when further increased taxation of labor becomes politically and economically difficult, by cutting the social safety net. This is bound to jeopardize social stability. Even governments with significant budget surpluses—like the United States until the aftermath of September 11—seem unwilling to protect the weak against the cruelties of the market.

III. WHERE SHOULD POWER RESIDE?

Into whose hands are the powers to *set* society's goals being delivered as the forces of globalization continue to expand? Virtually everyone concedes that markets are a useful instrument for *implementing* certain goals. As mechanisms for delivering goods and services to the people at the lowest possible prices, they have yet to meet their match.

But for implementing many other goals and for setting the goals of society, unfettered markets may not be the best instrument. Unregulated markets often lead to spoiled environments. Nor do markets provide for the national or collective defense. They do not eliminate the scourge of unemployment. They rarely distribute income and wealth in accord with most people's conception of fairness. And they're not usually designed to protect other cultural values. Markets don't care for fairness or community, but only for efficiency.

Who then ought to set society's goals? How are today's globalizing communities and nations governed? To what extent do their governance structures hold decision-making powers accountable for the consequences of their decision? Three schools of thought give very different answers to these questions.

The Washington Consensus. This widely held point of view finds its leadership in the business community, the economics profession, and the IMF, World Bank, and World Trade Organization. The Washington Consensus supports a "top-down" structure of global economic governance when crises occur, as during the debt crisis of the 1980s and more recently during the Asian, Russian, and Brazilian currency crises. Perhaps the best illustration of this consensus has been the habit of these institutions to offer various kinds of debt relief, but only if the indebted countries agreed to adopt some combination of "stabilization" and "structural adjustment" policies that sharply reduce government services, free economies of regulation, and encourage exporting and direct investment. Members of this consensus applaud the growing power of market institutions and the weakening of governments, and favor strengthening key multilateral institutions like the IMF and WTO. Governments still have important roles to play, especially as providers of a legal framework, education, and stable fiscal and financial policies, but their importance is downplayed. Because this group says little about noneconomic goals, it leaves the impression that it favors policies that place economic growth and trade above other human values.[2]

The Washington Consensus has exerted enormous influence on the processes of change reflected in the global economic trends noted above. These trends strongly imply a heightened concentration of economic power in the world, centered especially in large transnational enterprises, a weakening of the countervailing forces of governments and civil societies, and quite probably a further separation of decision-making powers from public accountability for their consequences. Who sets society's goals in a world dominated by the Washington Consensus? It is still a pluralistic world involving enterprises, governments, and civil societies. But the balance of these forces seems now to be shifting in favor of businesses, whose interests are vastly more focused on economic returns than on the health of people and their communities.

The Human Development Consensus. This school of thought is best represented by UNICEF and the UN Development Program. It differs from the Washington Consensus primarily by its readiness to highlight the ill effects on human and community life of many globalizing processes. It is blunt about the fact that "market-friendly" development strategies usually produce losers as well as winners and that social cohesion easily is lost when societies fail to find ways to assist the losers with retraining, relocation, and/or income transfers. It rues the growing gap between rich and poor. The Human Development Consensus also has focused attention on the wastefulness of military expenditures and the human destruction wrought by the structural adjustment policies of the IMF and the World Bank.[3]

The Human Development Consensus thinks that an economic system can remain viable over time only so long as responsible governance structures establish mechanisms to counter the abuses of market or state power and the consequent erosion of society's natural, social, and moral capital. This suggests that it believes in a form of democratic pluralism not unlike the framework that guided the post–World War II economic boom of Western nations and resulted in the broad sharing of development benefits throughout their societies. Thus it supports a process of goal setting that actively seeks the involvement of all parts of society, including the civil society. Even so, it shares with the Washington Consensus a belief in economic growth through free and open markets, and therefore it too is hostage to economic power arrangements that produce outcomes especially favorable to business.

The People-Centered Consensus. This school of thought finds its leadership in various citizen alliances, such as the People-Centered Development Forum, the Third World Network, and the International Group for Grassroots Initiatives, rather than any official governance structure. It is deeply rooted in the institutions of civil society, including some church organizations. While the People-Centered Consensus acknowledges necessary roles for markets and governments, it insists that the people must take precedence over the interests of either the corporation or the state. It therefore stands in opposition to the patterns of globalization that concentrate economic power in the hands of transnational corporations beyond the reach of public accountability.

Adherents of the People-Centered Consensus favor economic and political *de*-centralization, so that people retain the rights to organize and to partici-pate in the decisions that affect them. In order to achieve this goal, they pre-fer greater community self-reliance—a drawing back from the deepening entanglements of globalization, not to the exclusion of specialization and trade, but with greater effort to nurture and control the use of local resources. Because the People-Centered Consensus regards the limits of the earth's finite ecosystem as more constraining than the other schools of thought, it also places greater emphasis on a means of livelihood adequate to assure every per-son's basic needs. Frugality for the well-off is a sine qua non of this point of view.[4]

The People-Centered Consensus draws strength also from the indigenous communities of developing countries, which resist the westernization of their culture. Their religious roots cause them to perceive their society's goals dif-ferently from, say, the elites who have allied themselves with the agents of globalization. For many of them, it is the dignity and sustenance of individual human beings that matters, more than growth or even development of the local economy.

Members of these communities wonder too if the free-market paradigm of the Washington Consensus is not an indirect method of organizing social and political relations and structures in society as well as a means of ordering the economy. It is not enough to have "friendly" economic markets and "socially concerned" business leaders. A society needs a healthy civil society *first*, lest the economic system be allowed to disrupt harmonious human relationships.

Thus, the kind of democratic pluralism preferred by the People-Centered Consensus probably implies markets with a significant degree of regulation and trade policies that link national economies to one another within a frame-work of rules that maintains domestic competition and favors domestic enter-prise employing local workers meeting local standards, paying local taxes and functioning within a well-developed system of democratic governance. For-eign competition is not excluded; it simply does not share the preferred status of locally owned businesses that are rooted in place and serve the community in many ways that imported goods and footloose investors cannot.

IV. A CHRISTIAN PERSPECTIVE

The Environment, Community, and Justice

Globalization is not a new concept to the church. It is prefigured in the Bible by the creation stories. What God has made is a unity; all belongs together. That creation is to be tended, protected, and nurtured by its human partici-pants, who have unique creation responsibilities because of uniquely bearing the image of the Creator. That responsibility involves caring for both "the garden"—the environment itself—and the relationships of the created beings. In the unfolding of the biblical message, a sense of the goodness of community extends to include ultimately all the earth's people and all future generations.

Thus the moral test of today's globalizing economy is whether it serves adequately the human enterprise and the larger creation. Few would doubt that international exchange has made life easier, more pleasant, and more interesting for those with the resources to participate. But huge segments of the world's population do not have such resources; worse yet, many are further impoverished by the ordinary functioning of the globalized economy.

Community is not encouraged by a competitive market system—even less so by its globalized version. Calls for free trade and free movements of capital, untouched by community constraints, are calls for individual, not community, values. This insistence on social and moral autonomy has caused critics in the church to denounce "the market society in whose logic God's grace and God's justice cannot appear."5 To acknowledge a sphere of life from which moral scrutiny is excluded is to abridge God's sovereignty and create an absolute that rivals God. Biblical faith acknowledges no such rival.

An economic system in which business profits and high consumption in one society are based on exploitative relationships elsewhere runs headlong into a basic biblical concern. The ability to manipulate people and to play God through money was vehemently condemned by the prophets: "I will not revoke the punishment; because they sell the righteous for silver, and the needy for a pair of sandals" (Amos 2:6). Such words still have a prophetic ring in a time when producers of apparel and sneakers search the world over for a labor force that will work for a few pennies less in the drive to cut costs while protecting market share and profits.

Nor can the pain of heavily indebted poor countries be easily dismissed by Christians guided by the biblical witness. In recent years, governments and banks have offered some relief. Still, in dozens of cases, the remaining debt cannot be paid or can be paid only by imposing enormous human suffering. The biblical message is unambiguous. In the seventh year or the forty-ninth year—"the year of the Lord"—there was to be a time of jubilee. Debts were to be canceled, family land returned, and the impressed and oppressed set free (Lev. 25; Luke 4:18–19). There is debate about whether the law of jubilee was ever formally administered in the life of Israel. Nevertheless, the principle is clear. No economic decision or arrangement must be allowed to impoverish permanently; it must not make the future hopeless. Within history, periodic corrections are to be made that will reestablish right economic relationships and restore freedom, opportunity, and hope. Such a principle has profound implications for the prophetic role of the church in today's global society.

The principle of jubilee is a reminder that biblical faith accords absolute status to no economic system. Nor does it sanction untended economic mechanisms. The biblical tradition assumes that an economy is subject to moral guidance and regular correction. That is no less true of complex international economic relations than of exchanges between individuals.

Facing such realities, the church should not pretend technical competence it does not uniquely possess. It can and should, however, engage in moral analysis of laws and economic proposals, denounce morally unacceptable economic outcomes, name the sin that is causing pain, and insist that more humane policies be sought and implemented. That is an authentic prophetic task of the community of faith in economic life—whether the market is local, national, or global.

Policies for Justice in a Globalizing World

The growth of the world economy could be a great advance for humankind. It could be the beginning of a many-centered world, in which different cultures and regimes could interact and cooperate without domination or war. But that is not the world that is arising around us in the vain attempt by proponents of the Washington Consensus to build a globally free market.

In a world in which market forces are subject to no overall constraint or regulation, justice and peace are continually at risk. Unregulated capitalism degrades the environment and kindles conflict over natural resources. It enriches the educated elites and owners of capital, often at the expense of less able and less mobile populations. By promoting only minimal government intervention in the economy, it neglects those in greatest need. And in expanding parts of the world, it locks nation-states into competition not only for markets but for survival. The global market as it is presently organized forces nations to become rivals for resources while creating weak methods for conserving them.

History confirms that free markets are inherently volatile institutions, prone to speculative booms and busts. Overshooting, especially in financial markets, is their normal condition; the recent implosion of the tech stock bubble is just the latest example. To work well, free markets need not only regulation but active management. During much of the postwar era, world markets were kept stable by national governments and by a regime of international cooperation. Only lately has a much earlier idea been revived and made into orthodoxy—the idea adopted by the Washington Consensus that, provided there are clear and well-enforced rules of the game, free markets can be self-regulating, because they embody the rational expectations that participants form about the future.

On the contrary, since markets are themselves shaped by human expectations, their behavior cannot be rationally predicted. The forces that drive markets are not mechanical processes of cause and effect, as assumed in most of economic theory. They are what George Soros has termed "reflexive inter-actions." Because markets are governed by highly combustible interactions among beliefs, they cannot be self-regulating.

Thoughtful people have a right to be alarmed by the evidence that freer markets are unstable and that not all people are prospering from their spread. Whole communities, whole regions, whole nations are being marginalized by the inexorable forces of change brought on by economic integration. Poverty is rising almost everywhere. Yet the power of governments to alleviate the suf-fering of those who are losing out is slipping away from them.

One evidence of this is that an appropriate balance is not being struck between the economic and noneconomic aspirations of human beings and their communities. Indeed, the evidence is mounting that globalization's tra-jectory can easily lead to social disintegration—to the splitting apart of nations along lines of economic status, mobility, region, or social norms. Globaliza-tion not only exacerbates tensions among groups; it also reduces the willing-ness of internationally mobile groups to cooperate with others in resolving disagreements and conflicts.

What then can be done to share the benefits of globalization more widely and to ameliorate its social consequences? The answer to this question is *not* to disengage altogether from the processes of globalization. That would be foolish as well as impossible. Many of the underlying changes that have occurred in the global economy are now irreversible. Rather, the question is how to engineer a new balance between market and society—a balance that will require greater human control over the processes of change and the shar-ing of its fruit.

The following recommendations are meant to help strike such a balance. They do not conform precisely to proposals generated by either the Human Development Consensus or the People-Centered Consensus, yet they draw from both groups. Nor do they represent a comprehensive blueprint for reform, which surely would include far more radical changes in the institu-tions of business, government, and daily living than proposed here.

V. WHAT WE CAN DO

Things that Governments Should Do

A rehabilitation of the modern state. In Liberia, Albania, Afghanistan, Tajikistan, Colombia, Siberia, Chechnya, and Somalia, the threat to peace and economic progress does not come from tyrannous or expansionist states. It comes from the absence of effective government of any kind. The Washington Consensus neglects the many ways unregulated world markets threaten cohesion of society and stability in governments. The World Bank's recent repudiation of the dogma of minimal government is welcome; but it falls far short of the need to provide the institutions necessary to assure security from destitution, unemployment, and exclusion.

A regulatory framework for coexistence and cooperation among the world's diverse economies. As it is presently organized, global capitalism is supremely ill-suited to cope with the risks of geopolitical conflict that are endemic in a world of worsening scarcities. If today's laissez-faire regime is not reformed, it is likely to fracture and fragment as mounting scarcities of resources and conflicts of interest among the world's great powers make international cooperation even more difficult. Free markets are creatures of strong governments and cannot exist very long without them.

More efficient and generous systems of social insurance. They would allow losers to secure more of the benefits of international economic integration and suffer fewer of its social costs. Indeed, the social welfare state is the flip side of the open economy; the more exposed the economy is to external shocks, the more certainly it will need a generous system of income transfers. Any movement towards freer trade and capital movements should be accompanied by more generous adjustment assistance policies, including unemployment benefits, retraining, and relocation subsidies.

Taxation of footloose capital movements. Generous and appropriate systems of social insurance must be financed in some way. If national sources of taxation are no longer adequate to this task, then it may well be time to consider taxation of footloose factors at the global level, with revenue sharing among nations. The most radical reform would involve outright restrictions on speculative capital transfers, with all their potential for abuse and corruption. A more moderate reform might include measures designed to regulate the timing of capital transfers or ones that increase the cost of speculative transactions. Similarly, a uniform tax might be imposed on intercurrency transactions, for example, the so-called Tobin Tax.[6] More exchange of information among tax authorities would be another step in the right direction. Better still, an international convention to restrict the ability of transnational firms to avoid taxation should be negotiated.

A new system of global safeguards. A new system is required to accommodate important differences in the social, political, and cultural preferences of nations. Multilateral institutions like the WTO should permit selective disengagement from the discipline of multilateral treaties, under well-specified contingencies, when countries need breathing room to satisfy domestic requirements that are in conflict with trade policies, for example, to assist labor reallocation or to protect the environment. Similar provisions should be made in treaties governing foreign direct and portfolio investment.

Reform IMF and World Bank conditional lending policies. These multilateral agencies should replace bankrupt structural adjustment efforts with policies and programs that more adequately meet the needs of the poor and promote sustainable, participatory, and equitable development. Among the conditions that should be included in loan agreements are these:

- Reduction of inappropriate levels of military spending
- Preservation of spending on basic needs, including education and health care
- Assurance of a safety net for those most severely affected by adjustment policies
- Prevention of adverse environmental effects such as deforestation and soil degradation
- A system for monitoring and correcting (as may be necessary) the effects of adjustment policies

These agencies also must be more accountable to the people affected by their policies and projects through increased transparency, greater access to information, and greater participation in the development of projects, programs, and policies.

What Churches Can Do

Redouble individual efforts to support self-determination. As individual Christians and their congregations contemplate development of covenant relationships with particular nongovernmental organizations or communities abroad, they should seek to support those whose projects are designed by the local community and controlled by its people. By the same token, individual Christians who hold stock in U.S.-domiciled transnational corporations should hold their companies accountable for conduct contrary to just and sustainable human development.

Encourage partnership relationships with local communities. All agents of development assistance, including USAID and the multilateral assistance groups, should be urged by churches to establish healthier partnership relations with local communities. The international mission programs of most mainline churches understand that partnership involves mutuality and cooperation and aims at increased self-reliance with respect to essential needs. Self-reliance comes through broad-based local ownership and control of productive resources, land reform (as necessary), and encouragement of sustainable agricultural and locally based business enterprises.

Support legislation that helps end sweatshops. The garment and textile industries are rank with labor exploitation, here and abroad. There is widespread noncompliance with labor, health, and safety laws, as well as stubborn unwillingness by many large retailers to monitor adequately labor practices by the contractors with whom they do business. Churches can help improve the lot of sweatshop workers by supporting local, state, and national legislation to regulate sweatshop practices. (See chapter 11, "Responding to Sweatshops.")

Support programs that forgive the unsustainable debts of impoverished nations. Recently the joint IMF-World Bank initiative for heavily indebted poor countries (HIPCs) was launched to much fanfare. Its terms and conditions expect applicants to demonstrate "good policy track records"—a euphemism for policies deemed appropriate by these agencies. Efforts to balance economic goals with other societal objectives are conspicuously absent from HIPC legislation. Recently, a forgiveness initiative for bilateral debts, along the lines of Jubilee 2000, has been announced by several creditor nations. Churches should study forgiveness initiatives, and their members should let their representatives know their views on them. (See chapter 13, "Should Debt Be Forgiven?")

Redouble individual efforts to live frugally and generously. Christians must lead the way to a basic reconception of the "good life"—one that is less materialistic and more frugal. The good life finds fulfillment in a genuinely caring and mutually supportive community in Christ and through faithful responses to God's call to restore creation and discover the contemporary meaning of doing justice, loving kindness, and walking humbly with our God (Mic. 6:8).

Discussion Questions

1. How have the linkages or interconnections of the globalization process impacted your life? On balance, do you regard them as advantages or disadvantages for a healthy Christian life?

2. Most people agree that markets are a useful instrument for implementing society's goals. But should they be allowed to set the goals for society? Assess the strengths and weaknesses of how the Washington Consensus, the Human Development Consensus, and the People-Centered Consensus set the goals of society. Which accords best with your understanding of how Christians should establish priorities for the goals of community?

3. Is it too late to expect justice in a globalizing world? Since much of the direction the global economy has taken is irreversible, how can a balance between market and society be negotiated? How might Christians play a role in these negotiations?

To Learn More

See "Dueling Globalizations: A Debate between Thomas Friedman and Ignacio Ramonet," *Foreign Policy*, fall 1999, 110–27. Friedman, a foreign affairs columnist for the *New York Times*, also wrote *The Lexus and the Olive Tree* (New York: Farrar, Straus & Giroux, 1999). William Greider argues for more managed globalization in *One World Ready or Not: The Manic Logic of Global Capitalism* (New York: Simon & Schuster, 1997). In his book *The Post-Corporate World: Life after Capitalism* (San Francisco: Barrett-Koehler, 1999) David Korten stipulates that corporate capitalism could unravel the cohesion of society. See also "The Face of Globalism," a special insert in the summer 2001 issue of *The American Prospect*. Refraining from taking sides, Dani Rodrik reexamines some of the faulty assumptions made on both sides of the globalization debate in "Sense and Nonsense in the Globalization Debate," *Foreign Policy*, summer 1997. For more about the roles of civil society and nongovernmental organizations, see "The Third Force. Civil Society's Challenge to Corporations and Governments," *World Watch*, Nov.–Dec. 1999.

13

Should Debt Be Forgiven?

In 1994, Juan Jose and Betty Chinchilla, small farmers in Colong-moncagua, Honduras, could no longer afford their traditional meal of red beans and tortillas, let alone the cost of the uniforms their children needed in order to attend school. Bean prices had risen dramatically, as had the prices of seeds and fertilizer they needed to plant crop. Ever since the government had adopted policies in the early 1990s to address Honduras' overwhelming foreign debt, Juan Jose and Betty, their family, and their neighbors suffered from hunger and little work. People in Colongmoncagua called these developments "paquetaso," or "hit over the head."

I. INTRODUCTION

For most of the last decade, many civil society and church organizations have called for banks, creditor governments and multilateral bodies to forgive the sovereign debt of the poorest and most heavily indebted developing countries. These calls usually are defended by appeals to fairness or justice. Each emphasizes particular aspects of the issue and of the benefits different parties receive from debt relief. Many interests and attitudes towards justice are on display.

Debtors and those who support them believe that the burdens of debt are too heavy and the poor are hurt more than others. Creditors and their supporters emphasize the sanctity of contracts and the losses suffered by depositors or taxpayers when debts are not paid. Little is heard about debtors who at great cost have honored their agreements. Honest people will inevitably differ in their response to the so-called debt crisis, depending on how they rank the competing claims and what they believe about the intentions of the claimants.

This chapter is an effort to clarify some of the confusing claims about developing-country debt and the consequences of its forgiveness. It brings an explicitly progressive Christian viewpoint to these considerations, including a ready acknowledgment that people of faith identify injustices far more easily than the ways to correct them. The issues of debt and its forgiveness, we have found, are vastly more complicated than we previously had expected.

II. THE DEBT CRISIS AND ITS EFFECTS

Origins of the Debt Crisis

In the two decades following World War II, governments of the newly emerging nations of Africa, Asia, and Latin America embarked on a strategy of industrialization based on activities protected behind high trade barriers that substituted domestic production for imported goods. Because domestic resources were considered inadequate for the large investment needs of development, countries often relied on foreign sources of funding to augment domestic resources obtained by saving.

Most of the foreign resources were borrowed, usually at low interest rates and with long maturities, from official lenders. Institutions like the World Bank, regional development banks, and most governmental assistance agencies took reasonable care to evaluate the projects they were lending to, in order to make sure they would generate increases in national income sufficient to service the debt and still leave a comfortable surplus. Most official lenders also monitored the long-term capacity of indebted nations to manage their borrowing sustainably.

By the late 1960s, however, lenders as well as some borrowers began to realize that prolonged protection was creating economic inefficiencies and strong vested interests in the status quo, stifling the potential for further development. Because most countries had small domestic markets for the goods of their import-substituting industries, investment opportunities began to dry up. Some governments of developing countries were reluctant to give up existing industrialization plans—plans through which they exercised some control—but under the circumstances they were compelled to adopt more outward-oriented trading policies that emphasized production of goods for export.

By and large, before 1970 developing countries were considered too great a risk to borrow from commercial bank sources. Virtually all of the debt accumulated by that time was owed to official lenders like the World Bank, the regional development banks, and the governments of the northern industrial countries. Debt problems—the inability or unwillingness of debtors to meet interest obligations—were relatively rare.

This picture changed dramatically as events of the early 1970s unfolded. The United Nations declared the Decade of Development, the Organization of Petroleum Exporting Countries (OPEC) sharply increased oil prices, and other prices followed them up. Awash in cash, the oil exporters looked for places to park it and found the commercial banks receptive. With it, the banks perfected the Euro-currency loan for developing countries. They believed Euro-currency loans were virtually risk-free for lenders because borrowing governments agreed to assume all the risks—often without really knowing the potential consequences. Banks also believed at that time sovereign governments could not go bankrupt.

Developing countries soon learned that they could readily borrow, not only to import oil, but also to increase other kinds of expenditures. This meant they could use borrowed funds to maintain domestic spending rather than be forced to adjust to the new realities of higher prices for necessary imports and the distortions of outdated development strategies. While some of the borrowing during this period was to ease the difficult adjustment process, much of it was to avoid making hard decisions, for example, cutting back on corruption or military expenditures. Commercial banks were much less careful than official lenders in their analyses of the use of their funds or of the extent of a country's borrowing from other banks. Indeed, banks often competed with each other to lend to these countries. When more sober voices in the development community urged caution, their advice was often ignored.

Higher oil prices normally would have depressed the economies of the United States and Europe during the 1970s; but recession was fought off with expansionary monetary and fiscal policies. As nominal interest rates held steady while inflation accelerated, real interest rates declined to nearly zero, making borrowing all the more attractive. Exports from many developing countries, especially commodities like ores and timber, also rose rapidly, reinforcing the sense that debt burdens were not getting out of hand.

Wrong! Oil prices jumped again at the end of the decade, requiring more borrowing by oil importers. But this time the industrial countries chose to fight inflation with monetary restraint. As a result, growth slowed, nominal interest rates more than doubled, and commodity prices fell. This meant that developing countries, particularly those with large commercial debt, found their debt service requirements shooting upward and their export earnings dropping fast at the very time banks were less willing to lend. The combination of slower growth, rising debts, and weakened assistance created a genuine debt crisis.

The Burden of Debt

The debt of developing countries had grown at unprecedented rates in the 1970s. Total debt increased eightfold, from $68 billion to $572 billion, between 1970 and 1980 and doubled again to $1,230 billion in 1987. The most spectacular rise occurred in publicly guaranteed commercial debt, though debt owed to bilateral and multilateral agencies also climbed significantly. By 1987 about one-third of all claims were held by commercial banks, two-thirds by official agencies. Most of the indebtedness of the lowest-income developing countries—a relatively small fraction of the total owed by developing countries—continued to be owed to official bodies.

It was clear by the beginning of the 1980s that most new foreign borrowing by developing countries was going to service old debt, rather than into new investments. Even this option was soon closed as banks, worried at last about their growing exposure, slowed their lending. Then in August 1982 Mexico defaulted on its debt payments, and people began to realize that, except for the fast-growing East Asian economies, few developing countries were generating enough additional domestic and foreign exchange resources to repay such large volumes of debt. Even worse, net transfers (net disbursements less interest payments) turned negative at this time. Negative net transfers meant that developing countries were transferring resources to their creditors, rather than the other way around.

Several factors combined to make the burden of all this debt excessively heavy. Debt obligations must be paid in foreign exchange (since most obligations call for payment in the currency of lending parties), and debtors must export to earn that foreign exchange. If the price of exports relative to imports—the terms of trade—moves against the debtors, earning foreign exchange becomes harder. That is exactly what happened: the terms of trade deteriorated for most debtors, because the prices of commodities they sold in foreign trade fell relative to other goods[1] and because technological changes reduced the demand for some primary products (e.g., fiber optics replaced copper in communications). Also, debtors' interest payments go up when world interest rates rise.

The International Monetary Fund (IMF) and the World Bank responded to the debt crisis by offering various kinds of debt relief, but only if the indebted countries agreed to adopt some combination of "stabilization" and "structural adjustment" policies. These policies generally required sharply reducing government services, devaluing currencies, lifting price controls, encouraging exports, freezing or reducing wages, and cutting some public sub-sidies—usually with the added purpose of transforming indebted nations into "market-friendly" economies. The effects on the poorest members of society were almost always adverse.

By 1990 the international financial community began to believe the debt crisis was over. More and more developing countries had negotiated new terms for some of their debts. Some of the poorest and most heavily indebted countries had also been forgiven some of their debt. Structural adjustment agreements were more numerous, putting the IMF and World Bank in stronger positions to dictate policies in indebted nations. Accordingly, inter-national lending by banks accelerated, bringing total developing-country external debt to the sum of $2.3 trillion by 1997, of which the lowest-income countries owed about $600 billion.[2] These obligations, as a proportion of each nation's gross national product and exports, were approximately double what they had been in 1980.

Then suddenly in 1997 the international financial community reassessed its risks and began withdrawing short-term loans and equity positions built up during the previous six or seven years, first from Asia, then Russia, Brazil, and other developing economies. The recession that followed in most of these countries once again threatened the ability of developing nations to service their external debt and imposed further pain on vulnerable people. The aus-terity prescriptions of the IMF for dealing with another debt crisis, moreover, failed to protect the most vulnerable.[3]

The results of public austerity are usually disastrous for the poor: rising unemployment, falling incomes, higher costs of living, declining levels of already low basic health care, and increasing deteriorations in living standards. Usually the heavier the burden of debt, the more vulnerable are the poorest and weakest members of heavily indebted societies. Nations that try to meet their contractual obligations to creditors necessarily use foreign exchange resources that otherwise might be allocated to the importation of fuels or other necessities on which the poor depend. Public budgets are inevitably squeezed by the need to service debt obligations.

Who Benefits from Expanding Debt?

For both borrowers and lenders, there were benefits from increased lending in the 1970s. Growth was an important goal of the development community, and the recycling of Euro-currencies was a ready source for financing it. The lenders profited from the fees and commissions on Euro-credit loans. Export-credit agencies, charged by their governments with promoting exports from national companies, eagerly extended credits. Even official lenders wanted to assist in the development process. The risks were borne by the depositors and shareholders of the lending institutions and ultimately by the taxpayers in the creditor countries, not by those doing the lending.

Countries that borrowed from banks gained additional budget resources to implement pet projects or avoid budget cuts. Individuals in strategic positions often earned commissions arranging the transactions. Politicians authorizing the borrowing often could not see beyond their terms in office to appreciate the need for repayments. Some officials were urged to borrow by eager lenders, while others surely recognized the opportunity for profit on their own. In some cases, extensive foreign borrowing financed the transfer by well-placed individuals of financial assets to safer havens.

Neither the individuals negotiating loans on behalf of lenders nor those working on behalf of borrowers had much incentive to be cautious. Others bore the risks and the responsibility of repayment. Most acted in good faith; but many were unduly optimistic, shortsighted, and poorly informed about the extent of the risks. Some, of course, were unscrupulous; the temptation to excess was widespread.

This is not to say that expanding debt is undesirable under most circumstances. On the contrary, debt usually is an essential ingredient of economic development. The issue, rather, is whether borrowed resources generate sufficient gains in productivity and income to pay the interest and eventually retire the loan, while leaving a lasting surplus. In addition, loans from foreigners must produce enough foreign exchange to meet these requirements.

During the 1970s and 1980s most of the economies in Asia expanded their exports and managed their debt well. Their growth strategies emphasized labor-intensive exports and helped considerably to reduce poverty in a region that contains the largest number of poor people in the world. A majority of developing countries elsewhere in the world, however, failed to adjust easily to new circumstances. Their economies were not as flexible and responsive as several of the Asian countries; some governments were shockingly corrupt; their ability to borrow was severely constrained; and the adjustment measures mandated by the World Bank and IMF as a condition of further lending often were poorly designed for unique situations. So they endured a decade of stagnant or declining growth, wrenching economic and social change, and increasing poverty throughout the 1980s.

Who Pays When Debt Is Reduced?

When borrowed money is not employed productively, funds to repay it must come from other resources. In the case of public debt, this essentially means from general taxation. Thus, how the tax burden is distributed among the

people becomes an issue. A debtor with appropriate monetary and fiscal policies can spread the burden of debt repayment relatively evenly across the economy. Even then, raising the revenue means higher taxes, cuts in public
spending, and probably higher interest rates—all factors likely to slow economic growth. And the domestic resources must be converted into foreign
exchange, which bids up its price and devalues the domestic currency.

When economies are not well managed, governments often resort to deficit
finance to maintain spending at levels higher than available revenues. When
they do cut spending, they tend to focus on targets that adversely affect productivity or victimize the poor. Inflation is the usual result, undermining the
economy still further. People who are able to protect themselves find ways to
move money overseas, avoid paying taxes, and fight to ensure that their real
incomes do not fall.

The poor are the least able to protect themselves in such circumstances.
Nearly all segments of society are forced to pay the debt service and to suffer
economic decline, but the poor are least able to absorb decline in incomes.
Despite increasing efforts to protect the poor in some countries, they still suffer disproportionately.

When debts are rescheduled or reduced by agreement of the creditor institutions, part of the debt-service burden shifts to them in the form of losses
from missed interest and principal payments. If the debt is simply rescheduled
and interest is paid on schedule, the direct costs to lenders are relatively
minor—the time taken by rescheduling, lost interest if rates are reduced, and
the forgone returns on money tied up in the loans. When interest is not paid,
the income losses to the creditor are greater.

Commercial banks also suffer indirect costs from rescheduling or writing
down outstanding loans. They must carry high reserves against developing-
country debt, which eats into their capital and reduces their earning capacity.
During the 1980s, the market perceived a substantial risk in bank exposure, so
the value of bank stocks fell dramatically, passing on the losses to shareholders. Since bank stocks are widely held by the public, including pension funds
and other institutional holders, it is not easy to tell how the burden of these
losses was distributed. In some cases, tax regulations were modified to facilitate sharing of the burden with taxpayers in order to protect the stability of
the financial system.

III. EXPERIMENTS IN DEBT FORGIVENESS

From the outset of the debt crisis in 1980, governments in the North recognized that default by developing countries might threaten the collapse of the

world's financial system. Thereafter, they intervened with increasing frequency with bridging loans to ensure that debtors could service their debts and not default. The large banks were pressured quite openly to continue lending to debtors when their best instincts were telling them to withdraw. That, indeed, was the central tenet of the Baker Plan, announced in 1985, which called on multilateral agencies and commercial banks to increase their lending to heavily indebted countries. The banks did not respond positively, however, and these efforts ran out of steam by 1989.

By 1989, the muddling-through policies of the preceding years were seen as inadequate means for restoring genuine development in the South. The so-called "debt overhang," it was thought, had to be removed in order to encourage investment in export industries and a larger voluntary flow of finance from North to South. Thus the Brady Plan offered heavily indebted middle-income countries an opportunity to reduce their outstanding debt in return for their commitment to ongoing adjustment programs. Negotiations between banks and debtor countries would be carried out on a case-by-case basis, and the IMF would be responsible for supervising adjustment programs.

About the same time, increasing amounts of debt relief were granted to heavily indebted lower-income countries by official lenders through the so-called Paris Club. Here too the IMF and World Bank normally monitor reform programs required as a condition of debt reduction. These negotiations also were on a case-by-case basis. The World Bank established in 1991 a special facility to make grants to low-income countries for the purpose of purchasing commercial debt at deep discounts in order to clear their accounts.

Recently the World Bank announced the so-called HIPC Initiative (Highly Indebted Poor Countries Initiative), which provides a more comprehensive framework for burden sharing among all creditors to reduce the debt of the HIPCs to a sustainable level. The objective is to help them achieve "overall debt sustainability," thus providing an exit from the rescheduling process. Debtor countries have to show a track record of "good policy performance" as monitored by the IMF and the World Bank during the first three years of eligibility. If their performance is deemed satisfactory, then during the second three years the Paris Club will provide rescheduling equivalent to up to 80 percent of the net present value of Paris Club debt. The process got off to a very slow start, but recently the number of qualifying countries has begun to multiply. Of the forty-one developing countries classified as HIPCs,[4] twenty-three now have been offered debt relief of approximately $20 billion under the HIPC protocols. Another twelve countries are being considered for debt relief. The process is taking more time in these countries, as many are in the throes of civil conflict.

These debt cancellation offers to date are far from generous. Each debtor country, for example, must first design a Poverty Reduction Strategy Paper (PRSP) in consultation with the IMF, World Bank, and nongovernmental organizations (NGOs). This requirement may delay debt reduction while countries assemble high-quality plans. It takes time, especially for a cash-strapped government, to assess the nature of poverty, consult with the groups affected, assign priorities to potential responses, and draw up plans. Yet speed is vital in resolving debt crises. In addition, the HIPC Initiative's definition of sustainable debt—the amount of debt a country is supposed to be able to man-age—is rather arbitrary and probably too high. For example, the HIPC Ini-tiative aims to cap a country's annual debt-service payments at 15–20 percent of export earnings. Still another problem is that the debt-cancellation condi-tions are so stringent they usually engender domestic political opposition. Debtors uncommitted to poverty reduction could fabricate PRSPs they have no intention of implementing, in order to obtain debt relief, as NGOs in Kenya fear is happening there.

IV. ISSUES IN DEBT FORGIVENESS

Debt forgiveness is not a free good. Since almost the entire debt of the HIPCs is owed to official creditors, it may be helpful to ask who benefits from, and who pays for, the reduction of debt obligations.

First, consider a country already in default of some or all of its debt obliga-tions. For it, the immediate effect of forgiveness would be small—reducing the stigma of being a deadbeat, relief from the need for continual negotia-tions, and a modest cash flow equal to the interest payments that would actu-ally have been made. In the long run, the burden of debt repayments or rescheduling would be avoided. What actually happens to the cash saved depends on what the government decides to do with it. It could spend it, reduce taxes, or retire other debts. If the current government is the one that led the country into the debt crisis, and if it intends to follow the policies used before, then additional resources probably won't be well spent for develop-ment and poverty alleviation.

Now consider a deeply indebted country that has been making substantial payments of interest and principal on its external debts. Because the funds released to its government are much larger than for a "non-performing" nation, its opportunities are more substantial. Even so, it too has the choice of spending it, reducing taxes, or reducing debts still further. Whether the gov-ernment is able to direct the gains from debt reduction into productive invest-ment and poverty alleviation depends again on the policies it pursues, much more than on the degree of debt reduction.

Most of the burden of debt reduction falls on the creditor, except to the extent that creditors deny future lending to the borrower or harden the terms of any future lending—a real possibility. If the lender forgiving the debt is a commercial bank, the burden at first reduces its income and then is likely to lower stock values, maybe cause job cuts, reduce taxes paid to government, and quite possibly make banks less willing to take risks lending to developing countries. With so many probable consequences, it is hard to be sure who ultimately bears the burden.

When official agencies forgive debts, the burden falls initially on the budgets of creditor institutions, leading to larger deficits or smaller surpluses in their budgets. Governmental agencies may make up for lost revenues by raising taxes, reducing expenditures, or pushing up interest rates. Where export-import bank loans are involved, countries have to make explicit budget transfers to offset debt losses. Multilateral agencies usually end up asking for additional contributions from their members. Also, the costs of debt reduction almost always count against the overall aid budget, reducing the pool of grants and loans available for assistance to developing countries.

Then there is the problem of "moral hazard." Much of the debt accumulated in highly indebted countries is the result of bad economic policy, bad judgment, or corruption. Lenders often worry, therefore, whether their willingness to write down debts will be seen as a reward for bad policies. If so, their actions may encourage bad behavior, while countries that follow better policies, make the necessary sacrifices, and service their debts are relatively disadvantaged. This is not a message that either commercial or official lenders want to send. Accordingly, most negotiations over debt reduction are long and arduous, requiring complicated protocols over how borrowers behave in the future. After Mexico defaulted on its external debt in the 1920s, forty years went by before it could borrow again in the international capital market.

V. A CHRISTIAN PERSPECTIVE

Forgiving Debts in Ancient Israel

Debt forgiveness was an important practice in the ancient Near Eastern world. The issue then, of course, was personal indebtedness rather than the debts of nations in international affairs. Even so, the social history of debt forgiveness is relevant to current discussions of international indebtedness.

Debt forgiveness in the ancient Near East was primarily an instrument of kings or monarchs to secure soldiers and revenue. Since usury was common, often at 20 percent per annum or more, there were many debtor-slaves. This clearly weakened a society from within, leaving it prone to attack from foreign sources. When rulers needed soldiers to counter the corrosive effect of widespread debt, they typically forgave debts by decree. Or if they were afraid that their land was being ruled by an oligarchy of the wealthy, they would counter it with an "economic order" decree, restoring the normal predebt state of affairs—including more widely spread self-sufficiency, a freer and more independent fighting force, and a larger share of the land's rent for the government, rather than letting it pass into the hands of creditors. When creditors tried to circumvent an economic order decree, the monarch would counter with royal decrees.[5]

In ancient Israel, the idea of debt forgiveness was transformed by the idea of jubilee—the idea that continues to name debt forgiveness proposals today—into a system for ensuring that the evils associated with indebtedness not become permanent. By making jubilee a divine decree and a matter of the calendar, Jews took the institution of forgiveness out of the hands of monarchs and governments, who sometimes abused it. "The LORD spoke to Moses . . . 'The land is mine; with me you are but aliens and tenants'" (Lev. 25:1, 23). Not only were the rich foreigners who indentured Israelites strangers, so too were the Israelites "aliens" on God's land. They were already God's "slaves" and could not belong to another.

As an institutionalized form of forgiveness, the Old Testament concept of jubilee called for all slaves to be set free, land to be returned to the original owners, and debts to be cancelled in the seventh or fiftieth year. The theological base of the legislation is that the land, the whole land, belongs to Yahweh. "Purchase" of land, or acquiring it as settlement of a debt so that it leaves the hands of the original family to whom it was assigned by God as stewards, was really not purchase to own, but purchase of "usufruct"—the right to use the land or to obtain the produce from it. This was decreed by God as a "calendar" year. The calendar was a sacred/sacral institution that had to be observed by the faithful, in one way or another.

While such laws may not have been implemented effectively in Israel, they nevertheless testify to an important moral and economic ideal. In God's envisioned world, no person, no family, and by extension no nation is to be permanently impoverished. Peonage is never an acceptable result of debt. Furthermore, it is an operative principle of Scripture that when economic loss and distortion occur, there is to be a restoration. From time to time within history, there is to be a determination of what rightly belongs to whom, and it is to be returned. Economic relationships are never to be allowed to make life hopeless.

Searching for a Christian Response Today

In addition to the themes of forgiveness and jubilee, Scripture speaks power-fully to the circumstances in which heavily indebted developing countries now find themselves.[6] Consider its message of salvation, redemption, deliverance, and liberation. The Old Testament is in large measure the story of God's actions to redeem Israel. The freeing from bondage in Egypt and from cap-tivity in Babylonia are the prototypical expressions of God's commitment that God's people shall be free—out of the clutches of the life-holder. Liberation was of the nation, not merely of individuals. Israel, of course, was to be a light to the nations. Ultimately what God sought for Israel was the goal for all peoples and nations. The New Testament formalized that concept, noting that in Christ "there is neither Jew nor Greek." God's outreach and liberation are for all. Therefore, a worldview that is biblical cannot be indifferent to the bondage of any people or nation. If debt holds nations captive and oppresses people, it ceases to be merely a financial concern and becomes a spiritual condition call-ing for deliverance.

Justice is another principle emphasized in Scripture: "But let justice roll down like waters, and righteousness like an ever-flowing stream" (Amos 5:24). It is a basic biblical theme that God has made a commitment to stand with and seek justice for the poor and oppressed. The poor benefit little from the huge debt incurred by Third World governments. So it is wrong that the poor should bear the burden of repayment. Such a conviction is bound to put the biblical faith community at odds with the commercial banking commu-nity. Some will say that the church has no right to urge its moral perspectives on business structures that may or may not be owned and operated by Chris-tians. But justice is never accepted as the responsibility of the faith commu-nity alone. Rather the Bible sees justice as the responsibility of all peoples and systems.

Still another relevant theme is that biblical faith rejects idolatry: "[Y]ou shall have no other gods before me. You shall not make for yourself an idol, whether in the form of anything that is in heaven above, or that is on the earth beneath, or that is in the water under the earth. You shall not bow down to them or worship them; for I the LORD your God am a jealous God" (Exod. 20:3–5a). Idolatry, of course, is not limited to what can be carved in wood or stone. That is a mere allegory for the god-shapes that dominate our minds and our lives. Any ideology, system, or nation that is given absolute standing in the society or creation is an idol. Our economic system becomes an idol when we accept the assertion that it is closed, fixed, and unchangeable.

There will be no long-term solution to the debt issue without a change in the way we and others think about economic order. John Calvin's great contribution to economic life was not to endorse free enterprise or money-lending, as is so often assumed. His contribution was to have such confidence in the sovereignty of God that he did not fear the passing of feudalism and the dawn of a new economic order. He was free to embrace the future and to wrestle with its new requirements.

Such a spirit of confidence in God and openness to new possibility will stand us well in our own time. The hidden blessing in the debt crisis may be that it will push the world toward a new global order. The challenge is to create humane alternatives to what the world has become and to move beyond the notion that normal mechanisms or invisible hands can be counted on to make things right. Justice is a conscious commitment and a chosen relationship, not an accidental or automatic outcome of self-interest.

VI. WHAT WE CAN DO

From the perspective of progressive Christians, the record of painfully slow response to the problems of heavily indebted countries—countries whose people are struggling to meet basic needs—is neither wise nor fair. While the reluctance of commercial creditors to extend additional loans or to write off delinquent accounts is understandable, the foot-dragging by official creditors is more mysterious. To be sure, they do not wish to reward regimes for having made foolish decisions or for engaging in corrupt practices; nor do they want to encourage bad policies in the future. But they are in far better position to recognize the pain that excessive debt imposes on vulnerable people and to do something to relieve it quickly.

We believe that creditor governments and the multilateral lending institutions must find new ways to insulate the poor people of heavily indebted countries from the costs of debt remission. Poverty alleviation is probably the most powerful argument for some form of debt reduction, and it is likely to command wide support. Yet the balance of power in most indebted countries rests with the elites who have garnered most of the benefits of debt accumulation. Thus official lenders will have to insist on protections for the poor as a condition for debt remission. Otherwise, it is harder to argue that the depositors and taxpayers of creditor countries should willingly suffer losses.

The record of movement towards debt remission may have been sluggish in the past, but it nonetheless is evidence that official creditors are increasingly willing to consider some form of debt reduction in the most heavily indebted countries. Indeed, a sudden rush during 1999 of new proposals to remit the debts of the most heavily indebted poor countries suggests a fresh desire on the part of creditor institutions to prove their seriousness and compassion.

Following a meeting of the finance ministers of the G-7 countries in February 1999, for example, the United States pledged a total of $920 million in debt relief over four years as its part of the effort. Whether this trend will continue will depend in large part on the willingness of indebted nations to grant them something in exchange. The chief reason the official creditors want a quid pro quo is their wish to avoid establishing perverse incentives.

The problem with this, of course, is the kinds of quid pro quo they have insisted on in the past when lending more money to the developing countries. The structural adjustment remedies they have required in the past have almost always led to cuts in government services, particularly for the poor. The economic meltdown in Argentina is only the most recent illustration of the adverse consequences of the IMF's enforcement of rigid rules. Progress towards just and sustainable human development is not possible without significant alterations in the policy reforms required as a condition of more lending or debt remission.

Progressive Christians recommend that the International Monetary Fund and the World Bank, in collaboration with other official and private creditors, replace traditional structural adjustment requirements with adjustment programs that better meet the needs of the poor and promote sustainable, participatory, and equitable development. Such programs should at a minimum:

- Reduce inappropriate levels of military spending
- Preserve spending on basic needs, including education and health care
- Assure the presence of a safety net for those most severely affected by adjustment policies
- Prevent adverse environmental effects such as deforestation and soil degradation
- Include a system for monitoring and correcting (as may be necessary) the effects of adjustment policies

Further, we are convinced that the multilateral creditor institutions and governments of the North can easily afford to reduce the debts of the most heavily indebted poor countries. The present value of debts owed them by the poorest nations currently is about $125 billion. The IMF's share of this total is much less than the unrealized capital gain on its gold holdings. Similarly, the World Bank could readily absorb a full write-down of its claims out of its special reserve funds. Commercial bank creditors already have written off of their balance sheets most of what is owed them, so a full write-off would be easily absorbed. The United States, likewise, isn't so foolish as to count its claims on poor nations at face value; these loans are already carried on the books at about 10 percent of their face value. The situation is analogous for other creditor governments.

The Jubilee 2000 Campaign

It would be difficult for individual Christians or even denominations to do much to further these goals by themselves. Fortunately we can support an existing movement. An international coalition named Jubilee 2000 called for definitive debt relief for all of the HIPCs by the year 2000. While its goals are vastly more ambitious and expeditious than the World Bank's HIPC Initiative, it also endorses construction of remission packages on a case-by-case basis that takes account of individual circumstances and the record of debtors and creditors. Eschewing supervision by the IMF and World Bank, it calls for appointment of an independent commission on which the debtors, creditors, international financial institutions, and international financial community would be fairly represented. In the longer view, this commission might even act as an arbitrator in cases meriting a declaration of international insolvency.

More specifically, the Jubilee 2000 platform calls for the following:

- Definitive cancellation of international debt in situations where countries with high levels of human need and environmental distress are unable to meet the needs of their people;
- Definitive cancellation of international debt in a way that benefits ordinary people and facilitates their participation in the process of determining the scope, timing, and conditions of debt relief, as well as the future direction and priorities of their national and local economies
- Definitive cancellation of international debt in ways that do not perpetuate or deepen poverty or environmental degradation
- Definitive cancellation of international debt that acknowledges the responsibility of all parties and is transparent and participatory, in order to prevent recurring cycles of indebtedness

Progressive Christians can embrace the Jubilee 2000 campaign as a significant step forward on the road to a just and sustainable resolution of the debt crisis. It is *not* a call for cancellation of all debts, even for the HIPCs, as some supporters have erroneously argued. By calling for a case-by-case approach to debt remission, it acknowledges the uniqueness of each situation and allows for injunctions against unsound policies for managing the economy and its debt. It emphasizes the need to recover resources that have been stolen by corrupt regimes. It places special emphasis on the protection of the most vulnerable against adverse effects of debt remission. And it properly calls for full participation by ordinary people in negotiations leading to debt remission.

The Jubilee 2000 program is *not* a comprehensive solution for the debt crisis, however. It focuses exclusively on the debts of the forty-one HIPCs whose debts are owed almost entirely to official creditors. It therefore ignores the debts of middle-income developing countries—debts that are many times

larger than those of the HIPCs and whose disposition is much more conse-
quential for the global economy. For example, Indonesia, Nigeria, and Pakistan are not included in the HIPC Initiative, even though they are as indebted
and poor as eligible nations. It is perhaps not a coincidence that these three
countries are the largest debtors among the poorest countries. Nor does the
Jubilee 2000 program give more than a glimpse of the kind of economic structures and policies towards which it wants the world to move.

But it is a promising call for justice in an unjust world. It has been endorsed
by the U.S. Catholic Conference, the National Council of Churches, several
major denominations, Oxfam International, Bread for the World, the World
Council of Churches, and the World Alliance of Reformed Churches.

In sum, should Christians support the forgiveness of debts? Yes, but only
on a case-by-case basis that reduces poverty, protects the environment, and
avoids perverse incentives in the future. Debt relief must be structured carefully to avoid rewarding interests that have acted irresponsibly in the past and
to reduce the rewards of shortsightedness or selfishness in the future. Debt
cancellation should be accompanied by conditions that clearly promote
human development, especially among the poor.

Discussion Questions

1. By most measures, at least forty-one developing countries are so deeply
   in debt to external creditors that it is reasonable to suppose they will
   never be able to pay off the debt. Yet the creditors seem reluctant to write
   off the debts. Is this a Christian response?
2. The current debt crisis poses two problems: how to treat the symptoms
   and how to cure the illness. Because recent debt-reduction initiatives are
   one-time offers, they treat only the symptoms. They do far too little to
   change the systems that created the crisis in the first place. What should
   Christians be doing to promote longer-term cures?
3. Much of the debt accumulated in highly indebted countries is the result
   of bad economic policy, bad judgment, or corruption. What kinds of conditions ought Christians to urge upon creditors before they consider the
   cancellation of uncollectable debts? How different are these conditions
   from those imposed by the IMF when it makes "structural adjustment"
   loans?
4. Do you support the objectives of the Jubilee 2000 campaign? As Christians, what else would you suggest be included in its stated objectives?

To Learn More

The best up-to-date introduction to the debt crisis is Nancy Birdsall and John
Williamson, *Development and Debt Relief: Is Enhanced HIPC the Solution?*

(Washington, D.C.: Institute for International Economics, 2002). See also David Roodman, *Still Waiting for the Jubilee: Pragmatic Solutions for the Third World Debt Crisis* (Washington, D.C.: Worldwatch Institute, paper no. 155, 2001). A good assessment of the adjustments imposed by creditor on debtor nations can be found in Tony Killick, *Aid and the Political Economy of Policy Change* (New York: Routledge, 1998). Bread for the World often publishes background papers on debt relief; it is the best U.S. interpreter of the Jubilee 2000 movement. For a radical critique of debt, see Susan George, *The Debt Boomerang: How Third World Debt Harms Us All* (Boulder, Colo.: Westview Press, 1992). The World Bank annually publishes *Global Development Finance* with analysis of debt conditions generally and by country with summary tables.

14

The Church and Environmentalism

Our church got into environmental issues when I decided to do a raise-the-flag-see-who-salutes sermon on Earth Day. I did a children's time of discovery on loving the earth and being God's caretakers. The kids got it in two seconds and were cheering for Creation and booing the boobs who trashed it. My sermon was on seeing beyond easy, politically correct, no commitment necessary, recycling as satisfying environmental activism and environmental justice. I had done an informal "pollution survey" of the church and asked if anyone else was concerned. I talked about the future of children and the world. I talked about what had happened to marine mammals on the coastline, and how they were like canaries in the mine, warning us of toxic changes. I talked about the difference between stewardship and trying to dominate the earth, and asked if anyone wanted to meet after the worship service to discuss these matters. Forty people showed up and eighteen of them set about writing the church's environmental policy. They led three classes, took several field trips, met with the power folk in the environmental movement, and eight months later the Session adopted the policy after a full congregational reading and discussion. There is now a "Stewardship of Creation" Commission active in a range of programs—everything from recycling to pollution inventories for homes and offices of members—and we are members of an Interfaith Coalition for Green Planning.

Letter from a Presbyterian pastor in California

I. INTRODUCTION

We begin this chapter with a story about remedial action rather than about the environmental crisis, because everyone is supposed to know that there is an environmental crisis. The depth of that knowledge, of course, varies greatly, and though we cannot possibly cover the complex range of environmental problems that presently confront us, we will offer a few items to remind us again that planet Earth is indeed in trouble largely because of what we humans have unthinkingly done to it. Almost everybody now knows terms like "global warming," "ozone hole," "endangered species" and "acid rain." Many recognize that those are important problems but feel that sufficient progress is being made in protecting the environment that they need not worry too much. Or if they don't feel that way, they may blame the politicians for failing to take responsibility and may not respond as did the congregation described above.

It is important to state the problems as accurately as possible, because predictions of disasters that don't occur do more harm than good. Pessimists fifty years ago were predicting that we would run out of food by the year 2000, but this has not happened. Starvation in the Sudan or Mali is more the result of war, politics, and distribution problems than of the ability of the world to grow food. (See chapter 15, "Global Food Security.") Due to better emission controls on cars, smog in Los Angeles is somewhat less than it was a few years ago. Americans take pride in our productive economy and especially our ability to grow food efficiently. Such pride and these trends make it easy to be complacent and hard to think seriously about certain hidden problems. Told that one-third of all people on Earth have inadequate drinking water, people sometimes respond in the spirit of American know-how: "We can fix that!" But it is the complexity, hiddenness, and interrelationships of environmental problems that give us trouble, that slow us down, that challenge us.

Scientists in Florida can now pick up traces of African topsoil in the air. Scientists in Hawaii can similarly pick up traces of Chinese topsoil. Why does this happen? The loss of forest land around the world is tremendous, about the size of a football field every second. In the developing countries ten trees get cut down for every one that is planted. This means water is not retained in the land; it means fires in Indonesia; it means topsoil blowing away. The earth loses 25 billion tons of topsoil a year, roughly equal to all the wheat lands in Australia. There may be about a fifty-year supply left.

One-third of all crops now require irrigation, and we are using seven times the water we used in 1900. Ten percent of irrigated lands are affected by salt water leaching into the soil. One ton of grain requires one thousand tons of water. Though people are now being better fed, 1984 was the high point in harvest of grain per person. Production per person has fallen 6 percent since then. The world's population is six billion, and the least we can expect by 2050 is another five or six billion. Many think that is very close to or beyond the "carrying capacity" of Earth, that is, the population Earth can sustain indefinitely. Because the population doubling time is exponential, the world population has grown more since 1950 than it did in the previous four million years. It cannot double more than one more time without disaster. (See chapter 16, "The Global Population Crisis.")

Understandably the developing countries envy and want to achieve the American middle-class standard of living, with cars, refrigerators, and television sets. And yet, if everyone on Earth consumed the way Americans consume, we would need ten planet Earths to supply our present world population. The world has used up more natural resources since 1955 than it did in all previous human history. With 4.5 percent of the world's population, the United States produces 72 percent of all hazardous waste and consumes 33 percent of the world's paper. Our Sunday newspapers alone eat up about 500,000 trees a week and, though recycling has increased commendably in many places, most of this paper does not get recycled. Americans use one million gallons of oil every two minutes. If we continue to use oil in the next decade at the rate we presently use it, we would need to discover more oil in the next ten years than has been found in all previous history. Something like five million tons of oil per year winds up in the ocean.

The problem then is not just food. Primitive people, eons ago, used up 2,500 calories a day, all in food. An American on a strict diet may aim at the same calorie intake. But in fact the average person in the world today uses up 31,000 calories a day, most of it in the form of combustible fossil fuels. The average American uses six times that, or seventy-five times what the primitive person used up. A head of iceberg lettuce is fifty calories. But it takes 400 calories of energy to grow it in California's fertile Central Valley, and 1,800 calories to ship it east.

One of the lessons that environmentalism teaches us is that everything is related to everything else. Burning so much oil, we pollute the air as well as the water. A hundred million Americans still live in urban areas where the quality of air is not up to Environmental Protection Agency (EPA) standards. Global warming is causing unanticipated and hard-to-calculate climate changes. The shrinking Amazon rain forest provides half the world's oxygen. The widespread use of chemical pesticides has affected water quality, while crop losses to insects continue to increase, because the insects that are herbivores breed faster than the insects that eat other insects. In other words, pesticides upset the balance of nature. The widespread and routine use of antibiotics in raising cattle and fowl has meant that many disease-causing bacteria have developed immunity to antibiotics. In Africa, the Sahara desert expands and mosquitoes move northward. Malaria and tuberculosis are making a surprising comeback. The human incursion into forested lands is related to the fact that a hundred species of plants and animals become extinct every day. We have lost more species in our lifetime than in all the rest of the history of Earth. The one hundred thousand tigers that lived on Earth at the beginning of the twentieth century are now down to about five thousand.

We could go on and on until you scream, "Stop!"—if you are not screaming already. Hundreds of books have been written on different aspects of today's environmental problems. The beginning of the modern environmental movement was in the 1950s, when the chemistry of the electron capture detector (ECD) first found traces of DDT in Antarctic penguins and in human mothers' breast milk. That led to Rachel Carson's *Silent Spring*; and the rest, as they say, is history. We have made progress, but much more remains to be done. Among the many problems we face are the ozone hole, acid rain, deforestation, species loss, pesticides in soil and water, and beach pollution (350 U.S. closures and warnings in 1998). But, simply by way of example, let us look a bit more deeply, but still briefly, at just four of the problem areas: nuclear waste, ocean fishing, water supply and global warming.

II. CURRENT ENVIRONMENTAL PROBLEMS

Nuclear Waste

In 1986 the disaster of a reactor explosion at Chernobyl in Ukraine (then the Soviet Union) reminded the world of the dangers inherent in nuclear power. Even now, scientists are by no means agreed on how many deaths Chernobyl brought about. Estimates ranged from 31, the number of immediate on-site deaths, to sixty thousand; but one study eight years later showed that children born 120 miles away had twice as many DNA mutations as do other children. The partial meltdown in 1979 at Three Mile Island in this country and the 1999 nuclear accident at the Tokaimura nuclear plant in Japan, where two hundred persons were exposed to injurious radiation and three hundred thousand were endangered, have kept public concern alive, as has the recent outpouring of medical complaints from two generations of workers at the Hanford plutonium-making complex in central Washington.

Nearly forty years after construction of the first U.S. nuclear plant, Congress in 1982 passed the Nuclear Waste Policy Act to cope with radioactive waste from the nuclear power and nuclear weapons industry. This act specified that two permanent high-level nuclear waste sites were to be established, one in the west and one in the east. In 1987 work began on the Yucca Mountain, Nevada, site, the idea being to place seventy thousand tons of waste in stainless steel containers a thousand feet underground. The project was to be completed by 1998. But after a few years the completion date was postponed to sometime between 2010 and 2015, and the eastern site was postponed indefinitely. One problem was a 1993 earthquake twelve miles from Yucca Mountain; there are thirty-three earthquake faults in the area.

In 2000 the Department of Energy held twenty or more public hearings on its plan to ship radioactive waste to Yucca Mountain. By rail and truck the waste would travel through forty-three states, past about fifty million people. Many objections were raised and many fears voiced. Meanwhile, at least forty thousand tons of spent nuclear fuel pile up at about eighty above-ground sites at nuclear plants around the country, and the utilities responsible are suing the government for storage costs. The U.S. Senate in February 2000 passed a bill to make Yucca Mountain a permanent site, but President Clinton threatened a veto on the grounds the measure weakens the ability of the EPA to set limits on permissible radiation. The nuclear power industry supported the bill; both Nevada senators and most environmentalists opposed it. The House held off.

The stand-off continued into the Bush administration. The Bush energy plan called for a national nuclear waste depository site without naming Yucca Mountain. New Energy Secretary Spencer Abraham was forced to extend the public hearing period. Loud objection to Yucca Mountain came from Nevada citizens and officials. The governor and U.S. Senator Harry Reid pledged to block legislation. To a cheering crowd, the mayor of Las Vegas rather melo-dramatically announced he would personally arrest any truck driver hauling radioactive waste through his city.

As a partial alternative to a federal depository, thirty U.S. utilities had ear-lier gone together to build a temporary private radioactive waste facility on the Mascalero Apache Indian Reservation in New Mexico. Some Apaches opposed the development, and in 1995 the New Mexico legislature passed a bill to prohibit the storage of spent nuclear fuel in the state until adequate emergency plans could be developed or there would be assurance that a fed-eral waste site would be available when the Apache facility closes, or in forty years, whichever comes first. Because the nuclear power industry has proved to be a loser economically, the Nuclear Regulatory Commission (NRC) wor-ries that safety may be slighted as plants try to cut costs. Some reactor pres-sure vessels have become "embrittled" and some boiling waste reactor core shrouds have been cracking. A single inspection of these problems can cost up to a million dollars. The NRC has projected a 50 percent chance of a core meltdown at some nuclear plant in the next twenty years. It costs $158 million to $317 million simply to decommission a nuclear power plant, which is usu-ally more than the original cost of building it.

A newspaper account in January 2000 called attention to a related problem. A 10.5-million-ton mountain of uranium tailings sits near Moab, Utah, a by-product of twenty-eight years of uranium milling operations by Atlas Corporation, which filed for Chapter 11 bankruptcy in 1998. Radiation from the mountain of waste material is beginning to leach into the Colorado River, a source of drinking water for southern California. Federal authorities and the states of Utah, California, Nevada, and Arizona are eager to remedy the problem but apparently equally eager to get someone else to pay for it. Bills were introduced in Congress to give responsibility for the cleanup to the Department of Energy, but they did not specify funding and, in any case, were not passed.

The discussion so far has concerned high-level nuclear waste, a term which applies to spent fuel from nuclear power plants. Low-level nuclear waste is a term that applies to every other form of waste that is radioactive. Though much low-level waste comes from hospitals, laboratories, and universities, the greatest part comes from nuclear power plants. The twelve-year abortive struggle over the proposed Ward Valley low-level depository in the California desert has involved the U.S. Department of the Interior, the California state government, antinuclear activists, environmental groups, Native American tribes, local politicians, members of Congress, the governor of California, and the president of the United States. The story is too complex to tell here, but the relevant point is that some environmentalists oppose Ward Valley on the grounds that it would involve a hidden subsidy to the nuclear power industry. They also express the more substantive concern that radioactive tritium and other metals might for a thousand years migrate to the Colorado River, a present source of drinking water for millions of people.

Nuclear waste is a problem that ought to have been thought out before the first peacetime plant was built; but it wasn't, and now it hangs like a heavy weight around our collective necks.

Bad as it is, irresponsible as it has been, our policy on nuclear waste is not the only problem with nuclear power. Earthquakes can be a threat to existing nuclear plants. As one Nobel physicist sarcastically warned, "No acts of God can be permitted." Another threat is terrorist bombings, a consideration much elevated since September 11, 2001. It is immensely expensive to decommission a nuclear power plant, and even decommissioned plants, as environmentalist Amory Lovins says, "remain dangerously radioactive for far longer than societies last." Early on, power companies refused to build nuclear plants unless Congress passed a law limiting their liability in accidents. That was a warning of dangers ahead. The law expired in 2002, and vigorous political battles over renewal can be expected. On the other hand, the problem of global warming, discussed later in this chapter, has given nuclear power advocates a new lease on life, for nuclear power does not generate greenhouse gasses. Our market economy has not proved highly rewarding for the 103 nuclear plants that presently exist; but nuclear advocates, hoping to justify enormous past investments, and minimizing security risks, can be expected to be increasingly vocal.

Ocean Fisheries

Middle-class Americans, concerned to lower their cholesterol level, or perhaps worried about mad cow disease, have been eating less beef and more fish. Since raising and grazing cattle is an expensive and inefficient way to provide protein to hungry mouths, this trend may seem to be a good development. Meanwhile, however, the supply of fish in the world, relative to human population, has been going down and down. According to the UN Food and Agriculture Organization (FAO), the total catch of ocean fish increased from 18.5 million metric tons in 1950 to 73.5 million tons in 1996, an increase of close to 400 percent. Some of this increase is attributable to the rise of fish farms, but there are limits to this enterprise. There have been recent complaints, for example, that Thai fishermen, who grow shrimp in pens, must catch fish in the wild, dry them, and grind them into meal to feed the penned shrimp. The process has become counterproductive, in one case taking five pounds of wild fish to produce one pound of farm fish. From 1986 to 1996 both the quantity and value of farmed fish increased about 40 percent, but after that the value and quantity of farmed fish began to fall.

Studies of particular species of fish suggest that overfishing has become critical. Sixty-nine percent of all species are either fully exploited or overexploited and on the decline. In the late 1980s the total catch of all fish began to level off and at the same time the catch per capita began to drop. To keep production up, fishermen began to travel greater distances and began to catch fish of lower value. High-tech fishing sharply reduced the supply of fish. A worst-case scenario was a fisherman who sometimes dynamited coral reefs to collect fish, thereby destroying for decades or longer important feeding grounds.

The development of high-tech fishing methods is impressive and has brought economic rewards to certain corporations like Tyson Foods. Massive factory trawlers the size of a football field, aided by satellites, sonar, and spotter planes, can pull in 550,000 pounds of fish per day. They sail around the world, dominating the small fishing boats. The Georges Bank off of New England was at one time the world's richest fishing ground. In the 1970s a thousand factory trawlers could sometimes be seen there on the horizon. But now cod, herring, haddock, and flounder are largely fished out in the Atlantic off New England. The same thing has happened to pollock off Russia, anchovies off Peru, and Caribbean reef fish and red snapper in the Gulf of Mexico. Overfishing off New Zealand has cut the supply of orange roughy. The Maine lobster industry seems to be an exception, largely because the industry has assimilated a long tradition of careful regulation.

There are people who fish for a living, especially in traditional fishing ports like Gloucester, Massachusetts, who care deeply about protecting ocean feeding grounds. Their small boats are low-impact and are compatible with respect for the environment. They view with disdain the factory trawlers that make it harder and harder for the fish to hide and reproduce in a sustainable way. The Magnuson Act in 1976 imposed the first restrictions on ocean fishing, but it required periodic renewal and allowed "individual transferable quotas" (ITQs) by which limits on catches were often evaded by the trading of allowable quotas between fisheries. By the mid-1990s the big ships were poised to return. Congress in November 1997 renewed the Magnuson Act and imposed a four-year moratorium on ITQs. The local fishing industry and environmental groups cooperated in lobbying Congress to this end. In August 2000 President Clinton signed bipartisan legislation that created a sixteen-member commission to recommend a long-term strategy to protect the oceans and restore fisheries. Its report was due in 2002, but not available at the time of writing.

Squid used to be ignored as "trash fish" because they spoiled easily. But now the large flash-freezers on the big trawlers can freeze squid while still at sea. A federal grant to promote the catching of "underutilized species" helped stimulate the boom in squid fishing, and squid dishes began appearing in restaurants. But too few people reflected on the food-chain effect. Major types of squid have a shorter life span than many realized, and they spawn only once. Larger fish feed on squid. Some experts fear that the depletion of squid will have a serious effect on all sea life. Whales, seals, and dolphins have already been driven closer to shore because of the exhaustion of traditional feeding grounds.

Much research needs to be done on the complex interrelationships of ocean ecology. But Congress has not been generous in supporting such research. Regulation is difficult because it is hard for governments to keep up with technological changes, and most ships do not have on-board verification of conformity with regulations. There was, for example, a 1986 moratorium in commercial whaling, administered by the fairly weak forty-four-member International Whaling Commission. Norway and Japan continue to defy the moratorium. Japan has used the loophole of "scientific research" to justify killing whales—389 in 1998.

As the Atlantic cod has virtually disappeared, for a time the number of fish caught in the southwest Pacific and east Indian Oceans shot up dramatically, but these areas are now "fully exploited." The Black Sea has seen an almost total collapse of fishing. One effect of more aggressive fishing is that more and more immature fish are caught, leaving fewer mature fish to reproduce. Pollution of fishing areas from toxic runoffs has been another problem. Global warming affects fishing negatively.

Protecting Water Sources

Water is easy to take for granted if the taps flow when we are thirsty. But an adequate supply of safe drinking water requires an enormous network of installations and institutions, usually invisible to water users. Moreover, we in the developed world need to take seriously the fact that vast populations around the world, even when they have water, lack safe drinking water.

The developed world is not without its own problems of water quality and quantity. Moviegoers took heart from the triumph of virtue in *Erin Brockovich*. In that film, based on life, residents of Hinkley, California, suffering from cancer because of chromium 6 (hexavalent chromium) in their water finally received financial compensation. But chromium 6 raised its ugly head again in 2000, when it became known that water agencies were not required to test for chromium 6, and California state legislators began to call for hearings and legislation. (Chromium is benign in nature, but certain manufacturing processes turn it into toxic chromium 6.) It seems no one was sure what level of this chemical in water is safe. The state Department of Health Services, using emergency powers, ordered chromium 6 testing in ground water. Some legislative action may yet occur.

Scientists in Britain found that in eight rivers near sewage treatment plants, fish had significant hormonal damage. All of India's fourteen major rivers are badly polluted. Three-fourths of China's major rivers are unable to support fish. Ninety percent of Europe's rivers have high nitrate concentrations, mostly from agrochemicals. The Willamette River in Oregon doubled in toxic chemicals in a two-year period in the 1990s, including ten thousand pounds of known carcinogens. The EPA and General Electric have been in a struggle for years over the cleanup of polychlorinated biphenyls (PCBs) in the Hudson River in New York and the Housatonic River in Massachusetts. Fish in the lower Hudson are inedible. The Coeur d'Alene River in Idaho was thought to be pure again after a $200 million cleanup job of mining residues. Then in 2000 it was discovered that sediments contaminated with lead, cadmium, zinc, and arsenic had spread over fifteen hundred square miles of the river basin. In 2001 the Santa Ana River, a major source of drinking water for Orange County, California, was found to be threatened by perchlorate, a component of rocket fuel that can cause thyroid damage. Wells in nearby Riverside County were found to be contaminated by perchlorate.

As to quantity of water, there are numerous examples of water depletion. The Ogallala aquifer, which for fifteen thousand years has lain under the Rocky Mountains and spans parts of eight states, is one of the great aquifers of the world. It waters one-fifth of U.S. irrigated land. But the water level of the aquifer has in recent years been dropping ten feet a year and continues to do so. Total depletion amounts to a volume eighteen times the annual flow of the Colorado River. The acreage irrigated by the Ogallala aquifer peaked in 1978, and predictions are that 40 percent of the land it irrigates will have to come out of irrigation by 2020.

In the U.S. Northwest, rainfall has been 45 percent below normal (this may or may not be related to global warming). As a result, Bonneville Dam authorities face an excruciating choice. Some Columbia River water is usually held back in reservoirs for spring and summer release to aid salmon and trout; but in 2001 there was not enough water. If the requirements of the Endangered Species Act are met, power generation will have to be cut back by a thousand megawatts, enough to power a city the size of Seattle.

The world situation is worse. A report by the UN-sponsored World Water Forum meeting in Stockholm in August 2001 predicted that one in three people would not have access to enough water by 2025. Currently, it pointed out, water shortages affect 450 million people in twenty-nine countries. Conflicts over water will soon be more important than conflicts over oil, said Dutch Crown Prince Willem-Alexander, chair of the Forum. A 1998 study by the Johns Hopkins School of Public Health pointed out that there is no more fresh water on Earth than there was two thousand years ago, when the population was only three percent of its present size. In the twentieth century, while the population tripled, water withdrawals increased more than six times. The Johns Hopkins report called for a "Blue Revolution" to conserve and manage freshwater supplies, so naming it to supercede the Green Revolution of the 1960s, which increased agricultural production and fed millions, but at a cost of chemical pollution and overemphasizing single-crop economies.

Northern China is running a chronic water deficit, with overpumping averaging thirty billion cubic meters a year, and the water table dropping 1–1.5 meters a year. A Worldwatch Institute study of China found that it depends on irrigation to produce 70 percent of the grain used to feed its population of 1.2 billion, but more and more water is being drawn to cities and to industry. Three hundred of China's 617 cities are facing water shortages. Rivers run dry and aquifers are depleted, and more grain imports are needed, raising the prospect of increasing world grain prices. Higher grain prices can become life threatening for the 1.3 billion of the world's people who live on one dollar a day or less. Nine Indian states are running major water deficits totaling an estimated 104 billion cubic meters a year.

We could go on and on with American and worldwide statistics on water, but the information above is enough to suggest the dimensions of the problem. Many of our readers will already have installed low-flow toilets, cut down on lengthy showers, and fixed leaky faucets. (The average American family of four uses ninety thousand gallons of water a year, including thirteen gallons per day per person washing clothes. One leaky faucet can waste seventy-five to several hundred gallons a week. A leaky toilet can waste fifty gallons a day.) We need to encourage water-saving practices. But we also need to support United Nations efforts to protect and purify fresh water around the globe. We need to vote for legislators who take water problems seriously. One California water official and his legislative allies have been trying for ten years to see enacted a simple law that would require new subdivisions to identify long-term reliable sources of water before being built. As of 2002 it hadn't happened, despite one new community of fourteen thousand almost going dry.

Global Warming

It has been known since the 1890s that the so-called greenhouse gasses (carbon dioxide, chlorofluorocarbons, hydro-chlorofluorocarbons, methane) trap heat on the earth's surface. To a degree this is good—we need the sun's warmth. But too much of a good thing, and the warming gets out of hand. Humans shoveling snow during a record snowfall find it difficult to believe that the earth is warming up. What they and we need to know is that global warming is not inconsistent with highly erratic weather. The recent increase in droughts, fires, floods, and hurricanes is affected by, though of course not completely caused by, human activity. Deforestation can directly cause floods and mud slides and indirectly contribute to global warming, since trees absorb carbon dioxide. Global warming can indirectly change weather patterns in ways that increase hurricanes. One scientist has said, "The weather is like a giant beast and we are poking it with a stick." According to "chaos theory"— perhaps better called nonlinear theory—highly relevant to climatology, small initial changes in a process can produce enormous changes later in the process, changes that, because of the number and complexity of causal factors, are impossible to predict with precision.

This complexity is one reason that scientists were so long unsure that global warming was actually occurring. Moreover, it has allowed defenders of the status quo—that is, the way we currently burn fossil fuels in cars and industry and power plants (a primary source of carbon dioxide)—to stubbornly deny the need for change. But the scientific community is now quite sure of the global warming thesis. A group of 2,500 scientists from fifty-five nations formed the International Panel on Climate Change (IPCC) in 1988 under the aegis of the

United Nations. In 1995 the panel's second report, noting a one-degree Fahrenheit average increase in temperature in the twentieth century, concluded, "The balance of evidence suggests that there is a discernible human influence on global climate." Its February 2001 report confirmed the earlier premise even more decisively. The 1990s were the warmest decade ever recorded and included the five warmest years.

There is little dispute on the above data, but there is still dispute over the degree to which human activity, especially the burning of fossil fuels, has contributed to this warming trend. Skeptics, often applauded by the oil and gas industry, point out that there have always been great fluctuations in warming and cooling patterns. That is true, but certain correlations must be taken seriously. Studies that go back 450,000 years show that the earth has been warming for five hundred years, but 80 percent of the warming has occurred since 1800, roughly correlating with the industrial revolution. Meanwhile, a University of Michigan team drilled 616 wells all around the world and was able to measure carbon dioxide levels hundreds and thousands of years ago. Levels were never above 280 parts per million until the eighteenth century—the period of the invention of the steam engine and the internal combustion engine, and the increased burning of coal and oil in industry—when levels began to rise. The current level is 370 parts per million, a 31 percent increase in three centuries. If the trend continues, this percentage would double by the end of the twenty-first century. These carbon dioxide measurements roughly parallel heat levels. A recent study by the National Oceanic and Atmospheric Administration (NOAA) and a separate study by the Scripps Institute of Oceanography have found a close correlation between rising air temperature and rising ocean temperatures.

In November 1999 a research team drawn from three American universities, NASA, the NOAA, the Hadley Center in Britain, and the Russian Arctic and Antarctic Research Institute published in *Science* the results of a lengthy study. The researchers concluded that there is only a 0.1 percent chance that Arctic melting over the last forty-six years is the result solely of natural causes—that is, unaffected by human-caused global warming—and only a 2 percent chance that the last nineteen years of melting could have been naturally caused.

Global warming affects coral reefs, very important for marine life, which at the present rate of deterioration may be devastated in thirty years. As noted above, malaria-carrying mosquitoes are already migrating northward. Whole strains of DNA disappear as tropical forests recede. Polar ice has thinned 40 percent in the last few decades. Glaciers are retreating in every part of the world. The largest iceberg every recorded broke off from Antarctica in 2000. In a complicated chemical reaction involving the relationship of temperature, fresh water in ice, and the salinity of oceans, the Atlantic Gulf Stream is threatening to move off course, warming Greenland and freezing northern Europe. (Because the Gulf Stream causes differences in climate, we forget that Rome and Chicago, Oslo and Anchorage, Paris and northern Minnesota share roughly the same latitude.) It is counterintuitive, but due to global warming, penguins have been moving north! Melting polar ice may put New Orleans, Bangladesh and the Seychelles Islands under water.

In 1992, from concern over these developments, 166 nations met in Rio de Janeiro in an Earth Summit and worked out a Framework Convention on Climate Change, basically a plan for negotiating a climate treaty. This plan was signed by President George Bush and approved by the U.S. Senate. The parties agreed to hold greenhouse gas emissions at 1990 levels until 2000, by which time they could negotiate a new treaty. The new treaty, to go into effect by 2002, would aim to reduce emission levels. China, India, Indonesia, Malaysia, and other developing countries immediately let it be known that in their view this was not fair to them. They produced a small fraction of the world's greenhouse gasses, yet had a large portion of the world's population, mostly poor. To prevent any growth in emissions would, for them, deny any economic growth and be a condemnation to continual poverty. Meanwhile, the Rio signatory nations were highly uneven in their pledge to hold the line at 1990 emissions. Eastern Europe actually lowered its emissions, but this was because, with the breakup of the Soviet empire, the economy was collapsing and production was low. Western Europe, because of high energy prices and more efficient production technology, saw emissions go up only slightly (Britain actually saw a drop at the end of the decade). By 2000 the United States, the largest producer of greenhouse gasses, had increased emissions by 13 percent, and the public was buying gas-guzzling SUVs at a great rate.

Then in 1997 many nations met in Kyoto, Japan, and, using the Rio framework, worked out the Kyoto Protocol. Vice President Gore represented the United States. European nations agreed to an 8 percent reduction in greenhouse gasses, to be achieved between 2008 and 2012, the U.S. agreed to a 7 percent reduction, Japan agreed to a 6 percent reduction, and the average for all nations was to be 5.2 percent. The protocol would go into force when fifty-five nations ratified it, including all thirty-nine of the top industrial countries, which account for 55 percent of all emissions. President Clinton signed the agreement in November 1998, but the Senate did not approve it. (The often misunderstood term "ratification" means a treaty has been signed by the president "with the advice and consent of the Senate.") The position of opponents in the Senate has been that we should not commit ourselves to such reduction until Third World countries agree to exactly the same terms. Moreover, according to a unanimous Senate resolution, no potential agreement is acceptable that would "harm the United States' economy." The argument seems to minimize the fact that the overwhelming proportion of greenhouse gas emissions comes from North America and Western Europe. The United States, with 4.5 percent of the world's population, emits 1.5 billion tons per year of carbon dioxide, about a quarter of net total emissions worldwide.

After several other pretreaty conferences, a meeting in The Hague in November 2000 broke up in some disarray when U.S. delegates and northern Europeans disagreed sharply over pollution-credit-trading proposals. The rationale of pollution credit trading is that nations above the agreed-upon emission level could buy credits from a nation below the level, provided the worldwide level is not exceeded. The Europeans would support some credit trading, but not to the degree the Americans insisted on. One projection held that only one-fourth of U.S. reductions would be direct. The other three-fourths would be covered by credits bought from Russia and other low-producing Eastern European countries.

The sixth such negotiating meeting was scheduled for May 2001, in Bonn. At the request of the United States, the meeting was delayed until July, because the new President Bush had already called the Kyoto Protocol "fatally flawed," and the Americans promised to offer an alternate treaty. No such alternate treaty was provided. After a decade of work by 180 nations, the dismayed Bonn delegates nevertheless felt obliged to go ahead and approved the Kyoto Protocol without U.S. involvement, slyly adding a provision that would allow for "voluntary" participation by the United States. Whether it will ever go into effect is open to question. The United States was counted on for about 40 percent of the financing. Even some liberals think the Kyoto mechanism is impractical. Since September 11 the Bush administration has launched a global antiterrorism campaign and put global warming and other environmental issues on a back burner. In February 2002 the Bush administration announced its plan for reducing greenhouse gas emissions; it is predicated on largely voluntary actions by emissions producers.

Gloomy spirits on the left may say that all the remedial steps are too little and too late. But common sense has a claim to make. Economists show that while doing something effective about emission limits by mid-century may cost the huge sum of 2 percent of our gross national product, doing nothing will cost 6–20 percent over a longer period. Can we look that far ahead?

III. A CHRISTIAN PERSPECTIVE

In the area of public policy Christians need to see their policy positions as expressions of faith, not as some kind of separate enterprise. In this endeavor we walk a razor's edge between being just another political pressure group and articulating theological positions at such a level of generality that they fail to connect to specific policies.

A starting place is the words of the psalmist: "The earth is the Lord's and all that is in it, the world, and those who live in it" (Ps. 24:1). God is the creator and we are the creatures. The creation is "very good" (Gen. 1:31), even apart from human values and interests (Ps. 104). This does not mean that evil is absent from the world but that the world was created as an expression of the goodness of the creator and serves God's redemptive purposes. The planet has been created as a habitat to be shared by all, and God's concern covers the whole. The writer of Deuteronomy describes Palestine as

> a good land, a land with flowing streams, with springs and underground waters welling up in valleys and hills, a land of wheat and barley, of vines and fig trees and pomegranates, a land of olive trees and honey, a land where you may eat bread without scarcity, where you will lack nothing, a land whose stones are iron and from whose hills you may mine copper. You shall eat your fill and bless the LORD your God for the good land that he has given you. (Deut 8: 7–10)

The claim that humans are created "in the image of God" (Gen. 1:27) carries both an honor and a responsibility. The "dominion" given to humankind by God (Gen. 1:26) does not justify domination or despotism. The land is always God's land, entrusted to humanity to "till and keep" in a responsible way. The holiness code of Leviticus includes a soil conservation mandate to let the land rest every seven years. We are to "subdue" Earth not for self-glorification but to protect nutrition, health, and well-being. Moreover, the God of the Scriptures is a "lover of justice" (Ps. 99:4); upon this faith is built a tradition of concern for the weak and the poor. Although concepts of justice are not explicitly applied to nonhuman life in the biblical texts, it is wholly consistent with those texts that they should be. God cares for all flora and fauna (Ps. 104), for sparrows (Matt. 10:29; Luke 12:6) and the lilies (Matt. 6:28–29; Luke 12:27). And what we have done "to one of the least of these who are members of my family," we have done to Christ (Matt. 25:40).

> Every cell of every organ in my body is part of a larger living system that is me. Similarly, each of us, with all life, is part of a larger living planetary system. Earth is our larger self, our large body. . . . Earth is not a planet with life on it; rather it is a living planet. The physical structure of the planet—its core, mantle and mountain ranges—acts as the skeleton or frame of its existence. The soil that covers its grasslands and forests is like a mammoth digestive system. In it all things are broken down, absorbed and recycled into new growth. The

oceans, waterways and rain function as a circulatory system that moves life-giving "blood," purifying and revitalizing the body. The bacteria, algae, plants and trees provide the planet's lungs, constantly regenerating the entire atmosphere. The animal kingdom provides the functions of a nervous system, a finely tuned and diversified series of organisms sensitized to environmental change.[1]

Seeing the connectedness of all living things leads to a new attitude toward economic growth. Heedless, uncontrolled growth is more cancerous than constructive. Too many Christians, while deploring individual selfishness and seeking forgiveness for it, nevertheless have found it easy to accept an economic order that is described in the language of individual self-interest but in practice justifies the profit of global corporations at the expense of environmental and cultural dislocations. Most Christians rejoice in the recent success of the American economy in producing an abundance of goods and services and hope that these benefits can be shared with the whole world. But the prevailing economic model, relying on increasing specialization and a steadily growing market, does not take into account the social cost of extracting raw materials in a destructive way or the costs of emitting toxic wastes into the environment. "Full-cost pricing" that incorporates the cost of environmental damage and depletion has been neglected. Christians are still paying too little attention to the damage they do to God's creation. With its emphasis on individual satisfactions and individual success, the current economic model ignores the notion of communal goods and the good of the physical earth.

Environmentalist-theologian Bill McKibben says: "We are engaged in the swift and systematic decreation of the planet we were born into. And does God look at our actions and pronounce them good? I doubt it. Forget the sterile debate about whether we were given dominion over the planet. Grant that we were. The question is, what have we done with that dominion?"[2] He cites the familiar words of the book of Job, in which God speaks to Job:

> "Where were you when I laid the foundation of the earth?
> Tell me, if you have understanding.
>
> . . . .
>
> [W]ho laid its cornerstone
> when the morning stars sang together
> and all the heavenly beings shouted for joy?
>
> Or who shut in the sea with doors
> when it burst out from the womb?—
> when I made the clouds its garment
>
> . . . .

and said, 'Thus far shall you come, and no farther,
and here shall your proud waves be stopped'?"
                            (Job 38:4, 6–9, 11)

The great change is that now, except for earthquakes and volcanoes, "acts
of God" have human responsibility mixed with them. And even earthquakes
kill almost no one apart from the crumbling buildings inadequately made by
humans. Floods and droughts and hurricanes are partly our doing. "If we create a world without wilderness—and that is precisely what we are doing—then
we lose a critical locus for the radical encounter with the divine."[3]

IV. WHAT WE CAN DO

If Christians believe that stewardship of God's Earth means only such things
as not wasting water with the garden hose, recycling the daily newspaper, and
contributing annually to an environmental organization, that will not solve the
dilemma facing humanity—helpful as those modest measures may be. There
are many, perhaps too many, environmental organizations: the Audubon Society, the Environmental Defense Fund, Friends of the Earth, Greenpeace, the
National Wildlife Federation, the Natural Resources Defense Council, the
Nature Conservancy, the Sierra Club, the World Wildlife Fund, and Population Connection, to name but a few. They are vital and do good work, but each
has its special issues and special constituencies. On some legislative issues they
split into two or more camps. For example, the Environmental Defense Fund
and the Nature Conservancy support the policy of buying and selling "pollution credits," by which companies may delay conformity to some emission
limits by trading with other companies that are below those limits. They feel
this is a reasonable way to move gradually toward stated goals. This policy
presently operates in the United States and, as we have seen, was the subject
of disagreement in the Kyoto negotiations. The Friends of the Earth and the
Natural Resources Defense Council oppose this policy as conceding too much
to producers and unfairly harming particular geographic areas.

A tremendous educational effort affecting large masses of people will be
required if the sinister trends discussed here are to be reversed. This effort
seems to fly in the face of our economy's emphasis on growth and ever-expand-
ing consumption. But such an effort is not impossible. People must come to
see the seriousness of the crisis and also be given some hope that fundamental change is possible. With the development of the microchip and the introduction of the information age, it is possible to see at least the outline of an
economy that grows in service and education and sustainable community

activities without growing in consumption of trees and oil and mineral deposits. People throw up their hands when hearing estimates that cleaning up the physical damage we have done to the earth could take $800 billion. They should acknowledge that this amount is about one-tenth of what the world spends on armaments, the military, and violent confrontation. The expenditure is not impossible. It is our imagination that is too limited.

As political pundits often say of environmental issues, these things are on the radar screen, but they are not front and center. Voters don't want to hear a great deal on the subject. Sadly, the pundits are probably correct. Mainline Christian denominations are also caught in this atmosphere. Devout Christians are often of the opinion that the church as an institution should "stay out of politics." They are part of a venerable American tradition that sees politics as a dirty business. One of the paradoxes of democratic systems is that the more people believe politics to be dirty, the dirtier it becomes. Many denominational offices in Washington are well-informed on environmental issues, and some denominations have excellent publications on environmental issues that see eco-justice from a biblical perspective. But local churches may not be disposed to give such agencies and publications support. They see church bureaucracies, like governmental bureaucracies, as too far away.

Nevertheless, the church is in a good position to help in this transformation to wider environmental sensitivity. It is neither necessary nor possible for every church member to lead a crusade, but we can all let our senators know that global warming is to be taken seriously. Just as there are higher and lower forms of religion, there are higher and lower forms of politics. With vision, the church can be an effective agent of higher politics in the service of higher religion. The church helped in the nineteenth century's great moral fight against slavery. It helped in the civil rights movement of the 1960s. The environment is a different kind of problem. It is not a direct moral confrontation between individual persons over what justice is. But it is, like those racial struggles, a moral issue involving the meaning of justice, justice for the impoverished, justice for those at risk in an unhealthy environment, justice for our great-grandchildren, and justice for all God's creatures on Earth.

Discussion Questions

1. How do we understand God's grant to humankind of "dominion" over the earth and its creatures?
2 What are the most practical steps that we can take to reduce our consumption of fossil fuels?
3. Can we convince peoples in the developing world to limit their consumption if we do not limit our own consumption? Can we grow in the consumption of services without growing in using up resources?

4. Why is the international control of fishing so weak?
5. Who should take responsibility for nuclear waste cleanup?
6. Why has there been such a long delay in acknowledging global warming?
7. What are the effects of global warming?
8. What steps can be taken to move toward "full-cost pricing"? Do most people yet understand this concept?
9. Is a limit on population beyond our control?
10. What do you think of McKibben's idea of "decreation"?
11. Do you find it easy or hard to think of everything on Earth, all species and Earth itself, as one family?
12. Has your congregation taken steps similar to those described in the congregation on page one?

To Learn More

Those interested in further reading might consult John B. Cobb Jr., *Sustainability: Economics, Ecology and Justice* (Maryknoll, N.Y.: Orbis, 1992). This book relates the ideas of Christian justice, conversion, and eschatology to the current environmental crisis. Sallie McFague, *The Body of God* (Minneapolis: Fortress 1993) re-envisions God and the cosmos, seeking to change our attitudes towards the environment in crisis. Larry L. Rasmussen, *Earth Community, Earth Ethics* (Maryknoll, N.Y.: Orbis, 1998) uses international discussions of sustainable development and synthesizes insights from religion, ethics, and environmentalism into a single vision for creating a sustainable community.

Michael Brower and Warren Leon, *The Consumer's Guide to Effective Environmental Choices* (New York: Three Rivers Press, 1999) is a helpful book about consumerism and provides environmentally friendly buying habits. Jill S. Schneiderman, ed., *The Earth Around Us: Maintaining a Livable Planet* (New York: W. H. Freeman, 2000) is a group of essays from prominent scientists who discuss environmental problems and ways that individuals can actively work for change. The Worldwatch Institute's annual publication *State of the World* and the excellent bibliography in Evan Eisenberg, *The Ecology of Eden* (New York: Knopf, 1998) are both good resources.

15

Global Food Security

In mid-February and early March of 2000, Madagascar was impacted by two massive storms, the cyclone Eline and the tropical depression Gloria, which eventually flooded the vast Limpopo River valley of Mozambique. The only railroad that traverses a very productive Madagascar food-growing region and connects it to a major port city was damaged by nearly two hundred mudslides. Several hundred meters of rails were undermined. Consequently, food supplies ceased to flow to the cities and surrounding villages. At the same time, the livelihood of one hundred thousand people was in jeopardy. The many landless rural people who had employment on farms or served as porters who carried farm products to the railway had to contemplate the necessity of burning more forests in the highland as a desperate step for survival. This in turn would further the destruction of the unique flora and fauna of the region. National and regional governmental resources were inadequate to rebuild the railroad. Until several international agencies responded to this challenge, the future of these rural people, the producers of food and subsistence farmers, was in doubt.

I. INTRODUCTION

No issue can be more important for humanity in any age than how to feed people. In earlier centuries this problem has been a local one in each region of the world; today it has become global. Thus far, on a global basis the race to produce enough food to meet demand has been successful, but there have been some terrible failures in getting this food to those who need it. Furthermore, for thousands of years much of the production of food has not been on a truly sustainable basis, and the increased production of recent decades has accelerated the loss of essential resources and the destruction of fragile ecosystems. In the next hundred years it will be difficult to find ways in which to increase food supply to keep up with demand. The necessity of doing so on a sustainable basis will become ever more apparent. Even if we succeed in producing food sustainably in the quantities that are needed, there will remain the problem that many people may not be able to buy it. This chapter will consider (1) the crisis in production and the threat of absolute shortfalls, (2) the problem of distribution, and (3) the Christian contribution to reflection on these matters and to constructive action.

Already in much of the world there is critical food insecurity. Projections of present patterns indicate that this situation is likely to grow much worse in the coming century. It is urgent that we understand what is required for food security and then do what is needed.

How should food security be defined? Food security is achieved when all people at all times have both physical and economic access to nutritious food to meet their dietary needs for a productive and healthy life. In view of this definition, is it possible to achieve food security for the entire human family? At present, no one knows. But at the outset of this discussion, concerned people need to be reminded that as a global community we have not yet even asked the question in a large enough way. The question of global food security in the twenty-first century is indeed a large one. We are considering it first in terms of the sustainable production of sufficient food and then in terms of enabling everyone to acquire the food they need.

II. THE THREAT OF FOOD SHORTFALLS

To avoid shortfalls of food for the human family in this new century, we must overcome the social and technological legacies of colonialism and its contemporary expression in the current globalization of the food system. Indeed, we need to change practices that have dominated agriculture for seven thousand years. During this entire period people have replaced the complex ecosystems of nature, which include many perennials, with a single crop grown on cleared land that must be replanted every year. The result in most places has been erosion and the degradation of the soil. Indeed, humanity has yet to design sustainable food systems.

At present, the prospect of adequate healthy and nutritious food for the human family in the twenty-first century is dim. An unprecedented world population of six billion, which is still growing rapidly, makes an enormous impact upon natural resources. Accompanying this growth are the increasing number of grazing livestock across the earth's rangelands, depleted fisheries, deforestation, and pollution of air and water resources from food-production systems predominantly based on chemical inputs. These systems are heavily dependent on fossil-fuel-based fertilizers for meeting the fertility requirements of the high-yielding varieties of corn, wheat, and rice. Cropland soil loss from wind and water erosion worldwide is now estimated to equal four tons per person per year (24 billion tons of soil). Chronic neglect of the physical, social, and economic infrastructures for serving the rural people, who are the world's primary food producers, is another troubling factor.

The story about Madagascar with which this paper began is an encouraging one. It shows what thoughtful people can do in response to a crisis. But the reality of the island's situation is not a happy one. Nowhere can we better observe environmental degradation and the resulting poverty of the majority of citizens. This has resulted from a history of deforestation, poorly designed agriculture, and governmental ineptitude. The future of Madagascar is bleak. If radical changes and new commitments are not in place soon, the prospects for Madagascar foreshadow what will happen to the world as a whole during this century.

If we are to understand our situation and find direction for the future, we need to learn from agricultural history. No writing on this subject provides greater insight than *The Conquest of the Land in Seven Thousand Years*, written in 1939 and published by W. C. Lowdermilk, the first secretary of the U.S. Soil Conservation Service. Despite changes in names of countries, political boundaries, and conservation technology, this publication still has significance for all peoples concerned with maintaining and improving global food systems. Lowdermilk's immediate mission was to find out if the experiences of these older civilizations could help in solving the serious soil erosion and land use problems in the United States, then struggling with repair of the dust bowl and the gullied South. He studied the record of agriculture in countries where the land had been under cultivation for hundreds and even thousands of years. He discovered that soil erosion, deforestation, overgrazing, neglect, and conflicts between cultivators and producers of livestock have helped to topple empires and to wipe out entire civilizations. He learned also that careful stewardship of the earth's resources, through terracing, crop rotation, and other soil conservation measures, has enabled other societies to flourish for thousands of years.

At the beginning of this new century, slightly more than 50 percent of the world's population lives in seventy-five food-deficit nations. Of these nations, thirty-five (twenty-five of which are located in sub-Saharan Africa) are severely affected. Approximately 675 million people subsist on far fewer than 2,200 calories per day. Their natural-resource context is that of shortages of water and deterioration of croplands, rangelands, forests, and plant and animal genetic reservoirs.

The causes of food shortfalls of this magnitude are many. Some are old and lingering; others are relatively new. Reaching the goal of global food sufficiency for the human community during this new century requires that we (a) deal with old and lingering causes of food shortfalls, (b) with new ones, and (c) make a radical departure from a long history of annual monoculture. In its place we need to develop an agro-ecology—based on perennial polycultures, carefully integrated with livestock (preferably indigenous species) and, where possible, agroforestry—that will give priority attention to the health and economic stability of rural communities and national populations.

Old Causes of Food Shortfalls

The old and lingering causes of food shortfalls are many. Most of the food-deficit nations are located in the tropics, and a foremost cause of food shortfalls is the fragility and relatively infertile nature of tropical soils, which are typically only two to five inches deep. Most are lateritic in composition (formed by rock decay), with high concentrations of iron and aluminum oxides. When cleared of the forest and grass cover, which in part, hold these oxides in suspension, these soils oxidize rapidly, transforming them into a rock-hard surface. Tropical forests are nothing more than tree-covered deserts.

Until the early 1960s, Western colonialism dominated most of this tropical world. Temperate-zone agricultural technologies and industries of the northern-latitude colonial powers were imposed onto the tropical world, not for domestic food production, but for the production of commodities for people and industries of the colonial powers. Consequently, crops such as sugar cane, highland coffee, cocoa, peanuts, corn, sisal, hemp, and cotton were emphasized, and commercial production of beef was set into motion. Agricultural research, roads, bridges, and storage facilities were created to enhance this kind of production. In nations that are former Western colonies, the results are food shortfalls and cropping systems that, over time, have proved both environmentally ruinous and destructive of traditional rural communities.

During the colonial period, there was no advanced training of tropical peoples in the science of agriculture and environmental management. Consequently, leadership for rural community and agricultural development for sustainable and self-reliant domestic food systems is nearly nonexistent.

Coupled with this deficit are the twin problems of ill-defined development policies and priorities and governmental ineptitude. International competition for national alliances during the Cold-War years further inhibited the emergence of leadership and infrastructure for domestic, sustainable (regenerative), self-reliant food systems.

Prior to the colonial period, most areas of the world were largely self-reliant in the production of necessities. The colonial powers systematically destroyed this self-reliance, so as to make the colonies economically as well as politically dependent on them. After the former colonies became politically independent nations, the global economic system continued, and even intensified, the breakdown of economic self-sufficiency. This has also limited the ability of new nations to exercise political self-determination. In a healthy community, there is a great deal of mutual dependence. But a healthy community is comprised of people who take some responsibility for one another's well-being. Dependence on the decisions of distant corporations seeking primarily maximum profits undermines community rather than extending it. A global market is not a global community. One major change required for food security in the twenty-first century is a return to self-reliant agriculture. (See chapter 12, "The Globalization of Economic Life.")

Throughout this chapter the term "self-reliant" refers to food and fiber production systems that are relatively independent of imports. These systems do not depend on external supplies of petrochemically based fertilizers, pesticides, fungicides, and herbicides. To be self-reliant a farming system needs to be as independent as possible of international supplies of fuel and of replacement parts for mechanized equipment. Self-reliance involves technologies of plant and animal breeding that are independent of international seed suppliers and sperm banks. It assumes that adequate supplies of food are produced within a nation's boundaries, so that the nation is not dependent for necessities on imports or on global transportation facilities. Although such independence does not exclude trade in surpluses of nonessential foods, when these can be produced and transported in sustainable ways, the goal of self-reliance points in the opposite direction from the now-dominant approaches to the production of sufficient food.

The currently dominant system is based on the theory that each region should produce for the world market what it can grow most competitively regardless of its consequences for the environment, rather than produce what its own people need and the environment can sustain over the long run. Each region exports these crops and imports what it needs from elsewhere. As a result, the availability of food today in many parts of the world depends on a fossil-fuel-based transport system. In the industrial world, our food now travels an average of fifteen hundred miles. Within decades the oil and natural gas on which this depends will be too scarce and too expensive for the present system to survive.

But it is not only our transportation system that depends on oil. The now-dominant direction of agricultural development was set in the post–World War II period by what is called the green revolution. Advanced technology was used greatly to increase yields of rice, wheat, and maize. It accomplished this almost exclusively by breeding varieties of these grains designed to respond to heavy inputs of nitrogenous fertilizers, which are derivatives of fossil fuel. *Major world food systems are now completely dependent on petrochemical inputs.* Part of the challenge in the twenty-first century is to develop a postpetroleum global food system that reverses both the dependence on long-distance transportation and the dependence on petrochemical-based nitrogenous fertilizers.

New Causes of Food Shortfalls

Overarching all of these lingering causes of food insecurity is the unprecedented growth in human population, consumption, and waste. During the past fifty years, world population has tripled. Rural poverty fuels this growth, since children are needed for farm labor and the security of the poor in old age depends on support by their children. Population growth, in turn, worsens the poverty. (See chapter 16, "The Global Population Crisis.") In some cultures, poor farm families divide their land among their sons, resulting in ever-smaller plots. Elsewhere, those who do not inherit land add to the competition for work in the cities. Approximately 150 million people in the world are unemployed. Nine hundred million jobs pay less than a living wage. Two billion people survive on less than two U.S. dollars per day.

Meanwhile the growing affluence of the richest 20 percent of the world's population leads to increasingly wasteful use of food. Much of the food purchased by grocery stores, restaurants, and even families is thrown away. It is difficult for those with modest needs to purchase in small quantities, and restaurants compete with one another to serve large portions.

Today the avoidance of food shortfalls faces new problems. The world is running short of *water for irrigation.* Forty percent of the world's food supply is produced on irrigated land, which constitutes about 5 percent of the earth's total cropland. China and India are facing critical water shortages. Across almost all irrigated land, surface water and aquifers are being exploited in unsustainable ways, and the irrigated lands are suffering from salinization and water logging. (See chapter 14, "The Church and Environmentalism.")

AIDS is taking a tremendous toll on men, women, and children who are food producers. In much of Africa, AIDS is decimating agricultural and rural community leadership. The impact of this growing epidemic upon food production and the management of soil, forest, and water resources has yet to be adequately determined.

Climatic instability is increasing and remains little understood and highly unpredictable. Scientists do know about the accumulation of fine dust particles at high altitudes, increases in carbon dioxide, and the depletion of the ozone shield, particularly over the polar regions. All countries need to adopt the United Nations' "precautionary principle." According to this principle, when new products or procedures—which may have destructive consequence—are proposed, the burden of proof should be shifted from those who oppose their introduction to those who support it. Following this principle would slow the worsening of climatic instability (drought, typhoons, tornadoes) and consequent outbreaks of pathogenic and insect crop infestation, which are new causes of food shortfalls. It is better to be safe than sorry.

Today the precautionary principle is relevant to *developments in biotechnology.* Scientists are introducing new genes into many crops, a process called transgenetic engineering. For example, it is being used in an effort to improve the nutritional value of rice. Within the past four years, more that forty million acres of transgenetic corn, soybeans, cotton, and potatoes have been planted in the United States. Opponents cannot prove that the wider consequences will be seriously harmful, but there is certainly no assurance that they will be benign.

One example of the risk is the introduction of bacillus thuringiensis (Bt) into corn. Bt produces an insecticidal protein that is lethal to the European corn borer. This protects corn from one of its major enemies. Scientists from Cornell University and Iowa State University have now provided strong evidence that the pollen from this corn kills the larvae of monarch butterflies. No one knows the long-term effects of this toxic protein on other insects and on soil microorganisms.

A second example is Monsanto's engineering of soybeans to resist the effects of the popular herbicide Roundup; this makes it easier to control weeds without damaging soybeans. However, there is a clear possibility that the genes added to soybeans will migrate into a wild cousin and produce superresistant weeds that would inhibit the growth of future soybean plantings.

Genetic manipulation of food represents uncharted territory. Many questions remain unanswered. Are these new foods safe for human and animal consumption? What are the environmental risks of introducing new genes into existing crops? Are agricultural biotechnic and classical breeding methods the same? On the other hand, what are the risks—such as pathogenic infestations resulting in massive crop losses—if we do *not* take advantage of these new technologies?

Clearly, much additional research is essential. Conflicts of interest exist when industry determines its own level of safety review for food products it seeks to promote. There are also conflicts of interest when scientists with investment in, or funded by, bioengineering companies take part in the evaluation. For these reasons, the National Academy of Sciences advocates strong regulations of genetically engineered products consumed over extended periods of time. Indeed, precaution should be the watchword. This new field of scientific inquiry and food crop development raises complex issues requiring thorough discussion. In any case, if applications are very cautious, bioengineering may help, but it does not offer the basic solution to the problem of providing sufficient food on a sustainable basis in the next century.

At this early moment in the history of transgenetic engineering, there is no way to predict how these genes will express themselves in different organisms as a result of genetic drift. Wes Jackson, of the Land Institute near Salina, Kansas, raises this question: "If, in time, a transgenetic organism proves to be dysfunctional, do we have an exit strategy?" Our sciences are creating new organisms that by definition have no history within ecosystems into which they are being introduced. The introduction of transgenetic plants into global food systems raises, in the long term, the question of global food security and of safe and healthy food. Like nuclear power and DDT, transgenetic engineering has hazards. A system replete with unknown dangers does not contribute to security.

The global reach of *corporate industrialized agriculture* works against efforts to achieve a regenerative, or sustainable, and self-reliant food system, particularly in food-deficit nations. The goals of such agriculture have little to do with food security as defined at the beginning of this chapter. Such agriculture has little to do with feeding the hungry, although it is sometimes promoted as a contribution to this end.

In recent years, the quest for food security has been complicated and derailed by social unrest. Many nations have experienced increased incidences of *civil war and ethnic conflict*, a major consequence of which is disruption of the food production system. Food cannot be produced and distributed during civil strife.

Another obstacle to the achievement of sustainable production of adequate food is *the way productivity is measured*. The focus of research for the development and maintenance of food supplies is on the maximization of yields per acre or animal unit. The full costs of resource depletion and environmental and social stress are not calculated in the equation of profit and loss. The issues of animal welfare are also not considered. Productivity measurements are deceptive. We need more realistic measures for cost/benefit analysis for achieving a sustainable global food system.

Problems caused by *international debt repayment* have emerged as a recent factor contributing to food insecurity. Pressure placed upon food-deficit nations to service their debts has contributed to the perpetuation of old colonial cropping systems. For example, crops such as cocoa, tea, coffee, tropical fruits, cut flowers, spices, and vegetables destined to northern countries are produced for the fundamental purpose of earning foreign currency that is then committed to servicing old debts. For many countries, the necessity of debt repayment retards the development of self-reliant domestic food systems. Recently the issue of debt forgiveness has become a matter of widespread public discussion, and a beginning has been made with a few countries, but the problem remains enormous. (See chapter 13, "Should Debt Be Forgiven?")

Needed Responses to the Problem of Shortfalls

The total problem outlined in the preceding sections is not simply the sum of the individual causes of food shortfalls. The multiple causes interact with one another and complicate the task of responding to any one. Instead of dealing with the causes singly, we need a radically new strategy. To achieve global food security for the human family, we must move toward the development of a sustainable, or regenerative, agriculture.

During and immediately following World War II, demographers recognized the unprecedented reality of rapid human population growth. Because the need to increase food production dramatically was clear, the green revolution was set into motion. The intent was to increase crop yields three- to fourfold. By so doing, the problem of anticipated food deficits could be resolved, at least on a short-term basis.

And so it was. International research centers were established, with a particular focus on the breeding of high-yielding varieties of rice, wheat, and corn. Skilled plant breeders, geneticists, agronomists, plant pathologists, and entomologists were recruited. Their research developed a packaged delivery system of miracle seeds, associated with fertilizers and pesticides. High-potential areas (fertility, rainfall, topography, and rural infrastructure) were targeted. The results during the past fifty years are impressive. Nobel prizes were awarded and the goal of addressing the immediate need of increasing food production was met. The green revolution deserves appreciation for its great achievements.

On the other hand, the green revolution cannot provide food security for the coming century. It made agriculture dependent on fossil fuels, led to the loss of thousands of indigenous plant varieties—in spite of a great deal of effort in recent years to collect and preserve remaining varieties—and dislocated thousands of farmers who, for one reason or another, could not take advantage of the new technologies.

To achieve adequate and sustainable food production in the twenty-first century will require a radical departure from the approach of the green revolution. In contrast to the comparatively simple approach of the first, the strategies of the second green revolution will be complex. They will focus on the development of sustainable, and therefore socially just, food systems across very diverse environments. They must create a productive agriculture within poor natural resource areas and among people who are still on the margins of society. The rural unemployed and landless must be brought into food systems. The experiences and wisdom of indigenous peoples need to be incorporated into the design of sustainable domestic food systems. After decades of undermining of rural communities, we must do what we can to nurture them.

To accomplish this complex goal, the strategies of the next green revolution will involve the recruitment of leadership from across a wide span of disciplines that will include not only plant breeders and agronomists but also those representing the social sciences. A profound interdisciplinary analysis of agro-ecosystems is required, along with the development of massive biodiversity in crop and livestock production appropriate for croplands, rangelands, and forests. The emphasis should be on the rehabilitation of stressed ecosystems within which an agro-ecology can evolve. This strategy moves far beyond the dominance of the biological sciences. If the vision of global food security, with its underlying commitment to the evolution of a sustainable or regenerative, self-reliant food production, is to become a reality, then the first priority in research and development will be reaching the marginalized sector of national populations.

Obviously, the next green revolution, designed to be regionally specific and focused on marginalized landscapes and peoples, must address issues that were not taken into consideration during the first green revolution. The needs are many: self-reliant soil nutritional management; water management, including surface and underground resources; mangrove and coral reef protection; reducing pollution from farms; regional genetic-resource (biodiversity) maintenance; alternatives to slash-and-burn agriculture; the development and maintenance of mountain agriculture; changes in land-tenure traditions; innovative market accessibility; careful farming designs for the integration of crops and livestock, including the maintenance of wildlife habitat. We also need national and international policies that give priority to developing essential rural infrastructures, including public health and educational services, as well as roads, railways, bridges, and storage and processing facilities for agricultural products.

The agenda is long. The needed second green revolution, if it is to reach or approximate the goal of adequate supply of food globally, must focus on food production with justice, be ecologically benign, and be economically viable. The challenge is to understand production efficiencies in ways that measure all of the production, social, and environmental costs. We must move beyond the present paralysis in production research, our dependency on fossil fuels, and the mindset that some must produce more in order to feed others. We must give priority to the ability of people to feed themselves sustainably, rather than to production of crops for the world market.

III. THE DISTRIBUTION OF FOOD

The Problem

The preceding sections have devoted primary attention to the production of food. Without sufficient production, food security is obviously impossible, but it is not sufficient. Indeed, until now the cause of hunger has rarely been that no food was available for a price. The cause has been that those who needed it could not pay for it. Poverty, rather than absolute food shortfalls, has been the primary, immediate reason that people have gone hungry and have even starved to death. Without drastic and complex action on the part of humanity, absolute shortages will vastly worsen the situation, but there are also complex problems involved in getting the food to those who need it most.

Especially in poorer countries large portions of the crops never become available for purchase. Occasionally, crops are not even harvested because of political disturbances, low prices, or erratic weather. The breakdown of transportation, as illustrated in the opening story of Madagascar, contributes to the failure of food to reach markets. Still more critical is the lack of suitable storage facilities. In some cases as much as half of the grain decays or is eaten by rodents.

Nobel laureate and economist Amartya Sen has argued persuasively that poverty—rather than absolute food shortages—is frequently the underlying cause of hunger. A survey taken early in the 1990s, for example, showed that almost 80 percent of the children identified as malnourished in the developing world lived in poor countries where food was available. When people lack sufficient income to meet basic needs, their access to food in the marketplace or to land and credit to produce their own food is very limited. Poverty also deprives people of other basic needs, such as available health services, education, and a clean environment, the lack of which in turn increases the likelihood of hunger. Unsafe water, for example, leads to diarrhea and an inability to absorb available nutrients, while a poor education lessens the chance for a job and the income needed to buy food.

Chronic food insecurity for poor people is often made worse by seasonal fluctuations in prices and availability. Small variations in diet can be fatal to children already at risk. The extreme form of this risk is widespread famine as a result of a breakdown of food production, food distribution, or the flow of income with which people buy food. Perhaps as many as 30 million people died in the Chinese famine of 1959–61, and hundreds of thousands in the recent famines in sub-Saharan Africa. A relatively small number of people die from outright starvation, but many of those weakened by hunger die of infectious diseases.

Cultural factors also lock people into poverty, undermining their access to appropriate nutrition. Throughout Africa, Latin America, and Asia, women are often denied access to land ownership, credit, agricultural training, and social privileges in general, even though their labor raises more than half of the food produced. Hungry women bear children who are made hungry by their mothers' inability to breast feed or care for them. In this way malnutrition and poverty are continued from generation to generation.

As economic development takes place, moreover, increases in income are not shared evenly across most societies. Those suffering most from poverty and hunger are the most likely to be left behind by the globalization processes, skewing still further the nutritional patterns that condemn poor people to unhealthful diets. The more affluent citizens of developing countries are likely to eat too much food that is high in fats and wasteful of resources. As their consumption of meat and processed foods increases, prices rise and the poor find it still more difficult to purchase food.

A good illustration of the impact of higher incomes on diets is found in China. Production of food has leveled off due to soil loss, water shortages for irrigation, and conversion of agricultural land for industrial and urban growth. But, due to greater affluence in a significant segment of the population, demand for food is increasing. More grain is required to meet growing demands for swine, beef, and dairy products. It is forecast that China will be importing upwards of two hundred million metric tons of grain from Australia, Argentina, Canada, the United States, and Western Europe. This will produce global shortages and raise grain prices everywhere. Several other nations that are now experiencing rapid economic growth will also contribute to the growing per capita demand for food and fiber. Consequently, most of the present food-deficit nations will be outpriced and in serious trouble if they cannot feed themselves. Also there will be far less food in global storage facilities to meet emergency needs following inevitable regional events of drought, civil strife, crop pest infestations, flooding, and frost.

Poverty and hunger in rural areas are driving many desperate people to move to the cities, despite their lack of urban, industrial skills. Demographers estimate that sometime between 2020 and 2050 more than half of the human *population will reside in cities*. Even today, many of the world's largest cities have inadequate infrastructures for food processing, preservation, and distribution. Food security involves not only the sustainable production of adequate food but also the ability of these vast populations to buy it. Food security is a two-sided coin.

Needed Responses to the Problem of Food Distribution

If poverty is among the central causes of food insecurity, poverty reduction is crucial for food security. Until recently, the conventional approach or strategy for reducing poverty was economic growth. It was believed that opening markets and encouraging technological advances cause economies to grow and that eventually all the people would share in this new wealth. The rapid growth of international trade, international finance, and multinational corporate enterprises bears witness to the global dominance of this thinking.

Unfortunately, economic growth too often speeds up the exploitation of resources and pollution of land, water, and air, *increases inequality* of wealth, and *fails to protect vulnerable groups*. At the very least, policies for economic growth must include efforts to *narrow* the economic differences between people through effective programs such as land reform, progressive taxation, and education and health care for all. Nearly all the countries that have significantly reduced poverty in recent decades have embraced some version of this strategy.

In addition, widespread malnutrition requires a variety of specific policies in order to move toward a condition of food security. For example, people may eat more poorly than their incomes allow because of ignorance. This is most true of vitamin A, a shortcoming that can be corrected with better nutritional education. Fortifying the foods people already eat with micronutrients such as salt and iron also improves nutrition. If properly targeted and implemented, supplemental food programs can improve nutrition, as can food-price subsidies that make basic foodstuffs more affordable to the poor.

The world is in the midst of a nutrition crisis, and its toll on human development is staggering, yet largely unrecognized. Reversing the trend toward worsening diets requires that nutrition, long treated as an afterthought by many national leaders, become a clear priority. For this to happen, policy makers need to see hunger and overeating as partly the product of human decisions—societal and individual—that government policies can influence.

IV. A CHRISTIAN PERSPECTIVE

The awesome agenda spelled out above raises a fundamental question about the achievement of global food security for the human family. Are the production of sufficient food on a sustainable basis and its distribution to all who need it a pipe dream or a possibility? This is a faith question. Given the magnitude of the problem, coupled with the breadth and complexity of strategies for response, nothing less than a global commitment, similar to that made for the reconstruction of Europe and Japan following World War II, will suffice. We have the human and financial resources to address the challenge. Can we generate the will?

All of this chapter is written from a Christian perspective. The preceding sections contain many practical proposals about how to think and act. In conclusion, we want to give explicit attention to the biblical vision and some theological considerations. In the concluding section, we will consider what actions we are called to take as Christians, collectively and individually.

The Biblical Vision

We have used the Bible so much as a resource for personal faith and for the faith of our churches that we have too often overlooked the rich resources that it offers for giving direction to such public joint ventures as food security. In fact, however, much of the Bible focuses more upon the history of a people in all its social and political dimensions, including its food security, than on individual piety.

First, clearly, is the prophetic voice that the Bible offers in the call for justice to the poor, specifically applied to the control and distribution of food that have been discussed above. Isaiah and other prophets spoke sharply against those who built up great estates at the expense of the small farmers: "Ah, you who join house to house, who add field to field, until there is room for no one but you, and you are left to live alone in the midst of the land! . . . Surely many houses shall be desolate, large and beautiful houses, without inhabitant" (Isa. 5:8–9). The prophets were speaking to a smaller-scale version of the industrial agriculture that characterizes our time.

This theme is familiar to us, though we have often held back from applying it to our own situation. But there is much more to be found. Most biblical people, particularly those who gave us the Hebrew Scriptures, lived close to the land; they learned in their faith that they were not to lord it over the land but to serve it as faithful stewards. Quoting Deuteronomy 11, Richard Cartwright Austin observes: "The most difficult part of farming in Canaan was not the physical labor but obedience to God and moral sensitivity to intricate natural relationships."[1] Austin goes on to point out that the land was not simply a commodity to be exchanged at will, but a responsibility of the whole covenant community. He cites the underhanded way King Ahab took possession of Naboth's vineyard (1 Kgs. 21:1–16) as an illustration of how seriously the Hebrews took their covenant tradition and the agricultural ethics that developed from it. This tradition "evoked a loving relationship with the landscape. Farmers, vinedressers and shepherds touched the land with feeling, remaining sensitive to its character while cultivating it for their needs."[2] Much of this sensitivity can be found in traditional farming communities all over the world, and the preservation or recovery of such awareness is a major challenge to the churches.

Perhaps the noblest expression of the biblical land ethic is expressed in the year of jubilee (Lev. 25), the vision of a renewed liberation of the impoverished and those heavily in debt, once every fifty years, when the land was to lie fallow for a year and when each family would return to live on the land originally allotted to it, even if it had been lost in the meantime. An extension of the Sabbath rest, the year of jubilee spoke of the renewal of both land and people. Probably never fully implemented, this vision still remains as an ethical challenge to those of us who derive our faith from the Bible. Today's push for the cancellation of the international debt of impoverished countries gets part of its inspiration from this tradition.

In the New Testament, we find in Jesus a continuation of these themes. In the prayer he taught his disciples the first two petitions echo the central concerns of this chapter. We are to pray for daily bread. Since the whole prayer uses the first person plural, we are to pray for the daily bread of all. The second petition is for the forgiveness of debts, echoing the jubilee tradition. Among the central signs of following Jesus are feeding the hungry and giving water to the thirsty. In the early churches, all were responsible to meet the needs of those unable to care for themselves. Sharing in the breaking of bread and the drinking of wine was from very early times the heart of Christian community.

Theological Considerations

The insights we derive from the Bible are shared with many people of good will. Indeed, the teachings of most traditions lead to a concern for food security. Few can look forward complacently to a world of declining production, in which only the rich are able to procure the food they need for a healthy diet. It would be all too easy to draw together theological reasons for our concern about food insecurity.

Hence, it may be more important to ask questions about the present situation: Why is the kind of analysis offered above still so rare? Why are public policies still shaped by quite different ways of thinking? Why are we Christians still so deeply involved in systems that will result in increasing food insecurity? Why are we not more concerned?

Part of the answer is sin. Because of greed, we often prefer immediate profits for ourselves to the long-term well-being of all. Because of sloth, we prefer to continue with the habits to which we have grown accustomed, instead of making the needed changes.

Part of the answer is ignorance. Many people simply do not know the facts. Some of this ignorance is itself culpable, since we should inform ourselves about issues of such importance to the human family; much of it is innocent, since many have had little opportunity to learn.

Furthermore, the results of actions taken in the past, reflecting both sin and ignorance, have created institutions and structures that are entrenched in our society. They leave little room for individuals to make significant changes, however badly these are needed. We can think of them as among the "principalities and powers" against which we are called to struggle.

But by no means are all of the obstacles to change found in sin, ignorance, and the structures they have produced. They are found also in honest disagreement with persons who view matters in different ways. These differences are theological or ideological. Those who view matters in terms of different patterns of understanding and reflection come up with different pictures of what is now happening and different judgments of what is needed.

An example of this difference can be found in the work of Amartya Sen, whose impressive research we noted above. An economist whose concern for the well-being of people generally, and especially of the poor, is not in doubt, he views the issue of food sufficiency in terms of projecting the statistical trends of the past. He notes that there has long been anxiety about population growth outstripping food production, and that in fact food production has increased faster than population generation after generation. Accordingly, he encourages us not to worry about the sufficiency of the future food supply.

Why do Christians, looking at matters through Christian lenses, come to different conclusions? We suggest two related reasons. First, the Bible has schooled us to think in historical terms that lead us to consider the particular circumstances under which the growth of food production has occurred and to ask whether these circumstances will continue into the future. Second, belief in the God who created and is creating all things leads us to think of all things as part of a single created world. We do not believe that this world is well understood when people break it into parts and analyze each part separately. Our faith works against the fragmentation of thought—so characteristic of contemporary universities—that leads to abstracting one set of considerations from the wider context.

As a result, we are not satisfied to project past developments into the future on a statistical basis. We ask how the remarkable increases in production thus far have occurred and whether similar methods can work in the future. We inquire about the cost of these increases and whether increased costs of that kind can be borne in the future.

More concretely, when we examine the green revolution that so greatly increased yields of rice, corn, and wheat in the past half century, enabling the world to feed a rapidly growing population, we note its social and ecological costs. We also see that it has made agricultural production dependent on rapidly diminishing resources—oil and soil. We fear that even the present level of production will be threatened in this century by reduced availability of these resources. More generally, we see that single-minded efforts to increase yields do not deal well with the complex long-term problem of food security. For example, supposing that transgenetic engineering will be the miracle solution for world food insecurity may, in the end, increase the insecurity.

We note that those who simply project past increases into the future often pay little attention to the costs of these increases. Viewing matters historically and holistically, we conclude that a profoundly new approach is needed. Developing this approach will require inputs from people with many different kinds of experience and knowledge: natural scientists, social scientists, economists, and historians; traditional farmers and modern agronomists; visionaries, inventors, administrators, politicians, and entrepreneurs. It will require a willingness of all of them to expand their horizons and habits of thinking and to learn from one another. And it will require all of us to be willing to make changes in the way we live, even when they seem costly. As people of faith we will encourage such moves in whatever way we can.

There has been a similar problem with respect to the distribution of income. Economists have focused most of their attention on increasing the wealth of nations. Many suppose that concern for distribution slows economic growth. They prefer to believe that this growth is good for the poor, even when the evidence does not support this. Christians, on the other hand, direct attention primarily to the effects of policies on the poor. Policies directed toward overall growth have failed to benefit the poor; this fact is more apparent, and more important, to Christians.

V. WHAT WE CAN DO

Jesus made very clear that to share the good news involves expressing love by addressing the needs of the hungry. However daunting the task of achieving food security, as Christians we cannot give up. We are "victims of hope." Our faith laughs at impossibility and shouts out, "It shall be done!" Throughout history seemingly hopeless situations have been transformed. In our own time, against seemingly insuperable odds, African Americans ended legal segregation throughout the American South. Contrary to almost universal expectations, South Africa achieved abrupt transformation from apartheid to majority rule, peacefully and with few acts of vengeance.

Today, food shortfalls and poverty impact more than half the world's human family. The spectacle of a hungry world and of the diminishing health of the biosphere itself has become, for a vast number of Christians, a moral outrage. Born within this emotion and ethical evaluation is the concept of sustainability, which integrates the ethical idea of transgenerational as well as interspecies justice. The foremost question for us now is, How can we meet our needs for food, shelter, education, health, and recreation in our time without jeopardizing the ability of future generations to meet their needs in their time? More narrowly to the point of this chapter, How can we provide healthy and nutritious food for our generation while working to guarantee food for the future? These are proper issues for the Christian community of today. If the human family is to avoid global catastrophe, these issues must receive much higher priority than they have received thus far.

One of the basic challenges involved in the idea of global food security for the human family is that of reenergizing our preaching, liturgy, public prayers, and Christian education with the concerns, so eloquently identified in Matthew and Luke, of setting at liberty the oppressed, giving sight to the blind, and feeding the hungry. Educational and worship materials produced by our church agencies need to confront, in imaginative ways, the dominant contemporary preoccupations and lifestyles of affluent Christian people that contribute to the food insecurity of the global poor. Education about food security in our contemporary world and about the prospects for future generations is essential for mobilizing the Christian communities. Certainly this commitment must unfold in the seminaries.

Christians need to advocate international commitment to make real a global food security system. In the United States, many churches are creatively linked to the ecumenical national policy advocacy program known as Bread for the World. Every congregation, be it Roman Catholic, Orthodox or Protestant, should be a part of this impressive lobbying group. As citizens become aware of the need and complexity of achieving global food security, policy formulations and advocacy will be enhanced and made more relevant. Policy development, legislation, and application require an enlightened electorate. To move the nation and the churches beyond relief activities so as to engage in moral and structural change for sustainable domestic self-reliance in food, our so-called "hunger funds" should be allocated as follows: 20 percent for emergency relief, 40 percent for programs for sustainable self-reliance, 20 percent for awareness building and lifestyle change, and 20 percent for public policy advocacy and implementation.

Beyond educational and policy formulations, Christians are challenged to accept responsibility for personal lifestyle changes and to contribute to overcoming the causes of food deficits and to developing comprehensive strategies for the creation of an entirely new and sustainable global food system. We will ask new questions: How might Christian people (and all affluent people) live more simply and walk more tenderly upon the earth? How might people in more affluent regions consume less, share more, and avoid waste and pollution? How might young people become aware of their gifts and of the importance of their vocational decisions? How might church camping experiences for both youth and adults be influenced by theological and biblical studies that address the needs of Earth and its human and nonhuman creatures?

When Christians think there is nothing they can do that will matter, they should remember the parable of the Mustard Seed: "The kingdom of heaven is like a mustard seed that someone took and sowed in his field; it is the smallest of all the seeds, but when it has grown it is the greatest of shrubs and becomes a tree, so that the birds of the air come and make nests in its branches" (Matt. 13:31–32). The first small steps that we take individually will move us personally off a destructive path and can have an impact on the economy and government policy—especially if entire congregations participate. For example, eating less meat and more fruits, grains, and vegetables not only helps the earth but is also more healthful for humans and can be more economical for home budgets.

Americans need to understand the full cost of beef production. Historically, the United States has had a food grain surplus. Feeding food grains to beef and dairy cattle has been a way to dispose of the surplus production of our prairie. Consequently, feedlots were invented. One of the many negative results is the buildup of marbling of muscle tissue, or fat, of the beef that we consume. In most nations, fatty beef is considered a poor grade, not prime. A cow has the wonderful ability to produce milk and meat from grass. A cow does not have to be a competitor with humanity for grain. Yet we have made it so, at great cost both to the environment and to human health.

Christians can teach children about what's behind the food on their plates. We can help them to pay attention to the choices they make about food and the related aspects of their lives. We can make the table blessing before each meal a way to give thanks to God and to educate the family about the world's food needs.

Christians can support local efforts to feed people in their own communities, such as food banks, soup kitchens, and Meals on Wheels. We can share fruit from our backyard trees with local food pantries or pass along our extra zucchini and tomatoes. We can contribute to reputable humanitarian organizations providing food aid and food policy advocacy, such as Oxfam and Bread for the World.

Christians can find out whether the stocks they own are part of the food security solution or part of the problem. When we invest, we can ask, Are we making money off of someone else's hunger? We can support constructive corporate policies with our investments and our votes. If a corporation is part of the solution, we can let the management know we approve. If it is part of the problem, we can communicate with the management to encourage change. If change is not forthcoming after reasonable efforts, we can sell the stock and let the company's board know the reasons.

We can let our state and federal officials know that we think issues related to food security are important and that we expect our representatives to give preference to food security for all people over policies that benefit only one segment of society. The mission of the churches in the world is to reach out and serve the hungry, the poor, and the oppressed. Wherever Christians work—be it in education, law, politics, industry, the arts, or sciences—they can share insights about priority needs in ways that contribute to reshaping the concerns of their workplaces.

Caring about whether or not there will be global food security in this new century is a tangible way for Christians to express gratitude for their moment in the history of the earth. Caring about the future of all members of the human family is what makes us human. Caring about the food crisis and working for food security in the comprehensive way that has been outlined in this chapter is our Christian calling. This caring leads to study of both how to produce enough food in a sustainable way and how to overcome the poverty that is being increased by some of our current policies.

Caring transcends enlightened self-interest. Christians are motivated not by fear but by love and vision. Faith gives us the possibility of attempting and accomplishing the things that often seem impossible. Faith energizes so that we can ask big questions for a lifetime and act on the answers that we find.

Discussion Questions

1. Do you believe the world can produce enough food on a sustainable basis to feed the much larger population expected by the end of this century?
2. If the rich have to share with the poor in order that all can eat, is it possible for this to occur?
3. Are you personally willing to change your eating habits if this is required for food security for all?
4. Are there any actions that you are now prepared to take that might move the world toward food security?

5. Do you agree that it is better to promote more self-sufficient food systems instead of growing crops chiefly for export?

To Learn More

The Worldwatch Institute has published good materials relevant to food security: Lester Brown, *Who Will Feed China?* (Washington, D.C.: Worldwatch Institute, 1995) and "Facing the Prospect of Food Scarcity," in *State of the World 1997* (New York: Norton, 1997); Brian Halweil, "Where Have All the Farmers Gone?" *World Watch* 13 (Sept.–Oct. 2000): 12–28; Gary Gardner and Brian Halweil, *Underfed and Overfed: The Global Epidemic of Malnutrition*, Worldwatch paper no. 150 (Washington, D.C.: Worldwatch Institute, 2000).

W. C. Lowdermilk, *Conquest of the Land through 7,000 Years* (Washington, D.C.: U.S. Government Printing Office, 1975) gives a history of how humanity has farmed, identifying lessons we can learn from past mistakes. Barbara Ward and Rene Dubos, *Only One Earth: The Care and Maintenance of a Small Planet* (New York: W. W. Norton, 1972) deal with our resources and how we can adjust our lifestyles to change that trend.

We suggest four books attempting to change the way we think about agriculture: Wes Jackson, *New Roots for Agriculture* (Lincoln: University of Nebraska Press, 1985); Gordon Conway, *The Doubly Green Revolution: Food for All in the Twenty-first Century* (Ithaca, N.Y.: Comstock Publishing Associates, 1998); Eric T. Freyfogle, ed., *The New Agrarianism: Land, Culture, and the Community* (Covelo, Calif.: Island Press, 2001); and Victor Klimoski and Lance Barker, eds., *Abundant Harvest* (St. Paul: Minnesota Consortium of Theological Schools, 2001).

Several books deal with agriculture and international development. Nobel Prize winner Amartya Sen has written *Poverty and Famine: An Essay on Entitlement and Deprivation* (Oxford: Clarendon, 1981) and *Development as Freedom* (New York: Knopf, 1999). World Commission on Environment and Development, *Our Common Future* (New York: Oxford University Press, 1987) and World Bank, *Investing in Health* (World Development Report, 1993) are reports by international governmental agencies.

16

The Global
Population Crisis

In many parts of Africa, feral children roam in bands, thieving and scrounging for the barest necessities for life. Their parents are dead, victims of AIDS and other scourges. In some cases, the oldest in a band of forty is ten years old. No adult cares for these children, no one teaches them. Their language development is minimal, they are malnourished, many are sick. But they will live to produce children. Even with all the deaths, the population keeps growing. In other parts of the world, the feral child problem is so great that the police shoot them on sight, at night.

I. INTRODUCTION

The rapid growth of world population is one of the major problems humanity faces today. Population growth significantly affects nearly every area of our lives and acts to magnify other problems that cry out for solutions. Christians need to be alert to this critical problem facing our planet and those who will follow us, and then work with others in addressing it in a way that is compatible with God's love and concern for creation.

Today there are more than 16,000 babies being born in the world every hour. In that same hour, of course, some 6,000 men, women, and children die, so the net growth is a little more than 10,000 people every hour. This means that daily there is a net increase of 250,000 people in the global population, 90 million more people every year—with 90 percent of them living in the so-called developing countries.

Population grows like compound interest. For example, if you had $1,000 and simply added 7 percent (or $70) to it each year, after ten years you would have $1,700. However, if you received compound interest at 7 percent, in ten years you would have virtually doubled your investment. The doubling time of the world's population is decreasing at an alarming rate, from hundreds of years to, most recently, fifty-eight years.

The world's swelling population plays a significant role in many global calamities:

- Famine-ravaged people in Africa
- Civil wars in Europe and Asia
- Firewood crises in many Third World countries
- Ten of thousands of street children running wild in South American cities
- Acid rain in wealthy countries where overpopulation and overconsumption join hands to destroy our ecosystems
- Global warming

Cutting down population growth will not automatically solve all problems humanity faces, but if population continues to grow as it is doing, an increasing number of potential calamities will be impossible to avoid.

The way in which nations make a transition in bringing their population down to a sustainable level differs with each country. Many interrelated factors, besides available contraceptive methods, determine the speed and the depth of that change, such as the political will, the national educational level (especially for girls and women), the cultural patterns, the natural resources available, and the economic opportunities (especially for females and the very poor).

In contrast to the demographic transition that took place in Europe and North America in the last two centuries, it now appears that nations will not be able to experience sustained economic development until they reduce their fertility rates. Not only must they achieve a total fertility rate approaching 2.0 or lower; they also need to open their government to the citizens, make government institutions available to women, cut down on corruption, adopt a fair market economy, and address the too frequent inequities between the minuscule group of the very rich and the massive group of the very poor.[1]

II. THE GLOBAL SITUATION AND PROSPECTS

Growth Patterns

One thousand years ago, because of high mortality rates around the world, humans had a high fertility rate to balance the births and deaths. Just one hundred years ago, it was common for families in our own country, especially those who lived on farms, to have ten or more children. But the last hundred years have seen many changes: the mortality rate has been rapidly reduced by modern medical techniques; now farmers have more tools to do their work; many families have moved to the cities, where large families have proved to be very expensive; a higher standard of living has also brought fewer births and vice versa.

In 1900 this country had a population of 76 million. During the twentieth century the birth and death rates were close to balancing—but not before the population reached 275 million by mid-2000, which is more than double the 1940 population. Dr. Joel Cohen of Rockefeller University estimates that if this country continues to have one million immigrants each year, the United States will grow from today's 275 million to roughly 760 million before the population stabilizes. If, however, immigration rates are reduced to 400,000 per year, the population will probably stabilize at roughly 304 million.[2]

There are thirty countries that have brought their growth rate to zero. These are all European countries, except for Japan.

However, many countries, especially among so-called developing nations, got a late start at balancing births and deaths. Although many of them are now making valiant efforts to rectify this, the past rapid rate of growth saddles them with a population that often exceeds what the country can sustain. For example, Kenya is currently doubling its population every eighteen years. If Kenya continues to grow at over 4 percent per year in the next fifty years, its population will grow from 30 million to 240 million.

Thailand has greatly reduced its current rate of growth through thirty years of excellent family planning programs. Even so its population grew from 14 million in 1947 to 61 million in 2000. Currently it takes fifty years for the population in Thailand to double, compared to fifty-eight years needed for the world population to double.

Prospects

In 1950 the world had a population of 2.6 billion. This grew to 5.2 billion in 1989, doubling in just thirty-nine years. By mid-2003 the world population will be over 6.3 billion. At the present rate of growth it is expected to reach 9.3 billion by 2050. Thanks to valiant efforts by the UN, the People's Republic of China, and many groups deeply concerned about this problem, the growth of human population has been slowed to 1.2 percent a year. Even so, before the world's population levels off and quits expanding, it could grow to anywhere between 9 and 12 billion by 2050 depending on several factors:

The availability of contraceptives. How well contraceptive services are made available to the 300–400 million women who do not now have access to effective contraceptive methods and services will play a large role.

The impact of religion. Currently religion often hinders response to the problem. For example, Catholics continue to maintain a pronatalist stance, which in theory, at least, refuses contraceptives and abortions to their followers. Although church teaching has little effect on population growth in Europe and the United States, it often inhibits the development of sound policies in many other nations. The future of the one-billion-member Muslim world is difficult to determine as well. Muslims now average about six children per completed family, more than any other religious group. This may not be related directly to their religion as much as to their poverty and the inferior status of women in their societies.[3]

The education of girls. Educated women marry later and have fewer children. In Pakistan, the World Food Program gives each girl who attends school classes at least twenty days a month an eleven-pound can of cooking oil for her family. This same incentive is offered to teachers. The program is working, since cooking oil is the most expensive item in a Pakistani diet.

The status of women. In some cultures, women say, "I am nothing in my culture unless I bear children—in fact, unless I bear sons. I was nobody until I married, so I married young and the babies started coming." All over the world, when women live constrained lives with little education and few personal options, when their culture conveys prestige on them only through marriage and childbearing, especially of sons, and when all things female are devalued, fertility is high. The state of a woman's reproductive health depends on how she answers these questions: Can a woman control when and with whom she will engage in sexual relations? Can she do so without fear of infection or unwanted fertility? Can she choose when and how to regulate her fertility, free from unpleasant or dangerous side effects? Can she go through pregnancy and childbirth safely? Can she obtain a safe abortion on request? Can she easily obtain information on prevention and treatment of reproductive illnesses?[4]

III. RESULTS OF POPULATION GROWTH

Social Problems

Population growth, even when it is not the major cause, tends to exacerbate many social problems.

- Millions of babies are born into this world each year under conditions in which they suffer from the many forces that create disaster, such as war and civil strife, misguided national policies, trade barriers, environmental degradation, poverty, and gender inequality. The quality of life for such children is usually low, but their death rate is high. It is estimated that each year seven million children under five years of age die in this world.

- Social services are swamped when populations escalate, creating such problems as overcrowded schools—or even preventing schooling entirely. There are reportedly some 130 million children worldwide with no access to primary school—90 million of them being girls. This latter fact does not bode well for population stabilization in the near future.
- Mass migrations often occur in regions of the world that have excessive population growth. Several years ago this was seen in Ethiopia, a country where contraceptive usage is illegal. More recently, in Rwanda and Burundi, the most densely populated region of Africa, the population has doubled since 1970, fueling competition for land, with the deadly result that 800,000–1,000,000 people were murdered in just three months in 1994.[5]
- Health problems tend to escalate at a faster rate in expanding populations. For example, in 1980 we would not even have heard the terms "HIV-positive" or "a full-blown case of AIDS," since it was not until the next year that the virus and disease became known. And yet, according to the Joint U.N. Program on HIV/AIDS, as of the end of 2002 there were 42 million people infected with the HIV virus. During 2002 AIDS caused the death of over 3 million people. Population pressure increases the incidence of disease and reduces the ability of communities to deal with outbreaks of serious epidemics.
- The adverse psychological factors of living in crowded conditions must be recognized. In the more than 1,000 slums in the city of Bangkok, Thailand, the effects on both adults and children of the combination of crowding and poverty are vividly apparent.

Ecological Problems

The combination of overpopulation and overconsumption is making a substantial contribution to the destruction of the world's life-support systems. What we are doing is like shooting holes in our lifeboat. Earth's natural resources are finite, but we tend to treat them as if they were infinite. Some think the present population of our planet already exceeds its carrying capacity; others think we are getting close to that number.

- While the world population was doubling from 1950 to 1995, the *demand for natural resources* was growing even more. The need for grain tripled, the consumption of seafood quadrupled, water usage tripled, firewood demand tripled, the use of lumber more than doubled, and the burning of fossil fuels increased nearly fourfold.[6]
- *Severe climate changes*, often a direct result of human activities, are taking place. Although the rate of increase has slowed somewhat in the 1990s,

the carbon dioxide emission level in the world is still over 2 percent a year, which is bound to have adverse results for future generations.[7] The negative results of the greenhouse effect are gradually increasing. At the same time, even though the production of ozone-depleting substances is decreasing in the developed world, the important ozone layer is still being depleted.

- *Water* is absolutely essential to life, but the underground aquifers of this planet are being used beyond their natural rate of replenishment. "Unless wealthier countries reduce consumption levels and all countries move more quickly to create the conditions needed for population stabilization, water scarcity will lead to great human and political insecurity. By 2025 . . . as many as 3 billion people could be living in countries experiencing water stress or chronic water scarcity."[8] Already, native populations in many areas are denied water for part of each day so that tourist hotels can have water.

- *Land used for growing food is shrinking* at the same time that more food is needed for the extra 90 million people being added annually to our planet. There are many ways in which agricultural land is lost: building of roads, erosion, reduced supplies of water for irrigation, the decreasing time for leaving land fallow (especially in developing countries), and the expansion of cities. For example, the city of Bangkok, Thailand, was projected to expand by 51,000 hectares (more than 125,000 acres) between 1984 and 2000, an increase of 40 percent. If 80 percent of this expansion engulfs agricultural land (a reasonable estimate), the reduction in rice production will be equal to the requirements of more than 300,000 people each year.[9]

- *Cutting down trees* for fuel and building purposes results from overpopulation in some countries, such as Haiti. The resulting serious erosion reduces the carrying capacity of the land even more.

- *War* and its destruction can also erode agricultural land.

IV. POPULATION STABILIZATION

Factors Involved

There are several positive factors that can help control rapid population growth. Among these are late marriage, new mothers nursing their infants for a longer period of time, rising educational standards (especially for girls and women), better mother and child health programs, broad-based economic development, and effective contraceptive programs that emphasize the involvement of men as well as women. The ideal, of course, is to have all of these working together.

There are also negative factors that can cut down population growth, such as epidemics (e.g., HIV/AIDS) with large numbers of fatalities, warfare in and between countries, malnutrition, and severe famine. These factors, in and of themselves, have not been known actually to stabilize populations. In modern times, however, if global population growth continues at a fairly high rate for a long period of time, some of these negative factors may significantly curtail population growth.

Contraceptive Programs

Culturally acceptable and fully understandable contraceptive programs that are specifically geared to the group to be served have been an important factor in bringing down the human growth rate in many areas. Such programs are not the only solution to this problem, but without them there is virtually no way to reach zero population growth without counting heavily on abortions, as was done in Japan and Europe. When severe population pressure is relieved by means of contraceptive programs, families and nations have more viable options for achieving their development goals.

Contraceptive programs that are developed out of a true concern for the total welfare of families and nations should be integrated with other health programs, giving special emphasis to providing the best possible health care to mothers, infants, and children. The contraceptive service will then be more logistically attractive, since basic health services are becoming more prevalent in most countries.

The availability of all services must be made known and clearly understood. It must be established that each couple is making an informed, thoughtful choice. Follow-up checks should also be made to be sure there are no problems.

The most important aspect of any successful contraceptive program is not the technology used—although the best possible technology should be made available—but the loving, concerned people who provide the service.

The Chinese Program

The People's Republic of China has been forced to adopt a drastic family-planning program out of sheer necessity. After suffering a severe famine with countless deaths in 1970, the Chinese, with 22 percent of the global population but only 7 percent of the world's arable land, came to realize that they had to take immediate steps to curb the population explosion. The program they developed, which included late marriages, a stress on education (especially for women), and available contraceptive services for men and women, is credited with preventing some 240 million extra mouths to be fed between 1970 and 1990—and no doubt many millions more since then.

The Chinese faced a major problem in instituting their one-child-per-family policy. If an urban couple only had a girl, she could not carry on the family name, thus challenging their deep-seated cultural desire to maintain continuity for the patrilineal family. In rural areas, where land is handed down to a son, it became a double burden to have a girl, although in most cases those couples were allowed to have one more child in hopes that they could have a son. Even though it was unlawful to do so, there are reports of girl babies either being aborted or left to die, in hopes that the couple could then have a son.

Even though their program works hardship on many individuals, we must recognize that the nation is seeking to balance the reproductive rights of the current generation with the survival rights of the generations to come. It is now estimated that, in spite of these strenuous efforts, the population, which was 400 million in 1970, will probably increase to 1.6 billion by the year 2050—a fourfold increase in just eighty years.

The People's Republic of China is learning, as all other nations should learn as well, that the spigot of population growth cannot be turned off in a short period of time. If the Chinese had implemented a balanced family-planning program in the middle of the twentieth century, they may not have come to the place where they would have to enforce such harsh policies just to survive as a nation.

Other Examples

Norway and Thailand are countries that devised population policies before their numbers caused severe conditions and were thus able to significantly reduce their total fertility rates (the number of children a woman has in her lifetime). Brazil has also launched a concerted mass media effort on behalf of family planning and has upheld the small family as the norm. At the same time, such countries as Italy, Spain, Portugal, and Greece have achieved population stabilization without specific national population policies.

The United States

The United States does not actually have a population policy, even though at the Cairo Conference on Population and Development in 1994 we agreed to establish such a national policy. For such a policy to be accepted in our country, there needs to be a national will. In order for that will to develop, there must be a recognition of the urgency of the problem and a determination of all sectors of the society to work in harmony to solve that problem. A national policy would deal with several areas:

- Men must play a much greater role in choosing contraceptives and making sure they are properly used. Experiments in producing male contraceptives have not been promising so far, and more needs to be done. China is successfully using "plugs" and a new type of vasectomy that has minimal intrusion. These need to be studied.
- Often global pharmaceutical companies aid in creating overpopulation by promoting drugs that prolong life, while avoiding the development of effective, low-priced contraceptives.[10] While life-prolonging drugs are glamorous and profitable, contraceptives are not. Also, the threat of enormous litigation liabilities along with the climate created by extreme antiabortionist and "pro-life" groups make companies think twice before getting involved in any way with contraceptives.
- Since the 1970s, treatments using fertility-enhancing drugs and techniques have caused their own population explosion. As of April 1996 there were thirty-nine sets of quintuplets in this country, with another set born about every eight weeks. Of the women who receive fertility treatments and then get pregnant, 25 percent have multiple births. Thus the number of quadruplets, triplets, and twins has escalated sharply since the 1970s, with one case of surviving septuplets.[11]
- Since the birthrate among the native born is close to replacement levels, the growth in population in the United States is now primarily a result of immigration. The increase is compounded by the higher birthrates among immigrants, although there is a tendency for this to decline in the second and third generations. But there is also a strong tendency to adopt an American consumer lifestyle. Since the United States as a nation is the creation of immigrants, since we celebrate the diversity of cultures brought by them, and since we recognize a responsibility to offer sanctuary to refugees, the issue of immigration cannot be discussed only in the context of population growth. (See chapter 9, "The Immigration Dilemma")
- The United States must aid the UN, national governments, and various nongovernmental organizations (NGOs) in their attempt to bring about population stabilization worldwide. Cutting down on the amount of aid given for family-planning programs around the world clearly increases the number of abortions and maternal deaths, as well as population. Further, we should not tie strings to financial aid for family planning, except to specify that the programs truly serve the people and are fully accepted by them.
- Last year there were some 1.2 million abortions performed in the United States. This number is down slightly from the previous two years. Abortion is not a desirable form of population regulation. But the ability to choose abortion as an option must remain a decision between a woman and her doctor, and abortions must continue to be legal, safe, and inexpensive—and we hope rare—in the United States.
- We must work to cut down on teen pregnancies. Sex education programs given at an early age and continued through high school must be a commitment of all educational leaders. A high percentage of teen pregnancies occurs among girls living in poverty who have been

abused and have low self-esteem. Men, who are sometimes much older
than these girls and take no responsibility or blame for their actions,
often prey upon these vulnerable girls. Our nation must seek the best
solutions to rectify these problems as quickly and thoroughly as
possible.

Developing Nations

Since 90 percent of the world's population growth is in developing nations,
often among people living in preliterate and tradition-bound cultures, special
consideration needs to be given in creating effective and compassionate programs which are tailor-made for each local group. Protestant missions in
developing countries have developed some very successful population-stabilization programs.[12]

   We have learned certain things from these programs that can be replicated
by other groups seeking to develop meaningful family-planning programs
among preliterate people:

- There must be cultural sensitivity. This includes using the language of
  the group to be reached and providing all services in ways which are culturally understandable and acceptable.
- The program must be devised and operated by the local group. Involvement of local leaders increases the potential effectiveness of the program and keeps the focus of the program on the total welfare of the
  receptors.
- The needs of the receptor group must be given primary consideration.
  One program among seventy thousand Lahu, Akha, and Lisu tribal people in north Thailand found that family-planning and primary health-
  care services had to be taken to the villages where the people lived. When
  special services, such as tubal ligations, could not be taken to them, special arrangements had to be made for providing them in hospitals and
  clinics in nearby towns.[13]
- The alternative forms of contraception, with all of the pros and cons,
  must be carefully presented to the people, and then each couple should
  be allowed to choose the best method for their own needs or to reject
  them all. Truly informed consent is imperative for a successful
  program.
- When possible, family-planning programs should be integrated with
  health services and community-development programs, provided, of
  course, there is a felt need on the part of the recipients.
- Highly motivated paramedics from the population to be served can be
  trained and sent to even the most remote villages. There are not enough
  trained doctors to provide contraceptive aid to all the millions who want
  it so desperately. Using paramedics saves costs and gets the services to the
  people in the shortest time possible.

V. OVERCONSUMPTION IN AFFLUENT COUNTRIES

The focus of this chapter is population. However, one of the main reasons for concern about population is that the larger the population, the greater the pressure upon the resources of the planet available to support human life. The total pressure is a multiple of population *and* per capita consumption of scarce resources. Hence, to deal with population without recognizing that it is only one part of the problem is distorting. Although population growth in poor countries does exert heavy pressure on the local environment, often the environment of those countries suffers more from exploitation by transnational corporations for the sake of supplying goods to the affluent.

To put the issue vividly, consider a Bangladeshi farmer and a Stanford University professor. While the farmer may subsist through hell and high water on the produce from his own plot, the professor can keep eating only if railroads and trucks keep running and electricity and natural gas continue to be distributed.[14] Americans since 1950 have consumed resources equivalent to the resources consumed by all of humanity up to 1950. The richest countries, with 20 percent of the world's population, account for 80 percent of all private consumption; the poorest 20 percent of the population account for only 1.3 percent.

Given this vast difference in levels of consumption, small increases in population in affluent countries constitute as great a problem for the planet as do much larger population increases in poor countries. Technologies developed to meet the appetites of the affluent often intensify the damage done by their consumption. The per capita resource consumption and production of waste in the United States is the highest in the world.

Many affluent countries have ceased to grow in population, but not the United States. Accordingly, population issues are important here, but more important are issues of consumption. Reducing consumption of scarce resources in the affluent world is as important for the future of the planet as slowing population growth worldwide.

VI. A CHRISTIAN PERSPECTIVE

The Jewish Scriptures were written at a time when the human population was relatively small. God's command in Genesis 1:28 to "be fruitful and multiply" was experienced as fully appropriate. Having large families was a great blessing. God's promise to Abraham was that his descendants would be innumerable (Gen. 22:17 and 32:12). Christians who favor pronatal policies can refer to many passages that celebrate a large progeny.

However, there are two reasons for Christians to hesitate to draw conclusions about current practice from these texts. First, other creatures were also given the command to be fruitful and multiply. Today the growth of human population is leading to the disappearance of many other species, and habitat for many others is shrinking rapidly. Practices appropriate to a thinly populated planet are not suitable in a crowded one.

Second, in other respects we do not make the customs and the values of the patriarchs normative. In the interest of having large families, they practiced polygamy. They viewed wives and children as possessions, along with flocks and herds. Israel outgrew these practices and attitudes and moved to monogamy, which is taken for granted in the New Testament as the norm. In the teachings of Jesus and Paul there is no special celebration of large families. So far as we know, neither of them married. Paul seems to have thought the celibate state preferable. Many early Christians expected the end soon; accordingly there was little emphasis on family life.

We cannot take either the patriarchal or the apocalyptic pattern as normative for us today. Hence we look to deeper levels of biblical teaching as our guide. Our perspective on the population crisis will be grounded in an unwavering faith in God's love and care for the world and all its people. This love has a concern for the welfare of humanity through space and time. We Christians, having been transformed by that love, must recognize the perilous condition overpopulation and overconsumption have created for all people; under God's guidance we must seek creative and compassionate ways of alleviating the situation without delay.

Moving from faith in God's love for the world and all its peoples to a specific vision of how to meet the world's population crisis involves several factors:

- In our culture we tend to focus on individual rights and consider them to take precedence over the rights of the whole society. We often view society as providing a neutral framework within which each person can explore his or her freedom at will. However, Christ teaches us to pray, "*Our* Father . . . give *us* this day *our* daily bread . . . forgive *our* debts as *we* forgive." The Bible and the best of Christian tradition teach us that we are called together in Christ, not only to develop our own individual abilities, but to strive for a deeper mutuality that will further the fuller life of all members of the community. We must be willing to give up certain individual rights if by so doing we will serve the needs of the group.
- Christ said that the greatest commandment is to love God with all one's heart, soul, strength, and *mind*. Our minds tell us that there is no quick fix for the population crisis, because the network of problems is complex and long-term. Our minds also tell us that any time lost in bringing about a balanced population and stopping ecological degradation is time that

can never be regained. As Christians we have the responsibility to analyze the situation carefully and then apply the very best solutions we can think through.

- Christ also said that we are to love our neighbor as we love ourselves. Certainly overconsumption and poor stewardship of the world's natural resources are not valid responses to that command. Love demands that we accept certain limits, for the welfare both of today's neighbor and of the neighbor who will be living on this earth a hundred years from now.

VII. WHAT WE CAN DO

We are daily faced with choices related to population. There is bound to be a serious conflict between the needs of *today's* people and the needs of *tomorrow's*. We as Christians must keep both groups in mind.

By using the best methods possible, we must help to lower the human birthrate to the level of the human death rate (or slightly below) as soon as possible. If decisions are delayed and the problems become worse, options for effective action are severely reduced. The worst aspects of the present population explosion will be seen only in fifty or a hundred years.

There is a significant time lag between beginning effective family-planning programs and reaching zero population growth—about seventy years. Too often, significant social changes are made only in the midst of a terrible crisis and only after many innocent people have had to suffer. If we truly love God with all of our minds as well as our hearts, we will seek meaningful solutions before this crisis gets any worse.

Christian leaders must keep the urgency of population stabilization before their own people, as well as pressing our nation and the nations of the world to encourage one- and two-child families. Each country must choose the method that meshes with its culture. Outsiders can sometimes furnish needed technology, but true population stabilization must grow out of the will of the people of that country.

As individuals we can support organizations that are working around the world to improve the status of women. This includes offering contraceptive services to women who want them. We can encourage our government to be much more generous in its support of the efforts of the United Nations in this field. We can encourage subsidies to research designed to help women limit their families and discourage subsidies for fertility-enhancing research. We can support legislation that would limit litigation in cases of frivolous lawsuits related to the use of contraceptive devices or medications that have been approved by the FDA. We can also work to keep abortions safe and legal. (See chapter 3, "Reflections on Abortion.")

At the same time that we support programs to limit population growth in humane ways all around the world, we can also attend especially to the problems for which we are most immediately responsible. For most of us affluent Americans, these are more matters of consumption than of having too many children. Population growth in the United States is a serious problem more because of per capita consumption than because of absolute numbers. Hence, while we continue to work for population stabilization in this country, our primary response to the problem should be to reduce consumption.

Reducing Waste

There is no clear standard for overconsumption. Nevertheless, it is possible to identify ways to reduce it. All of our households, institutions, businesses, and industries generate waste. Thoughtful attention to this can reduce waste, as can recycling, buying recycled products, and producing less waste to begin with.

Efficient use of resources can make a huge difference. Far less electricity than we have been using in the past can accomplish all of its purposes in lighting, heating, and operating machines. Using the new technology as it becomes available encourages business to produce more and better equipment. Constructing buildings that need less heating and cooling helps. Whole cities can be built that require far less energy in order to operate. Eating lower on the food chain can ease pressure on the environment and is healthier.

Frugality and Generosity

We can go beyond avoiding waste and act in many ways to consume less. We can dress for the cold in the winter and use less heat, and we can dress for the heat in the summer and use less air conditioning. We can live in smaller houses and have fewer second homes. We can landscape in ways that require less water, fertilizer, and insecticide. We can get along with fewer clothes. We can share equipment with neighbors. Some can experiment with communal living. We can sometimes repair goods instead of buying new ones.

One function of frugality is directly to reduce pressure on the environment. A second function is to direct our money to meeting the needs of the less fortunate and to other worthy causes, either by giving money directly or by reducing the time spent in earning it and then giving the time saved.

Energy Sources

Knowing that our present sources of energy are being rapidly exhausted and that in the meantime their use is harmful to the environment, we can devote ourselves individually and collectively to shifting from fossil fuels to solar power, especially direct solar power. This includes generating energy through harnessing wind power and tides. In this way we can reduce our consumption of exhaustible resources and leave more for others.

Meanwhile the most practical means of meeting additional energy needs today is through greater efficiency in production and use. National and state laws and policies should encourage this, rather than the construction of new facilities. Timothy E. Wirth, undersecretary of state under President Clinton, believes that the United States could save $400 billion a year—enough to wipe out the federal deficit—if its energy use were as efficient as Japan's and Germany's.[15] (See chapter 14, "The Church and Environmentalism.")

Taxation

Taxes are needed to raise money for public use. They can also be used to direct society away from damage to the environment. By taxing natural-resource extraction and importation rather than labor, a nation can encourage reduced use of resources and increased employment of workers. At present the United States subsidizes the cutting of its forests and the extraction of minerals from beneath the surface. This encourages resource exhaustion and damages the future. If these costs were dramatically increased, prices would rise, but efforts would be directed to more efficient use of lumber, minerals, and oil. Since taxes on labor would decline, people would be able to pay higher prices where new technology was not able to obviate them. People cannot make informed purchase decisions unless all goods reflect the true cost of their entire lifecycle—such items as the use and ultimate disposal of natural resources, the manufacturing cost, and the transportation cost—both subsidized and nonsubsidized.

The Economy

If we are to adopt policies that reduce overconsumption, we must dethrone economic growth as our primary commitment. This growth entails growth in consumption—especially by the affluent—just what we do *not* need. Yet all of our economic policies are geared to increasing it.

We must rethink our commitment to a unified global market, which is advocated simply for the sake of growth. It speeds up the exhausting of resources globally, while on the whole the poor do not benefit. This global market renders more difficult the task of establishing socially and environmentally desirable goals within the nations affected by it, including our own.

Discussion Questions

1. Does population growth affect you personally? If so, how? Do you feel that the problem is as serious as depicted in this chapter?
2. In your community, what is the greater problem, population growth or overconsumption? Are there groups or organizations who are working to solve either of these problems?
3. Is the biblical argument above sufficient to provide a solid basis for Christian action? Are there other Bible passages that would support or contradict the position presented in this chapter?
4. Some Christians, reading the same Bible, have criticized the United States, where abortion is permitted, for having a "culture of death." Is the view on population growth presented in this chapter susceptible to their criticism? Can the two positions be harmonized? How would you discuss these issues with someone who held these beliefs?
5. How does a woman's position in society affect her childbearing habits, both positively and negatively? How could we impact population growth through policies dealing with women and women's rights? Is there anything in your own community that you can do to further women's issues that would lower the birthrate (for example: sex education, scholarships and mentoring programs for underprivileged high-school girls who would be facing these decisions, abortion counseling)?
6. Some people in the Third World feel offended that we, in the First World, would fund programs to discourage them from having children. They see it as another form of imperialism. How could that be a valid feeling? Do you feel that this chapter could be seen that way? How can our lifestyle change that idea (or cause even more bitterness)?
7. Reflect on your own consumption compared to someone in a Third World country. At the community and personal level, how can you reduce the stress placed on our environment that would be equivalent to reducing population growth in a Third World community?
8. Can we reduce consumption of scarce resources sufficiently by reducing waste and increasing efficiency, or do we also need to tighten our belts?

To Learn More

Among the best treatments of the topic from the Christian perspective is Susan Power Bratton, *Six Billion and More: Human Population Regulation and Christian Ethics* (Louisville, Ky.: Westminster/John Knox Press, 1992). There is a video, "Population and People of Faith: It's About Time," produced by the Institute for Development Training, 475 Riverside Dr., 18th Floor, New York, NY 10015.

A recent study published by the United Nations Population Fund, *Footprints and Milestones: Population and Environmental Change: The State of the World Population 2001* (New York: United Nations), discusses population as well as consumption issues. Paul R. Ehrlich wrote a popular, alarmist book that awakened millions of Americans to the population crisis: *The Population Bomb* (New York: Ballantine Books, 1968). He and his wife, Anne H. Ehrlich, updated their concerns in *The Population Explosion* (New York: Simon & Schuster, 1990). A harsh and controversial analysis of what drives population growth is found in Virginia Abernethy, *Population Politics: The Choices that Shape Our Future* (New York: Plenum Press, 1993). The "Report of the Independent Commission on Population and Quality of Life," a truly global approach based on hearings in many countries, is found in *Caring for the Future: Making the Next Decades Provide a Life Worth Living* (Oxford: Oxford University Press, 1996). Recent books providing sober informational proposals for slowing population growth include Lindsey Grant, *Too Many People: The Case for Reducing Growth* (Santa Ana, Calif.: Seven Locks Press, 2001); Nancy Birdsall, Steven Sinding, Allen C. Kelley, eds., *Population Matters: Demographic Change, Economic Growth and Poverty in the Developing World* (Oxford: Oxford University Press, 2001); William Hollingsworth, *Ending the Explosion: Population Policies and Ethics for a Humane Future* (Santa Ana, Calif.: Seven Locks Press, 1996).

Web Resources:

www.npg.org/reading.htm —Negative Population Growth
www.zpg.org —Zero Population Growth

These two organizations working on the population issue both have good resources and have chapters around the country to promote their concerns.

(www.un.org/esa/population/) is the UN link for information on world population.

Population Coalition (www.popco.org), networking for a sustainable future.

Appendix: A Short Political History of the American Christian Right

I. INTRODUCTION

Well into a new century it may give us some perspective to chronicle and reflect on the recent history of the American Christian right in general and the prominent organization, the Christian Coalition, in particular. Among the questions worth raising are these: What have been the political strengths and weaknesses of the Christian right? What have been the sources of its appeal? What should our attitude toward the Christian right be? Many important theological issues related to these questions could be, but will not be, examined in this short and perhaps sketchy history. We can say that in an ambiguous or even paradoxical way the Christian right has seen itself as an oppressed minority at the same time that its influence on national politics has been disproportionate to its numbers. Though no single personality type or theological view can be said to characterize believers of the American Christian right, they have been united by opposition to rather particular designated enemies: abortion doctors, gay and lesbian persons, feminists, liberal schoolteachers, and artists and entertainers regarded as indecent. There does seem to be a heavy emphasis on biblical literalism and also the apocalyptic symbols of "the last days" that American life is said to be approaching.

It is of interest that various polls have shown about two-thirds of Americans consider themselves Christian, but less than one-third of these say they attend church regularly. A number of Christians who accept the label "born again" has fluctuated from one-fifth to one-third of respondents, including at least one president.

II. FUNDAMENTALISM

Many evangelicals are not fundamentalist, and some evangelicals are not politically conservative. In recent usage, evangelical has come to mean those who stress a personal relationship to Jesus, who feel salvation lies in being "born again," perhaps at a specific moment, who accept biblical authority in matters of faith and practice, and who feel the necessity of "witnessing," sharing the faith with others. Billy Graham is an example of a conservative Christian who is evangelical, but does not care to be called a fundamentalist. Jim Wallis of *Sojourners*, the periodical and the organization, is an evangelical who is politically "liberal" or "progressive," as are the publishers of such magazines as *The Other Side* and *Green Cross*. The Sojourners' Call to Renewal in the church casts a fairly wide net. On the conservative side, although Jerry Falwell and Pat Robertson have shared a similar political agenda, they have different worship styles. Falwell is more the Bible-based fundamentalist. Robertson is more the Pentecostal and charismatic, that is, relying on the Holy Spirit and ecstatic worship. Many casual observers do not realize that evangelicals and Pentecostals, but not dedicated fundamentalists, tended to vote for Robertson when he ran for president in 1988. (These terms of course have different meanings in different historical and theoretical contexts.) Some extreme racist groups like the Aryan Nation are often considered on the "far right" and may employ Christian symbols, but they will not be included in this historical sketch.

The term "fundamentalism" was coined in 1920 and referred back to the Niagara Bible Conference of 1895 and the publication between 1912 and 1915 of a series of twelve pamphlets called *The Fundamentals: A Testimony to the Truth*. The Niagara Conference declared that the five essentials of Christian belief were (1) the inerrancy of the Bible, (2) the deity and virgin birth of Jesus, (3) substitutionary atonement (the sacrifice of Jesus as propitiation for human sin), (4) the bodily resurrection of Jesus, and (5) "dispensationalist premillennialism"—the coming battle of armageddon to defeat the antichrist, followed by the second coming of Jesus. The group also denounced the theory of evolution, higher criticism (that is, the analysis of the historical and literary context of the books of the Bible that arose out of modern secular historiography), Catholicism, Mormonism, and much more.

What may be especially noteworthy is how recent this usage is. Harry Emerson Fosdick preached a sermon in New York City in 1922 entitled "Shall the Fundamentalists Win?" which question he answered with a resounding "No!" The World's Christian Fundamentals Association (founded in Philadelphia in 1919) led the attack on a Dayton, Tennessee, high school biology teacher, John T. Scopes, who dared to teach a scientific approach to evolution. A Tennessee law, passed early in 1925 after WCFA lobbying, had forbidden such teaching. This resulted in the famous "monkey trial" pitting defense lawyer Clarence Darrow against three-time presidential nominee William Jennings Bryan. Scopes lost and was fined a hundred dollars; but Darrow won nationwide support in calling this "the first case of its kind since we stopped trying people for witchcraft." Popular ridicule of the trial seemed to confirm Fosdick's prophecy.

But fundamentalism survives and revives. Among the Niagara tenets fundamentalists still cling to, perhaps the most difficult to maintain is the assumption of the inerrancy—and by implication univocity—of the Bible. This also means a literal rather than symbolic understanding of such things as the creation of the universe in seven days, as told in Genesis. Fundamentalists generally hold—despite contrary evidence that seems obvious to most of us who try to read the Bible carefully—that there are no discrepancies among the four Gospels; that the parables of Jesus have simple and singular meanings; that the book of Revelation can be applied straightforwardly to explain the causes of current or future events. Against the best biblical scholarship they hold that Moses wrote all of the Pentateuch, that David wrote all of the psalms, that Paul wrote all of the letters originally attributed to him. But, as we shall see, the most prominent leaders of the Christian right do not necessarily engage in detailed defense of fundamentalist, or even conservative, positions on biblical exegesis. They seem to be more interested in politics than they are in biblical criticism or theology.

Many followers of the Christian right view politics with mixed feelings and may also be little interested in theology. Nevertheless, the Christian right tends to monopolize the word "Christian" so that one may hear in their conversation, "She used to be a Catholic, but now she's a Christian." The fundamentals of fundamentalism may not be examined very closely by those who claim the name. It is a mistake to think that the Christian right appeals mainly to rural and traditional societies and to uneducated people. Sociologists and political scientists have found surprising strength of the Christian right in suburban, middle-class areas, where many have attended college and income levels are moderately high. The Christian right does not, in fact, appeal to the very poor.

Peter Beinert has studied Olathe, Kansas, until 1960 a small, rural village, but now, thanks to freeways and urban sprawl, a Kansas City suburb of 80,000. He finds the Christian right support there is a phenomenon of parental anxiety about schools, which seem disturbingly different from the schools of the parents' childhood memories. They remember schools that taught "facts," not values, because parents, teachers, and everybody else shared the same values. Now they fear schools are "not teaching with them but against them." They are fearful of sex education and the redefinition of "family." New—or different—races and religions have appeared as part of the wider public scene. The public schools reflect the pluralism and multiculturalism of the larger society, which brings the alarming notion that "truth is relative." They simply want their kids to know right from wrong, in a very basic sense. These are the fears and hopes to which the Christian right appeals.[1] It must also be noted that the Christian Coalition has been, especially in the early 1990s, quite shrewd in responding to, and providing local leadership for, immediate, practical political concerns such as the need for a new stop sign, lack of a crossing guard at a school, and an unresponsive school board. In such cases the expression of religious concerns comes later rather than sooner.

III. CHRISTIAN RIGHT GROUPS
PRIOR TO THE CHRISTIAN COALITION

Glenn Utter and John Storey, editors of *The Religious Right: A Reference Handbook*, give information on sixty-six organizations on the religious—largely Christian—right.[2] A complete listing of groups on the right would be too encyclopedic for inclusion here. But a few deserve brief comment. In chronological order of founding:

The American Council of Christian Churches (ACCC) (1941, Valley Forge, Pennsylvania). The ACCC was set up by Carl McIntire (1906–2002) initially as a protest against the "too liberal" Federal (after 1950, National) Council of Churches. McIntire, most seem to agree, was autocratic, doctrinaire, self-righteous, and intolerant. He was suspended from the ministry by a predecessor of the Presbyterian Church (U.S.A.) in 1935, whereupon he set up his own denomination, the Bible Presbyterian Church. His radio broadcasts began in 1955, and in 1956 he was expelled by the ACCC, his own organization. (The National Association of Evangelicals was organized in 1942 to offer a more moderate alternative to McIntire.) After time out for some political team play with Sen. Joseph McCarthy, in which he displayed his conspiratorial tendencies and virulent anticommunism, McIntire came back to the ACCC's executive council, only to be dropped again in 1969. In 1971 most of the faculty and half the students at his Faith Theological Seminary, Philadelphia, walked out in protest of his high-handed leadership and unrelenting advocacy of total military victory in Vietnam. The ACCC still exists, publishes Fundamental News Service, and is affiliated with the Council of Bible Believing Churches (Denver, Colorado, founded 1968).

The Christian Crusade (1948, Tulsa, Oklahoma). Encouraged by McIntire, Rev. Billy James Hargis (b. 1925) captured many headlines with his somewhat paranoid anti-communist agitation and efforts to get the United States out of the UN. His Christian Crusade Newsletter captions each issue with "All I want to do is preach Jesus and save America." In the 1950s he and McIntire developed a plan to float balloons containing Bible messages over Iron Curtain countries. In the 1960s and early 1970s he became more involved with conservative political campaigns, often labeling campus radicals, antiwar protesters and black power advocates as communists. For "health reasons," after a sordid sex scandal, in 1974 he resigned as president of four-year-old American Christian College in Tulsa and cut back Christian Crusade activities; but he still conducts yearly Bible conferences and in 1994 celebrated conservative Republican victories.

Campus Crusade for Christ (1951, Orlando, Florida). Campus Crusade began at UCLA and currently has Bible study groups and conferences for college and high school students and faculty, military personnel, and prisoners in the United States and abroad. Longtime president Bill Bright was originally bankrolled by Texas silver tycoon Nelson Bunker Hunt and organized college "cell groups," using the terminology of early communist recruiters. Though nominally nonpolitical, Bright's Third Century Publications has included in its lists manuals on how Christians can become politically active.

The Christian Anti-Communist Crusade (1953, Long Beach, California). Fred Schwartz (1913–98), an Australian psychiatrist, came to the United States at the invitation of Carl McIntire and followed the pattern of Hargis in making anticommunist appeals; but after moving his organization to Long Beach he de-emphasized fundamentalist Christian appeals, maintaining in his books and congressional testimony that Christianity is of importance as the only alternative to communism. A study of the Crusade in the 1960s found its members were 71 percent Republicans and 9 percent Democrats; they were quite educated, but only half attended church regularly.[3] In the 1970s Schwartz's organization was active in India, the Philippines, Korea, Taiwan, El Salvador, and Chile, among other places. The end of the Cold War vitiated the appeals of both Hargis and Schwartz.

The John Birch Society (1958, Appleton, Wisconsin). The Birch Society was founded by candy manufacturer Robert Welch (1899–1985) and named for "the first casualty of World War III," a Baptist missionary killed by the Chinese Communists in 1945. Against communism, the UN, government in general, and the liberal theory of democracy, Welch called Dwight Eisenhower, among others, a "knowing agent of the communist conspiracy," and even Ronald Reagan was seen as a "lackey" of Communist conspirators. Birch came from a fundamentalist Baptist background but pushed no one view of Christianity. Welch stepped down as president in 1983; that same year, John Birch National chairman, Congressman Larry P. McDonald of Georgia, was killed as one of the passengers in the Korean airliner that strayed into Soviet territory and was shot down by a Soviet fighter. The memorial service for McDonald in Constitution Hall turned into a three-hour political rally with anticommunist speeches by Jerry Falwell, Admiral Thomas Moorer, Congressman Philip Crane, and Howard Phillips, chairman of the Conservative Caucus. Phillips called for "Godly retribution," and urged cutting all ties with the Soviet Union, expelling all Soviet citizens from the United States, and pulling out of the UN. President Reagan had been invited to attend but declined. Today the organization still supports a speakers bureau and seminar program but is a shadow of its former self.

The Eagle Forum (1975, Alton, Illinois). This is the organization of the redoubtable Phyllis Schlafly, a longtime conservative spokeswoman, an early 1960s Goldwater supporter and a Catholic. Her Forum was organized in the aftermath of the 1973 Supreme Court's abortion decision, in Roe v. Wade. The EF supports "traditional morality," which means no abortion, no public school sex education, no Equal Rights Amendment, mothers at home, and school prayer. But ahead of strictly religious concerns are a strong military, lower taxes, and higher tax exemptions for children. Schlafly was prominent at the Christian Coalition's God and Country Rally at the 1992 Republican Convention, along with Coalition leaders, Vice President Dan Quayle, Jerry Falwell, Pat Boone, Henry Hyde, and others. In 2002 Schlafly continues weekly radio broadcasts, and her Eagle Forum website regularly addresses the evils of illegal immigration, fast-track trade agreements, foreign aid, environmental legislation, and the like. Her program *Court Watch* marshals statistics on what she regards as good and bad judicial decisions.

Focus on the Family (1977, Colorado Springs, Colorado). This is a support organization for James Dobson (b. 1936) and his radio program of the same name. Dobson (not to be confused with one-time Moral Majority activist Ed Dobson) is a Presbyterian, former professor of pediatrics at University of Southern California, and advocate of traditional family structure. He emphasizes traditional Christian values but, unlike most radio evangelists, rarely refers to biblical texts. His book *Dare to Discipline* was quite popular. He is heard on 1,450 radio stations and has a staff of family counselors and others estimated at 700. Originally nonpolitical, his monthly magazine, *Citizen*, deals with political issues. Its circulation is over 100,000 but cannot compare to the magazine *Focus on the Family*, which is said to reach two million. Dobson served on six government panels during the Reagan administration, most notably the Commission on Pornography headed by Attorney General Edwin Meese. He has been a supporter of Gary Bauer's Family Research Council (see below). Recently he has been on the national commission to study the effects of gambling. Dobson made headlines in November 2001, when he successfully appealed to the national Salvation Army to reverse the decision of the

Western jurisdiction of the Salvation Army, which granted its employees standard benefits for same-sex domestic partners.

Concerned Women for America (1978, Washington, D.C.). Organized by Beverly LaHaye, it claims a half million members. It has lobbied Congress and state legislatures for new religious freedom legislation, for antiabortion legislation, for AIDS testing for marriage license applicants, and against the Equal Rights Amendment and condom advertisements. Working with Schlafly's Eagle Forum, it claimed credit for defeating a Vermont equal rights amendment in 1986. It has provided legal representation to Christian parents who challenge public school policy and has conducted political training workshops and educational programs on traditional American values.

The Religious Roundtable (1979, Memphis, Tennessee). The Roundtable was founded by Edward McAteer (b. 1927) with the avowed aim of recruiting fundamentalist ministers into politics in order to save Christianity and Western civilization. It was active in organizing ministers in support of Ronald Reagan in 1980. Its National Affairs Briefing at the GOP convention in Dallas in 1980 was attended by Ronald Reagan, but the anti-Semitic tone of some speakers proved to be a political loss for all involved. It has been a vocal opponent of child abuse, homosexuality, and pornography. McAteer, a Southern Baptist layman, was a marketing specialist for Colgate-Palmolive; with Paul Weyrich (see below) and fellow Conservative Caucus leader Howard Phillips, he worked diligently to arouse political interests among fundamentalists. For a time Pat Robertson, Jerry Falwell, and television evangelist James Robison were on the Roundtable board. The organization's influence declined after McAteer ran unsuccessfully for the U.S. Senate in 1984.

The Moral Majority (1979). In its brief life, the Moral Majority was perhaps the best known of Christian right organizations. The name, invented by Paul Weyrich, probably derived from Richard Nixon's earlier evocation of "the silent majority." The Moral Majority claimed considerable influence over the national political agenda in the early 1980s, but the aggressive lobbying activities of its leader, Jerry Falwell, against abortion rights, gay rights, pornography, and the Equal Rights Amendment and for school prayer, generated much hostility and some ridicule. Most of its activities were shifted in 1986 to a new organization, the Liberty Federation, and Falwell resigned as president in 1987. The Moral Majority went out of existence in 1989. Raised by hill-country bootleggers in central Virginia, Falwell was born again as a Christian in 1952, went to Missouri's Bible Baptist College, and came back to Lynchburg four years later to establish an independent Baptist church in a vacant bottling plant. The congregation numbered thirty-five members in 1956, but by the early 1980s it drew around twenty thousand, and Falwell's *Old-Time Gospel Hour* reached an estimated twenty-one million listeners through 681 radio and television stations. He was generating roughly one million dollars per week of income, enough to start Liberty Baptist College, with three thousand students, a seminary, a children's day school and a home for alcoholics—an operation with sixty-two assistant pastors and thirteen hundred employees. The money-raising suffered greatly in 1987, due to the largely unrelated Jim and Tammy Bakker scandals, which was a factor in terminating the Moral Majority. But Falwell himself was responsible for alienating much support. In 1986, for example, he spent five days in South Africa, praised the apartheid government, and called Bishop Tutu a "phony." He then flew to the Philippines, lauded the Marcos dictatorship, and said the Philippines was "paradise."

Paul Weyrich (b. 1942) has been called the Christian right's point man. A Roman Catholic of blue-collar origins, he has been not so much a religious leader as a political conservative leader who has been a force in politicizing religious leaders. He was involved in the formation of the Religious Roundtable, the Moral Majority, and the Christian Coalition. His political bent was shown by his attempt to broaden the appeal of the Christian right's social objectives, by restating them in terms of a secular "cultural revolution," which led to a disavowal by Edward McAteer of the Religious Roundtable. He has tried to bring conservative Catholics, Protestants, and Jews together, without conspicuous success. A front for his activities in Washington, D.C., is the Committee for the Survival of a Free Congress, which has spawned such offshoots as the Free Congress Research and Education Foundation. In 1973, with the backing of beer tycoon Joseph Coors, he helped found the Heritage Foundation, a conservative think tank that has thrived to this day. He has worked with Richard Viguerie, whose direct-mail political empire began with a list of Goldwater contributors in 1964, Howard Phillips of the Conservative Caucus, Terry Dolan of the National Conservative Political Action Committee, Reed Larson of the anti-union National Right to Work Committee, and Senator Jesse Helms.

The Family Research Council (1980, Washington, D.C.). The Council began as an affiliate of James Dobson's Focus on the Family. The president, Gary Bauer, served as an aide to Education Secretary William Bennett and as a policy adviser to the president in the Reagan administration. Bauer, who in 1999 became a candidate for president of the United States, has emphasized such issues as the evil of abortion and teen pregnancy, the virtue of alternatives to public schools, tax benefits for parents with small children, and welfare reform. Bauer grew up in Kentucky's "sin city," Newport—once noted for gambling, drinking and prostitution controlled by a Cleveland mob. The son of a poor, working-class, alcoholic father, as a high school student Bauer in 1961 joined a group of ministers bent on cleaning up the town of Newport. The campaign succeeded, launching Bauer's attempts to clean up wider regions.

The American Coalition for Traditional Values (ACTV) (1983, Washington, D.C.). ACTV was founded by Tim LaHaye (b. 1926), whose wife, Beverly, organized the Concerned Women for America. The first executive board contained, among others, Jerry Falwell, James Dobson, James Robison, Jimmy Swaggart, and Bill Bright. When information surfaced that some of its financial support came from Sun Myung Moon's Unification Church, the adverse publicity led LaHaye in 1986 to announce its disbanding. But the organization still maintains an office in Washington, and LaHaye is prominent in Christian right circles. With his wife he authored a book on marriage and wrote another book attacking secular humanism. When living in San Diego in 1980 he set up a branch of the Moral Majority called Californians for Biblical Morality. He was honorary cochairman of Jack Kemp's campaign for the presidency in 1988 but was forced to resign when anti-Catholic and anti-Jewish statements in his published works were disclosed. A California chapter of the ACTV called the Traditional Values Coalition, led by the Rev. Lou Sheldon of Anaheim, remains active in opposing gay rights, condom distribution, sex education in the schools, and abortion. Sheldon gained advantageous publicity when a worship service in his church was interrupted by gay-rights activists.

Tim LaHaye has become more literary or, perhaps, theological in recent years. With coauthor Jerry Jenkins he has written a series of novels collectively called *Left Behind*, after the first title in 1995. *The Rapture* was a bestseller, and *The Indwelling* (2000) sold two million copies and was number one on the *New York Times* best-seller list two weeks after its release. The novels feature handsome airline pilot Rayford Steele, disappearing people, and the antichrist using the UN as his tool. In January 2002 LaHaye began a School of Prophecy, a one-year program attached to Jerry Falwell's Liberty University.

Operation Rescue (1984, Summerville, South Carolina). Organized by the energetic and brash Randall Terry, this group has become notorious for its picketing and demonstrating outside family planning clinics. Though it officially disavows violence, the intense emotionalism of this organization's actions has certainly contributed to individual acts of violence, including the shooting of abortion doctors. Jerry Falwell joined a Terry Atlanta "rescue" in 1988. Court decisions in 1989 and 1992 that allowed qualified state restrictions on abortions took some steam out of Operation Rescue as a movement, but by 1995 over 43,000 arrests had resulted from such demonstrations. By 2001 the organization had changed its name to Operation Save America, and its leaders had rejected Terry as an "evangelical hypocrite" based on his personal behavior. The annual organizational conference in Wichita, Kansas, that year went ahead without Terry.

The above are only thirteen of sixty or more Christian right organizations. We will look at the Christian Coalition in greater detail below. The above survey may be enough to suggest that there is considerable overlap in leadership and probably membership, that a considerable number are transient, that narrowly conceived and often negative issues rather than broad purposes seem to characterize their orientation, and that all have had their ups and downs.

IV. THE CHRISTIAN RIGHT AND THE SEPARATION OF CHURCH AND STATE

Religious leaders, like politicians, must respond to popular concerns. Supreme Court decisions, by virtue of their great particularity and their necessary focus on specific individuals and specific cases, often take on symbolic overtones as targets of opposition. In our political system, the Supreme Court has the last word, and despite, or because of, attempts to insulate the courts from popular passions, defeated contestants are rarely in a mood to grant anyone (else) the last word. On the other hand, to use "Moral Majority" as a positive symbol implies a belief in democracy, which is rule by majorities. It is the American tradition to attack politicians, but when a majority of citizens support a politician, it makes it harder for critics to attack him or her. (Robert Welch could attack everybody because he avowedly did not believe in democracy.) But the Supreme Court is a nondemocratic institution in a democratic system; its justices are appointed for life. Progressives have used the courts to advance civil rights when legislative action was slow. These factors may help to explain in some measure why the Christian right seems particularly to enjoy attacking the Supreme Court or, better said, to enjoy their own outrage at Supreme Court decisions that go the wrong way. Accordingly, it may help our understanding to note a few of the decisions that arouse their ire.

The first clause of the First Amendment to the U.S. Constitution, which is also the first clause of the Bill of Rights (Amendments One through Ten), pertains to religion: "Congress shall make no law respecting an establishment of religion, or prohibiting the free exercise thereof." As is evident, this text is a limitation on Congress and not initially on the states. Several Christian right leaders say that we were from the beginning a "Christian nation" because, though the First Amendment limited the national government, there were state churches, that is, tax-supported, in several of the states. This is perhaps the grounds on which Pat Robertson stands when he says there is nothing in the Constitution that requires the separation of church and state, even though the courts began applying the First Amendment to the states (through the Fourteenth Amendment's protection of persons' "life, liberty and property" against state action) in the 1920s. The only mention of religion in the body of the U.S. Constitution is Article VI, which bans any religious test as a qualification for office.

The religion clauses did not become major issues for the states until the late 1930s and early 1940s, when a series of Jehovah's Witnesses cases made them so. In 1938 the Supreme Court first held that a city could not forbid Jehovah's Witnesses from handing out tracts door to door. In 1947 it held that New Jersey was not establishing religion by paying for school buses to parochial schools.

The decisions that irritated Christian conservatives began in 1962, when in Engel v. Vitale the Court declared that the non–denominational public school prayer approved by New York State's Board of Regents was unconstitutional, being an establishment of religion. The next year in Abingdon v. Schempp the Court outlawed laws in Pennsylvania and Maryland that required Bible reading in public schools. Religious conservatives were outraged, seeing this not as freedom of religion but an attack on Christianity. About this time Mel and Norma Gabler in Texas began a protracted series of attacks on the Texas Education Agency for its approval of textbooks that teach evolution. In Stone v. Graham in 1980 the Court declared unconstitutional a Kentucky law requiring the posting of the Ten Commandments in public elementary and secondary schools. (See chapter 1, "Religion and the Public Schools.")

Roe v. Wade in 1973, which established a right to an abortion in the first trimester of pregnancy, was not directly a religion case, but the Christian right regarded it as such; perhaps no case has been subject to more vocal criticism or a more declamatory defense. The followers of Operation Rescue's Randall Terry often compare him to Martin Luther King and usually recite Psalm 139:13–16 at their protests, while holding aloft signs invoking God's judgment against "baby-killers." Jerry Falwell and Richard Viguerie, among others, were very upset when in 1981 President Reagan nominated Sandra Day O'Connor to the Supreme Court, for as a state senator in Arizona, she had cosponsored a family planning expenditures bill. The White House staff actually welcomed criticism from the Christian right. The polling data they lived by showed a growing unpopularity of Falwell. Such data also showed that the Christian right had not been responsible for Reagan's election in 1980, so they resented the right's repeated efforts to take credit for that election.

In 1992, after Christian right lobbying, Colorado voters passed a sweeping state constitutional amendment denying any "protected" rights for homosexuals (Aspen, Boulder and Denver had recently adopted gay-rights ordinances). In Romer v. Evans in 1996 the Supreme Court, by a somewhat surprising 6-3 vote, declared the initiative amendment unconstitutional.

It must not be thought that all federal judges are unsympathetic to the

Christian right. In 1987 Federal Judge W. Brevard Hand of the Southern District of Alabama ordered the banning of thirty-one school textbooks on the basis that they violated the First Amendment by teaching "the religion of secular humanism." (He was overruled by the Circuit Court.) And in a bitter dissent in Romer v. Evans, Justice Antonin Scalia scolded his colleagues by reminding them that in Bowers v. Hardwick (1986) they had upheld the right of Georgia to criminalize consensual homosexual behavior.

V. KEY FIGURES IN THE RELIGIOUS RIGHT

Pat Robertson and the Organization of the Christian Coalition

Marion Gordon "Pat" Robertson (b. 1930) was born in Virginia, the son of Senator A. Willis Robertson and a devout Baptist mother. He was a Phi Beta Kappa graduate of Washington and Lee University, studied at the University of London, served with the Marines in Korea (1951–52) and graduated from Yale Law School in 1955. In these years he displayed, it was said, "a fondness for women, whiskey and poker."[4] But influenced by a fundamentalist friend of his mother, he was born again in 1956. By 1959 he had completed work at Biblical Seminary (later renamed New York Theological Seminary). Returning to Virginia, he purchased a television station in Portsmouth and launched the Christian Broadcasting Network (CBN) in 1960.

In a few years he developed a formula. Needing $7,000 a month to cover costs, he enlisted seven hundred listeners who would pledge $10 per month. The TV program of the 700 Club deliberately copied the format of Johnny Carson's *Tonight* show, and fund-raising boomed when a young Jim Bakker joined the show in 1965 (he later set up shop in Charlotte, North Carolina, with his own *PTL—Praise the Lord*—show). By 1975 CBN claimed 110 million viewers (though a *New York Times* study showed this to be a vastly inflated figure). In 1979 Robertson opened an expansive headquarters building and CBN's Regent University at Virginia Beach. By 1987 he employed 4,000 people and had a campus of 380 acres. His social concerns reflected exactly the standard Christian right parameters: against abortion, homosexuality, pornography, and the Equal Rights Amendment; in favor of prayer in the public schools and tax credits for private schooling.

Various Christian right groups were active in the 1982 congressional elections, but the economy was languishing and their preferred candidates did not do too well. Reagan's White House pushed a school prayer amendment, and a majority in the Senate (but not the two-thirds needed) supported it. The White House and the Christian right were more successful with "equal access" legislation, allowing religious groups to use school facilities. The new alliance of pols and the pious also held together in their support for Bob Jones University, denied tax-exempt status by the IRS for its racially discriminatory practices. (In 1983 the Supreme Court upheld the IRS.) Reagan designated 1983 the Year of the Bible and appeared at National Religious Broadcasters' conventions.

In 1984 for the first time Pat Robertson and Jerry Falwell were invited to appear on the stage of the Republican National Convention. Who was using whom is difficult to determine. Before long, Robertson had superseded Falwell as the leading spokesperson of the Christian right. In Robertson's book *The Plan*, he says the idea for making a presidential bid came to him in 1984. He prayed over several weeks about it, and again and again came God's answer: "You will not want to do this, but you should do this."[5] He decided to seek the Republican nomination for president in 1988. Speaking before church audiences, Robertson hinted at the command of God. Before secular audiences and in public communications, he did not mention it, because the one time he did, it was reported in the *Washington Post* and stirred up a flurry of negative publicity. His statement to the *700 Club* on October 2, 1984, that "there is nothing in the U.S. Constitution that sanctifies the separation of church and state" has remained a political weight around his neck.

From Robertson's point of view, the leading Republican contenders, George Bush and Bob Dole, were unreliable. He regarded Jack Kemp as his primary competition for the support of the Republican right. Robertson's strategy was to picture himself as the true heir of the Reagan ideology and to focus on the one-fourth of the GOP convention delegates who would be chosen in party caucuses as opposed to primary elections, where he knew he was not as strong. If he got the nomination, he would run hardest in the winner-take-all states, especially in the South, where traditional Democrats were still "moral conservatives." He prepared a video, *Pat Robertson: Who Is This Man?* in which he was portrayed as the originator of relief and literacy programs. No mention was made of the Christian Broadcasting Network. The terms used in the video were getting back to "traditional morality" and to "foundational spiritual convictions." He and his followers were torn between the appeals of two contradictory positions: (1) America is a Christian nation, and (2) real Christians are a persecuted minority in a decadent nation. As the campaign went on, his speeches spoke of the threat of "secular humanism," but rather than enunciate specific evangelical tenets, he referred broadly to the "Judeo-Christian heritage." He tried to turn opponents' attacks on religious intolerance around by accusing them of "Christian bashing." His "family-based solutions" to economic problems were vague. His proud conservative boast, "I have no intention of taking some liberal as vice president to balance the ticket," made party pragmatists uncomfortable. Venturing into foreign policy, he defended Oliver North's escapades in Central America and repeated familiar alarms about the Soviet threat and the dangers of communism, this as the Soviet Union was about to collapse.

Robertson actually beat out George Bush in the Iowa caucuses. But reporters, tired of hearing the same stump speech over and over, would pounce on anything out of the ordinary, and political novice Robertson gave them some choice bits. He promised to fire most of the 100,000 federal employees who serve at the pleasure of the president—a wildly inaccurate figure. The Jimmy Swaggart sex scandal broke at a very bad time for Robertson. He suggested the Bush campaign was somehow responsible for its disclosure, though there was nothing to substantiate this charge. He said there were Russian missiles in Cuba, when there weren't. Robertson later conceded, "My mistakes went up geometrically in relation to the measure of my jet lag and fatigue."[6] In the New Hampshire primary, a state without much Christian conservative organization, Robertson came in an embarrassing fifth, after Bush, Dole, Kemp, and Pierre du Pont. Robertson foolishly, and against the advice of his professional advisers, loudly made the South Carolina primary a crucial test case, believing South Carolina was where Christian conservatives were strongest. But South Carolina had become Bush territory by virtue of the governor's support and the skill of Bush organizer Lee Atwater, a South Carolina native. Robertson got only 19 percent of the vote, trailing Bush and Dole.

After his defeat at the national level, Robertson looked elsewhere, toward state campaigns, local school boards, city councils. To this end the Christian Coalition (henceforth CC) was created in 1989. A bright young historian, Ralph Reed, an admirer of Lee Atwater, came aboard as executive director (see below). In theory the CC does not endorse candidates, but it distributes "Congressional Scorecards" listing votes on issues of importance to the Christian right. Before the 1994 election, the CC claimed to have distributed 29 million Congressional Scorecards and 40 million voter guides, mainly through churches. It publishes a monthly newsletter and a bimonthly newspaper, *Christian America*. In the 2000 election (see below) the number of CC voter guides fell off sharply, and some other groups on the right were writing and distributing their own.

Ralph Reed

To an indeterminate degree, the early success of the CC owed much to the political skill of its executive director, Ralph Reed (b. 1961). Reed was born in Virginia, not far from Robertson's first broadcast studio. The son of a Navy doctor, he and his family moved many times during his childhood. He says he became a political junkie reading history and observing the Republican and Democratic National Conventions in Miami in 1972, when he was eleven years old. After high school in Georgia, he entered the University of Georgia, where he wrote a conservative column for the student newspaper (until fired for plagiarism), worked with young Republicans, and got a Senate internship in Washington, D.C., earning his stripes in the 1984 Senate campaign for Jesse Helms. Despite his affection for practical politics, he meanwhile had enrolled in graduate school at Emory University and picked up a Ph.D. in history in 1986, expecting a career as a college professor. A merely nominal Methodist, he smoked and drank in college, but in 1983, attending an evangelical church in Washington, D.C., he was born again—though he refers to it as "a faith experience," or "faith commitment." "More than shifting my ideology, my Christian faith [now] caused me to shift my tactics." He began to talk to former enemies and pray for them, he "tried to bridge differences. For someone trained in the old-fashioned school of political hardball, it was quite a transformation. Some of my old foes were speechless."[7]

Reed says he had an "epiphany" in January 1988, when his then-candidate Jack Kemp lost out to Pat Robertson's forces in one of the Georgia Republican caucuses.

> My candidate had been trounced, but I was nevertheless euphoric about the outcome. Why? Because my own dream of bringing religious values and conservative principles into the political arena after two generations of liberal dominance seemed possible for the first time.[8]

Even though Reed had worked for Jack Kemp, Robertson admired both his organizational talent and his religious conviction and asked him to become executive director of the CC. After they conversed at the Bush inaugural, Reed had sent Robertson a memo on how to organize Christians state by state and county by county, and it appealed to Robertson's instincts at the time. A shrewd political strategist and smooth talk-show guest, Reed had more flexibility and more generosity toward opponents than did Robertson. His 1994 book, *Politically Incorrect: The Emerging Faith Factor in American Politics*, an articulate defense of CC positions and strategy, made a splash. One of Reed's techniques, he said proudly, was to schedule meetings in rooms too small for the anticipated audience, so that he might comment on the "surprising" upsurge of interest.

The CC and other rightist groups were upset in 1989 when newly elected President Bush appointed pro-choice Louis Sullivan as secretary of health and human services and named too few evangelicals to other positions. Early in 1990 Reed flew to Orange County to energize CC recruits. He met with James

Dobson of Focus on the Family and had to assure him that Robertson had no intention of running for president again. Robertson's new mode of operation was further indicated in 1990 by his organizing in Virginia the American Center for Law and Justice, a kind of ACLU of the right. Its aim, he said, was to "litigate for . . . as many years as it takes to restore America's Godly heritage." It provides legal defense for anti-abortion demonstrators and Bible-quoting teachers in the name of free speech, sometimes putting it on the same side as the ACLU, though its fund-raising literature pictures the ACLU as the evil enemy (along with the American Jewish Congress, People for the American Way, and NOW).[9] The Center had a hand in drafting President George W. Bush's Faith-Based and Community Initiative program in 2001 (see below).

VI. ELECTORAL STRATEGIES

Despite their disappointment with Bush, the Christian right swung behind him in 1992. Supported by the CC, Jerry Falwell and Tim LaHaye cochaired an Evangelical Leaders and Laymen Coalition for Bush-Quayle '92. The CC mobilized its 300,000 members and distributed forty million voter guides to forty thousand churches. Technically, they were nonpartisan, but they were clearly designed to promote conservative candidates. But this was not enough to save Bush, who got 38 percent of the vote to Clinton's 43 percent. The Perot campaign got 19 percent. The presence of Perot helped get Clinton elected, but Perot was pro-choice and did not appeal to the Christian right.

In California, the Christian Coalition made a vigorous effort to capture the Republican Party in 1992. Governor Pete Wilson was too moderate for them. The CC distributed 3.9 million voter guides on "family issues" to fifteen thousand California churches. It focused especially on eight of twelve key Assembly races. Said Reed: "I can't think of another election year where there is so much at stake. . . . If we win the [California] Assembly races, that would be a very big blow for Governor Wilson. The ice would be very thin under his seat."[10] Christian right leaders rather bluntly told Wilson he had better play ball with them or he would be defeated in 1994, but Wilson maintained his hold on the party and he was reelected in 1994.

After the 1992 election, Robertson gloomily told his *700 Club* that "radical feminists" Barbara Boxer and Dianne Feinstein were taking over the Senate and Bill Clinton was putting gays in the military and gays and women in the Cabinet. To Robertson, "it seemed that God Himself had lost the election."[11]

But 1994 was different. The congressional races in 1994 proved to be a boon for the CC. A good enemy can be a powerful organizing tool; Clinton proved to be a good enemy for the Christian right, as did his surgeon general,

Jocelyn Elders, a black woman who was outspoken on sex education and drug legalization. Said Reed, "The conservative community, largely asphyxiated during the Bush years, awoke from its slumber like Rip Van Winkle on steroids after the Clinton inaugural."[12] He claimed that the CC went from 250,000 in 1989 to 1.6 million in 1995, figures that are probably exaggerated. But the independent *Campaigns and Elections* magazine in a 1994 study concluded that the Christian right was dominant in eighteen state Republican Party organizations and a contending force in thirteen more.

The 1994 Election

The Clinton administration was stunned when in 1994 Republicans captured both houses of Congress for the first time since 1952 and a majority of statehouses became Republican. Governor Mario Cuomo was upset by George Pataki in New York. Georgia Congressman Newt Gingrich had formulated a Republican "Contract with America" that became the basis for the legislative agenda after he was elected speaker in January 1995. (Ralph Reed announced that the Christian Coalition would support the Contract, even though it did not mention abortion or school prayer.) The press, remembering the relatively weak showing of the Christian right in 1992, was also surprised. As one commentator noted, the Christian right had been discovered, then dismissed, by the media four times since 1979. The influence of the CC on Republican candidates was enhanced not only by the CC's good organization, but by the low turnout of voters in the primaries.

The best study of the Christian right at the state level in the 1994 elections is *God at the Grass Roots*;[13] seventeen scholars looked at eleven states. They found Christian right organization most effective in South Carolina and Oklahoma, somewhat less so in California and Texas, fading in Michigan and Virginia (where Oliver North was beaten for the U.S. Senate). The Christian right contributed to serious divisions within the Republican Party and hence to defeats of its candidates in Oregon, Georgia, and Florida. There were mixed results in Iowa and Minnesota. In general they found, in these states and the nation as a whole, that the political strength of the Christian right lay in its significant numbers, potentially a fourth of the electorate, plus its focused political commitment that could sustain much hard work. Its weakness lay in the difficulty of mobilizing otherworldly and often antipolitical types; the reluctance to form coalitions with non–true believers; their sometimes eccentric and difficult leadership; and the persistent opposition of the media, the entertainment industry, higher education, and the professions.

California may be taken as an example of state political activity by the Christian right in the crucial 1994 election. As elsewhere, Christian right activity was almost entirely within the Republican Party. The exit polls showed that 29 percent of California voters described themselves as evangelical Christians (17 percent said they go to church weekly), of whom 60 percent were Republicans. Fifty-four percent of the California electorate were secular or not religiously active. Most of the latter were liberal. (These percentages have not changed much since.)

Governor Pete Wilson had largely ignored the Christian right until the 1994 election. Both he and Senate candidate Michael Huffington were pro-choice social moderates. Under pressure, Wilson shifted somewhat to the right. He vetoed the California Learning Assessment System bill, feared by some religious schools, after which Lou Sheldon began calling him "my good friend." He supported Proposition 187, which made illegal immigrants ineligible for educational and public services. Indeed, he made this the crucial issue of the election, and Kathleen Brown, his opponent, could not make headway against it.

Huffington had scored quite low on the Christian Coalition's scorecard and supported gays in the military (four years later he revealed that he was gay). Nevertheless, by spending enormous amounts of money, he beat longtime Congressman William Dannemeyer in the 1994 primary 55 percent to 29 percent. Dannemeyer had Christian right support, but he had been beaten by Wilson's appointee to the Senate, John Seymour, two years earlier. After the primary, Huffington began to speak on Christian radio stations, and his wife, Arianna, publicly described her born-again experience. The National Abortion Rights Action League denounced Arianna Huffington as a "great pretender" on pro-choice issues, which had the unintended consequence of greatly boosting her husband's Christian right support. Seventy percent of self-designated evangelicals voted for Huffington, and 24% of his total vote came from that group. The race with Dianne Feinstein was quite close, and if his Christian right support had been a little higher, as high as Wilson's, he would have beaten Feinstein.

The year 1994 was big for the CC, yet its limits were shown by a very minor election in Vista, California. Having earlier captured a majority of the school board there, the CC incumbents so irritated the community by pushing the teaching of creationism in dogmatic and intolerant ways that they were thrown out in a special recall election in November 1994.

The 1996 Election

The budget of the Christian Coalition in 1996 was $27 million. Reed announced, "We now have what we have always sought—a place at the table, a voice in the conversation we call democracy and a vital and vibrant role in the future of our nation." But the year 1996 was not such a bountiful year for CC hopes. The whole Christian right was criticized when self-proclaimed messiah Sun Myung Moon addressed a Family Federation for World Peace conference in August attended by Ralph Reed, Gary Bauer, Beverly LaHaye, and the Crystal Cathedral's Robert Schuller, among others. CC spokesman Mike Russell rather defensively said of Moon's Unification Church, "They're working to strengthen the family and so are we. Ralph doesn't agree with every organization he speaks to." Gary Bauer said, "I disagree with the theology of many groups that I address—Jews, for example, who do not accept Jesus, or atheists." The fact that George Bush, Gerald Ford, Edward Heath, Bill Cosby, and Pat Boone also spoke to the conference was protective coloration for the Christian right, but the fact that Rev. Moon had given money to the CC and had received money from the South Korean arms industry was harder to live down.

In October 1996 the CC had to apologize for distributing sample voter guides that African American leaders in Texas branded as "race-baiting." The CC spun off a group called the Catholic Alliance, hoping to attract Catholics to their point of view, only to be criticized for the move by a number of Catholic bishops, who called attention to the CC's positions on welfare reform, immigration, and the poor. Americans United for Separation of Church and State (AUSCS), People for the American Way, and the new Interfaith Alliance, energized by the CC showing in the 1994 election, began to attack the Christian right more directly and scored some points. Barry Lynn of AUSCS tried to get Interfaith Alliance and AUSCS voter guides distributed early and simultaneously with those of the CC to show how partisan the CC guides were. He suggested that CC's guide violated IRS tax-exempt guidelines. CC refused to cooperate. "Ralph Reed is being arrogant," said Lynn.[14] But even Clinton, always calculating the odds, accommodated the Christian right to some degree when with great reluctance and in the middle of the night he signed into law legislation that allows states to refuse to honor same-sex marriages performed in other states.

After the supposed success of the Contract with America, few observers in early 1996 could have anticipated that by shutting down the government when the Republicans failed to approve his budget, Clinton could outmaneuver the Republicans and defeat Bob Dole as handily as he did. The favorite CC issues of abortion, homosexuality, and school prayer were rarely mentioned in the presidential campaign. Like George Bush before him, Bob Dole tried to woo the Christian right but could not succeed in speaking their language, even when, in September, he clasped hands with Pat Robertson and spoke to the CC's Road to Victory conference.

The cold calculations of political insiders in 1996 were that in 1992 at the presidential level, the Christian right had lost the GOP candidate more votes than they had delivered. The Christian right leaders who were prominent in the 1992 Republican Platform Committee were not invited back in 1996. Candidate Dole emphasized economic issues and his 15 percent tax cut rather than "social issues." Operation Rescue's Randall Terry said, "The Republican Party is the greatest moral impediment to righteous reform in politics. . . . They've manipulated the 'Religious Right' to their own ends. They throw us a bone, like the party platform, which the politicians promptly ignore. . . . The Republican Party is marked by betrayal and cowardice."[15] Paul Weyrich suggested a third party may be the answer.

Gary Bauer, perhaps thinking ahead to his race in 2000, did not give up on the Republicans. He attacked Ralph Reed because the CC's "Contract with the American Family" had not specifically called for a constitutional ban on abortion and criticized others on the Christian right who had plugged Colin Powell for president. Powell is pro-choice.

In House races in 1996, several favorite religious right candidates went down to defeat. Ellen Craswell was trounced in the Washington gubernatorial race. Perhaps most important, a parental rights initiative in Colorado that would allow parents to veto "liberal" school programs like sex education was defeated 58 percent to 42 percent. Nevertheless, Republicans gained two seats in the Senate and, though losing a few seats in the House, held on to a majority. Reed made the best of it: "For the first time in sixty-eight years a Republican Congress has been reelected and it would never have happened without conservative people of faith who provided the margin of victory."[16] He claimed that born-again Christians accounted for 29 percent of the vote, a figure larger than most experts would agree to. One conservative columnist suggested that the election of 1998 was simply the result of "moral relativism" having captured America, a theory difficult to prove.

VII. THE PRESENT CHRISTIAN RIGHT

The Post-Reed Coalition

To the surprise of many, Ralph Reed left the Christian Coalition in March 1997 and began a private political-consulting firm. (Reed made headlines again in 2002 during the Enron scandal discussions when it was aired that Reed had become a political consultant for Enron Corporation in 1997, with the apparent recommendation of Karl Rove, later to become President Bush's senior White House adviser. He remained with Enron until bankruptcy was declared.) There were rumors that Robertson had become jealous of Reed's fame; diplomatic to the end, Reed left without saying anything but good things about Pat Robertson. With the departure of Reed the CC lost not just organizing skill but a certain level of sophistication. Reed's position is that religion has been marginalized in America because of the failure of secular liberals and modern institutions to realize their own dependence on traditional religious values (a view more respectably advanced by Stephen Carter of Yale in *The Culture of Disbelief*). Robertson, by contrast, manifests what historian Richard Hofstadter once characterized as the "paranoid style" in politics, finding conspiracy and satanic influences in the way the powerful have suppressed religion.

The CC strategy of focusing on local races seemed to remain in place, but, without the young man's maturing influence on the older man, Robertson often reverted to impolitic statements characteristic of his 1988 campaign. Information surfaced that Robertson was using airplanes owned by his tax-exempt international relief organization, Operation Blessing, for flights to the Republic of the Congo on behalf of the African Development Company, Robertson's mining company. He gave late night TV comedians some new material by predicting that because Orlando, Florida, was flying rainbow flags, God would hit it with hurricanes.

In late 1997 Robertson brought a hundred CC leaders to Atlanta for some political talk. "If there is any press here, would you please shoot yourself? Leave. Do something." He praised New York's old Tammany Hall for its effective precinct organization: "There are 175,000 precincts in the country and we want ten trained precinct workers in each of them." Keeping a bit of Reed's pragmatism alive, he announced he wanted a "winner" in the 2000 election for president. He mocked Al Gore as "Ozone Al" and said House minority leader Dick Gephardt was unelectable. "I don't think at this time and juncture the Democrats are going to be able to take the White House unless we throw it away. . . . But we have to get a responsible person and we have to realize some strategy." An Americans United for Separation of Church and State spy in the room taped his remarks. Barry Lynn of AUSCS said the tape shows that the CC is "nothing but a hardball Republican machine with a thin veneer of religiosity." If the IRS, he said, "hasn't seen a smoking gun yet, this is the smoking gun." Arne Owens, CC communications director, said Robertson's remarks were "private" and reiterated that CC does not endorse candidates.[17] But the Federal Elections Commission sued the CC, accusing it of illegally spending money to promote Republican candidates. A month before the 1998 election, on a largely party-line vote, the House authorized an inquiry into the possible impeachment of President Clinton. This gave promise of an outcome the Christian right could celebrate to the skies. But it was not to be.

In January 1999 Robertson angered a number of his compatriots when he seemed to carry pragmatism too far, announcing that Clinton had won the public relations battle and the Senate should end its impeachment trial. Don Hodel, a former Reagan official who had replaced Robertson as president of the Coalition, was among the outraged and quit. Robertson had to take over once again as president.

The acquittal of Clinton by the Senate was a shock to the whole Christian right. Former Congressman Randy Tate (R-Wash.), who had succeeded Reed as executive director, admitted the frustration, saying that "it makes it tough to teach kids right from wrong, in the sense that the President doesn't know right from wrong." But he still expressed the hope that conservatives had influenced the mainstream of American politics. Paul Weyrich went much further, saying in a letter to several hundred on the right that American society is "approaching barbarism. . . . I no longer believe there is a moral majority. I do not believe that a majority of Americans actually share our values. If there really were a moral majority out there, Bill Clinton would have been driven out of office months ago." He suggested it may be time for the Christian right to abandon the effort to influence the American political system, time to "drop out of this culture. . . . The culture we are living in becomes an ever-wider sewer. In truth, I think we are caught up in a cultural collapse of historic proportions, a collapse so great that it simply overwhelms politics."[18] Ironically, the tone of this statement echoes in some ways the tone of left-wing radicals of the 1960s who advocated "dropping out" of a corrupt political system. To a lesser extent, and in a different way, it paralleled the conclusions of pacifist Christians like John Howard Yoder and Stanley Hauerwas, who have argued that the whole notion of a "Christian nation" falsifies the meaning of Christianity.

In June 1999 the CC acknowledged that it had been denied tax-exempt status by the IRS. It split into a Christian Coalition of America, which would concentrate on voter education and presumably maintain tax-exempt status, and a Christian Coalition International, which would be political and not tax-exempt. Executive director Randy Tate was demoted, and the chief operating officer announced that he would be leaving. Pat Robertson once again took over the helm.[19]

The 2000 Election and into the Twenty-First Century

While conservative religious issues have not ceased to be important in American politics, Christian right organizations have had fewer dramatic successes in the new century than in the late twentieth century. In the presidential election of 2000, George W. Bush benefited from extensive Christian right support, though he was not conspicuous in courting it. Such support was enlarged somewhat by the attack made on the Christian right by Bush's primary-election opponent John McCain, senator from Arizona.

In a different way, religion entered the presidential race when Vice President Al Gore named Connecticut Senator Joseph Lieberman as his running mate. Lieberman, a practicing Orthodox Jew, was the first Jew ever to be on a national ticket. In the campaign, he did not downplay his faith but celebrated his candidacy as a tribute to a tolerant and multicultural America and found considerable support in doing this. As expected, Gore did well in the industrial East and California, Bush did well in the South and Midwest. White Protestant support for Bush in Tennessee was a contributing factor to Gore's losing his home state and also the election. The election, as no doubt every reader knows, was an all-time cliffhanger, with Gore-Lieberman winning the popular vote, while the electoral college vote was virtually even and the winner undecided while the nation awaited the outcome of balloting disputes in Florida. The U.S. Supreme Court, after an appeal from the Florida Supreme Court (which had reversed rulings of the Florida secretary of state, who was a Republican), sided with the Bush lawyers and declared Bush the winner, barely in time for the inaugural. Despite intense feelings on both sides, civil war did not erupt, as it would in many countries, and the public accepted the decision with remarkable equanimity. The country moved forward.

Pat Buchanan, noted conservative Catholic, stressing abortion rights and opposing immigration, drew some Christian right support. He was a candidate of the Reform Party, started by Ross Perot. (Running as an independent, Perot had won almost twenty million votes in 1992. He drew only eight million in 1996). But the bitter schism revealed at the Reform Party convention between Buchananites and the remnants of Perot's movement severely weakened Buchanan's candidacy.

Four political scientists have given a succinct account of religious alliances at work in the 2000 election. They found that both parties courted religious constituencies with zeal and that patterns of partisan-religious linkages held up with remarkable consistency between 1996 and 2000. White evangelical denominations contributed 29 percent of the delegates to the Republican Convention, but only 7 percent to the Democratic Convention. Mainline Protestants were 33 percent of the Republican delegates and 23 percent of the Democratic delegates. About half of the Democratic delegates were religious minorities (Jews, black Protestants, Hispanic Catholics), whereas only 12 percent of Republican delegates came from these groups. White Catholics were 20 percent of the Republican delegates. The category of secular activists accounted for 5 percent of the Republicans and 14% of the Democrats.[20]

In the election, Southern Baptist clergy were more enthusiastic for Bush than they had been for Bob Dole in 1996. Gore campaigned unceasingly in black churches, stressing his Southern Baptist origins, and won 96 percent of black Protestant votes. Evangelical Protestants voted 75 percent for Bush, and 84 percent of regular church attenders in this group supported him. Catholics of European background were split evenly between Bush and Gore, but regular mass attendees went for Bush 57 percent. Minority religious groups went heavily for Gore: Hindus, Buddhists, and Muslims 80 percent; Jews 77 percent; Hispanic Catholics 76 percent; Hispanic Protestants 67 percent. Bush's support came from evangelical Protestants who were regular church attenders, plus traditional Christians and allies such as Mormons (3 percent) and mass-attending white Catholics (12 percent), all of which added up to about 60 percent of the Republican support. Black Protestants and secular voters each accounted for 19 percent of the Democratic vote. These patterns held up in congressional votes as well as the presidential vote.

Perhaps the appointment of John Ashcroft as attorney general was Bush's best gift to the Christian right. Son and grandson of pentecostal ministers, as senator from Missouri he had been a favorite of the Christian Coalition and similar groups. Though noncommittal on school prayer, on most other issues—abortion, school vouchers, gay rights, welfare, drugs, the death penalty, flag burning, immigration—Ashcroft mirrored Christian right thinking. It could not, of course, be anticipated how, after September 11, the war against terrorism would give Ashcroft media prominence almost equal to that of Defense Secretary Donald Rumsfeld and make him a lightning rod for alleged restrictions on traditional civil liberties protections in the name of antiterrorism. (See chapter 4, "Human Rights and Civil Rights.")

A Bush policy that reflected some Christian right thinking was his creation of a new Office of Faith-Based and Community Initiatives in the White House. The president invited religious organizations to apply for federal funds and administer them for various community welfare, public health, and homelessness programs. The program would ultimately need congressional approval, and while the House has approved, the Senate, by the end of 2002, had not, despite efforts of Senators Lieberman (D-Conn.) and Santorum (R-Penn.) to fashion a compromise that would not jeopardize anti-discrimination hiring laws. Assurances were made that, on the one hand, religious proselytizing of program clients would not be tolerated and, on the other hand, government regulations would not be allowed to compromise religious convictions of the faith-based groups involved—a narrow path clearly requiring a balancing act. Religious right groups were generally favorable, religious left groups were often skeptical, asking, for example, whether Protestant family planning programs or a Black Muslim food center would be likely to get funds.

The program suffered a setback when John Dilulio Jr., an outspoken academic and Catholic layman who had been appointed first head of the White

House office, apparently distraught by the political warfare the position entailed, resigned only a few months after being appointed. Bush did not appoint a successor until February 2002; he was Jim Towey, a Democratic administrator from Florida and a Catholic layman. Towey said that, despite the lack of legislation, the president would work administratively to advance the faith-based initiative. In October 2002, the Department of Health and Human Services made grants to twenty-one religious organizations totaling $24.8 million, including $500,000 to Pat Roberton's Operation Blessing International.[21]

Another of the new president's initial challenges was the issue of stem-cell research. On the one side were scientists and the public generally who believed that using stem cells from discarded fetuses was crucial to further medical progress on a number of diseases. On the other side were abortion opponents, usually allied with the religious right, who claimed stem-cell research was linked with pro-abortion sentiment and represented an assault on the sanctity of life. The Bush administration negotiated a compromise position that was able to win the support even of Jerry Falwell. Research could continue on existing lines of cells, but the use of federal funds for research beyond that was ruled out.

Falwell, however, proved to be an embarrassment both to the Bush administration and to other leaders of the Christian right, by remarks made after the September 11 attacks. Appearing on Pat Robertson's *700 Club* television broadcast immediately after those attacks, he castigated American decadence in familiar terms and said, "God continues to lift the curtain and allow enemies of America to give us probably what we deserve. . . . God will not be mocked." He mentioned "pagans, the abortionists and the feminists" and listed by name groups "who have tried to secularize America—I point the finger in their face and say, 'You helped this happen.'"[22]

Despite a storm of protest, Falwell initially was unrepentant, defending himself by saying he was "making a theological statement, not a legal statement." A spokesperson for the White House called the remarks "inappropriate" and said, "The President does not share those views." After telephone calls directly from the White House, Falwell publicly apologized, acknowledging that the words seemed "harsh and ill-timed" and regretting that his words "detracted from this time of mourning." Pat Robertson's reputation also suffered from this event, but in a different way. The day after the broadcast, he refused to answer reporters' calls. Then on September 17 he seemed to denounce Falwell, saying the remarks were "totally inappropriate," and protected himself by saying he had been caught off guard and had, "frankly, not fully understood" Falwell's remarks when they were first uttered. This led reporters to check up on the original broadcast to find Robertson saying "Jerry, that's my feeling. . . . Well, yes."[23] The whole episode made Falwell appear sincere but outlandish and made Robertson appear shrewd but deceitfully self-protective.

Such events, plus declining CC budgets, may have been a factor in the resignation of Pat Robertson as president of the Christian Coalition on December 5, 2001. At age seventy-one, he declared it was time for younger leaders to come forward. He wished to devote more time to his ministry. The *700 Club* would continue and Robertson would remain as chancellor of Regent University. He said that all of the ten-year goals of the Christian Coalition set in 1990 had been met. "Without us, I do not believe George Bush would be sitting in the White House or the Republicans would be in control of the United States House of Representatives." Not surprisingly, he failed to mention that his candidate for governor of Virginia lost, as did a number of other CC-endorsed candidates. The CC board chose Roberta Combs as new president. She had been executive vice president since 1999.

Combs has seemed to adopt the highly partisan style followed by her predecessor. In January 2002, on the CC website, she attacked Democrats for planning "to demonize America's mainstream families." Her source for information on the Democratic "plan" was a *Newsweek* story of December 31, written by Howard Fineman, reporting that congressional Democrats were planning to stress "ideals of tolerance" and criticize Republicans for linkages to an intolerant and extremist religious right. How this "demonized mainstream families" was not entirely clear. The reported Democratic statements were clearly partisan but claimed to represent the mainstream rather than demonize it or families within it. Though the Christian Coalition appears to be in decline, the above discussion of the 2000 election suggests that the political influence of the Christian right will be with us for some time to come.

VIII. THE CHRISTIAN RIGHT CULTURE

The above history has focused on the politics of the American Christian right. But it needs to be mentioned that the significance of the Christian right in the long run may rest more on cultural factors than on electoral success. Three areas illustrate this generalization: music, publishing, and homeschooling. Rough estimates are that 10 percent of the $10 billion-a-year music industry is devoted to contemporary Christian music, which is popular music, broadcast by well over a thousand radio stations.

Contemporary Christian music is not, by and large, music heard in old-line churches, though some hymn tunes provide the melodies. Contemporary Christian music has its own rock stars, its own record labels, and its own magazines, including, aptly enough, *Contemporary Christian Music*. Of course not all who listen to such music with regularity are of the political right; but themes of being born again, a personal relationship to Jesus, the coming rapture, and the sinfulness of the "other" culture are common.

In publishing, we have already mentioned the remarkable success of Tim LaHaye's novels. Other "Christian novels" published by Christian conservatives that have sold well are Pat Robertson, *The End of the Age*; Charles Colson, *Gideon's Touch*; and Frank Peretti, *The Oath*. Word Publishing in Texas has been the publisher of many of these works. The most popular evangelical magazine is *Charisma*, with a circulation of around 250,000. The Evangelical Press News Service in Minneapolis supplies material to almost three hundred local evangelical newspapers and magazines. Most communities in the nation have a Christian bookstore, businesses which, collectively, are said to do $3 billion a year in trade.

The Department of Education in 1997 estimated that there were between 500,000 and 750,000 children being homeschooled in America. Many of the homes involved are of Christian conservatives. The homeschooling textbook trade for Christian bookstores, mentioned above, is a significant part of their revenue. The mother is usually the teacher, but a number of Christian right educational materials suggest that the father should play the role of "headmaster" and be the primary teacher in subjects like politics and government, subjects that relate to authority. Bible study is generally an important part of the curriculum. On basic subjects of reading, writing, and science, homeschooled children generally score above the national average on standardized tests. To counter the criticism that homeschooling denies children socializing experiences, homeschooling families often get together for field trips and social activities. The distrust of public schools is partly academic, but perhaps even more based on perceptions of public school teachers and administrators as irreligious and too liberal.

IX. CONCLUDING REFLECTIONS

Politics, some cynic said, is the art of getting money out of the rich and votes out of the poor, each on the pretext of protecting the one against the other. A study of the Christian right can easily lead to such oppressive cynical feelings: this brand of Christianity can seem to be a front, a useful device for bringing in lots of money, providing a diversion such that the rich don't have to worry about the poor and the poor are given the wrong things to worry about. One of the most significant statistics, among mountains of statistics about recent elections, may be that the congressional candidates who spent the most money won over 90 percent of the time, and the percentage keeps creeping up. This suggests how central campaign-finance reform is to any healthy democracy in the media age.

Another interesting phenomenon is the degree to which the Christian right identifies the very concept of morality with sexual probity (in spite of or possibly in part because of the sexual behavior of evangelists like Hargis, Swaggart, and Bakker). There seems to be a special concern with homosexuality. Gaining power is said to require finding the right enemy, and many have commented that, with communism evaporating as an enemy, for the Christian right and some others, gays and lesbians make a convenient and profitable enemy, more convenient than the distant Chinese, which business leaders see as a market. More broadly, sexual misconduct in general has aroused deep-seated passions in the Christian right. Before it expired, the Moral Majority in its newsletter regularly indicted movies, women's magazines, television, and rock music as "pornographic," hinting at a societywide conspiracy: "we are being programmed, subtly but steadily, to accept gross sin and immorality as normal."[21] Though the conspiratorial notions are misplaced, if one pays attention to certain films and certain rap lyrics, it is not hard to understand concern for the decline of civility.

But concern for civility is one thing, and fear, even hatred, of those who are different is another thing. The latter can gain only a superficial connection to an ethic of Christian love and forgiveness, and that by clutching tightly a simplistic dichotomy between "right and wrong," understood as a set of absolute rules of behavior. The politics of the Christian right is a politics of nostalgia and fear. There is nostalgia for lost communities that in memory were placid and harmonious, paternal and hierarchical. There is fear of persons called "relativists," a label applied not only to unsavory characters but carelessly to many who are trying to respect the variety of viewpoints emerging in a new pluralistic world.

It is, of course, important to recognize that evangelical Christians are by no means all as rigid as those described above. Two political scientists from Westmont College surveyed forty-two West Coast self-designated evangelicals and evaluated their responses to forty-six statements culled from a wide range of evangelical and fundamentalist literature, left to right. They found that the responses quite clearly clustered around two poles, one of which gave the highest priority to correct belief, the other of which gave highest priority to right action. The first emphasized rules and doctrine. Especially important for them was belief in the inerrancy of the Bible, individual salvation, personal certitude and sticking to principle. The second group emphasized relationships and doing things for and with other people, agreeing to a high degree with the view that Christ died for people rather than for a principle. For them, God is dynamic rather than static. For this second group of evangelicals, other people's opinions were not the primary basis for judging them, and inerrancy was "a non-issue."[25]

Clearly we must fight the demons without demonizing opponents, and we must have confidence that ultimately by their fruits we shall know who is worthy. While skepticism is surely appropriate in contemplating the Christian right, Christian hope requires that we fight against cynicism, just as we must fight against its partner sentimentality. The human capacity for self-deception being what it is, many of the men (and the few women) who lead the Christian right are probably quite sincere in believing that they are following the authentic Christian path. They no doubt really care about families and children, as do liberals and moderates, though it sometimes seems they care more about children in utero than children after they are born. Despite being very busy raising money and organizing people, they may even read the Bible they talk so much about, though, if so, they must surely read it very selectively. The judgment of the Hebrew prophets against the unjust and the powerful and Jesus' gospel of forgiveness and inclusive love seem mostly subordinated in their speech to the ungodly idols of rigid and narrow sexual morality, capitalistic individualism, and exclusive nationalism.

Discussion Questions

1. What accounts for the appeal of fundamentalism? What are its shortcomings? What are its strengths?
2. Why did the American Christian right become prominent when it did?
3. Why did the Moral Majority disband? Why has the Christian Coalition until recently been more successful? Evaluate the leadership of Pat Robertson.
4. Why did the Christian right do so well in the 1994 elections? Why were its victories relatively short-lived?
5. What has replaced anticommunism as a target for the Christian right?
6. Have you had political or religious conversations with advocates of the Christian right? Should more such conversations occur? How can such conversations occur?
7. How does the Christian gospel as you understand it connect to the various positions of the Christian right?

To Learn More

William Clyde Wilcox, *God's Warriors: The Christian Right in Twentieth-Century America* (Baltimore: Johns Hopkins University Press, 1992) is a scholarly treatment with an excellent bibliography listing many periodical articles. Wilcox has updated this study in *Onward Christian Soldiers: The Religious Right in American Politics* (Boulder, Colo.: Westview Press, 2000). Another excellent history is William Martin, *With God on Our Side: The Rise of the Religious Right in America* (New York: Broadway Books, 1996). Perhaps the best introduction to the politics of the Christian right is Sara Diamond, *Not by Politics Alone: The Enduring Influence of the Christian Right* (New York: Guilford Press, 1998). Statistics on the declining influence of the religious right may be found in Andrew Greeley and Michael Hout, "Measuring the Strength of the Religious Right," *Christian Century*, vol. 116, no. 23 (Aug. 25–Sept. 1, 1999).

Randall Balmer of Columbia University is one of the foremost scholars of American evangelical religion. See his *Mine Eyes Have Seen the Glory: A Journey into the Evangelical Subculture of America* (New York: Oxford University Press, 1989).

A taste of Christian right thinking may be obtained from Jerry Falwell, *Strength for the Journey* (New York: Simon & Schuster, 1987); Ralph Reed, *Active Faith: How Christians Are Changing the Soul of American Politics* (New York: Free Press, 1996); Pat Robertson, *The New World Order* (Dallas: Word Publishing, 1991) and *The Turning Tide: The Fall of Liberalism and the Rise of Common Sense* (Dallas: Word Publishing, 1993).

Notes

Chapter 1

1. Lee v. Weisman, 505 U.S. 577–646, passim (1992).
2. Martin Marty, "Law without Gospel," *Christian Century*, vol. 116, no. 19 (June 30–July 7, 1999): 695.
3. Ronald J. Sider, "Making Schools Work for the Rich and the Poor," *Christian Century*, vol. 116, no. 23 (Aug. 28–Sept. 1, 1999): 802.
4. Perry Glanzer, "Religion in Public Schools: In Search of Fairness," *Phi Delta Kappan* 80 (Nov. 1998): 219–22.
5. Warren Nord, *Religion and American Education: Rethinking a National Dilemma* (Chapel Hill, N.C.: University of North Carolina Press, 1995), quoted in Glanzer, ibid.
6. Edd Doerr, "Religion and Public Education: In Search of Fairness," *Phi Delta Kappan* 80 (Nov. 1998): 223–25.

Chapter 2

1. Douglas Sturm, *Solidarity and Suffering: Toward a Politics of Relationality* (Albany, N.Y.: SUNY Press, 1998).
2. Peter Edelman, "Regarding Poverty—Take Two," *Nation*, Feb. 4, 2002.
3. United Church of Christ Synod Reform Resolution, 1999.
4. *Los Angeles Times*, Feb. 7, 2000.
5. Jonathan Peterson and Lee Romney, *Los Angeles Times*, Oct. 28, 2001.
6. Marian Wright Edelman, "Wages, Child Poverty, Welfare, Race, and Values," address at King/Drew Medical Center, Los Angeles, June 9, 1992.
7. Ibid.
8. Ibid.
9. Ibid.
10. *Los Angeles Times*, Aug. 31, 2001.
11. Sturm, 24.

Chapter 3

1. *Abortion Surveillance—United States, 1997* (Atlanta: Centers for Disease Control and Prevention, 2000), 1. (These are the most recent statistics available.)
2. *General Board Abortion Hearings,* Hearings of the General Board of the American Baptist Churches/USA on Abortion, Dec. 5, 1980.
3. Ibid., 53.
4. Susan Neiburg Terkel, *Abortion: Facing the Issues* (New York: Franklin Watts, 1988), 71.
5. Rita J. Simon, *Abortion: Statutes, Policies, and Public Attitudes the World Over* (Westport, Conn.: Praeger, 1998), 11, 20.
6. Wang Xiaoming, "Family Planning in China," *Women of China,* Aug. 1991, 14ff.
7. Garrett James Hardin, *Naked Emperors: Essays of a Taboo-Stalker* (Los Altos, Calif.: William Kaufmann, 1982), 137.
8. John M. Swomley Jr., *Theology and Politics* (Washington, D.C.: Religious Coalition for Abortion Rights Educational Fund, 1983), 3.
9. *Population Action International Reproductive Risk: A Worldwide Assessment of Women's Sexual and Maternal Health* (Washington, D.C., 1995).
10. Jan Goodwin, "In Nepal, There's No Abortion Debate, Just a Life Sentence," *Utne Reader,* Jan.–Feb. 1997, 68.
11. *New York Times,* Sept. 28, 2002.
12. *Bangkok Post,* Aug. 19, 1985.
13. *New York Times,* Feb. 17, 2002.
14. Goodwin, 71.
15. *Abortion Surveillance,* 1.
16. *Los Angeles Times,* Jan. 4, 1997.
17. *New York Times,* June 11, 2002, D. 6.
18. Terkel, 16–18.
19. *Time,* Mar. 9, 1970.
20. Terkel, 20–28.
21. Hardin, 138.
22. Swomley, 1.
23. Terkel, 30.
24. John Connery, S.J., *Abortion: The Development of the Roman Catholic Perspective* (Chicago: Loyola University Press, 1977), 31–32, 45.
25. Connery, 16–21.
26. Connery, chaps. 4–7.
27. Connery, 307; Terkel, 99.
28. Jane Hurst, *The History of Abortion in the Catholic Church: The Untold Story* (Washington, D.C.: Catholics for a Free Choice, n.d.), 21.
29. Hurst, 2–3, 26.
30. Beverly Wildung Harrison, *Our Right to Choose: Toward a New Ethic of Abortion* (Boston: Beacon Press, 1983), 124–44; Susan T. Nicholson, *Abortion and the Roman Catholic Church* (Knoxville, Tenn.: Religious Ethics, 1978), 3–13.
31. Harrison, 144–53.
32. Jane Dempsey Douglass, *Women, Freedom, and Calvin* (Philadelphia: Westminster Press, 1985), 79–80.
33. Hurst, 2.
34. *We Affirm.*
35. Presbyterian Church (U.S.A.) General Assembly Report 1992:27.024–6; *Church and Society,* "Freedom of Choice Act" (July–Aug. 1993), 47–48.

36. Terkel, 134.
37. John B. Cobb, *Matters of Life and Death: The Right to Kill, the Right to Die, the Right to Live, the Right to Love* (Louisville, Ky.: Westminster/John Knox Press, 1991), 73–74.
38. William R. LaFleur, *Liquid Life: Abortion and Buddhism in Japan* (Princeton: Princeton University Press, 1991), 218.
39. Cobb, 89.
40. *General Board Abortion Hearings*, 3.
41. LaFleur, 218 (his emphasis).

Chapter 5

1. Mark Peyser and Donatella Lorch, "High School Controversy," *Newsweek*, Mar. 20, 2000.
2. *Sacramento Bee*, "Bitter Split over Scouts and Schools," *Bee News Service*, Mar. 15 and June 4, 2001.
3. PlanetOut News Staff, May 12, 2000.
4. June Rivera Brooks and Stuart Silverstein, *Los Angeles Times*, June 9, 2000.
5. Associated Press, Feb. 4, 2002.
6. Anna Quindlen, "The Right to Be Ordinary," *Newsweek*, Sept. 11, 2000.
7. Walter Wink, "Homosexuality and the Bible," *Christian Century*, Nov. 7, 1979.
8. Ibid.
9. Ibid.
10. George F. Regas, "God, Sex, and Justice Revisited" A sermon at All Saints Church, Pasadena, Calif., Nov. 10, 1991.

Chapter 6

1. There are six trustees: the secretary of the treasury, the secretary of labor, the secretary of health and human services, the commissioner of social security, and two members appointed by the president and confirmed by the Senate to represent the public.
2. Henry J. Aaron, Alan S. Blinder, Alicia H. Munnell, and Peter R. Orszag, "Governor Bush's Individual Account Proposal: Implications for Retirement Benefits," *Issue Brief #11*, Social Security Network. The following analysis is based primarily on their work.
3. Costs of administering private accounts may be substantially higher for employers, the IRS, and money managers. Even the Cato Institute, a champion of privatization, sets the average in the range of 1.17 percent to 1.83 percent of assets per year.
4. The financial burden of private accounts on participants may be as large or larger than on their employers and money managers. For most people, at least some of the time, decision making is both time-consuming and painful. We often do not know enough to choose among the options presented to us; we often do not have enough time or motivation to attempt to make good choices; and we rightfully fear that bad decisions will haunt us in the future, tingeing our decision making with feelings of regret.
5. *Report of the 1994–1996 Advisory Council on Social Security*, 94.

Chapter 7

1. Joseph T. Hallinan, *Going Up the River: Travels in a Prison Nation* (New York: Random House, 2001), 216.
2. L. Gregory Jones, *Christian Century*, Mar. 8, 2000, 279.

Chapter 8

1. *Los Angeles Times*, Aug. 21, 2001, A5.

Chapter 9

1. Letter to John Adams in 1794, quoted in Wayne Lutton, *The Myth of Open Borders: The American Tradition of Immigration Control* (Monterey, Va.: American Immigration Control Foundation, 1988), 6.
2. Roy Beck, *The Case against Immigration* (New York: W. W. Norton, 1996), 40.
3. Report of the U.S. Commission on Immigration Reform, 1995.

Chapter 10

1. This is discussed in most introductory books on management; e.g., Harold Koontz and Cyril O'Donnell, *Management: A Systems and Contingency Analysis of Managerial Functions* (New York: McGraw-Hill, 1976), 34–37.
2. For information, contact the Financial Accounting Standards Board, P.O. Box 30816, Hartford, CT 06150.
3. John Seely Brown, "Research that Reinvents the Corporation," *Harvard Business Review* 69 (Jan.–Feb. 1991): 102–11.
4. Bill Saporito, "Cutting Costs without Cutting People," *Fortune* 115 (May 25, 1987): 26–30.
5. In Arie P. de Geus, "Planning as Learning," *Harvard Business Review* 66, no. 2 (Mar.–Apr. 1988): 70–74.

Chapter 11

1. National Labor Committee, "Facts and Figures of the Global Sweatshop Economy," 2001.

Chapter 12

1. Excerpted from "Who Went Under in the World's Sea of Cash," *New York Times*, Feb. 15, 1999, 1; and "Asia Feels Strain Most at Society's Margins," *New York Times*, June 8, 1998, 1.
2. See the World Bank's *World Development Report, 1991*.
3. See the United Nations Development Program, *Human Development Report*, published annually.
4. See David Korten, *When Corporations Rule the World* (West Hartford, Conn.: Kumarian Press, 1996).
5. M. Douglas Meeks, *God the Economist* (Minneapolis: Fortress Press, 1989), 37.
6. James Tobin, "A Proposal for International Monetary Reform," *Eastern Economic Journal* 4, no. 3–4 (1978): 153–59.

Chapter 13

1. An important reason for the fall in commodity prices was the glut in supplies brought on by the need to export, urged on by the multilateral lending agencies (see below).
2. The face value of the external debt is not a good measure of a country's debt burden, however, if a significant part of the debt is contracted on concessional terms with an interest rate below the prevailing market rate. The net present value (NPV) of debt is a measure that takes into account the degree of concessionality. The NPV of the lowest-income countries' external debt probably was closer to $125 billion.
3. By January 2000, most Asian economies had started to recover. But their recov-

ery seemed to have started without the fundamental reforms, especially in their banking systems, necessary for prolonged recovery. And by the end of that year, a full-fledged worldwide depression was already starting.

4. Angola, Benin, Bolivia, Burkina Faso, Burundi, Cameroon, Central African Republic, Chad, Congo, Côte d'Ivoire, Democratic Republic of Congo, Equatorial Guinea, Ethiopia, Ghana, Guinea, Guinea-Bissau, Guyana, Honduras, Kenya, Lao PDR, Liberia, Madagascar, Mali, Mauritania, Mozambique, Myanmar, Nicaragua, Niger, Nigeria, Rwanda, São Tomé and Príncipe, Senegal, Sierra Leone, Somalia, Sudan, Tanzania, Togo, Uganda, Vietnam, Yemen, and Zambia.
5. See Michael Hudson in *Bible Review*, Feb. 1999.
6. Adapted from the 201st General Assembly (1989) of the Presbyterian Church (U.S.A.), *The Third World Debt Dilemma: Searching for a Moral Response to Vulnerable People and Systems.*

Chapter 14

1. Michael Dowd, *Earthspirit* (Mystic, Conn.: Twenty-third Publications, 1992).
2. Bill McKibben, "Climate Change and the Unraveling of Creation," *Christian Century*, Dec. 8, 1999, 1197.
3. Ibid., 1198.

Chapter 15

1. Richard Cartwright Austin, *Hope for the Land* (Atlanta: John Knox Press, 1988), 90.
2. Ibid., 91.

Chapter 16

1. David Poindexter, *Population Press*, Nov./Dec. 1997, 1.
2. *Population Press*, Jan./Feb. 1998, 30.
3. Paul R. and Anne H. Ehrlich, *The Population Explosion* (New York: Simon & Schuster, 1990), 212–13.
4. *ZPG Reporter*, vol. 33, no. 1 (winter 2001): 13–14.
5. *Time*, Aug. 5, 1996.
6. Lester R. Brown, *State of the World 1996: A Worldwatch Institute Report on Progress: Toward a Sustainable Society* (New York: W. W. Norton, 1996), 4.
7. Brown, 21, 29.
8. Brown, 51.
9. Brown, 81.
10. Carl Djerassi, "The Economics of Contraceptives R&D," *Science* 272, June 28, 1996.
11. Donald D. Jackson, "People Say, You Poor Thing, and I'm Thinking, I Have Four Healthy Kids," *Smithsonian*, Sept. 1996, 30–38.
12. Paul W. Lewis, *The Introduction of a Family Planning Program to Akhas in Thailand* (Ph.D. diss., University of Oregon, 1978).
13. Ibid.
14. Paul R. and Anne H. Ehrlich, *The Population Explosion.*
15. Timothy E. Wirth, 1994, in testimony to Congress prior to the International Conference on Population and Development in Cairo (he was chair of the U.S. delegation).

Appendix

1. Peter Beinert, "Battle for the 'Burbs: Nostalgia and the Christian Right," *New Republic*, Oct. 16, 1998, 25–29.
2. Glenn H. Utter and John W. Storey, *The Religious Right: A Reference Handbook* (Santa Barbara, Calif.: ABC-Clio, 1995).
3. Raymond Wolfinger et al. in R. Schoenberger, *The American Right Wing* (New York: Holt, Rinehart & Winston, 1969).
4. Utter and Storey, 67.
5. Pat Robertson, *The Plan* (1989), 21, quoted in Duane Murray Oldfield, *The Right and the Righteous: The Christian Right Confronts the Republican Party* (Lanham, Md.: Rowman & Littlefield, 1996), 127.
6. Oldfield, 164.
7. Ralph Reed, *Active Faith* (New York: Free Press, 1996), 23.
8. Reed, *Active Faith*, 127.
9. *Los Angeles Times*, Dec. 30, 1992, E1, 5.
10. *Los Angeles Times*, Oct. 18, 1992, A1.
11. Michael d'Antonio in *Los Angeles Times Magazine*, Nov. 29, 1992, 28.
12. Ralph Reed, *Politically Incorrect* (Dallas: Word Publishing, 1994), 219.
13. Mark J. Rozell and Clyde Wilcox, eds., *God at the Grass Roots: The Christian Right in the 1996 Election* (Lanham, Md.: Rowman & Littlefield, 1997).
14. Barry Lynn, *Christian Century*, Oct. 16, 1996, 958.
15. James Penning and Corwin Smidt, "What Coalition?" *Christian Century*, Jan. 15, 1997, 37–38.
16. *Christian Century*, Dec. 4, 1996, 1192.
17. *Christian Century*, Oct. 8, 1997, 866.
18. *Los Angeles Times*, Feb. 27, 1999.
19. *New York Times*, June 10, 1999.
20. James L. Guth, John C. Green, Corwin E. Smidt, Lyman A. Kellstedt, "Partisan Religion: Analyzing the 2000 Election," *Christian Century*, Mar. 21–28, 2001, 18–20.
21. *Christianity Today*, vol. 46, no. 12 (Nov. 18, 2002), 25.
22. *Washington Post*, Sept. 14, 2001. CO-3.
23. *Washington Post*, Sept. 18, 2001, CO-4.
24. David Snowball, *Continuity and Change in the Rhetoric of the Moral Majority* (New York: Praeger, 1991), 84–85.
25. Susan Dodrill and Bruce McKeon, "The Meaning of Evangelical Political Beliefs: Consensus and Dissension within a Religious Subculture" (unpublished paper, Western Political Science Association, Mar. 18–29, 1993).